# The Letters of
## Teilhard de Chardin
## and
## Lucile Swan

# The Letters of
## Teilhard de Chardin

*With a Foreword by Pierre Leroy, S.J.*

*and Lucile Swan*

*Edited by Thomas M. King, S.J., and Mary Wood Gilbert*

*GEORGETOWN UNIVERSITY PRESS / WASHINGTON, D.C.*

*CREDITS*: All photographs used in this volume and on the jacket are the property of Mary Wood Gilbert and are used with her permission, except those separately credited on a given page.

Georgetown University Press, Washington, D.C.   20057–1079   U.S.A.
© 1993 by Georgetown University Press. All rights reserved.
Printed in the United States of America.
10  9  8  7  6  5  4  3  2  1
THIS VOLUME IS PRINTED ON ACID-FREE OFFSET BOOK PAPER.          1993

**Library of Congress Cataloging-in-Publication Data**

Teilhard de Chardin, Pierre.
    The letters of Teilhard de Chardin and Lucile Swan / Pierre
Teilhard de Chardin and Lucile Swan ; Thomas M. King and Mary Wood
Gilbert, editors.
        p.     cm.
    1. Teilhard de Chardin, Pierre, d. 1955—Correspondence.   2. Swan,
Lucile, d. 1965—Correspondence.   3. Philosophers—France—Correspondence.
4. Sculptors—United States—Correspondence.   I. Swan, Lucile.
II. King, Thomas Mulvihill, 1929——— .   III. Gilbert, Mary Wood.
IV. Title
B2430.T374A4   1993       194--dc20                              93-8648
ISBN 0-87840-522-4.   —   ISBN 0-87840-524-0   (pbk.)

*These pages are an effort to express an internal evolution deeply impressed by you.*

TEILHARD WRITING TO LUCILE

*December 15, 1950*

# CONTENTS

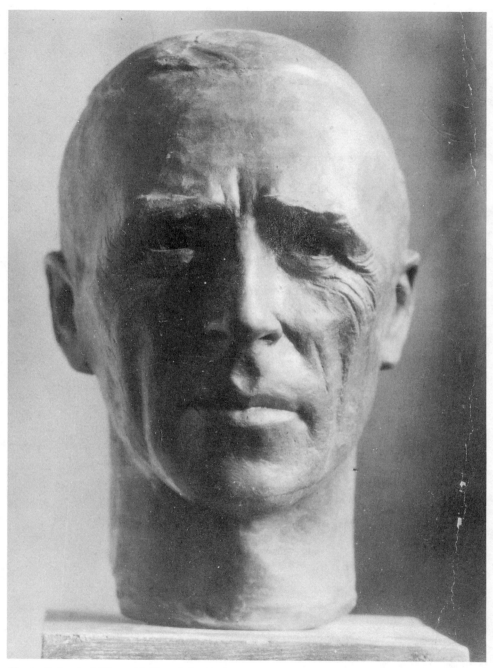

*Portrait bust of Pierre Teilhard de Chardin by Lucile Swan;
in the Museum of Natural History, Paris.*

# FOREWORD: *Memories of Teilhard*

This image, engraved in my memory over fifty years ago, is as clear today as it ever was. Why, I cannot say. It is something I fail to understand since the picture is quite an ordinary one.

It happened in Peking where I had just moved. I was living with Pierre Teilhard, a fellow Jesuit and colleague. We were alone in the new institute of geo-biology and our fraternal relations were fast turning to friendship. I was under the impression that we had no secrets from each other.

One day, as I was going to the French hospital in Legations Road, I saw to my surprise a couple coming towards me—a man and a woman walking side by side in silent thought. It was Teilhard and an American lady whom he had not mentioned to me. She was about the same age as he, a striking figure, though quiet in her bearing and dignified in the simplicity of her dress. It is this picture that remains in my mind.

I learned later that this American was Lucile Swan and that she was living opposite us in the same street. Her European style house was graced with a garden where I was to meet her several times. This was in 1940. Teilhard was to be found there often also, translating some of his articles into English. We all used to have tea together.

She was a sculptress and had modeled a face for the "Peking Man," an old fossil skull studied by Weidenreich at the Peking Union Medical College. This successful work had won her recognition in scientific circles. The bust was christened "Nelly" by us privately.

The pressure put on the Americans living in Peking by the Japanese army prompted a number of them to return to America. In 1941, Lucile made the wise decision to join them and departed in late August.

Letters made up for the absence and the distance. The value of the resulting correspondence between the two friends is left to the appreciation of the reader. In fact, it brought them together again, for the beginning of their friendship face to face had been somewhat strained. Lucile saw a contradiction between the evolutionary theories of Teilhard and his practice of chastity. "You admit the necessity of working thought out and with material in order to reach ideas abstract or God-like, but you deny the use of material (human) in order to reach the abstract or the God-like. You will say you deny only one part of human love but I think you are evading the question, for the physical is not only a very important but an essential part for the race."

Lucile was not mistaken: it is quite natural for the physical act to play its part in the manifestation of human love.

Neither was Teilhard wrong for he was fully aware of the power of "the feminine," that force of attraction towards union, not only among human beings but for the whole universe. His conception of union between a man and a woman went far beyond physical union. Some men and women are called individually to live the love of God in a different way. By denying themselves certain material pleasure, they seek strongly to give themselves totally to a loving God. Teilhard was one such person and everyone knows that he remained faithful until his death.

Lucile was not incapable of realizing the true value of her friend nevertheless. "What you are doing and what you have to offer is the most important thing in the world today."

*　　*　　*

Teilhard left Peking at the end of March 1946. He settled in his room on the Rue Monsieur in Paris with the firm intention of resuming the scholarly activities he had been pursuing before his [disciplinary] exile to China in 1926. An unexpected obstacle was to thwart his projects however. During the month of June 1947, he had a severe heart attack and, since his condition required extended hospital treatment, he entered a nursing home in the Rue Oudinot. I visited him frequently to see how he was getting on.

Meanwhile Lucile had arrived in Paris from America. She was staying in the Auteuil district and had let Teilhard know that she would be coming to see him. The appointment came at the wrong moment; he was unfortunately otherwise engaged.

Lucile discovered with bitterness that her friendship had been superseded. The new friend was Rhoda, the former wife of Professor Hellmut de Terra, a scientist whose acquaintance Teilhard had made in Burma.

Teilhard was anxious that his two friends should not meet. And to me was entrusted the job of explaining the situation to Lucile. She was extremely vexed but, with time, things settled down again.

*　　*　　*

Teilhard's influence on Lucile did not have the effect that might have been expected. Intelligent and independent, she went on to follow a swami in Vedanta contemplation. Here is what Teilhard wrote to me on the matter: "Lucile has found peace of mind in a group directed by a Swami. In such circles spirituality seems to me to be terribly vague. But is it not the only issue for countless people who do not manage to pierce that formidable, hardened, outer shell that theologians qualify by the name of orthodoxy?"

Teilhard returned to America for the last time in the autumn of 1954. There in New York he found the ever-faithful Lucile. He died on the evening of Easter Sunday 1955 while talking with other guests who were also visiting at the New York home of Rhoda de Terra.

*January 1992*                                                          PIERRE LEROY, S.J.

# PREFACE

Teilhard was an avid writer of letters—several thousand have been preserved. The present collection consists of more than two hundred letters or notes that he wrote to Lucile Swan and a selection from her replies and other writings. Apart from these letters of Teilhard, some were lost in the mails and some were destroyed by Lucile before her death; their contents and dates are not known. Most of the present letters were written in English; French passages have been translated; many letters were typed and many were not. They are published intact and exactly as written by Teilhard.

Teilhard did not save the letters he received, so the originals of Lucile's letters are not extant. But shortly after she began typing letters, she made carbons. Carbons of about forty of her letters remain (it is not always clear whether some carbon pages comprise an additional letter); the first of these is dated March 1937. Only selections from her letters are included; additional passages have been included from her private writings to bring out her character, her work, and their friendship.

Because of their many visits together, the letters tell only a part of their story. Some of this story is told in the entries from Lucile's Journal, her Line-a-Day, or in the notes that she sometimes wrote to herself. In these private writings she often addressed Teilhard, but it should be noted that in these she expressed her feelings more freely than in the letters she intended to send. She also retained several letters in which she believed she had spoken without sufficient reserve; selections from these are included.

The friendship of Teilhard and Lucile changed through the years. We have decided to let their own words tell the story. We offer only minimum interpretations and so allow readers to reach their own understandings. But through it all we find two people who cared for one another and hurt one another in ways they did not intend. Their story gives significant insight into one of the great original thinkers of our century.

Teilhard died in April of 1955 and Lucile died in May of 1965. Shortly before her death she left her Teilhard-related material to Mary Wood Gilbert, a much younger cousin who had spent time with her in France, Peiping, Washington, and New York. This other material includes: a small bookstand of Teilhard's, photographs (some reproduced here), a collection of articles he had published (mostly small printings for private distribution in China—many translated into English by Lucile), Lucile's account of her friendship, her journal, day-book, carbons of her letters, and a small picture of the Sacred Heart which Teilhard gave Lucile as she left Peiping in the summer of 1941. This collection is the basis of the following text. The small editorial notes connecting the letters are based on the writings of Teilhard, selected biographies, and the personal memories of Mary Wood Gilbert.

These letters are published with the permission of Teilhard's family and the encouragement of his close Jesuit friend, Pierre Leroy. Père Leroy was ninety-one years old in January of 1992 when he contributed the Foreword for this volume; he died in France four months later. The volume editors have collaborated in writing the connecting passages. Karl Schmitz-Moormann has authenticated the textual accuracy. French passages in the letters have been translated into English by Madeleine Betz of American University with suggestions from Nicole Schmitz-Moormann. Many people have contributed identifications for the Guide to Indexed Names (page 304 of this volume). We thank them all.

We are pleased to have been involved in producing this work.

THE EDITORS

# TEXTUAL EDITOR'S NOTE

Some of the letters in this volume are typed and many are written by hand. They are published exactly as written by Teilhard with the small irregularities in his French-influenced English and typical errors in spelling and grammar. Only obvious typing or writing mistakes have been corrected. Whenever there were small doubts about how to read a text, a note suggests alternative readings. Teilhard's punctuation is, even compared to the standards of French grammar, very personal. It has been left that way. My wife, in working long with the handwriting of Teilhard, has developed great skill in understanding his texts. By her persistent work this text is available in the present, critically reliable edition. Our work was made possible by the support of the Hellmut Ley Stiftung whose grants have allowed us the necessary hardware and part of the travel expenses.

*Bochum*
*October 16, 1992*

KARL SCHMITZ-MOORMANN
Dr. Phil., Dr. Theol.

# ACKNOWLEDGMENTS

In the twenty-eight years since Lucile's death I have tried many ways to get these letters before the public. In my view the correspondence leaves no doubt that Teilhard remained true to his faith and to his religious vocation—an issue that was sometimes sensationalized and trivialized during his lifetime and after his death, and one that Lucile was so determined to refute that she destroyed some of his letters since she felt they might be misunderstood.

Among those good friends who encouraged me to pursue publication were Herbert Morton who helped me organize the material into a readable account. My friend and colleague, Dr. Edwin S. Kessler, suggested that I contact Father Angelo d'Agostino, S.J. He in turn arranged a meeting with Father Thomas M. King, S.J., of the Department of Theology at Georgetown University.

From then on my hopes slowly became reality as Father King and Father John Breslin, S.J. together undertook to share my vision and publish these letters. To my several friends, both young and old, who helped me in the plodding work of proofing, etc., my heartfelt thanks for seeing me through the preparation of this book.

*August 1993*                                                                                      M.W.G.

# PROLOGUE: *Memories of Lucile*

My association with Lucile Swan, my mother's cousin, began when she lived with us for a while in 1924 and later spent a winter with my family in the south of France. She and I, the grown woman and the young girl, became fast friends. Then, ten years later at Lucile's persuasion, my mother brought my brother and me to Peiping. Just as Lucile and many others had succumbed to the beauty and richness of the city, so did we. We too decided to stay on in the ancient, great city. So we rented a house and settled in. Old Peking had become Peiping and now it is Beijing. The walls that had divided the city into three parts—the Chinese, the inner city with the legations, and the Forbidden City—are gone now. Then the sky was clear, the air came fresh from the Gobi Desert, and at night the stars were so close they really seemed reachable. Rickshaws were the ordinary mode of transportation; coal stoves heated most homes; electricity was available only in the inner city; mail from Europe arrived two months old; wireless was the sole method for fast international communication; passage from America by ship took the better part of six weeks.

The foreign population was various; it included the diplomatic corps, scientists, artists, photographers, explorers, tourists, and many people in business (tobacco, antiques, silks). There were also those contented sojourners like us, for whom Peiping remained one of the few cities unspoiled by modern life. The environment was not only exotic but one with a rich cultural heritage that offered stimulating associations among a people of ineffable vitality and an abundant sense of earthy humor. It was there that I eventually met Teilhard.

When Lucile Swan and a friend, Betty Spencer (later Mrs. John Carter Vincent), first arrived in Peiping in 1929 they had found life interesting and easy—a sharp contrast to their lives in Chicago and New York (Lucile had lived in New York after the dissolution of her marriage of twelve years to a fellow artist in Chicago.) They decided to stay and soon moved together into a house with the usual Chinese "accoutrements" of those times—a cook, a cook's helper, a number one boy, and an amah.

Shortly afterwards the two women met Teilhard at a dinner party, and later entertained him and their other new acquaintances. Lucile described the other guests of the evening as "drawn to his radiant and loving presence."

At that first meeting in Peiping their conversation, destined to continue for twenty-five years, began with Lucile's query, "What kind of an -ologist are you?" Teilhard answered that the more deeply he went into science, the surer he felt there was a God. This firmly expressed conviction, coming from a paleontologist-priest, laid open to her a new perspective for reconsidering beliefs she had not thought about since her days at an Episcopal boarding school in Sioux City, Iowa, where she had been born and reared.

After Betty returned to the States to think over whether or not to marry young Vincent (a consular officer in the American Legation), Lucile settled into

another house where she was able to change part of the temple the Chinese own-
ers had used for ancestor worship into her studio. There she modeled portraits in
clay—studies of prominent Chinese and Westerners, as well as Chinese jugglers,
sword dancers, and many other interesting passers-by. She was particularly apt in
'catching' children. Later she was asked to make a reconstruction of Peking Man.
She did under the supervision of Professor Weidenreich of the Peking Union
Medical College. Using a cast of the skull, called "Nelly" by Teilhard and his fellow scientists, Lucile modeled a head of the famed Pleistocene fossil. Unfortunately both were lost during the War.

Sometime in 1933 Lucile asked Teilhard to sit for a portrait. She began a
small head which, when finished, she did not like, and later destroyed it. He liked
to talk while he posed, but Lucile found she could not follow his ideas and work,
so they arranged to talk afterwards. Each day after the sitting, Number One Boy
Wong brought tea. Later she described how Teilhard came to love the 'Little King'
in her copies of the New Yorker magazine, and she was surprised at how quickly
he grasped the humor in this bit of Americana. She wrote in her diary:

> He so enjoyed all sides of life and had such capacity to live fully. Some-
> times after tea he would stay on until I was ready to go to a dinner party.
> He liked seeing the bright colored evening dress, but there was never the
> slightest sense of envy or unhappiness because he was not going also.

For her, each of their walks in the park was a "revelation of insect and
bird life." He imparted his knowledge so simply and clearly that it made everything ten times more alive and more meaningful. "Life is a constant discovery," he
commented. When Teilhard said, "Everything we do is important because we are
doing God's work," Lucile had a feeling of being part of it all and that "God
would be always with me. That we were building something—always, all the
time." She had begun her spiritual quest.

When they were both in Peiping, tea-time conversations became a daily
habit. In her little courtyard they talked constantly of ideas; and they watched figs
ripen on the potted trees and lettuce and tomatoes grow in the kitchen garden. On
Saturdays they sometimes picnicked in one of the city's parks. Lucile started a
second bust of P.T.—her nickname for him. This portrait is now in the Teilhard
room in the Museum of Natural History in Paris.

About 1935 she felt familiar enough with his ideas to articulate her reactions and opinions in one of her letters:

> I was deeply interested and sympathetic, and my very questions made
> him clarify his thought. I am not a Roman Catholic and so brought a dif-
> ferent point of view. So I would argue with him for my views, all of which
> was most helpful to him, and, after a certain amount of talk and reflec-
> tion, he would write another essay. He was amused to say he had pro-
> duced another "egg." And he always said it was my work too. This, of
> course, made me very proud and happy. He was like that with his Chi-
> nese science friends. Often he would write their entire article, but do it in
> such a way that they felt that they themselves had done it, and [they]

would cheerfully sign it without a qualm. He had no need to insist on "me" or "mine." It was the idea that was important. Now he could make the world more conscious of itself and its possibilities to grow and evolve with always Christ as the motivating power.

In fact, she began to think that he was offering the Church a way towards a spiritual regeneration. At times she wondered aloud if he ought to leave the Church so that he could speak out and write freely. She reported his reply, "Perhaps there are some dead branches to the Church, but those will be taken away. The roots and the trunk are strong and healthy. Besides the Church is the only international organization that works."

Teilhard would regularly bring a draft of what he had just written for her to read, and then he would explain and elaborate on it. Later, if it was in French, she would translate it. Then they would talk it over, and if it was clearly what he had intended to say, Teilhard would incorporate it into the whole of whatever paper he was writing. Lucile noted in her appointment book, Line-a-Day, that it was on June 13, 1940 that Teilhard brought her l'Homme, afterwards re-titled to Le Phénomène Humain. Lucile noted that "This was the work he had put his heart into and was the essence of all his writings. He was very happy about the book. I thought he felt this time there would surely be no objections and that it would be published." She said, "I was thrilled as I read it and every day we would discuss it and he would explain things to me."

They had one point of difference which over time became a subject they often discussed as their friendship strengthened. For Lucile, physical consummation was fundamental to the love between a man and a woman, a seal of what they felt for each other. Teilhard's consistent and continual response was a rejection of this point of view, offering in its place a redirection of the energy of sexual union towards God. He did not deny the dynamics of love between a man and a woman, and he believed that such love, although unconsummated, could bring them to God.

This was hard for a high-spirited woman such as Lucile to comprehend. To her love meant a physical expression of the body as well as of the heart and mind. Teilhard put the dilemma clearly when he wrote to her that she wanted love à deux while for him it could only be love à trois. I once asked Lucile if indeed there ever had been a physical confirmation. She replied, "Never."

During the War while she was in Chicago I took drawing lessons from Lucile. And after World War II when I lived with my husband and child in Washington where she had recently bought a house, we visited and walked together often. She spoke a good deal about Teilhard and his ideas, and speculated on the future—his and hers—and sometimes she read to me from his letters. When she moved to New York, I visited her frequently and was with her during her last illness in 1965. It was then she gave me Teilhard's letters saying, "Do with these as you see fit, but I want my side known."

In her last years Lucile had developed an interest in Vedanta in which she found many similarities to Teilhard's ideas. But not long before she died she told Swami Nikalananda, her mentor, that she had returned to her Christian faith.

During the twenty-eight years that have passed since Lucile's death I have read over these letters several times. At my first reading I had her admonition very much in mind, for, after his death her friendship with Teilhard had come into question and, in some quarters as of little consequence. Rereading them brought out different perspectives on their appreciation of each other. Romantic that Lucile was, she hoped to reestablish the friendship as it had been—as did he, although he always recognized the constrictions that his vows placed upon him and in the last years the impositions of illness and age, as well.

Reading over the letters also has sharpened my recollection of the one somewhat private time I spent with Teilhard. Sometime in the mid 1930s, when we were still living in Peking, I was invited to lunch with Jacques Bardac. We were three: Jacques, Teilhard, and myself. I was already acquainted with Teilhard's ideas because the work at Chou Kuo Tien was well known and Lucile frequently talked about his religious-philosophical ideas. And, as youngsters at home, my brother and I had often heard our father affirm Darwin's theories. So, when the conversation turned away from France's gloomy political situation (the Léon Blum years) I asked Teilhard about early man in China. He was as respectful to a curious high-schooler as to a colleague or a friend. He answered me seriously and wittily and engaged me in understanding those complex scientific problems imaginatively. We were gay—a word I was later to read in many of his letters to my cousin whenever he found people or events amusing, happy or stimulating. Looking back on this brief meeting, I treasure the memory of having known him—slightly, for sure, but truly.

A vignette from a friend of those times gives his impression of tea with Lucile and Teilhard. I quote from John Paton Davies:

> Like Paris and Florence of the same period, Peking in the 1930s attracted foreign artists, writers, and scholars. Among them was Lucile Swan, a sculptress from Chicago, by way of the South Pacific. She had left her husband on one of the French islands and was living in typical Peking fashion in a small house around a small courtyard behind a big red gate. Lucile was fine-featured, amply bosomed and hipped, perhaps in her mid-thirties and beloved by all who knew her. For she glowed with warmth and honest sentiment.
>
> On the several occasions that I went to tea at Lucile's house, there was present a Jesuit priest. I had known of him during my Yenching days. He was the eminent paleontologist who at that time had participated in identifying the fossil skull of *sinanthropus pekinensis*, the so-called Peking Man. His name was Teilhard de Chardin.
>
> Père Teilhard was a lean, patrician priest. Not the patrician of Roman marble or glazed porcelain. Rather, the jagged visaged aristocrat, rough cast in bronze. Which is what Lucile was doing.
>
> We sat in her living room and talked, not of theology and not much of fossils or sculpture. We talked mostly of what are regarded as unimportant things and were quite content with that. With these two, it is not precisely what they said so long ago that is fixed in the memory. What I

sharply remember, really as a spectator, was the unspoken communication. Shining from her face was Lucile's wordless affirmation that, withal (for there were lines of sadness by eyes and mouth), life was sweet and its delights were to be shared with friends to be cherished.

Père Teilhard's face, a noble construction of rugged angles and furrows and a sensitive mouth, illuminated what he said. And when he was silent it still uttered his moods, slowly sometimes, more often in flashes. He did not withdraw from those about him. He radiated outward to them gravely, merrily, inquiringly. And always with delicate consideration for the other and no concern for self.

These letters speak to me now of the steadfastness which both Lucile and Teilhard stood by their own individual values while trying to maintain their very real affection through a welter of distracting circumstances and conflicting emotions. In this age is it remarkable? Odd? Devotion is not a word often heard. They found the beauty of life in ways that were often not pragmatic.

*August 1993*                                                M.W.G.

# *The Letters of the China Years: from 1932 to 1941*

Pierre Teilhard de Chardin met Lucile Swan at a dinner party in Peiping in the Autumn of 1929. He was then forty-eight, a geologist, a French priest, and a Jesuit for thirty years. His doctoral studies in science had been interrupted by military service in World War I, during which time he developed the ideas that would later make him famous. In 1925 Church authorities had restricted publication of his religious and philosophical writings, but by 1929 he had gained international recognition for his scientific work in China. Lucile had just come to Peiping; she was then thirty-nine, an American sculptress and portrait artist from Iowa. With her husband, also an artist, she had worked in Chicago, New York, and Paris and had traveled widely, but her marriage of ten years had ended in divorce.

Lucile was immediately taken by Teilhard's gracious manner and ardent faith: "For the first time in years I felt young and full of hope again." She became part of the international community living in Peiping and met Teilhard at many social gatherings. Eventually Teilhard began regular visits to Mrs. Swan's home for afternoon tea. Teilhard's earliest extant letter to her is dated August 30, 1932.

*A bord du Porthos, August 30th, 1932*

Dear Lucile,

    *Tomorrow morning, we are in Hongkong, — and then, for me, China is behind, — geographically, I mean — for, by the heart, I have not left Peiping, nor the small studio under the green trees. —— I hope that everything is external and internal smile, for you; and that, gradually, more light, and more inspiration, will for ever rise and grow inside of you. —— Useless to tell you how it has been sweet and strong for me that our paths have been crossing and joining, so unexpectedly, where the East ends for me and the West for you. —— God did it, I hope, so that we could have more life for Him. ——*

    *Perfectly quiet journey, so far. A typhon has just been passing away, leaving behind a smooth sea and a cool breeze. I try to retake myself, and to think a bit, and to write. But who is living really, in the bottom of my soul? — the christian, the pagan, or the man?*

    *Yours ever*

    *Pierre T. de C.*

*You know my address: Laboratoire de Paléontologie du Muséum, 3 Place Valhubert (Paris V)*

*Paris, October 20th, 1932*

Dear Lucile,

    *To find yesterday, in the Museum, your letter of Sept.10th was a real joy for me. That means so much to me to feel your frank and strong friendship in my life; and I like so much to hear from you what you do, and what you think, in the quiet recess of your small temple! What you tell me on myself in this letter, is that "my friendship is better than my ideas", I have already heard several times, told to me by other friends. But do you really think that, but for those ideas, I would be the same as you like? — and, from another hand, do you think, also, that the best season for philosophy is not the strongest, rather than the weakest time of the life? We shall discuss the matter again, under your ever-green trees, after a few months. In any way your art is, I think, the sacred thread which, if followed, will lead you to the light which will be yours,\* in the right time.*

    *My journey to France was quiet. Crossing the blue water of the Indian seas, I have written a few pages on the opposite oriental and occidental ways, in the quest of some divine Unity: "La Route de l'Ouest". Some of my last Essays, I am more and more sure by new experience, would rouse something more than an ordinary interest, if I could have them printed. But, in that direction, I don't expect much more than new difficulties.*

    *Otherwise, I am already taken, here, in a whirl of business and social relations; — and, once more, I realize how hard it is to conciliate individual truth and world's conventions. —— On the whole, I feel happy, —— if not always*

---

\*The underscores used for emphasis in many of the letters are reproduced exactly as they were written in the correspondence of the two friends.

quiet. — *The work is going well.* — *I was right, I think, in coming back to Europe for a while. I wanted it, — brain and soul.*

*The last week, I had the great pleasure of meeting Jameson and Rose, in their small hotel, very close to my own place. We had a long chat, and agreed that we would perhaps feel better "at home", with you in Peiping. Jameson seems to be in very good form (his wife also), and extremely interested in his present life.*

*Any news from you will be precious to me.*

*Yours ever*

*Teilhard*

---

In the early days of their friendship they laughed a lot together. One source of their amusement was the cartoon character of the Little King in the *New Yorker* magazine which Lucile explained in English and parlor French. They also laughed at the tricks her two white fox terriers performed for a share of the tea cookies and chatted about their friends. In this friendly atmosphere Teilhard allowed himself more and more freedom to discuss his ideas for his own clarification. He also soon found Lucile's responses and questions stimulated him to further probing, in fact, he began to call her his "sounding board".

THE EDITORS

---

*Paris, January 23th, 1933*

*My dear Lucile,*

*Just a word, — but a word deep from my heart, — in answer to your letter of the Dec. 11th (which I have received today) — and also to your other letter of November 22th, — which I have left so long on my desk without any written answer. —— I plan to leave France the next Febr. 10th, via Suez, on the s.s. <u>Aramis</u>. But I wish you will receive the present letter a few days in advance to me, as a last greeting from France, and the first new of my coming back. — You are right, of course. In spite of the fact that the true ideas are <u>living</u> beings, their spring is something better still. This is the reason for which I strongly believe that the most essential and everlasting part of the world is made of our souls, and that the common center of the souls is a still brighter and loving soul.*

*So, my "holidays" are quickly shifting away. Holidays? or rather a whirl, — one of those whirls which, I strongly (or desperately?) believe, are the necessary path of the man towards some higher spiritual countries in the Universe. — Nevertheless, I was right coming back to France. You will find me just the same, I hope, — perhaps a bit wiser, — but not cooler. — I have met Davidson Black and Mrs Black, in London, last December. — Mrs. Jameson is still here, I think; — her husband busy and happy in Cambridge.*

*Excuse, please, these hurried lines. I am so glad to see you again.*

*Yours ever*

*P. Teilhard*

---

By early summer Teilhard was back in Peking where he worked until leaving for a scientific congress to be held in the United States in June. Probably it was during this pre-congress period that Lucile asked Teilhard to sit for a portrait. They began meeting regularly in her studio in the afternoons so she could maintain a sense of continuity in her modeling. It was also an opportunity for them to expand their friendship since he talked while she worked. In effect, his thinking aloud revealed facets of his personality that Lucile tried to catch in the clay.

These meetings-for-a-purpose established a rhythm continued over the years, long after this first small bust was finished — which, because Lucile was not pleased with it, she ultimately destroyed. However, in 1937 she did complete a larger head which satisfied her. It is now in the Teilhard Room of the Natural History Museum in Paris.

*Peiping, June 20th, 1933*

*Dear Lucile,*

*God bless you for your kindness and the treasure of your friendship. In return I pray Him to make me a pure light for you.*

*Dont worry because I am wandering.*

*I think that, for being perfect (and esthetic . . .) a friendship has to be harmonized so well with the conditions of both friends that it does not interfere with, but achieve, the line of the life of each of them.*

*And I think also that it grows ever stronger and sweeter when both, at the price of some sacrifices, are just helping each other to become closer to something divine above.*

*Be happy, —— and goodbye*

*Yours*

*Pierre*

*s.s. President Coolidge Sunday 26th\* June, 1933*

*Dear Lucile,*

*Just now (5 p.m.) our boat is skirting the first small islands of the Japanese coast: steep, woody, rocks emerging from the sea as a sunk range. Yesterday, we travelled in the fog. Today, an autumnal sun is shining over a perfectly smooth sea. This is a good start. — We are all well on board: the "three wise men of the East" (Dr. Grabau, Ting, and myself), the Star, and Hömer, — very gay, of course. The boat is most luxurious, indeed, — and not crowded so far, — so that we can enjoy an enormous place for walking, reading and talking. — As a matter of fact, those charming conditions are not the best ones for an intellectual or internal work. I hope however, when we leave Japan, to manage my daily occupations in a more methodical way. —— By mere chance, I hit this morning in an official document on the crudest possible expression of what I believe to be the fundamental mistake in the present mind of my Church: the very divide between the past and the future world; — something, clearly set, which I can not accept, and which I believe to be "illegitime" because an important alternative is overlooked. That gave me a kick. And I think I will write something down which can make the battlefield clear. No, I am not yet at the end of my road. But God has to help me. Truth does not break anything, I believe.*

---

\*Teilhard absent-mindedly dated this letter June 26th although the ship was apparently offshore Japan on a different day.

*Nothing new, besides. The journey down to Shanghai was very easy, thank to the American Express, — and Grabau is in a very good spirit. Mrs Woodland also, of course. So far, nobody interesting seems to be with us on the boat. But, after a few days, we will probably make some discovery.*

*Are you happy? — working? One of the charms of this trip is that I travel with a return ticket to Peiping. — You can send me a word to S. Francisco for the 8th september, c/o the Dollar Line, on the same "President Coolidge".*

*I will write you from Honolulu*

*Yours*

*Pierre*

*s.s. President Coolidge July 3d, 1933*

*Dear Lucile,*

*Day after to morrow, we are due to Honolulu. Just a few lines, here, for making you sure that I will not forget you, amongst the palms and the flowers!*

*Perfectly good and smooth journey, so far. The weather is a bit windy, — but the sky scarcely cloudy, — and the water so deep blue that you would "y tremper vos pinceaux". — Everything right, on board. But very few interesting-looking passengers. Practically we are living apart, we five; and most of the other groups are doing the same. Dr. Grabau looks in very good form. And Mrs. Woodland decided she had to stop immediately her breakfast, so quickly she would have become fat. — On the whole, we are perfectly idle. For my part, I wrote only a few letters and typed a short scientific paper. — In spite of this, I have the obscure feeling that something is moving or growing inside of me: as if, in the course of this new period of complete freedom, the true "myself" was escaping a little more, still, from a world of conventions. This new and direct, contact with the Unbelief of the world makes me more sharply conscious of what I believe (strongly) and what I do no more believe (equally strongly). — But what to make out of that? — How to propagate, in my condition, the sparkle I believe to feel in myself? — I dont see. But I wait, and I watch. — My dearest faith is that something Loving is the deepest essence of the growing Universe.*

*This letter will reach you shortly before you start for Dairen. Good luck! — I am sure you will like twice more your Pekinese house when you come back to it. —— And I shall be so happy when I, also, will enter it again. ——*

*I will send you a few news from Washington.*

*Yours.*

*Pierre*

---

During his travels, Teilhard worked on several scientific essays and reports that he was preparing for publication — eight altogether in France and in China during 1933. Most, but not all of these, were brief papers, but they included the well-known, illustrated memoir that he and Davidson Black wrote together. Entitled *Fossil Man in China — The Chow-Kou Tien Knowledge of the Late Cenozoic in China*, it also lists Chung-Chien Young [Yang] and Wen-Chung Pei as collaborators in the work.

*Dear Lucile,*

     *I arrived in New York day before yesterday, after a very quiet transcontinental journey. In San Francisco we did not stop but a few hours (from 9 a.m. to 6 p.m.), spent, in a nice little cottage, with old Pekinese friends (Mrs. Berry-Barker, the former "home-lady" of Dr. Grabau). In Ogden, [Utah] we parted from Grabau and Mrs. Woodland, on their way for the Yellowstone Park (!?). And, in Chicago, I did not stay more than a short time (from 9 a.m. to 9 p.m.). But, after doing some work in the Field Museum, I had two hours spare for calling at the Newbury Hotel in which I was so glad to meet your father and your mother, who were exceedingly nice with me (may I confess you that one of my best pleasures was to discover there a photograph of you, made some 15 years ago, but on which you look just as yourself now). I found your parents in very good conditions, exactly as you described me, — your mother so young under her white hair, and your father so full of life. I tried to make them understand, as much as possible, your present life, your work, your friends. And I went away with the absurd wish to find in the street a rickshaw which could drive me straight back to you. — I left Chicago one day before the Balbo's arrival, — and, from the Fair, I did not see but the fantastic light, along the railway. On my way back, I shall possibly visit more.*

     *Here, in New York, I have met again, with a real joy, several of my dear friends of the Natural History Museum: Granger, etc. But Roy has left a fortnight ago, for Moskow, where he tries to start a combined Russo-american Expedition in Russian Turkestan. He curses probably the japanese duplicity still more than the Chinese association "for the preservation of antiquities". — Several french friends (brought here by the [scientific] Congress) are reported here; but I did not see them, so far. — I expect Grabau here in two or three days. I did not like, positively, to see him wandering in the Yellowstone with Mrs. Woodland alone (he is so slow, and so heavy!). Hope that everything went well. —*

     *Here, I am living in a nice home of my Order, close to the Hudson River, at 50 meters from Broadway. This is supposed to be the intellectual center of my Society in New York. They know me more than I would have supposed, — and yesterday I had to talk hours on the most delicate matters. I did it cautiously, but frankly. One at least of the Fathers is able to understand, and to spread, what I think. It was some comfort for me to meet with such a friendly and sympathic group of confrères. This is the true spirit of my church, — very different from the stiff and timorous mind of Roma. And America is far from being (on the whole) a progressive intellectual part of my Order! That gives me some hope. But in the same time, that makes me a bit "mélancolique" to think what I could do if I was allowed to print my best papers. Those people do not know me but by almost insignificant parts of my work. —— God knows better, I suppose. ——*

     *We are on Sunday. Friday, the Congress opens here, and then we go to Washington [the District of Columbia, U.S.A.]. — Hope that you are going, yourself, to leave for Dairen. — Be happy. — You know that I don't forget you.*

     *Yours ever*

     *Pierre*

[a postcard] *Flagstaff (Arizona) Aug. 5th, 1933*

*Splendid excursion, with excellent friends. I don't forget Peiping! — Left Grabau in good conditions at Washington, after successfull Congress. — We meet again on the beginning of September at San Francisco.*

*Pierre*

*Arcata, Calif. August 16th, 1933*

*Dear Lucile,*

*I don't remember exactly whether I have sent you a word from Washington. In any way, you have received, I hope, my letter from New York (after my visit to your family in Chicago). Every thing is going all right, since that time. Presently, I write to you from a small town, near Eureka, on the Pacific coast. Just the sea between me and you. Are you "wise" and happy? I hope so. — I left the Congress party three days ago, in the "John Day Basin", the most wild part of Central Oregon. They are going to the Yellowstone, and back to the East. Myself, I took a place in the small car of a Chaney's student; and we are driving, both of us towards San Francisco, along the marvelous "Redwood highway": a good road, skirting the sea, amongst splendid groves of huge sequoia trees, 500 to 800 years old in average. I was specially anxious to get in touch with the geology of the Coast Ranges, — and this is a wonderful opportunity. Tomorrow, we are due to San Francisco. I will stay at Berkeley University [University of California at Berkeley], — and spend there the three weeks after which the President Coolidge will take me back to Shanghai (leaving the Sept. 8th). — I left Dr. Grabau and Mrs W. in Washington, — both in excellent conditions. I expect them in S.Francisco on the Sept. 4th. — The meeting between Dr. Grabau and his wife and daughter seems to have been a success. I will explain it to you longer, in a conversation. — Washington proved to be very hot and moist, and we had to search comfort in beer and ice-cream. In spite of it, I enjoyed really the place; and the Congress was very brilliant [the International Convention of Geologists, in 1933]. — On the July 30th, I left to the West, with a very pleasant party (40 people) including several good french friends. We had three cars (two Pullman and a special car for bagage, bath, etc.) for ourselves, — a real moving home. We went by St. Louis, Kansas City, Flagstaff, Los Angeles, S.Francisco, Klamath Falls [a city in S. Oregon], and Eugene (Oregon). The four days spent in the "painted desert" and the Grand Canyon, the two days in Crater Lake (Ore.), and the crossing of the Cascade Range amidst the forest of pines, close to high volcanoes clad with snow and ice, were the best parts of the way. — I felt a bit blue in parting from my friends; but now I look forward, to Peiping, — and to you.*

*Yours*

*Pierre*

[a postcard] *s.s. President Coolidge Sept. 22th, 1933*

*Dear Lucile,*

*I will send to you this card from Yokohama, day after tomorrow. May those lines bring you quickly my deepest feelings of friendship, and my joy of see-*

*ing you again, soon. — We are due to Shanghai on the Sept. 29th. I plan to stay
there a few days, and to reach Peking on about the october 5th. Dr. Grabau and
Mrs. Woodland are on board, both in excellent condition.*

> *Yours ever*

> *Pierre T.*

*Thank you so much for your letter in S.Francisco*

---

When Teilhard returned to Peiping, Lucile apparently was hoping still for some physical
confirmation of their friendship. But Teilhard wrote the first of the many letters which
explain why their friendship would be different.

---

[Peking] *November 14th, 1933*

*Lucile, my dear friend*
  *The other day, you told me that, under a certain respect, you "did not
understand me". Those words made me thinking a good deal. Because "not understanding" means sometimes suffering, or at least walking in the dark. Then, I
must try to express myself more clearly, for the sake of your happiness.*
  *The fundamental bearing of my life, you know it, is to prove to the others
and firstly to myself, that the love of God does not destroy, but exalt and purify
any earthly power of understanding and loving. I dream going to God under the
pressure of the strongest and the wildest spirits of the world.*
  *That will explain you, perhaps why, when I met you, I accepted you as a
marvellous gift. I thought (as I still more think now) that I had found a wonderful thing, which would help me to live more intensely, — so that I could give
myself more efficiently to the divine work of enlarging the World around me.
Thus I can be yours, really yours, in getting more spirit from you, and in growing
into a same spirit with you.*
  *But because your friend, Lucile, belongs to Something Else, he cannot be
yours — (and you would find very few left in him, of what attracts you, if he tried
to be yours) — just and merely for being momentarily happy with you.*
  *Do you remember a thought expressed in the short page I gave you when
coming back from America: ". . . to conquer the things, not for merely enjoying
them, but for converging with them into something or somebody ever higher".*
  *I know that I must look queer, or illogical sometimes. Why to take this
and not that. And if I do not take that, why not to stay like the others, confined
in a cell?*
  *Just because I am so foolish as to try to discover a new path, — along
which the World might breathe.*
  *Well for me. But what of the other? the other who perhaps does not see
nor feel the same Star as mine. Am I not making her suffering, by a subtle selfish-
ness of mine? — Do I really help her (as I would so much!) to be more full, free
and happy? —*
  *Sometimes, you will answer me.*

> *P.*

With the 1933 Christmas and New Year's festivities over, the sculptress resumed work in her Peking studio and the scientist set out to do fieldwork in and around Kwangshi in southeast China.

*On board, Jan. 7th, 1934*
[Dollar Steamship Lines]

*Lucile, dear,*

*Coming on the boat, day before yesterday, I had the joy of finding your letter, which is with me as a dear perfume of the best of Peking. I thank you so deeply for what you tell me. Yes, my dream is that we could be a little like a star, each for the other, by the presence, and just so much in the absence. A star, leading to the best of the Unknown, in front of us. You know how much I feel that the only important work in the World is the discovery (or rather the creation) of the Future. Now, can it be a more vital line in such a progress than to discover a new path and a new ground for the power of love? — Let us go ahead, the hand in the hand. The only danger, I think, would be, for us, to hope too little, and to trust insufficiently. —*

*I will send you this letter from Hongkong, where we are due tomorrow morning. Our plan is to go to Canton directly, by rail. As soon as I know something precise about our departure for the Kwangsi, I will drop you another word.*

*Everything all right, so far. We spent two days in Shanghai (the boat was a little delayed), — and still I had scarcely the time for seeing my friends. I met Lejay, — an extremely nice man, in spite of his nerves. And, before leaving, I had a very pleasant lunch to the Mac Hughes, with Petro and Barbara (who are living there).*

*The weather is a bit cloudy, but the sea perfectly calm. Gradually, I dress in a more and more light clothes. — And yet, you are still under the healthy frost of Peking.*

*Be happy, dear and precious friend, — and if ever you have the impression of any shadow, during those weeks, — just laugh at it. —— There is light, and only light, in front of us.*

*Yours*

*Pierre*

Lucile often challenged Teilhard on his chastity; in February 1934, Teilhard wrote an essay in response: "The Evolution of Chastity" (see *Toward the Future*, New York: Harcourt Brace Jovanovich, 1975, pp. 60-87). He began by claiming that chastity is the most sublime manifestation of all religions, but he finds the value of chastity poorly formulated for the modern world. He tells of a doubt originating in his own experience and magnified by the many sincere people he knew who saw no value in the restrictions of asceticism. Teilhard argued that asceticism could be justified only in so far as it developes into a mysticism.

In this essay Teilhard claimed that the energy of our interior life has roots of a passionate nature. "It is from man's storehouse of passion that the warmth and light of his soul arise, transfigured." So when a man approaches a woman he finds he is "enveloped in an indistinct glow of illumination." Should this love reach physical fulfillment, an inner flame will leap up to God; so the spiritual potentialities of passion are achieved. But Teilhard remains wary, for it seems "a sort of 'short-circuit' is produced in the dazzling gift of the body—a flash which burns up and deadens a portion of the soul."

the old
tantric
yogi talking

But when there is "no physical contact," there is "convergence at a higher level." So chaste "lovers are obliged to turn away from the body, and so seek one another in God." He tells of having "been through some difficult passages" in maintaining his chastity. But he believed he was not thereby diminished. This was the love he proposed to Lucile. The essay ends with a much quoted passage: "Someday when men have conquered the winds, the waves, the tides, and gravity, they will harness for God the energies of love, and then, for the second time in the history of the world, man will have discovered fire."

While working on the essay Teilhard wrote to a friend assuring him he was not writing "monologues in abstracto." He explained that these reflections on chastity are "the best I could tell myself and the other when three or four times in my life for long periods I was up against the wall (*Lettres intimes*, Paris: Aubier-Montaigne, 1973, pp. 263, 275).

*March 9th, 1934*

*Lucile, my dear friend,*

*Reading your letter has been one of the most precious minutes in my life. It was not only a "nice", but a glorious letter. You have entered more deep than ever, as an active seed, the innermost of myself. You bring me what I need for carrying on the work which is before me: a tide of life.*

*But, just because you are for ever such a dear treasure for me, I ask you to do your best for not building too much your material, or external, life, on me. You and I, we are two wild birds on the Mother Earth. May be, for years, our paths are going to run close to each other. May be, also, the wind is going to separate our external ways. . .*

*Sometimes, I think I would like to vanish before you into some thing which would be bigger than myself, — your real yourself, Lucile, — your real life, your God. And then I should be yours, completely. — Keep free of myself, if possible, Lucile, in having me.*

*Anyhow, if those things seem still to you too difficult, or too far away, — don't worry, and let the Life and the Light work quietly in you. Just try to keep the direction straight. And be patient (even with yourself), peaceful, and happy. — I know that what is born between us is to live for ever.*

*Your*

*P.*

Shortly after Teilhard returned from the field in 1934, Lucile had to go to Shanghai in order to see her mother off for the States. (Mrs. Charles Swan had been visiting her daughter in Peking for several months.)

*Peking, March 13th, 1934*

*Lucile, my dear friend,*

*Since you have left, three days ago, we had clouds, snow, and then an icy dust-wind. — And because you have left, I had a bit to fight for keeping my inside bright and warm. But this is only, I know, a passing depression. Close, or far, you are essentially for me brightness in the life, — a mere light, — as your name, in Latine, means. I hope that in the south, you have escaped any shadow, and that Shanghai is nothing but sunny, for you. — Might, tomorrow, the parting with your mother not be too hard for you!*

*My personal plans seem now to be settled as follows. Today I go to Tientsin. I come back to Peiping on Saturday. On thursday 22nd I leave to Shanghai by the same train of 8 a.m. as you. Then I stay in Shanghai, up to the 27th (arrival of Barbour). Then I don't know. But I will write to you again, before. — Evidently, we cannot join. Our trains will probably cross each other, somewhere. — But we shall meet here again, — before long, —— and pick up together the fruits of the absence.*

*When we parted, you observed that I looked somewhat "un-personal". That is probably true. The reason of it, I think, is that, when I look at you, I am searching something <u>in you</u>, which is deeper than you, — and which however is the very essence of you. But I don't believe that doing so (this is the only way in which I am able to look at anything in the world), I am missing anything in you. Nor do you, I think, miss anything in me. ——*

*Nothing else, besides. Did not see anybody, but Grabau and Black*

*So much yours*

*P.*

*P.S. I have open the box containing the special edition of "La Croisière Jaune". A very luxurious book, with pictures largely different from those of the small edition. A large picture of me. You shall see.*

*Yesterday, in a french review, I found those lines, from the well known Paul Valéry:*

*"La valeur vraie de l'amour est dans l'accroissement de vitalité générale qu'il peut donner. Tout amour qui ne dégage pas cette énergie est mauvais. Ceci suggère qu'il faut utiliser ce ferment sexuel vers des fins nouvelles. Ce qui croyait n'avoir à faire que des hommes tourne à faire des actes, des oeuvres. Production, après reproduction."*

"The true value of love is in the growth of the general vitality that it may give. Any love that does not release this energy is wrong. This suggests that this sexual ferment should be used for new purposes. That which was believed to be there to generate human beings turns to generate acts, works. Production, after reproduction."

*Is that not exactly what we have so often told? — I know very well Valéry. But I don't remember to have discussed this matter with him.*

*Peking, March 18th, 1934*

*Lucile, dear friend,*

*I send to you these few lines, à tout hasard, in the hope that they will reach you in the south. Yesterday, coming back to Peiping, I found with joy your precious letter of the 12th. I received it in my heart and in my mind. Yes, I feel sure that they are great prospects for us, in front. If I can give you something, you, in turn, you can help me and complete me, not only by the warm light of yourself, but also by your keen and strong sense of the reality. You have still to teach me a lot of things. And may be we shall do something for "dematerializing" a little the Matter around us.*

← ✳

*I feel deeply, today, this necessity for saving the world from its material darkness. You know already that Dr. Black passed away, day before yesterday. The apparent absurdity of this premature end, — the stoical, but blind, acceptance of this fate by the surrounding friends, — the complete absence of "light" on the poor body lying in the ice-room of the P.U.M.C., have deepened my grief, and revolted my mind. — Either there is an escape, somewhere, for the thought and the personality, — or the world is a tremendous mistake. And we must stop. — But, because nobody will admit that we must stop, — then, we must believe. To awake this belief must be, more than ever, my duty. I have sworn it to myself, on the remains of Davy, —— more than a brother, for me.*

*The end was nice, and simple. Black had the fallacious impression of getting much better. He had come to the Laboratory, seen several friends, talked cheerfully. Then, when he was alone, he passed away, close to his desk, between his maps and its fossils. Absurd, —— or wonderful.*

*Now, we try to save the boat. I have, for a part, to take the rudder. Dr. Greene asked me to do so. — The first clear thing is that we have to go on. The plans will not be altered. Most probably I will go to Shanghai (may be arriving on the 24 only), and we shall try to make the trip Nanking-Hankow. — In the meantimes, we shall search somewhere in the world an anthropologist for the study of our material. Every day, probably, the depth of the loss we have made will become more apparent.*

*But you will help me. ——*
*Be happy, and sure of me.*

*Yours*

*P.*

*(I suppose you have received my letter of last Tuesday).*

---

Teilhard put aside his own work to serve as acting head of the P.U.M.C.s laboratory until the Rockefeller Foundation sent out a replacement for Davidson Black.

---

*Peiping, March 21th, 1934*

*Lucile, my dear friend,*
*I have received this morning your two letters from Shanghai. I knew you were with me, during those sad days, — and I felt stronger. "God bless you" as used to say sometimes dear Davy.*

*I write those few lines in the P.U.M.C., and I will bring them at your gate, — which I did even not see since you left. — I wish that you should have a proof of my thinking of you, when you come back in your home.*

*I leave tomorrow morning. — Are we going to cross each other? — anyhow, as you say, we are always close, —— and closer.*

*Yours*

*P.T.*

*[P.S.] Mrs. Hempel will let you have the large edition of "La Croisière Jaune". —
(Look at the end for my picture!)*

Shanghai, March 29th, 1934

*Lucile, dear friend,*

    *Last saturday, arriving in Shanghai, I found your letter, waiting for me.
So, our paths have crossed in Nanking. I think I felt it, when I passed there! —
Anyhow, I am glad you have enjoyed your trip. And I enjoy thinking that you are
now back to your little home, under the trees. It is more easy for me to see you, in
my imagination, in those familiar surroundings, — in the studio. And the prospect of coming back to your gate will be as a brillant spot before me, in the course
of the present journey.*

    *I have been rather busy, here. And I am still in this tedious period of dis-
cussing and preparing things. I would like to be already somewhere on the field.
— Barbour has arrived two days ago. We plan to leave to morrow (or perhaps
day after tomorrow), for Hangchow probably, then Nanking, then Kulin, then
possibly Hankow. But this programm depends on so many people outside of ourselves that it is subject to alterations. — In any ways, we shall not be more than
4 or 5 weeks absent from Peking. — You will probably observe that it is a rather
long time. — But, as I told you, this survey of the Yangtze is probably the most
important piece of my work this year. I have to do it nicely, — for me, — and for
you. I shall feel more eager and happy, thinking that your approval is on me.*

    *From the Geological Survey's side, things do not improve. Conditions of
Dr. Wong have recently turned to be worse. He got a strong fever, for unknown
reasons. Yesterday, I have seen Dr. Dieuaide, back from Hangkow. He is still hoping. But the case is very serious. The coming of Barbour is a providential thing, —
specially for me. He has got a clear mind, an exact knowledge of the Chinese, and
he is deeply devoted to our work. We have to take largely the control of the ship,
this year. — Another thing I like in Barbour is that we agree perfectly, although
tacitely, he and myself, in our views on the deep and divine meaning of the world.
— Impossible, so far, to come in touch with V.K.Ting, —now in Hangkow.*

    *We had a terrible weather here: cold, rainy, windy. This morning, how-
ever, the sun is shining. So are you.*

    *I shall write you, the next week, from Nanking. My mail will be sent
there for a while. - May the Eastern joy and youth be with you! ——*

    *Yours*

    *P.T.*

*I have received a very nice invitation from Mrs. Mac Hugh, — but could not man-
age for going Tunsing Road.*

[a wire from Shanghai] *March 30th, 1934*

    *We leave tomorrow, for Nanking directly*

    *Yours*

    *P.T.*

*Lucile, dear friend,*
        *We left Shanghai last Saturday, — and since that time, we are working in the Nanking area. The three last days have been used in a somewhat longer trip to the Mao-shan, some 50 miles south-east. Using a "bus", we reached rather easily the proximity of the mountain. But then we had to use several more primitive ways for proceeding: chair, and chiefly foot. Two nights spent in a rather homely inn at the very foot of the Mao-shan. There is a famous temple on the top and we came at the very time of the pilgrimage. Hundred of peoples, coming up and down, — often in chair, — bringing yellow wreaths or childish objects, and also sticks: like in the Miao-fan-han. — I enjoyed very much the country, which we could see, at least one day, under a bright sun. The rocky hills, emerging from the flat rice fields spotted with pools, were positively poetical. I liked specially, along the slopes, the small houses, almost clean, conceiled in the middle of bamboo groves, amidst pink or red peach-trees. A few weeks later, the country must be lovely. I include in this letter an iris flower which was so nice when I picked it up, for you, on the Mao-shan slopes.*
        *The work itself is highly interesting. I enjoy deeply to study, and to try to understand, a China which is entirely new for me. Barbour is a great friend, and a keen physiographist* [a geologist specializing in topography]. *We have, he and myself, quite a different way of grasping the facts. But that is precisely an advantage. — We are probably going to stay here 4 or 5 days more. And then we shall proceed to Kiukiang and Kulin. But, for doing this, we have to wait for J. S. Lee* [a Chinese colleague and a paleontologist], *who has not yet written, from Peiping.*
        *My life is presently concentrated on gravels, terraces, topographical surfaces, etc. But you know that, for me, merging in those material things means only getting a fresher contact with the roots of the spirit. — The "spirit" is always there, and* you *with Him. And I feel that I am, in spite of the absence, coming closer to both.*
        *I hope that you are happy, —— and happily working. My mail will be sent here from the survey those days.*

        *Yours deeply*

        *P.T.*

*Nanking, April 10th, 1934*

*Lucile, dear friend,*
        *Your letter sent to Shanghai missed me (I will find it in Tientsin). But the last one (April 7th) came here one hour ago. And it was very sweet for me, to read it. I like you so much, Lucile. And you are so "straight" and courageous. I feel stronger and better, because you like me. And you are very powerful for giving me the light and the strength I need, — just because you are so frank, and because you* understand *me. Not to feel* alone internally *is the best of the life, isn't? - I have been pleased, and a little amused, that you should enjoy my wild face in the Croisière Jaune. I will positively write Williams to send me a copy for you.*

*A real joy for me was to know that you have started again your regular
and working life. I wonder which is going to be your next artistic inspiration. I
shall see it amidst your blooming flowers. — Go on in your art, and in everything
[that] is beautiful. But try to reach the bottom of its attraction and of its value.
Then you will be very close to your God.*

*I write you rather in a hurry. Barbour is packing and talking around my
room. We are leaving to morrow morning. A first stop in Nganking; — another
one (the important one) in Kiukiang (near Kuling). Then probably Hankow. And
then Ta-Tien-Shui-Ching Htg! — You can write me at the Central Post office
(Poste restante) Hankow for the 22th or the 23th. — I will send you a note from
the chief stations (Hinkiang and Hankow). —— The work is developing well. But
I realise that it is sometimes delicate to deal with the Chinese "susceptibilité".*

*Yours so deeply*

*Pierre*

*April 20th, 1934*

*Lucile, dear friend,*

*I write you on a boat, on the Yangtze. A lovely morning, sunny, with a
touch of fog on the low hills. We are due this afternoon to Hankow, — that means
to the Kinhan railway. I wish to have a letter ready, which I can send you immediately. Maybe I will also find a word of you, at the Post-office. ——*

*Since I wrote you, we have been going on, according our plan. A first stop
at Nganking, — an another, longer one, in Kiukiang, — which we have left yesterday evening. J. S. Lee had joined us in Kiukiang. Under his direction W. had an
excellent trip to Kulin, — just at the end of the cold weather. When we reached
the top of the Lu-shan, all the trees were still covered by a thick sheet of ice. But
the sun was already there. And the most part of our visit we had spring, or even
summer days. The Kulin mountains are really impressive, some 1,400 meters high,
and set between large lakes. You would have enjoyed the sight of the slopes, covered with pine-trees, oaks, and large bamboos. The hills were pink, or purple, or
yellow, with blooming azalés, rhododendrons and wild lilacs; and the "cigales"
[cicadas] were singing just as in June, in Peiping. The flower I enclose here for you
is a nice clematite, picked up along the shores of the Poyang lake.*

*We have been walking a good deal, all those days. Some 20 or 30 kilome-
ters each day, and not in a flat country! — I was surprised to find myself so little
tired. In fact, those days of work are rather an excellent rest for me. — We spent
two nights in very picturesque temples. But the food was rather terrible. In Kulin,
happily, there is an excellent foreign hill.\**

*The work is much interesting. We could not decide, of course, whether Lee
is right or not, with his theory of a glaciation of the Lushan. The features are
rather equivocal. But the formations are really big, and extensive. And I am
learning a lot in Chinese geology.*

---

\*Teilhard probably meant to write "foreigners hotel."

*Our plans in Hankow are still vague. I suppose we are going to stay there a week, — trying to build there a geological base. — But Peiping is not far away, anyhow. I will still write you when we have decided. —*

*And I feel that, on my return, I will realize still more how a precious friend you are.*

*Yours*

*P.*

---

Teilhard was in Peking only a short time before he left again to make a trip up the Yangtze.

---

*Hankow, May 16th, 1934*

Lucile, my dear friend,

It was a little distressing for me also, two days ago, to leave you. So, I went on, bringing with me your so precious letter, and now I want to answer it, from a Chinese hotel, in which we got stranded (somewhat by our own fault) yesterday evening. Your fan is beside me (a very useful thing), and I smoke a Chesterfield. Is not the atmosphere complete? — A very slight outer appearance of what you give me so completely inside, Lucile? - Yes, all this time, — and ever — I know, — I feel, that, in spite of the miles, your presence is with me, — or, still more truly, — in me. I enjoy this idea (perfectly "scientific", I believe) that distance does not exist but for what we call "matter". Gradually, — and according the proportion of a mutual love, — the spiritualized elements of the world are converging into a common and deeper center, in which nothing whatever can separate them. There I will find you, during those few weeks of absence. I know, this time, you had the harder part: staying, when the other leaves. I am certain however that, after the first moments are over, you will chiefly feel the strength, and the peace, of the unbreakable thing which has grown between us. And you will be still more rich and yourself when we meet again.

The journey, between Peking and Hankow, was perfectly quiet, — not too hot. And so far, here, we have no rain. But everything is rather warm and damp. People say, here, that the heat is exceptional, and will not last very long. All right. — Anyhow, we plan to leave for Ichang no later than tomorrow night. — This afternoon, we must go to the Wuchang University, where Young and Barbour will give a short lecture. This is a regular "corvée", — because the University is far. — But we can not avoid it. —

On the train, I exhausted the possibilities offered by the New-Yorker. — But I did not so much enjoy the "Little King" in the lift, because we could not laugh at it together. - Barbour had brought a number of "Hearst's International Cosmopolitan" (April 1934) in which (p.24), I found a very curious article by a man named C. G. Jung: "Does the world stand on the verge of a Spiritual Rebirth"? Try to read it, if you can. The ideas, substantially, are curiously akin to the mine. The impossibility, for a modern man (the more modern he is) to be satisfied by a work which has not a "définitive" value, is expressed there, in a very impressive way, by a technical psychologist. — I am sure you will be interested by those pages.

*[margin annotation: first encounter with (an article) C. G. Jung — ideas of]*

*Good bye, dear. Be happy. And don't forget, never, that what sweetness I force myself not to give you (in addition to the "strength"), — I do it in order to be more worthy of you. — Someday, I know, you will understand more fully.*

*Yours*

*P.T.*

I shall write to you before long.

Ichang. — May 23th, 1934

Lucile, dear friend,

I suppose, you have received, several days ago, my letter from Hankow. Since that time, we have been going on peacefully, in our trip. — We arrived here, Ichang [a **walled city and treaty port**] three days ago, — by a very good, and fast, steamer. Between here and Hankow, the journey is rather tedious. With the exception of the approach of the Tungting lake, and of the approach of Ichang, the [**Yangtze**] river is bending, endlessly, in a perfectly flat and unattractive country. — Ichang, on the contrary, is very picturesque. The town, built in a hilly and pretty landscape, appears, looking from the river, as a row of small and high banks of the Yangtze. — All three, we are sheltered in a very comfortable house, the Scotch Mission (friends of Barbour), in which a set of perfectly nice old ladies keep us properly fed with cakes and tea, the entire day. — Meanwhile, we try to work, in spite of frequent rain. Yesterday, on a launch of the Customs, we had a marvelous trip in the Ichang gorges. The water was high and strong, and the cliffs splendid. Everywhere, waterfalls were running down the precipitous walls, — and everything was so intensely wet and green. I thought that it was just a pity you should not be with me. Geologically speaking, this is one of the most famous sections in China, and I was glad to see it for the first time. — Today, we have been working around Ichang,— and I collected the orchid flower enclosed in this letter. We plan to leave day after to morrow, straight to Chunking, — a matter of three days, since the boats stop during the night. Then, probably, we shall come back, unless we decide to go to Chentu. ——

On the whole, I am satisfied, — because I see and learn a lot of things.

The only weak points, in such a half-touristic journey, is that the mind is not so alert as in the quiet laboratory work, — or as in a real trip in the wild. I feel rather difficult, under such circumstances to "find myself". I wonder, sometimes, where really I am. — But, several experiences have proved me that, after such periods, something new had been softly growing in me. — So I know that, when I come back to Peking, you will find me somewhat more myself, and yours.

In the meantimes, I like to have my thought wandering to Peking, — to your dear little home. Might every blessings come then down from Heaven! —

Good bye. — You could send me a word here (we shall be here back in a fortnight), or still more safely to Hankow (poste restante).

Yours

P.

*Lucile*

*And now you are away again two whole weeks — and I have only the same things to say to you — only more so. You've become more important in my life every day. Yes. The live, physical, real you, all of you. I want you so terribly and I'm trying so hard to understand and incorporate into my being your philosophy, your views on life. I read and reread and I think I understand, but <u>why</u> do they not make me feel them more deeply. I want to <u>so much</u> — I must for my own salvation — I can't have you. Not really, so I must learn your way of having each other.*

*China Navigation Co. S.S.*
*May 29th, 1934*

*My dear friend, L.*

*I have written to you a few days ago, from Ichang. Now we are on the Yangtze, a few hours before reaching Chunking. We took, at Ichang, a very small but nice steamer (Jardine Co); — young, and very agreable British officers; - and, in addition to ourselves, two first class passengers only: a dumb Japanese officer, and Captain Clavell Wilkinson, who is in charge of bringing you this letter. This way is probably scarcely slower than the mail; and I am sure you will enjoy to have a talk with this young man, with whom I felt really friend. —*

*Since we left Ichang, the weather has been perfect. And the gorges are just so wonderful as people say. For a geologist, the journey is really "unique". — Perhaps we came a bit late, for the scenery: flowers are passed, and, by high waters, the rapids are less impressive. But, still, the landscape is a pure marvel, — and so deeply chinese! I am always thinking that I should like so much to have you here, when we are passing a high pagoda-tower set on a spur of rock, or a gorgeous and intricated temple half conceiled amidst the cliffs and the trees, — or one of those curious cities hanging along the river's banks. — Tomorrow we will have to start a more serious work, on the field. Our plans are not yet very definite. We must have a talk with the Chunking's people, before deciding.*

*In the meantime, I discovered my soul sufficiently alert. I have been thinking pretty much. And, as a result, I feel more and more a passionate child of Mother Earth - and yours.*

*P.T*

*Wanhsien (Szechuan) June 8th, 1934*

*Lucile, dear friend*

*You have probably received the visit of Mr Wilkinson (with whom I have crossed the Yangtze gorges), — and he has probably also given you the short letter which I have given to him for you. He looks a very pleasant young man, and I thought you would like to have a talk with somebody who had seen me recently. -*

*Presently, we are in Wanhsien, in our way back to Hankow. Wanhsien is a picturesque city, slightly modernised, hanging (as so many other towns along the Yangtze) over the steep banks of the river. We stay here in order to study a very important fossiliferous locality, at one day in the mountains. On account of a heavy rain, we could not start this morning. Tomorrow will be better. I hope.*

*After three days we shall be back, and then take the first available boat to Ichang (where I expect to find my mail), and to Hankow. I don't think that we may be later in Peiping than on about the 20th. In any case, I will let you know, when the day of our arrival will be fixed.*

*On the whole, I am satisfied by the trip so far. From Chungking (another "hanging city", but strongly transformed by motocar-streets and ambitious shops) I went to Chengtu (280 miles by a rather good road), which looks as the Peking of Szechuan: no foreign houses, but exclusively low chinese roofs, half conceiled under the old trees. The french consul of Chengtu, Dr. Béchamp, is a dear friend of mine, extraordinarily brillant (artist, linguist, physicist and physician, etc.), — but somewhat sceptical and pessimistical. We had long talk, both together. Apparently he is just so far from believing in anything that I am myself a passionate believer (in certain things). But still we enjoy to be together, - probably because we can be absolutely true with ourselves when discussing the problems of the life. You would have liked the Béchamp's house, — full of Chinese embroideries and curios, — and very pretty (so much as a non married man is able to keep the things pretty). Every evening, we could, during two hours, listen to perfectly distinct talks and music, from our common Paris. This combination of the most refined humanity in the heart of western China was a kind of triumph on the life. — From Chengtu [capital of Sezchuan province] —— we had a trip, by motocar, to Kwanhsien, a picturesque little town which acts for the Thibetan area as Kalgan for the Mongolia. The town is built at the very foot of the snowy Szechuan Alps, - and works as a continuous market for exchanges between the mountain and the Chinese plain. —— Geologically, the journey has been highly interesting for me. My only "regret" is not to have been able going a bit further westwards. Still, I have crossed the entire Sezchuan, — a beautiful country which I will describe better to you when we meet again in your dear, little home. Useless to tell you, I think, how much I look forward for this happy day. My hope is to find a letter of you in Ichang, after a few days. Might those past weeks have been for you full, and happy!*

*Yours more deeply than ever*

*Pierre*

[Note to herself] *June 17, 1934*

*There was another dear letter from you three days ago and you say "more deeply than ever yours". I wonder what that means? But it is <u>more</u> and that is enough for me. You will be home just in a few days. It seems as if I couldn't wait. How to fill in the time, and what can I do and think to be more worthy of you, Pierre. I shall try. Of that I am sure, for I want your love so much that I will do anything to keep it and to make it grow. So that I may be a part of your very life as you are of mine, and I shall learn to control my emotions.*

*And then came your wire saying that you will be here Tuesday. I am so happy and feel so completely yours. I love you every minute of every day and that love is going to make me a better and I hope finer woman. I am on my guard not to do anything that would be unworthy of our friendship, and all the time I am more fully understanding and believing your ideas and they are becoming a part of me, so I must be better.*

*But I still love you so that it hurts - which is probably not the way you want me to love you - but Pierre I shall learn - and you will help me.*

*Loyang, July 18th, 1934*

*Lucile, dear friend,*

*We have arrived safely here this morning, 4 a.m., after a remarkly cool, and windy journey. Today, unfortunately (?) the sun is shining, and the day is warmer. But still, the conditions are sufficiently good; and we have found, near the railway station, a rather clean small inn, very quiet, - in which nobody tries to watch everything we do. The local officials, also, have been very kind. We plan to leave, tomorrow morning (or a day later) by motorcar, to the southwest - Some hundred kilometers, probably. Further, we hope to find mules.*

*This is the present, external situation. — Now I must tell you, internally, how much I have been, and deeply, moved by your letter. I read it several times, carefully, - and this has been my "inner" sun of yesterday. — Yes, Lucile I want your womanliness. And all the question for me is to know how I can get it without being of any undue trouble in your life. God (whom I dream you will gradually discover) will help us to find the path which we are finally searching for Him.*

*When we meet again, we shall have to talk again of your "trinal" conception of the perfect love. The problem, I told you, exists for me just as for you, — although, for some complex reasons, I believe to have to stick somewhat to an old solution. My line of answer, let me observe, does not exclude the "physical" element, — since it is not some abstract spirit, — but the "woman", — which I discover in you. All the question is to decide whether, amongst the natural "effects" which you alluded to, some have not to be avoided (in certain cases) precisely because they have, in themselves, something of an end, or of an achievement, or of an internal completion, which makes them rather a <u>terminal</u> stage than a <u>step</u> towards the only complete spiritual union. -*

*Anyhow, you are right in observing that life is constantly going on by "compromissions". But, then, we must understand that obeying those "contingencies" is not a mere expression of "bon sens". This submission expresses the faith we have that the most beautiful thing we can do by our life is to fill, as perfectly as we can, the place in which we happen to be in the Universe. — In our particular case, also, we can find some kind of happiness in thinking that what we have to suffer or to miss expresses (and pays for) the work of discovering something which is grand and new, — the "new discovery of the Fire". —*

*I hope, Lucile, that yesterday was not too much a cloudy day for you; — and that you found some mysterious compensation to the "breaking of the habit". I paid you mentally, and heartily, my visit, at 5 p.m. — God might help you in finding how I can "animate" your life without interfering in anything with its normal external course!*

*And God bless you for the sweet strength you have become for me!*

*I will write you again before long.*

*Yours*

*P.*

*I seem to have so few thoughts about God — there is still an inner resistance that I don't quite understand — Perhaps it is because so many recent Christians have been such dry narrow uninteresting people—most of my friends the people whom I consider to be <u>doing</u> things are mostly like myself — vaguely or strongly believing in a greater force and hoping by doing some good work and developing one's self to the best of one's ability to add to the sum total of good in the world — when we create this force for good we add something to the world and in this way we are doing our share and "loving God"——*

*I would like to love God in the way P.T. does — perhaps that will come in time — For certainly he has an inner strength and integrity that is unique — is it because of his feeling for God or just because he is that — probably both —*

*His "credo" — or whatever it is still seems to me the best expression of a faith that I have yet found —*

*Perhaps it is because I have been trying to contemplate and write about the spirit of the world, God, and also because I have read your notebook and realize how much of you is unworldly. And I wrote you just before you left in which I spoke of the "physical". Please don't think I mean just sex, although that is very strong. It would make a bond between us that would add a strength that I believe <u>nothing</u> else can give. However, that is only a part. I want to be with you and when you are well and when you are ill. Go see beautiful things with you and walk through the country. In other words, I want to stand beside you always, to laugh and play and pray with you. Don't you realize what a big part of life that is, and how that is what is right and normal and God-given. But I cannot. <u>Ne puis pas</u>.*

*Lucile, dear friend,*

*Just a few lines, in order to prove you that I don't forget you.*

*We are now at Lushih, a small "hsien", five days south-west of Loyang, along the Lo-ho. — We came here by carts, then by mules. And today we plan to leave, by chairs and mules, for Sichuan, a small town south of the Tsinling range.*

*Very picturesque and montainous country. Geologically, we have hit a critical and fascinating place, — much more interesting than I could hope. — Weather rather cool. Not too much rain.*

*Going to Sichuan will possibly delay us a little, may be a week. Still we hope to be back to Peiping not much later than the August 15th.*

*Hope you have received my letter from Loyang. — I enjoy the thought that you are probably quiet, — fundamentally happy, — and that you are going to take holiday, somewhere. -*

*<u>Yours</u> ever*

*P.*

*How I wish he were free so he could spread his beliefs of religion freely - they are so sane and intelligent and so appealing to the world of today —— which needs and <u>longs</u>*

*for the very thing that he has to give — whereas his church neither wants not condones it - Maybe something will happen if they would only kick him out! But I'm afraid he has been a bit too cautious — with a wee bit more daring he could be a flower to brighten the dark places and give man something solid to hold to in this age of catastrophies and sudden changes ——*

[Journal] *August 2, 1934*

*A letter this morning from P — which gives me <u>such</u> inner peace and happiness- translating now "Christianity and Evolution" and hope to learn from that - I realize how often the ideas just skim to the top of my mind and they do not penetrate way down and become a part of my consciousness - I shall keep at this paper until I have really digested it - It is hard for me to accept the importance - or if not the importance, then the <u>necessity</u> of Christ in religion- He seems to me too emphasized in a way that confuses the whole pan- theistic idea — (And I am a pantheist-)*

[Journal] *August 8, 1934*

*Because I decide I would like to believe in God, I expect to have Him suddenly and fully revealed to me — and I am distressed and doubtful when this does not happen - which is certainly a wrong and absurd point of view — Everything else in this world that is worth while has to be gotten (or maintained) slowly with work and thought — so why should I expect this most precious gift — of a feeling at-Oneness with God should come to me suddenly and fully made.*

*A human love seems to come suddenly and easily —— That is the glorious mira- cle and great joy of it - But to maintain the love — there is the great problem — and one that we are apt not to realize but expect the love to function completely and perfectly by itself —*

*P —— I shall work for <u>both</u> — I want yours as much as God's —*

[Letter to herself] *August 9. 34*

Pierre,

*How the days pass and yet how they repeat themselves — at least in the mean- time I have <u>seen clearly</u> how I can live, and function fully with you in the position that <u>you</u> would have.*

*The "light" that animates my life without having any very definite part in its daily routine - and I still inwardly fight against accepting this fully - I subconsciously hope that some miracle - or accident - will happen to make a <u>normal</u> relationship possible. I might say "ordinary" and then I can revolt against that.*

*No, it <u>cannot</u> be ordinary, Pierre, but it is so difficult to give up those old ideas. They aren't just <u>mine</u>. They are bred into my whole being. There is a little feeling of being traitor to <u>something very important</u> and <u>fundamental</u>, in giving up my views and accept- ing yours - and yet I know that I must and that I must substitute them for something finer.*

*And I remember in some Indian philosophy that I read a long time ago something to the effect that it is only by giving a thing up that we really get it. Sometimes lately it is hard to realize that <u>you</u> really will be back here soon again. That we shall be together again to laugh and talk and explore new paths.*

*It is so strange when you are away sometimes it is so difficult to touch you, you seem so very far away and then at other moments you are here completely. I can touch you almost—so strong is your presence. But I have gotten a great deal of inner strength since last winter. I think that your help is germinating something real and strong and that will be with me always.*

[Journal] *August 9, 1934*

*In looking over these pages there seems to be quite as much about P. as about God — I was thinking over that last sentence — "I want P.'s love <u>as much</u> as God's." And I don't believe it is true — God <u>must</u> come first — otherwise there is nothing for the other —But it seems to me they can go <u>nearly</u> hand in hand — as the more can help the lesser - so also the Lesser by becoming more pure can become a part of, therefore strengthening to, the More — "Pure" — what does that Mean —— less selfish —— less influenced by worldly motives ——*

*Peiping, August 17th, 1934*

*Lucile, dear friend*
    *As you can easily suppose, I felt a touch of disappointement, when, on the 14th, I found Spotty and Dungshi [Lucile's dogs] only masters of the house, at [Number] 1, Ta Tien Shui Ching (they received me, I must say, very affectionately). But, this impression was immediately swept away by the feeling that you were enjoying the endless green of Mongolia, — and still more by the reading of your precious letter, which has meant so much for me. Because, as you know, my dream is to help you in being more fundamentally happy, more conscious of yourself, more aware of the essential values of the life, more free. And, by your letter, I could see that you are gradually undergoing this "métamorphose". — Most evidently, we shall have still to meet the clouds, from time to time. But the climbing path, towards the glorious mountain, is already clearer, in front of us. Let us trust, fully, the highest possibilities of the life: they will never deceive us.*
    *As I have just told you, I am glad that you decided to go to Mongolia. Whatever might be the final success of the trip, you will feel better, and younger, just for having tried what you were planning for such a long time. And, on your return, the Peking's life will have new interest, and something like a new flavour for you. I have experienced it so many times, myself.*
    *Personally, I have made an exceptionally interesting trip. After I wrote you, from Lushih (I could not find, later, any other place from where I could send you a letter which would arrive before myself), we have crossed the Tsinling mountains, reached the northern border of the Hupeh, — and, from this latter place, travelled eastwards up to the Kinshan railway, south of Kaifong. The country was quiet, — but the communications rather uneasy. We had to use carts, mules, chairs, and finally rickshaws (for 4 solid days!). Very picturesque mountains and people; — and practically no rain. From the most essential, that is from the geological, point of view, I am "over-satisfied". Once more, I realize that I would have lost a lot if, at the middle of July, I had given up, by some weariness, the idea of making this trip.*

C'est beau,
C'est beau,
Si tu voyais
là haut au
fond là-bas

*I leave tomorrow for Tientsin. My plan is to begin my "retraite" sunday evening (19th). After this time, I will have (by decency) to stay a few days more with my colleagues. But I must be back in Peiping in the very first days of September. At the end of the month I shall write you, from Tientsin, a <u>few</u> lines, in order to let you know the precise day of my return (I prefer, from Tientsin, where I don't post my letters myself, not to write too much extensively and too much personally). — In the meantimes, I will be "with you" very closely. Trying to put myself deeper under the divine "influence" is a work in which I cannot separate you from me. ——*

*Thank you so much for the pages you included in your letter. We shall discuss them, in September, — and many other things, also. ——*

*Yours so much*

*P.*

[Journal] *October 14, 1934*

*The sun shines — the air is fresh and cool and I am deeply happy — it seems to me I love more completely every day — He is the man I've been dreaming to find all my life everything - except why did God put in that little joke of making him a priest!*

[Note to herself] *November 7, 1934*

*He has gone away for a week — so I turn again to my pen — I want to be more conscious of what he is and of what I can be for him — we have talked very deeply lately of him, his relations to institutions etc. — it is not all clear — sometimes it does not seem completely right — but is it possible to have things completely right here in this life — By trying to right one angle — may we not make another one so sharp it will cause great pain and sorrow — and yet by following the safe and happy mean — does not seem the <u>best</u> always — It's often by hard things that the great ideas are born into the world — Anyway the moment has not yet arrived — If I can help to keep the Divine flame more alive and bright in P. —— it will eventually show the Right Way.*

*Pengpu, January 3d, 1935, 5 p.m.*

*Lucile, dear,*

*We have just arrived in Pengpu, — and I will take the chance of this stop for writing to you in a readable way. — A day since I left you, — and this famous "2th" is over! I want to tell you again how I feel safe and sure that these weeks of absence are going to strengthen and to feed what is borne so deep between you and me. These last days, I believe, have been the most rich, and full, which we have ever experienced. There is no limit, I think, to this growing, mutual, "interpenetration" of the lives. Might you become even more happy and free by me, as you make me more alive and more true! ——*

*This first part of the journey is going its ordinary way: rather monotonous. We left the snow and the ice a long time ago. The weather is scarcely cool, — but so covered, and so grey. Maybe I will find Canton too warm, and long for the winter of Peking.*

*Yesterday, when I entered my car, I met the Rector of Tientsin, my friend P. Charvet, and we went on together, talking, up to Tientsin. In some way, I was glad to meet him, but in some way also, I "blessed" him, because I should have preferred to be left alone with my thoughts, and with you.*

*I spent this day reading your "brochures". An article on the Christ, by Charles Hall Perry, "the Man Amongst Men" interested me. The author is right, reproaching the Church to have too much forgotten the human side and teaching of Jesus. But do we not need a God for our human life? We shall discuss it. (I keep the paper). — Elsewhere, I noticed this quotation of "Dona Margherita", the "Woman behind Mussolini": "a woman does not influence a man by what she says, but by what she is". I think it is so beautiful and so true.*

*I will do my best for sending you a few lines tomorrow, when I know the time of departure of the Prest. Taft [an American ship bound for Hong Kong].*

*Be sure that you shall be everywhere with me, — as a smile and a light.*

*Pierre*

*Jan 12th, 1935*

*Lucile, dear,*

*I sent you my last letter from Hong Kong. And, as you see, we are still in Canton, — which we plan to leave tomorrow, by boat, for Wuchow (Kwangsi). I should have liked to start earlier. But we had to stay here a few days, waiting for Dr. Chang (the professor of Geology at Sun Yat-sen University) who is going to lead us during our journey. Chang is a great friend of Young, and we have been together in Mongolia, with Roy. To have him with us is an advantage which cannot be paid at too high a price. -In the meantimes, we had plenty to do here, inspecting the collections, and visiting the best geological sites around the city. I learn a lot of new things. — Everybody is really charming for us. Two days ago, I gave a short lecture in the University. And, yesterday evening, we have been offered a remarkable chinese dinner in the best restaurant of Canton. I thought, during this little feast that you would have enjoyed the place and the sight. So different from the small restaurants of Peking! — A long room, entirely open on a garden sheltered by great evergreen trees. — We found here a summer weather, sunny, scarcely too hot. People are going half naked. Many flowers, everywhere. I can scarcely imagine that you are still freezing in Peiping. And still I have better not to think too much of Peiping. I miss it, — chiefly because I miss you. — And yet, as you know, this feeling is not a depressing, but rather an "exalting" one. — I will ever do my best in the life for you, Lucile. ——*

*On the whole, Canton is a queer city, awfully noisy, swarming with human agitation, essentially Chinese. Practically all the old houses have disappeared, - replaced by half-foreign buildings: imagine a maze of magnified "Morrison streets". This is not specially artistic, but so full of lights, of life and of noise. - China seems to survive just the same under the new cloths. - Outside of the city proper, the growth of Canton is still more impressive. Everywhere, along the news roads, rise ambitious buildings: the new University (an enormous thing, in new chinese style, cf. PUMC or Yenching [a university in Peiping]), modern barracks with a constant buzzing of tanks and aeroplanes, innumerous memorials to the*

Revolution and Sun Yatsen. I get sick of this Sun Yat-sen[*] and of his statues "in redingote". A depressing god! - Such a poor change for the Christ. — The country itself is charming, with the red rolling hills, the pine-apple fields, the rice-fields, the huge banyan trees, and the constant going along the roads of tiny chinese so much like to Indochinese.

My time has been so much occupied from the chinese side that I did not go to Shamên nor to the American consultate. — Now, for our return, the plans are somewhat altered. We shall probably go back directly, by boat, from Wuchow to Hong Kong. This is shorter. — Yet, you can send me a letter c/o Dr. Chang, Dept of Geology, Sun Yat-sen University, Canton, (the letter will be forwarded) (unless you prefer to send it c/o Dollar Line, Hongkong, — waiting, — at the beginning of February).

Everything is all right, as you see. — I hope that you, you are happy, in spite of the absence. I am so full of you, Lucile. — How to thank you for what you are for me!

Evidently, I had no time for writing anything. On the Taft, Béchamp was always with me. — Still, my thoughts are progressing, I feel it, — specially concerning the value (and the emptiness) of the past. I think that I have crossed a critical point in my internal evolution, those past months, —— with you. ——

Yours

Pierre

*Nanning Jan 18th, 1935*

Lucile, dear,

My last letter was from Canton. Since that time, we have covered a long way; and, today, I write you from the Kwangsi chief town, way up along the Hsi-kiang (West River). From Canton to Wuchow, we used a small steamer,- and, from Wuchow to Nanning (about 400 miles), we used a private motocar, in order to see better the country. The road was excellent, the driver good, the small hotels perfectly decent, and we four (Young, Pei, Chang and myself) very gay. Since the arrival to Wuchow, the winter has arrived in the south: a cloudy sky, and a minimum of 7 centigrade. People look frozen, and go along the roads under a blanket, or with a small basket with burning charcoal on their belly. But, on the whole, it is not so cold. Only, as told us by von Steinen, the houses are mostly open, and there is no trace of heating system whatever. In a way, it is a pity to see the country without sun: everything is so tropical-looking: the huge green trees, the fruit, the red soil, the ferns, the bright birds. Today, the clouds seem thinner. Maybe this cold spell is coming to its end. —

Concerning my work, I am extremely interested. I begin to believe seriously that we understand the formations, in a way which will establish the connexion with the Yangtze and with the North. Each day brings a new light on our views. Once more, I realize that it is good to make an effort in order to see some-

---

*He was a Chinese revolutionary leader (1867–1925) who founded China's first republic. His "cult" was well established by that time.

*thing more, - in spite of the tendency to stay in a very comfortable place. And, all the time, I like to come back to you, in my thoughts, as to the best of the rest. I hope so deeply that for you absence is not too hard, but, on the contrary, brings you a clearer and better appreciation of the great hope which is in the front of our life! — We plan to stay here, and around Nanning, four days, — and then to go to the North. Impossible to foresee clearly the date of our coming back. I hope we can reach a President [a Dollar line ship] at Hong Kong on the 12th Feb., - and Peiping before the 20th February. A bit later than I thought.*

*Yours ever,*

*Pierre*

*Kweiling (Kwangsi), Jan 28th, 1935*

Lucile, dear

*My last letter was from Nanning, — close to Indochina. Now, we are almost in the north of the Kwangsi, not very far from the Hunan. This is the extreme point we planned to reach. The next step we do will be along the way back to Canton. Now it is sure that we shall catch the "President Pierce" on Feb. 12th. —*

*Everything is going well. Each day brings an opportunity for new observations which seem to confirm our views concerning the Tertiary and Quaternary Geology of S. China. - In prehistorical matter, we did not find any Choukoutien. But, here as in Nanning, we have excellent evidences of an ancient culture (cave-dwellers, shell-eating people) which marks an interesting stage in the prehistory of China. Unfortunately, all the caves have been "devastated" by fossil-hunter Chinese, so that a few patches only of the deposits are preserved. On the whole, I think that this journey will have cleared lot of questions left unsolved by the geologists of Canton. So, you see, I have been right in asking you the sacrifice of those few weeks, - and you have been a courageous and helpful friend. Your spiritual "presence" has been comforting me, all this time.*

*From a picturesque point of view, we are in one of the most famous and strange places of China. All around Kweiling, — and far south, — the country is a forest of high pillars or needles of limestone (about 80 or 90 meters high), forming a most extraordinary landscape. Those are the remains of a highly dissected limestone plateau. Amongst this maze of fantastic rocks, emerging from a brick-red soil, the rivers run, a transparent, jade-green water. The pity is only that the country is so much deforested. - Here, the vegetation is not so much tropical as in Nanning. No more palms, nor cycas [a* large plant, also called cycad] *in the rocks. But still we are in a country of oranges, mandarins, and pomalos. — Weather cloudy, and almost cold. The houses are mostly open, — and there is no fire, except for the fire-bowls.*

*Everything all right, also, with Chang, Young, and Pei. Yet, I begin to long for the society of white men, and I shall be extremely glad when I see Hong Kong again. — Our plan is to go, by boat, straight from Wuchow to Hong Kong. If you have written me to Canton, I will have the letter forwarded to Hong Kong. —*

*I hope deeply that you are strong, wise, and happy. — This is apparently the last letter I can write to you before my return, — unless I do it again from Hong Kong. ——*

> *Yours*
>
> *Pierre*

*Hong Kong 8 February, 1935*

*Lucile, dear,*

*I wonder how long before me this letter will reach Peiping. Anyhow, I try my chance for sending you those few lines before I return. — We have arrived yesterday evening from Wuchow, — and we have to wait up to the 13th, here, before leaving. That's the trouble with a return-ticket! — We are due on the 15th in Shanghai. I will probably have to stay there up to the 16th, or the 17th. — On the 19th (or the 20th, at the latest), I shall see you again. — As I told you in my last letter, we did not pass by Canton on our way back. But, if you have sent me a letter there, I hope to receive it tomorrow. I am rather anxious to know what you did and felt, during those last weeks.*

*My last letter was from Kweiling. - Since, the journey has been interesting, — even successful. — We came back along a river, on a small sampan: 4 days on the water, included the new Chinese year. We had our crackers, and the lady of the sampan performed all the small chinese rites, incense, candles, food to the ancestors, etc.*

*Here, I have met the Champeaux, with pleasure. — I expected to find also Béchamp: but no news of him. He has "evaporated".*

*A bientôt, dear. And believe me*

> *Yours very deeply*
>
> *Pierre*

*[Dollar Steamship Line] February 14th, 1935*

*Lucile, dear,*

*Just a few lines before my arrival, — so that you might be sure that I am coming, — and that I have well received your four dear letters (two forwarded to Hong Kong, from Canton, — and the two others found on the President Pierce). — They were so precious for me, those long letters, in which I could read so clearly the gradual deepening and strengthening of our mutual feeling! - Yes, this is the distinct rising of the bright hopes which are in front of our lives, under as well as across the sky. Too often, you know, I feel anxious, because I wonder whether I am right and wise in trying to reconciliate together Earth and Heaven. - But when I happen to experience (as in our case) that breaking some respected boundaries means a torrent of new life, — then I feel safer and stronger; — because, you know it also, I don't believe fundamentally in anything but in the awakening of spirit, hope, and freedom. Yes, we shall talk about Erasmus, Bailey Willis, and even B. Russell (whom I dislike instinctively, in spite of his worshiping by V.K. Ting). — I like to be contradicted, as well as to be approved, by you, so dear! -*

*We are due tomorrow (Friday) in Shanghai. I should like to take the Peiping's train the same day. But that would not be understood, nor admitted, by many friends (inside and outside of my Order). So, I have decided to leave (at the latest), Monday, -arriving in Peiping Wednesday the 20th. I shall see you the same day, - and I would be too glad to have the dinner with you, the same night.*

*The few days spent in Hong Kong were very pleasant. I enjoy this beautiful rocky coast, and its ever-green cover, and its "incessant" movement of steamers, from and for every part of the world. — Every night I used to have dinner with the Champeaux, at the top of the Peak, — and it was delightful, at 11 p.m., to enjoy, from those heights, the sight of the town and of the harbour: looking down at a second sky. — Béchamp passed last saturday, coming from Haiphong, but went straight to Macao. He sent me a letter, asking me to join him there. But I had no time.*

*Finally, I did not write my paper on the "Discovery of the Past". But I feel that this new child wants more and more to come to birth. The fruit is almost entirely ripe, I think. —*

*Instead of writing those pages I had to spend my time in making a report (now practically ready) on my Kwangsi trip: a rather good paper, I think. — When Breuil comes, at the end of the month, I am afraid that my dear "matinées de travail" will be terribly upset. —*

*I think your plans for your journey abroad are perfectly wise. — Personally, I am always decided to leave as soon as possible after the April 15th. The date depends chiefly on the Breuil's plans. - Hope to find a final answer of de Terra in my mail, next wednesday.*

*A bientôt, dear,*

*Yours*

*P.*

[Journal] *February 14th, 1935*

*I have been pretty wise and I have not been depressed — but my friend — the salt has gone out of life when you are away — You must help me to see a way —— Friendship is no doubt the highest form of love — and also very difficult — my primitive woman instincts are so strong — to learn how to control this love is so difficult — but oh my beloved what a worthwhile line of effort —*

[Journal] *March 10, 1935*

*Yesterday we walked together in Central Park — It was so beautiful and so completely right being there with you — you answer and satisfy every need and desire — Friday we talked again of the same subject and you said some things which made everything more clear — It was so simple and yet made several things clear to me — I asked for "bread" — meaning some of the ordinary things that an ordinary man gives to his woman — But we are trying to find a new path — a finer higher way to love — and if we miss some of the ordinary things - it is the price we must pay —— and how really very small a price compared to what we get — I don't know that no one can have all, that every thing has its price - and what prices people pay for such shoddy goods! But here I get the very best in the world and have cried because there was a small price to pay!*

Lucile left for the States a little more than a month after Teilhard returned to Peking. His March letter was most probably the farewell note they customarily wrote for one another, so that the one leaving had a message to take on the journey.

*Peiping, March 29th, 1935*

*Lucile, dear,*

*This time, you are leaving, and I am left behind. This is the hardest part. But I am glad it is my share: because, you know, I would like so much to take on me any pain from your life. — My dream and my hope, is to be for you a strength and a joy only, Lucile. Anything else, which should make you less happy, or weaker, reject it as untrue, as "un-existant": it would not be myself. — We have met in the light: more light will be the proof that we are getting always closer.*

*And now you have left, and you are already facing those eight months of internal adventure: a new conquest of the world under a new spirit. Keep your mind and your heart open, and faithful. Here again, any depressing thought, any suspicion, against God, the Life, or our friendship, would be untrue. You may come across external difficulties: inside nothing is really able to threaten your essential joy. — That is the treasure which does not rust: an everlasting interest discovered in the World at the deepest and personal heart of everything.*

*You are going East. After a few days I am also leaving, West. Is that not as if, by our two lifes, we were making the symbolic gesture of "encircling" the Earth? - Be sure of that: the separation of today is not the end of anything: just a start for the new life. ——*

*God bless you, precious*

*Pierre*

*Peiping, Saturday April 6th, 1935*

*Lucile dear,*

*This morning, I have received your letter, "très attendue", of April 1st; and I want to tell you immediately combien elle m'a été douce. I needed this letter, I must confess you, because the pink charms of the Pekinese spring made me feeling a little sick, in your absence. But now that I know that you have left China sufficiently strong, happy, and chiefly hopeful, this kind of shadow has almost disappeared, — and I can enjoy more directly the joy and the strength of our mutual and common conquests. Because, really, the meaning of our friendship is to discover and to conquer, — ourselves, each other, and the great world around us, — is it not true? — I will, all along these months, tell you what happens to me, in the course and in the line of this "our" development. And next january will positively find us higher and closer than ever, — just because we have parted when we had to do it. And then, also, we shall feel still more sure each of the other, because we shall have tried our wings, — those wings which have been growing so délicieusement in your nest during the past year. —*

Since I left you, on the Tientsin's platform, eight days have already passed. — We were only two days in Tientsin, Breuil and myself. On Sunday night we were back in Peitang [the Jesuit house in Peiping]. And since the routine has been going on — except that I feel still a little lost at 5 p.m. [teatime]. Weidenreich has arrived yesterday, — a very decent old Herr Professor, who pleases me really. He seems very clever in his anthropological line, — but will evidently rely entirely upon me for the geological side of the problems. His wife is a typical, short, rounded, german lady, - but agréable and evidently extremely witty. — I will have to see him as much as possible those days. Finally, I cannot go to Japan (my japanese friends are leaving Tokyo too early), — so that I have decided to go directly from here to Paris, — leaving Peking on the "2th" of May, and reaching Paris on May 15th. Reservations are already made. With the exception of the end of the "Semaine Sainte" (Eastern) which I shall spend in Tientsin with Breuil, I will not leave Peking this month (except for Choukoutien, with Weidenreich).* But even that makes a very short time. I prefer.

Today, I saw Rose who told me that your house is rented! So you were right, not worrying about this question. — Personally, I like to pass at the entrance of Ta Tien Shui Ching, — but I did not yet risk myself further. — Grabau has been operated, five days ago. He looks a little thin and weak. But everything seems to be all right with him. ——

God bless you, dear. And might the big ocean be always smooth and bright for you.

Yours so much

Pierre

Today (Sunday morning)

We are going to the Ming Tombs (Breuil, Pei & myself). I will think of you at each blossom of tree, I think.).

Peiping, April 14th, 1935

Lucile,

I felt a "shock of joy" yesterday, when I received your letter from Kobe. And so many nice things in this letter: that you have a pleasant trip, that you are so well fed, — and above all, that you are happy and hopeful inside. I too, you must be sure of that, I have this curious and sweet experience that you have been "growing" in me, during this last fortnight: becoming, in some way, a kind of living atmosphere, permeating my feelings, my thoughts, my desires, and my plans. Yes (I have told it to you in my last letter) I have been (and I am still) a bit lost, every day, at 5 p.m. But even this pain has something enjoyable in itself, since it makes more tangible for me the place you have been taking in my Universe, — for ever, Lucile. —

---

*Young and Bien also went with them later (from April 23 to 25) to Choukoutien, 37 miles southwest of Peiping and the site of the 1929 discoveries of the skull, jaws, and teeth of extinct Peking man (*Sinanthropus pekinensis*).

*1935 photograph of Teilhard and Breuil at the Ming Tombs.*

*Now, after a fortnight, I am going to leave, too. Better so. — These 2 weeks will be rather busy. Next wednesday (Sunday, today, and I write you from the Peitang), we are going to Tientsin, Breuil and myself. Next Sunday (Easter) or rather Monday, we come back here; and I have to go to Choukoutien with Weidenreich. And, the following week (2nd of May) we start our trans-siberian journey. In the meantimes, I have many papers to finish, — and a lot of "red spots" to distribute on my maps. — One thing makes these last days more simple: I will not have to part from you, when I leave Peiping. And, on the contrary, your strength and your presence will accompany me. ——*

*I wrote you last Sunday, just before going, with Breuil, to the Ming-tombs. A very pleasant day, — but so pleasant that a crowd of Chinese were also enjoying it in the same way as ourselves. In addition, the roofs of the main tomb were in full repair: dust, heaps of lime and of broken tiles. The spell of the place was broken. Yet, the country was lovely, with so many trees white and pink. No rain, since you left. I do not remember to have ever seen such a marvelous spring in China.*

*Grabau is still in the hospital, — but improving very fast. — I saw Rose last thursday (lunch to her house, with Breuil and St. Bennett). Nothing new on this side of Peiping. Last Monday, big cocktail-party given by Fortuyn in honour of Weidenreich. Ida Pruitt was here, back from Shantung. "Half Peking went away since Lucile has left", she told me. — Last friday, paying a visit to Mrs Black, I saw the two puppies (more or less the cousins of "Tunghsi") given by Seaholm. They were perfectly amusing. — Yesterday night, very gay party given by Fieschi. I had to explain everything about Man and Apes. This is the chronicle. The Hoppenot's have left for a fortnight trip along the Yangtze gorges. Mrs Wilder has been rather seriously ill in Nanking.*

*Now, you are on the big blue water of the Pacific.*

*"Que l'océan vous berce de ses lames," amie. Je voudrais être le Monde pour que tout soit toujours doux autour de vous. Mais Dieu peut faire cela, Lui, et Il sait toujours combien vous m'êtes chère. - Reçu, avant-hier, une très bonne lettre d'I. Treat: elle a passé 5 semaines avec son ami (allant avec lui en N<sup>elle</sup> Calédonie, et retour à Tahiti), et pense vaguement rentrer à Paris en automne.*

"May the ocean cradle you in its waves," friend. I would like to be the world so that everything would always be gentle around you. But God can do that, and He always knows how dear you are to me. Day before yesterday I received a very good letter from I. Treat: she spent five weeks with her friend (going with him to New Caledonia, and returning to Tahiti) and thinks vaguely of returning to Paris in the autumn.

*She had received your letter (and my photo), and she says; "I think your friendship with L. Swan an excellent thing. It is the sort of friendship that keeps you still aware of the tenderer things of this world." A bientôt une autre lettre, Dear. (I shall number them, so that you will notice if some is lost).*

*Pierre.*

*Everything is going all right with Weidenreich. He is an extremely able man in his anatomical line, — and very sympathic. ——*

Lucile dear,

It was such another joy for me to receive your 2nd letter from Japan (April 10). It came just after I had sent my letter 2. Since that time, I went to Tientsin, back here, and the day after to Choukoutien, where I come from today. — A terrible weather today: the wind is blowing hard and hot, and the air is yellow of dust and sand. No hope for a drop of rain, it seems. In spite of the tender green of the trees, I prefer to think that you are on the blue sea, today. And yet, I could not help being deeply moved, an hour ago, when I passed the entrance of your street: shall I, before I leave, make a pilgrimage at your gate? - probably. I did not dare to approach it, since you have left.

Everything is going all right, besides, for me. But I am already caught in the whirl of the departure. In this line, also, I prefer you have left first. I could scarcely see you, if you were here! - At the Survey, I hope to leave everything as much ready as possible for the continuation of the work and for my own publications. I appreciate Weidenreich each day more, who evidently, from his side, is more and more caught by the interest of his new position. — Decidedly, the last fragment of skull found in CKT (do you remember when I told you about my discovery in the Lockart Hall?) belongs to a true Sinanthropus. — Things are gradually taking a definite shape, in our investigations.

And now, in a week, I am leaving, with Breuil directly by Mukden and Manchouli. I go ahead a little blindly. I think I have to go: I go. That is all. This new journey I regard (and will more and more regard) as a renewed gift of myself to the Life (enlightened by you, Lucile). What am I going to meet in France and in India? I do not know. But I firmly hope to find more faith in the world, and more contact with the spirit of the world. — The world, I think, waits for me now in Paris, and at the foot of the Himalaya. I obey, — and, doing so, I think that I become closer to you. This is my only reaction to the life, presently.

Next Saturday, dinner of the Nat.Hist.Society, at the Peking Hotel. Breuil is the speaker. I have asked Rose and Miss Dolleans (the french "archivist") and Dantremer (Banque d'Indochine) to come. There is no "Grabau table" this year. Grabau himself is much better now; but he will not leave the Hospital before a few days. — I did not see much of your friends since you left: only Rose, practically, 2 or 3 times. She is a little afraid, these days, not to get the money she expected (at the divorce) for the education of Michel. It seems that this divorce-business is terribly slow. — I met also Magd-Lloyd in the Peking Hotel. She insisted for having me at tea: but I dont think I will have time for it. — Before I leave, I will have a tea with Mac and Timp (and probably miss you terribly). — Did not see Betty.

My next letter will be from Paris, — addressed to Chicago. — God bless you, precious friend, for all you give me.

Yours so much

Pierre

Today, at Cook's, I met Mrs Hayes: she had just received a long letter from Mrs Woodland, who seems in much better moral conditions. Mrs Woodland is now in

Scotland. *She plans to reach Boston the 10th June (c/o Dr. Philip Grabau, 280 Fairmont Ave., Hyde Park, Boston, Mass.)*

[Journal] *May 1, 1935*

*You admit the necessity of working through and <u>with</u> material in order to reach ideas — abstract or God-like — but you deny the use of the material (humans) in order to reach the abstract or God-love — you will say you deny only <u>one</u> part of human love — But here I think you are evading the question — for the physical is not only a very important part but an <u>essential</u> part for the race - I thoroughly agree that human love should become something much finer more spiritual than it is now but it must be <u>through</u> human love — not denying it — it is like telling someone to stop eating in order to become more spiritual —— (which would be true for many) but as a principal — Buddha himself tried and found absurd — no my dear on that point we do not see "eye-to-eye" — and I think that <u>there you</u> refuse to cast off your clerical teachings and look at the facts <u>honestly</u>. You have faced all sort of ideas brought to you by your science — But I still feel that you have refused to face that idea because your life has made it possible for you to evade it. And it is by such people as you that it should be faced and <u>helped</u> not denied ——*

*Lucile
Sue are
right in
this !.*

Peiping, May "2nd", 1935

Lucile dear,

*Just a word before I leave the Peitang for the station. - Everything all right. But "il m'en coûte un peu" to leave Peiping, - where I had the impression of having you, still a little.*

*Anyhow, we must face the future, only. It is in the future, that we have to achieve the triumph of our mutual conquest. I will do my best for being what you love in me. —*

*I leave Peiping in the glory of the peonies. — We had a terrible sandstorm. But the sky is blue again. Sunday last I saw Betty (very gay and majestic) at MacDonald's, who took a good picture of me, which I will send you from Paris. —*

*The divorce of Rose is to be pronounced the next week ... unless she withdraws, because the Jim's propositions are too little. —*

*Grabau is back (today) to Tou Ya Ts'ai Hutung. He will have to exercise before being able to walk as before.*

*I don't number this letter: too short.*

Yours

Pierre

---

Teilhard arrived in France after traveling for more than two weeks on the Trans Siberian railway.

---

Paris, May 18th, 1935

Lucile, my dearest,

*Day before yesterday, when I reached Paris, I found the smile of your letter (of Easter) waiting for me on this other side of the world, — and I caught it with the same deep joy as the real one on the threshold of your little pekinese* *home. You mean so much for me, Lucile, — you, the very expression of my new life, — the last season of my life. — Are you not, now, one of the few who understand me <u>as I am</u>, in the truth of myself? After a few days, maybe, I will make my readjustment to the old West. Presently, I feel still somewhat lost in my ancient environment. Never so much as during the two last years did I cut, consciously and unconsciously, the connections with my past: and now, coming back to the frame of this past, I scarcely can find myself in the middle of the most familiar things; so many are looking so terribly old. — In short, so far, I have experienced more mist than thrill. And still, my friends are receiving me gloriously. So much of hope they build on me. Am I really able to fulfill this hope? — Helped by your active sympathy, I think I will. But I have to retake possession on myself, and to fix more clearly my aims. Finally, this trip to Europe was probably more necessary for me than I thought. In my next letter, I shall be, I hope, in a better position for explaining you my internal reactions. I have but little doubt that I am going to reach a new level of "passion for the world", and of fighting optimism. But the "assimilation" of new elements has first to be achieved, before I can clearly see in the spiritual world, in front of me. I need a renewed expression of myself. I will get it from a renewed faith in Life. ——*

*I sent you a short letter before leaving Peiping. — The journey was interesting, - but spoiled by the numerous (ten!) customs along the railway.* Since Shanhaikwan up to France, the traveller has the feeling to be an undesirable and suspicious man: closely watched all along by the police. — Siberia was still grey, with ice piling along the rivers. We spent 5 hours in Moscow. Clouds of airoplanes in the sky, and a <u>dull</u> crowd of rather cheerful people in the streets: an enormous factory. We need a transformation (and <u>not</u> a suppression) of luxury in the modern world, as urgently as a transformation (and not a suppression) of the spirit of war. To fight for Beauty, amongst Beauty. ——*

*So far I could judge, an huge wave of heavy paganism and of human "depersonalisation" is spreading heavily over Europe. France looks depressed. I am not "déconcerté" by this stage of evolution. But we have to overcome it: the truth is further, in the same line. ——*

*Next time, I will discuss a little more the appreciation you quote me from the Sappho's book. — I do not accept it. Love is the primordial strength of the world. But precisely on account of that, there is no energy where a transformation is more needed, and more going on. We must love more, — but for this increase of love, we have to discover larger fields of expansion and deeper zones of interpenetration of the life. This is the way we are trying, Lucile.*

*I send you this letter to New-York, where you are staying up to June, I think.*

*Be happy, — and God might help you in discovering your life, forward.—*

*Yours so much*

*Pierre*

---

*These inspections were usually conducted in the train carriages and often at night.

[P.S.] *Here a picture of myself, by Mac.*
*On the way, I read "Ann Vickers", of Sinclair Lewis, — when I learnt more about the Brevoort!*

*Paris, June 4th, 1935*

Lucile, dearest friend,

Open on my desk are your two last long letters, the one you finished before landing in America, — and the one you wrote after your first days in New-York (I found it yesterday only, in the Museum). Such a joy for me to feel this permanent contact with you, — and such a joy also to feel you so alive, and so well surrounded by your friends! I told you already, Lucile: I would like to be the world, to make it so sweet and so strong all around you. — At the end of this letter, I will try to answer somewhat your philosophical questions. But first I must give you a few details on my parisian life. On the whole, gradually, I emerge again. And although there is something, now, in myself, which makes me unable to become a mere "Occidental" again, I have the impression to be more comfortable with the people and the things, here. In the same time, my mind is more vivid, and I begin to be more conscious of the various currents of life around me. Politically, France has apparently reached the final stage of "décrépitude". But, below the mouldering frame of the old "principes républicains", there is surely a rising of fresh energy eager to build something _new_. Since the war, I had been always feeling that the real spiritual divide in the world did no more coincidate with the conventional boundaries still expressed by social classes, national frontiers, and religious orthodoxies. I wonder whether today Humanity is not actually splitting into the believers and the misbelievers in a Future of the Universe. And I feel more decided than ever to join the first ones, for the conquest of the world. - On the other hand, in the course of this new closer contact with my Order and my Church, I did not discover myself so far apart internally as I was afraid from Christianity. And the reason for this better sympathy (or lesser antipathy) lies in my ever-growing appreciation of the value of Personality (I do _not_ say "individuality") in the structure of the Universe. Presently I stick to Christianity (in spite of so many deciduous elements in Christianity) because Christianity is around us the only collective stream of living thought saving and promoting the idea of a _Personal Whole_ in the world. This is already written in "Comment je crois". But, when I wrote it, I did not realize how deep, rich, and "envahissante" should be this view in the next period of my life. Most probably, my next paper will be on the Personal structure of the Universe. - Now I must come to more external news. As you may suscept, I have seen a large number of friends, of all kinds, - and I scarcely succeed in answering letters and telephone-calls. Jacques is here, in a comfortable flat, surrounded by a brilliant circle of highly aristocratic ladies, and just the same: simple, charming and gay, always "tendrement dévoué" to Mary. He still hopes to come back to Peiping, but nothing is absolutely sure in this line, so far. - Tomorrow, I have lunch with Haskin. - A week ago, I spent a few days in my familial home, in Auvergne. I found my sister in slightly better conditions (although the doctors wonder how many months she has still to live, - but she has always deceived the previsions of the doctors.),

*[handwritten margin note:]* Not individual but personal *

*and so alive in her mind that the meeting was almost gay. My two brothers (the "country-man" and the "parisian") were there: a complete reunion of what is left of the family.- Now, I am going to stay in Paris, with the possible exception of a few short trips (perhaps to London, at the beginning of July, for the Centenary of the Geological Survey of England).*

*Coming now to the chief questions included in your last letter, I would answer as follows:*

*(1) When I speak of "action", I mean this particular type of action (the <u>true</u> one) by which we <u>give</u> ourselves to the creation and to the worship of a <u>greater</u> than ourselves. Now, in this special line of effort, we can "refuse ourselves", we can "not-act", unless we recognise that it is <u>worth</u> acting. My thesis is that it is <u>not worth acting</u>, unless we act <u>for ever.</u>*

*(2) I agree with Wells, at some extent, that: "Man is immortal, but not Men". But the question is precisely to decide whether "Man" can be understood, finally, as differing from a convergency of the<sup>*</sup>*

*Paris, June 16th, 1935*

*Lucile dear,*

*Since I wrote you my last letter 5, I have twice found something from you waiting for me in the Museum (your letters of May 26th and June 1st). And it was such a joy for me, each time, to catch again, in these pages of your dear handwriting, your spirit and your heart, always moving and growing. I enjoy the way in which you have been greeted and comforted by so many friends. So you have been right, really right, in breaking for some time the "lure" of Peiping! Yesterday I have received a letter from Dr. Treat (she plans to be back in France at the end of August): she also realizes that she needs the contact with the more vivid parts of our human world, whatever she will have to suffer of it. In your case, happily, the contact means hope and new inspiration. Again and again, I am so glad, - for you and for me!*

*So far I am concerned, things are going in Paris the same way: the whole day, practically, I meet friends, of any kind, - and I am far from meeting everybody I ought to see. Slowly, I find myself back in the familiar big city. Yet, the lack of a positive work to carry on here, and the feeling of an impending departure (I have booked my place on S.S. <u>Cathay</u>, P & O., leaving Marseilles for Bombay on Sept. 6th), give to the whole business something like a touch of inconsistancy and irreality.- In addition to a few scientific contributions, my best personal achievement, so far, has been to reach a clearer internal view of new possible developments in my "philosophy". Une "philosophie de l'union", basée sur une analyse de la structure personnelle de l'Univers, me parait être à la fois ce dont notre pensée moderne a le plus besoin, et l'oeuvre à laquelle je suis le plus prêt à collaborer. I come more and more to this conclusion by talking with my friends, and by watching their reaction (<u>most</u> favourable) to my "Comment je crois". Possibly, as a title for a new paper, I will choose this one, - somewhat*

---

*The rest of Teilhard's June 4 letter was not found among Lucile's papers.

*"provocant": "La Structure de l'Esprit", (I will mean by this that the birth of each higher spirit is in a strict dependancy of the unification under him of more elementary spirits. "Provocant", I say, because traditional thinkers have always accepted the idea that spirit is "simple", and hence structure-less (and hence <u>unfit</u> for union). - As you see, "La découverte du Passé" is still waiting for better times (but not entirely forgotten).- So theoretical they would seem to be, these present ideas of mine are not far, nor so independant from political reactions. Not only for internal life, but just so much for international understanding, we need a "Philosophy of Union". As you have probably seen in the papers, France is more and more lost and depressed: the political "régime" does not work any more. A new engine is clearly necessary, - but we have no engineer. Everywhere, in the country, small groups begin to rise, each of them with a special periodic paper (Esprit, La Terre <u>Nouvelle,</u> l'Humanité <u>nouvelle,</u> etc.): the trend of the thought is in each case distinctly the same, directed towards a spiritual rejuvenation of the world. Something is evidently coming. But, in addition to the birth of a new spirit, we need a <u>technician</u> for re-adjusting the Matter around us: and this is a most difficult side of the things. —*

*As yourself, probably, I feel much concerned, these days, with the new developments of the Japanese intrusion in China [begun in 1932 when the Japanese first invaded Manchuria]. What is going to happen to the Survey, and to the Choukoutien work? I have no idea, so far, - and, from this respect, I hate to be in France, just now. I think that the best move for the Survey should be (if possible) to keep in Peiping at least the Cenozoic Lab., even if it decides to remove to Nanking the most part of its library and of its laboratories. But I am afraid that, for a question of face, even Dr. Wong will prefer to retreat southwards with everything, . . . unless (as I almost hope) it is already late. - If necessary, I am decided to drop India, and to come straight back to China. - As soon as I have news, I will write you. The last letters of Young and Pei (I received them the last week) were full of exciting things: new discoveries in Shantung, - a new and perfect jaw of Sinanthropus-child, etc! -*

*In your last letter from the boat, there was a point (concerning our pet-discussion) which I forgot to answer. You object once more that I am denying, by chastity, one of the fundamental laws of the Universe. - I told you already how <u>hesitating</u> I am in the position which I still keep because I have the dim impression that it preserves and saves a deep tendency (and a hope) of the World. Now, from this hesitating point of view, I believe that I do not deny the very essence of any universal law. Evidently, procreation is necessary for the world, so long this world will not have reached <u>as a whole</u> its point of maturity. But procreation is <u>not</u> the only, nor the <u>final</u> object of love: love is for <u>union;</u> and a superior type of union between man and woman is possibly to be searched, discovered (and gradually accepted) <u>above</u> procreation. In other words, there is possibly a progressive distinction to be established for a man between "Feminity" and "sexuality" (at the ordinary meaning of the word) . . .*

*— Now, a few social news. I have met Jacques twice more; always very gay, — but, the last time, a bit anxious for the future of his Bank in North-China. — Nirgidma is on her way back from Palestina. She has been sent by newspapers*

*to Morocco, Egypt, etc., in order to study the islamic question (why she, a Mongol?), — and I heard that some of her articles have been already published. I expect to see her at the end of the month. -A fortnight ago, I had lunch à Neuilly with the "Pirate" and his most respectable family. In such occurences, I become myself a member of the family, and I appreciate just so much as before this warm friendship. Monfreid hopes to re-integrate Abyssinia with the Italian troops; and for complex (personal and political) reasons, he speakes, writes, and lectures as a convinced supporter of Mussolini. — War is expected to start there in August.*

*I have to stop here, by lack of time. Be happy, dearest, - and God bless you.*

*Yours*

*P.*

*I am really sorry for Malvina Hoffman. — I will perhaps try to come in touch with her.*

*Paris, June 30th, 1935*

*Lucile dear,*

*Here, I answer your sweet letter of June 9th, the last one you wrote me, apparently, before going home. I am so deeply pleased to see how vividly you are reacting and expanding in your native environment. Yes, let us go, both of us, towards a better discovery of the world, ahead. Everything would seem to be an impossible mix-up, presently, in the world. Yet, everyday brings me a new evidence that we are playing our part in the birth of something great. I think that in no other times tension for life has been so strong.*

*So far I am concerned, weeks are passing on in a terrible speed. Did I tell you that I have booked a place on s.s. Cathay, P&O., leaving Marseilles on Sept. 6th? (arriving in Bombay on Sept. 19). I feel as if my time in France was already over; and I just begin to be again in touch with people and things! — Anyhow, I feel that, for me as for you, this contact with the West was a good thing. I have met a large number of friends (known and unknown), this month. And it was a real comfort for me to realize how, in spite (or in account) of the fact that I am living far away, in the "legend" of the Far East, my influence has kept growing on the thoughts of many followers. By a friend of mine, I had "Comment je crois" "stenciled" in many copies; and I spread it generously: a safer and possibly more efficient process than waiting for a problematical printing. In the meantime, my ideas are slowly improving and finding their shape and organization, for "une métaphysique de l'Union". — I am doing very little geology, I must confess; and although I am more deeply convinced than ever that life is discovery, I feel everyday less bewitched by the lure of the Past.*

*Naturally, I am rather anxious to know what is happening in Peiping. Nothing, evidently, to be afraid of concerning the safety of the town. But I wonder what step is going to take the Survey. At the worst (I mean, if the direction migrates to Nanking), some organisation is bound to stay in Peiping, at least for Choukoutien. Am I going to have to bridge, at some extent, Chinese and Japanese geologists in China? — As soon as I know something, I will write you. I told my friends, in the Survey and in the P.U.M.C. to cable me, in case they want me back immediately. - Nothing to do presently, but to wait, - and to hope. The strength which is borne between us, Lucile, is bigger than everything in the world, — because, I am sure, God is there.-*

*Yesterday, I had a more special thought for you, not only because it was the St. Peter's day (and do you not achieve me?), but because I went visiting with Le Fèvre (the writer of the Citroën expedition [la Croisière Jaune]) the studio of an italian sculptor, Pinienta. This man is working more or less in the same artistic line as you. But I wish you would see how he succeeds, by some "artifices" (eyes closed, stylisation of some details in the hair, slight inclinations of the head, etc) in breaking the monotony of a buste. If you have a little time to spare in Paris, Le Fèvre would enjoy to see you, and to introduce you to his friend (address of Le Fèvre: 14 bis. Rue Schnapper, St Germain en Laye, Seine et Oise. He comes to Paris in 20 minutes, with his car). Another sculptor I know is Raymond Delamarre, 11 rue Borromée, Paris (the author of the monument for the defense of the Suez Canal, at Ismailia). His wife is a very good friend of mine: just use my name. We have now, in Paris, a wonderful Italian exposition, mostly paintings: a number of sculptures and "tableaux" have been sent by Mussolini — Unfortunately, the show will be closed when you come this fall.*

*Day after tomorrow I am going to London (Centenary of the Geol. Survey of Great Britain) for three days. I shall meet several friends, and see the results of the pre-historical researches in Palestina. — I have just been interrupted by a long and marvelous talk with two young colleagues of mine!*

*Many thanks for the clipping concerning de Terra.*

*Goodby dearest,*

*P.*

*Paris, July 11th, 1935*

*Lucile, dear,*

*Here I answer your dear letter of June 21, — the first written in Chicago. That was a new joy for me to be sure, and to think, that you were back and happy at home. Try to catch, at its "maximum", the best of this rejuvenation of yourself in your native environment, — and do not let yourself, if possible, turn impatiently towards the future. Time is required for fruits (do you remember the figs?), — and life has to be picked gradually (à mesure). Now you are accumulating (and I too) the supply for a further common progress. Now, in spite of the geographical distance, we are conquering each other. Think of that, when you want "so dreadfully" to anticipate time, — and let gently the interest of your present life take the place, or even become the expression, of your desire. — I am glad you can work, just a little; this is the salt you need with your present food. —*

*So far I am concerned, nothing new. I go on, meeting people, and making very little science. Last week, however, I have spent three days in London, for the Centenary of the British Geological Survey. England was so sunny, so green, and so gay. I have seen a number of friends. The real reason of this trip, for me, was to see, in a Laboratory of the suburb (just close to the house of Darwin, a delicious spot in the Kent), the old skeletons dug out, the past years, in Palaestina. I went there with the discoverers (Mrs Garrod and McCown), and was charmingly received by Sir A. Keith, one of the most attractive figures of scientist I have ever seen. He had just enjoyed, a few days before, the visit of Malvina Hoffman, en route for Norway, - and we had a "salade" of the fruits she had brought to him! - To morrow, I leave also Paris, for three days, going to the house of a friend, near la Loire. I will be back on the 15th, just a day after the famous 14th, - which is apparently going to be rather quiet, in spite of the huge political demonstrations. Neither party ("fascists" nor "anti-fascists") seems to wish a clash. — Yet, conditions are rather tense, the weak government being caught between two opposite armies: the "Croix de feu", and the "Front commun" (left wing, and communists). — My plan is to stay in Paris up to the beginning of August, and then to go for a fortnight in my family. —*

*Finally, the best personal result of this time spent in France seems to be the clearer view I have reached of the new developments still open to my "constructions" of the world. I wish to find, at least the next winter, in Peiping, sufficient leisures for drawing a first sketch of my "Métaphysique de l'Union"; and now again "La découverte du Passé" insists in myself for coming to birth, with a renewed energy. I would like to show you something ready, when we meet in Peiping! — Your quotation of "Paganism and Christianity" was most interesting (I wonder and like how serious books you are reading!). So curious that, from so different sides, people come to the same conclusion! -*

*From Peiping, I have no letters since the last move of the Japanese. But, as an answer to a letter of mine, Weidenreich has cabled, July 3rd: "Dont worry; letter follows". So it seems that there is no serious administrative trouble. Greene has definately resigned, I heard. - No news from Rose, nor from Alice. - Here, Nirgidma is back from Tunis; But I could not see her, so far. (address: 5 rue des Sablons, Paris XVI.)*

*Good bye, dearest. I am so glad to hear that you become an "important person"! - Be happy, and quiet, and chiefly keep in you an overwhelming faith in the divine world. God bless you.*

*Yours*

*P.*

*Paris, July 20th, 1935*

*Lucile dear,*
*A few days ago, I have received your precious letter of July 5th. I am so glad that you feel happy in your family. Surely, you are <u>accomplishing something</u>, just because you are living more, and making other people more alive. Keep your heart and your mind open to the best of the world around you, — and do not worry if you have the impression of not being able to concentrate: now you are absorbing food. — I am always interested by your "religious" reactions. Recently I had to try the value of "Comment je crois" on an English friend (a scientist) who, after becoming a catholic (from a Protestant), has left the Church, because she had the feeling she could not live in it fully and sincerely. Now, she writes me that she follows up to the faith in immortality (inclusively). Further she does not like, or she cannot venture: (1) because preservation of Personality (although she*

*wants to believe in it) does not seem to her "necessary" (for the structure & equilibrium of the World, if I understand her correctly); and 2) because she does not see clearly the relations between Universal Christ and historical Christ. - Is that not approximately your own position?- Concerning the necessity of a preservation of Personality, I feel more and more convinced that I am right. Concerning the <u>proportion</u> of historicity necessary for supporting the Universal Christ, I confess my hesitations (just as for the <u>proportion</u> of flesh necessary for the completion, the full health of spirit). We shall try to go further in the problem, next winter.-*

*Two days ago, I have received a letter from Weidenreich (of July 4th). The Cenozoic Laboratory's life is not going to be altered by the political conditions (the great question will be to get a new grant of the Rockefeller foundation, next autumn: Dr. Houghton has promised to do his best); but it seems that the <u>other</u> branches of the survey start their migration to Nanking, — I do not know clearly at what extent. This move was easy to foresee since two years. But it will seriously disturb our work. Grabau is probably cursing the Japanese ten times more than at usual! By the way, I have no news of him nor of Alice (nor of Rose). — On the whole, dont be anxious on the matter: in a way or in the other, things will readjust themselves; and the work of C.K.T. cannot be stopped. —*

*Nothing special in my life. I go on, rive gauche and rive droite, meeting many people (from communist leaders to "marchands de canons"), talking, - and wondering whether I am doing really any serious work. Anyhow, my ideas are making some progress. But how difficult would it be, if, instead of giving some general aims to spirit, I was asked to give a practical opinion concerning the best technical way for improving the political and economical conditions of the world! . . Who are the most efficient for promising an international agreement: socialists or fascists? . . . Really I don't know. The only thing I care really for is to find, "n'importe où", faith and hope in the future.*

*Yesterday, for the first time, I met Nirgidma (5 Rue des Sablons, Paris 16.), back from her trip to Morocco, Tunis, Egypt, Arabia and Palestina (she went even to Mecca, as a Moslem pilgrim! "Uninteresting", she told me). She looks very healthy, and much attracted by Africa. Her wedding with "Philippe" is theoretically fixed for November or December. But, evidently, she is afraid by the "bourgeois" surroundings of her possible new family: she still wants to wander (as any real people does, is not?). Try to see her, when you pass. —*

*On August 6th I will go to Auvergne, to see my family, for a fortnight (address here or in the Museum, during that time). Then I will be very close to my departure.*

*God bless you, dearest.*

*P.*

*In the P.U.M.C., Greene has resigned, and
is replaced by an executive Commity of 3 (!):
Dr. Maxwell, Dr. Lyon, Dr. Wu.*

*Lucile dear,*

    *Here, I answer your letter of July 15th, which I have received with the same joy as the other ones. Don't get "nervous", dear, because you may have the feeling that you are accomplishing nothing. Your chief work, just now, is to come in touch with the western world, — and to make your own people happy. Time will come in which you will realize and use what you are accumulating during your present rest. The great wisdom (and not the easiest one) is to catch, and to receive, (and to love), life just as it is, and gradually ("telle quelle, et à mesure"). I really believe that there is no deeper "contact" between God and ourselves than by the <u>rhythm of time</u>, which we can not either stop, nor make quicker, — the rhythm of the birth of the world.*

    *Don't worry, neither, if you feel still somewhat difficult to grasp what I mean by the "Universal Christ". Just let grow, in your mind, the interest (le goût) in the value of Personality, -and also the clear view that Personality (in a higher meaning) is not bound to "individuality": Gradually you will understand what does mean the <u>love</u> of God. Your plan is good to read again, in a new spirit, the Gospel. But, in many parts of the Gospel, you will find chiefly the Man-Jesus. For discovering "my" Christ, see specially John, - and also (in his best parts, which cannot hurt you) Paul: beginning of the Epistles to Ephes. & Coloss. In Peiping, I will show you the best places, (I have filled, in the old times, a full note-book of them).*

    *Speaking of Peiping, I thank you for the news transmitted from the Seaholms. Poor Wong! Day before yesterday came to me the first letter from Rose. She seems extremely "soulagée" by being free — Michael was in Peitaiho with Germaine, and she was working hard on the Chinese folklore. Her plans are the same: to speed up the Michael's preparation in autumn, and to go with him to England, next winter. — No news from Alice. Rose was told that Grabau looks splendid, and that Mrs Licener would stay on if Mrs Woodland would not return. — I wonder, in the reality, what Grabau is feeling and thinking about the partial shifting of the Survey to Nanking. His position is somewhat worse than mine. — Mrs Hempel has written me a few vivacious lines, on July 17, just before leaving for her short trip to America. Concerning the transfer of a part of the Survey to Nanking, she says: "I do not believe that it will be too bad for us if Dr. Weidenreich's plan which he will submit to the Rockefellers Foundation will go through" (what we hope).*

    *I am glad to know your own plans. — Personally, I am leaving after a few days to my own country (more "adieux" to do, and possibly, alas, several definitive ones: my mother is not strong, and my sister worse. I hate these "adieux"; — but thinking of you will help me, Lucile, because I have to be always the best of myself for you). — On the 20th I will be back to Paris, — and then leave, for Marseilles, on Sept. 4 or 5. My address in Bombay (September 20th and later) is: <u>St. Xavier's College</u> (Bombay). Breuil's address, in Paris: <u>52, avenue de la Motte-Picquet, Paris VII</u> (Phone: Suffren — 35.19). — You will reach Dr. Treat by*

*[margin annotations: * / Personality not bound to Individuality --- the "good parts" of Paul.]*

*my dear friends Bégouën (they would like to see you), <u>26, Rue Raynouard, Paris</u> <u>XVI</u> (Phone: Auteuil 27.19). She is arriving from Tahiti in the middle of August, and will have to face a very difficult sentimental problem. My hope is that she will not break definitely with her husband: they need terribly each other on a certain plane, higher than sex. — Nirgidma has moved: 75, <u>quai de Conti</u> (no telephone): her marriage with "Philippe" is theoretically decided for the end of the year. But she does not seem really enthusiastic.*

*Everything is all right for me. Yet, I long for being again myself, at a regular work.*

*Good bye, dearest*

*P.*

*Auvergne, August 13th, 1935*

*Lucile dear,*

*The day I left Paris (a week ago) I heard from the Museum that a letter has arrived for me, from Chicago (from you, evidently). But I had no time for getting it, so that I cannot answer you properly this time. Now you are spending your last weeks with your family. I hope you do not feel anything but comforting, and sweet. I would like to make everything sweet around you, Lucile.*

*Personally, I am now, for a fortnight with my family in old Auvergne. Last week, I spent three full days with one of my brothers (the "countryman"), in a very pleasant residence along the Allier river, amongst the same big oaks which I knew when I was ten years old. Presently, I am in the family house, on the slopes of the mountains, facing a wonderful landscape, — with my mother and my sick sister. After three days, I go to another place (also in Auvergne), belonging to my parisian brother. -Then I come back to Paris (on the 20th approximately), and I make my last preparations before leaving France. This is the external side of my life.*

*Internally, I enjoy rather this rest in my native land. Yet, for several reasons, I do not feel perfectly comfortable. First, on account of the shadow of my close departure. But also because I cannot readjust myself to an old frame which has turned to be almost impersonal to me: in a way, I do not find myself again in these familiar landscapes, or rooms, or furnitures, or scents, or noises, — but I have only the impression of looking curiously from outside at a child or at a young man which "happens to be myself". — And, chiefly for my poor mother (but <u>not</u> for my sister), I am still this young man! — Better to be away.*

*On the whole, conditions here are not specially bright. My mother (83 years old) is perfectly preserved mentally, but her legs are very weak. My sister fights bravely against T.B., but fever does not stop. Both of them have the feeling (probably wrong, — but they have it) that we shall never meet again. I realize more and more clearly that I did the right thing in coming back to France this year. But, when time comes for leaving, then you have to pay.*

*Nothing new, besides. Just before I left, I had lunch with Nirgidma in her charmant appartement, 15, quai de Conti (facing le Vert-Galant, between la Monnaie et l'Institut). She was a little depressed ("no interest in life"), although — everything seems rather well in her life; — and a bit anxious, because, since 4 months, she did not receive a single letter from her mother in Peking; and strangely frigid (apparently) concerning the wedding (in November?) She plans to spend a fortnight in Tunis very soon. But probably you will meet her when you cross Paris, — in October. —*

*Goodbye, dearest. I will write you next week, from Paris, when I read your letter. —— Be "strong, and wise", and happy!*

*Yours*

*P.T.*

Paris, August 25th, 1935

*Lucile dear,*

*Here I answer your <u>three</u> last letters (July 25, Aug 2, and Aug 14.), the last one arrived yesterday. I found the two first ones a few days ago, on my return from Auvergne, where I have spent, on the whole a happy fortnight. Leaving my dear sick sister and old mother was evidently a bit hard, — yet, less hard than I have feared. Sometimes I hope that really I shall see them again. And also, they are, both of them, so deeply convinced (and I think they are true) that some other better personal life is awaiting us on the other side of the world, that, for them, there is no fear of any parting for ever. And why not, after all? — If the best of our personality has to be preserved across death, is this preservation possible without the preservation of our connexions with such other personalities who have become a real part of our ownself? — Should I be "complete", Lucile, without you? — My best time, in Auvergne, was with my two brothers. Each of them has a very fine estate: — old houses, full of familiar scents and noises, — surrounded by quiet fields and large oaks. Life is not easy, just now, for a gentleman farmer. Yet, the apparent quietness is still there; and I enjoyed it deeply.*

*Presently, I am in Paris, very close to my departure. These last days, by luck, are not so feverish as they used to be when I was leaving France in winter. Very few people are left in town, by this time of the year: most of my "adieux" are already made. I plan to leave Paris on Sept. 5th, directly to the "Cathay" - and Marseilles on Sept 6th. — The boat is due to Bombay on Sept 19th. Address your letters: "St. Xavier's College, Bombay". Probably I will join de Terra in Rawalpindi before October, but my mail will be forwarded. After Sept. 15 you will receive my news in London and Paris, according to your directions. — May this end of your visit in America, Lucile, be just so sweet and comforting as the beginning. After all, if your family comes to China the next year, this is scarcely a separation. Anyhow be sure that I stand very close to you, Lucile, during these days, in which we experience the same things, you and I. — In my next letter, when I have left, I will try to make with you the computation (le bilan) of those last 4 months; at present, I feel a little lost in a complex whirl of hurried thoughts and hurried impressions. A positive fact is that I need to be again at a personal and creative work, — for being really again myself.*

*My last letter of Peking is from Weidenreich (august 2nd). We seem to work successfully in keeping the Cenozoic Lab. alive. In a way, I should prefer to come back straight to China; but my duty is evidently not to miss the opportunity of India. — Pei arrives Marseille at the end of the present week, — but goes*

* So he doesn't really believe this idea of a personal life on the other side ? or does he?

*straight to the Pyrénées, where Breuil is waiting for him. So, I shall not see him. -*
*This afternoon, I have an appointment with Nirgidma, who, judging by her letter,*
*feels badly depressed. I wonder what is the matter with her: she is really success-*
*ful socially, — she writes <u>very nice</u> things in the papers. Yet she has no interest in*
*life. I wonder whether she is really going to marry Philippe; and sometimes I*
*think she would have better not. - Don't forget her address: 15 Quai de Conti, VI.*

*I have come back to Paris just in time for seeing Ida Treat (now in*
*Bretagne: she asked me your address in Chicago). She looked very well, and per-*
*fectly decided to marry her navy-officer. Hope she will be happy! — As generally,*
*she had not a cent, but does not mind. She hopes to publish in England and Amer-*
*ica.*

*Good by, dearest. I have got a fine little book for discussing with you and*
*the dogs, next winter: "Essays of a Biologist", by Julian Huxley. - You shall see.*

*Ever yours*

*P.*

*No news from Alice?!*

---

Two weeks later Teilhard wrote to Lucile from aboard ship, en route to India.

---

*Before Malta. Sept 8th, 1935, S.S. Cathay*

*Lucile dear,*
*I feel rather angry with myself, — because, with the idea of writing you*
*more at leisure, I postponed so well my answer to your dear letter of August 20th*
*that I have left France without any word to you! And here, aboard, I got your pre-*
*cious lines, written August 16, — a blessing for the beginning of my journey east-*
*wards. Thank you so much, Lucile, for your beautiful and comforting friendship.*
*Don't agree too easily with myself, dearest. Keep the best of yourself. As my*
*present topic is, more and more: "L'union différencie". There is a full metaphysic,*
*ethic and mystic, contained in those three words.*

*So, I have left. — Those somewhat dreadful days of parting are over. And*
*now, sliding on the deep blue, between white Bonifacio and red Sardinia, the*
*Cathay brings me toward a new stage in my life! No retreat. Might God keep me*
*on the way (at least morally) up to the end of my life! In spite of many progres-*
*sive talks, I felt a bit uneasy, and weak, during those past three months in which*
*I had nothing serious "in doing". Now, it seems as if I was breathing more freely,*
*— as you like me —.*

*Nothing particular to tell you, concerning my last fortnight in Paris. I*
*wrote you already (am I wrong?) about my meeting with Ida Treat (penniless, as*
*usually, — but rich in plans for writing articles and books, - eager, and decided to*
*marry "André", the naval officer). The eve of my departure, I had an hour with*
*Nirgidma, always in quest for an aim in her life. She was in better spirit than a*
*week earlier, because she had found a way for going to Tunisia (where she hopes*
*to get, in the course of a fortnight, the material for an interesting publication).*
*Still she is not happy, in the deep of herself; — and if she marries Philippe, there is*

*no real love between them, but only sympathy. She is very anxious not to miss you in Paris, in October. — Besides, I have met several good friends (in my Order). Really, I feel ashamed when I realize how much they build on me, — because (and that is __true__, Lucile) I am conscious of so little in myself! What comforts me is to think that my strength, if not in my own value, radiates from the truth of what I believe to __see__. And this is the best success I can dream for my life: to have spread a new vision of the world.*

{ *a new vision of the world*

*The Cathay is a rather nice boat, — but in which everything looks so much "half category": people, rooms, etc. Just a piece of middle England. Of course, this hasty judgement might turn to be unfair after a few days. But I do not care very much; I am decided to work, before Bombay: fixing up a Memoir of Pei, and writing "La découverte du Passé" (in a somewhat different term from my first scheme). The only trouble is that the boat is full up, — and consequently the decks crowded. But I will manage in spite of that. (An amusing detail: a place having to be filled, in the dining-room, at a four-seats table occupied by three (perfectly unoffensive) girls, the chief-steward has decided by himself to give me this "poste de confiance": you will smile. —*

*Now I wonder where this letter is going to join you. I will mail it today from Malta. But where to address it? — I could not read exactly the place of your hotel in New-York. So, I try again Chicago. Later, I will use Cook and the American Express when you are in Europe. ——*

*Good bye, dearest.*

*P.*

*My congratulations for your beginnings in type-writing. — I am sure you are going to find this way of writing most convenient, even for letters.*

---

Teilhard arrived in Bombay on September 19 to join the Yale-Cambridge expedition that studied glaciation of the Pleistocene and tried to knit together the geology of India and that of China.

---

*St. Xavier's College. — Bombay, Sept 23, 1935*

*Lucile dear,*

*I hope you have received, somewhere, my letter n.13, which I sent from Malta (Sept 8th) to Chicago. This time, I wish these lines might reach you at your arrival in England, to tell you how close I feel to you during your long journey back to Peiping. I hope that parting from Chicago was not too hard, for yourself, nor (chiefly!) for your family. Left behind people are always in the worst position. — Now I enjoy thinking that you are travelling in a new and interesting world of things, friends, etc. But you come to Europe just for the climax of the present crisis with Italy. I still think that we shall not go to the war.* At the worst, you could come back to China by Siberia. —*

---

*Unfortunately, Teilhard misjudged events. Italy invaded Abysinia (Ethiopia) ten days later.

*Personally, I have arrived the 19th in Bombay after a perfectly quiet trip. The Red sea was very hot, however, — wind blowing from North. Gradually, my first impressions concerning the passengers turned to better. Amongst the British returning to India, I discovered a score of perfectly sympathic men, — and in addition an Australian, in the tin business of Malaya. I enjoyed sincerely talking with them, — and may be we shall meet again, someday.*

*Bombay is an extensive, but rather uninteresting city, in spite of many ambitious buildings in the anglo-indian part of the town. The monsoon is just over, and consequently the heat is growing. But I enjoy rather the sight of the big blooming trees, and of the palm-trees, and of the green parrots so talkative and busy. Tropical surroundings have always appealed to me. — In St. Xavier's college, I was very kindly received. In addition to my spanish colleagues (I do not like them specially) in charge of the college, are several Belgians, Dutch, and also a French, with whom I have immediately felt very friendly. We have long talks together, about India, France, and also more philosophical subjects.*

*And, this evening, I am leaving by the "Frontier mail", arriving day after tomorrow in Rawalpindi (Pendjab). The British of the Expedition, Dr. Patterson, will wait for me, there; — and the day after, I suppose, we shall join de Terra in Srinagar (Kashmir), — a 8 hours trip by motocar. Then, the real work will begin, at last. — I will let you know the developments.*

*In the meantimes, I wish you any kind of luck for your staying in Europe. Finally, I wrote, on the Cathay, a few pages on "La découverte du Passé". I wonder whether they are right or not. Anyhow, I made my mind more clear and free on the subject; and this was my first aim. I have sent a copy to France: for publication? — You will read my text, in January, - and we shall discuss. —*

*Goodbye, dearest. —— I think you are more precious to me than ever.*

*P.*

---

After visiting her family in Chicago and friends in the East, Lucile sailed for England in September, her first stop on the way back to Peking. From a houseboat on the Jheluma River in Kashmir, Teilhard wrote to Lucile about the work they were to do in northern India.

---

*Srinagar (Kashmir),*
*Oct 2nd, 1935*

*Lucile dear,*
*I have just realized that, if I wish to reach you in Paris, I must write you at once, and by air-mail. Time is running so fast!*
*I hope you have well received my letter n.14 from Bombay (sent to London, c/o Cook, on Sept. 23). At that time, I was perspirating in a tropical atmosphere. Today, I am in the Kashmir's capital, on a houseboat, among deep carpets, comfortable armchairs, and obsequious high-"enturbannés" boys. Weather is sunny and cool. And, on both sides of the broad, green, valley, an unlimited line of snow-capped peaks make a white barrier in the blue sky: the Pir Panjal (15,000*

*feet) south, and the Central Himalaya, north. I think I would enjoy ten times more this extraordinary scenery, if you were here; and I know that you would make me ten times more aware of the endless picturesque sides of this curious city where the most luxurious India is coming in contact with the thibetan wilderness. An incredibly wealthy maharadjah has here his palace; and strange-looking, dirty, people come everyday, down the Pamir and Karakorum passes, with their caravans of yacks and poneys. For a week, I have been brought four years back, to the time of the Citroën Expedition. In some way, the tracks of the Haardt's motocars are still to be seen on the Kashmir's roads. And, at the same time, they are so many common features between the Kashmarian landscape and the Sinkiang's oasis in which I have been living exactly at the same time of the year. . . Here, however, everything looks greener and richer than in Aksu. In the bottom of the valley, gigantic maples-looking trees (a kind of "plantane") turn red under the first touch of autumn, and roads are bordered by tight rows of high poplars. Higher, along the slopes big walnut-trees and apple-trees (red with apples) surround the small villages. Still higher, the dark belt of the fir forests, — the home of bears and mountain-monkeys. And then the "prairies": and then the barren rocks; and then the snow. —And, over all that, the mysterious spell of Central Asia. I think that everybody, coming here, is attracted by going more and more northwards, up to China. Yet, tomorrow, we are turning back, to Rawalpindi. This time, my work is in India. —*

*Now, after so many descriptions, I must explain you more clearly how the matter stands with the present expedition. Everything seems all right. My two associates, Prof. de Terra (from Yale Univ.), and Patterson (a young man of Cambridge), are very charming companions, and have already reached many important results. More specially, they have carefully studied the glacial formations of Kashmir as a key for the interpretation of the Himalaya's foothills, — and that is precisely in order to understand their views that I have come up to here. — Now, we are going to spend October in Rawalpindi and West Punjab. Later, I will move eastward to the Simla area; then to Calcutta, and possibly Madras. In any way, the work will end before Christmas, since de Terra has to leave for America in January. — I will let you know everything, from time to time. -*

*I hope to find my mail day after tomorrow, in Rawalpindi. May I have a letter of you! Now you are approaching England. I like so much to think that you are going to breath the air of Paris. — The trouble, only, is that I don't see clearly where to address you my letters, now. Maybe your next letter will give me the name of your boat, so that I can write you in Ceylon. Otherwise, I will address to Peking ! ——*

*Goodbye, dearest. God bless you*

*P.*

*As you see, I am still eager for Geology.
But, in the same time, I realize more and more
that I do not belong any more "to the Past"!* ✗

"I do not belong anymore to the past"

*Rawalpindi, Oct 7th, 1935*

*Lucile dear,*

> *I wrote you a few days ago. But this time I want to send you at least a few lines, answering your dear letter of Sept. 12 (New York) which has arrived today. I am so glad that you feel again happy and active, after the parting from your family. When this letter will reach you, in Paris, I hope you will be in "full life". — Thanks for having told me about Mrs Woodland. I write her today, in Peiping.*

> *Here everything is going all right. The last days, spent around Rawalpindi, have been specially interesting. Lot of old stony implements at the base of a formation which looks exactly as the chinese loess. Tomorrow, we leave for a fortnight trip in the Punjab's bad lands. Then we come back here. December will soon arrive, I guess. In the meantime, weather is gradually cooling. Yet, my arms are quite burnt by the sun. But this is all right. To be on the field makes me younger than the streets of dear Paris. — I am happy to be on the work, again; and I realize that, once more, I have been right in taking the chance of a new field for research.*

> *I hope that the Suez Canal will not be closed this month! Then you could come back by Siberia (a very easy journey), or round Africa (what a wonderful trip!). This Abyssinian business is an awful thing; and although I admit that Abyssinia has to be taken under some control, the Mussolini's hypocrisy goes over the limit. Exactly la fable du Loup et de l'Agneau. We shall have lot of talking about these things, next winter. By the way, did you read "Fountain" by Ch. Morgan? I read it on the boat, and bring it to you. — An ample matter for discussion, also!*

> *I leave you for packing. — Goodbye, dearest, and might God bless your journey.*

> *Yours*

> *P.*

*Let me know, by air mail, when you pass Ceylon, or eventually Bombay. Before the November 1st you may address: c/o Postmaster Rawalpindi. Later, address: St. Xavier's College, Bombay.*

---

While working near Rawalpindi (and afterwards in the Punjab), Teilhard received a letter Lucile had written and mailed from London. Subsequently, she went briefly to Paris and then in mid-October sailed from Antwerp for China.

---

*Rawalpindi, October 29th, 1935*

*Lucile dear,*

> *And now you have already left Antwerp, and you are sailing for Peiping! I realized it only this morning, in checking the dates you give me in your precious letter from Paris which came a few days ago. — And this constatation has made me so conscious (and so "feeling") of the fact that we are actually at a few weeks only of being together again. Lucile, yesterday I have received the "explosion" of*

*London.* Why do you ask me to forgive you anything about it? You are so true in what you say, — so yourself, — "si belle", dearest, —that it is rather my part to pray you to forgive <u>me</u> for the somewhat extraordinary path along which I have asked you to come with me. And yet, I still believe it; — We are making together a wonderful discovery, Lucile! In the meantime, let us not discuss too much about words. You know how and how deeply I love you, Lucile. Let us go on, developping, along the rich and always new and fanciful lines of the life, the beautiful thing which is borne, above all name, between us. That what is really new has no name, — isn't true? — Well, I have enjoyed immensely your two last letters, — each in its way. And I am only sorry that the present one will not reach you before Shanghai, — not so far away after all. I will think of you, at the middle of November, when your boat will skirt India: since months we shall not have been so close each to the other. — Everything you told me about Paris (concerning yourself and our friends) was for me delightful. I am so glad you have seen and appreciated the Bégouëns: they are such a treasure. For Nirgidma, I too I feel anxious. Evidently, her place would be in Asia. Anyhow, they are gradually so many new things and people in common in our lives, yours and mine. I like to feel it. —

Here, everything is going on, all right. Since my last letter (October 7th) I have spent a fortnight with de Terra in the half desertic area of the Salt-Range, living in tent or in bungalows, moving with cars or camels. An extremely dry and rocky hilly region, where every plant is thorny or pricky, trees or grass. And yet, light and sky are so beautiful that I liked it. The first days were very hot. Later the wind went north; and since that time the mornings are almost chilly. But the middle of the day is still warm: my arms are completely tanned. Tomorrow, we are leaving to Campbellpore on the Indus Valley, north of here. Last week, we have located there a promising fossiliferous site, which we must excavate. Relatively to Rawalpindi, Campbellpore marks a new step towards desert and Central Asia: landscape is almost a chinese one. And every site, here around, is so pregnant of very old "aryan" history, so poetical. A great, ancient, human past is a good platform for jumping in the Future. Today, we meet Sir Aurel Stein, the hermit of Kashmir. I am curious to see this man who has got a so marvelous insight of ancient Central Asia. — On the whole, we are making marked progresses in our own geological and prehistorical work, de Terra and I. I shall explain you all these things between Spotty and Dungshi. The main fact is that I am tremendously glad to have joined de Terra this season. I did not realize how much the present trip would complete and achieve my knowledge of Asia. Really, as we told so often, the great thing is to obey life. — My plans ahead are rather vague. The clearest part of them is that I shall be in Calcutta before Xmas, and leave Ceylon at the very beginning of January (perhaps a bit earlier). If so, I should be in Peiping on about the 20th of January, - somewhat later, maybe, than you would like. Be sure that I will not loose time on the way. In December, you might address your letters: c/o RV F. Lechien, Archbishop's House, 32, Park Street,

---

*The "explosion" refers to an emotional outburst of a frustrated Lucile. Perhaps she had wanted to join the expedition to India.

*Calcutta. — By the way, I have been amused and interested by your reaction against the New York priests; you will explain me. In some way, you know how much, generally, I react <u>as you</u>. But there is also something deeper, not to be forgotten. — And also we shall discuss Abyssinia. I hate the Italian hypocrisy,- and their boasting for the capture of Adowa [Asmara]: Goliath proud to have defeated naked David. And I hate the silence of the Vatican, too. And yet, Abyssinia could not remain as it was. — Things are so complicated, sometimes. — My most friendly regards to the Petros, and to the Peiping's friends (Grabau, Alice, Germaine, Rose, etc.) I have been much distressed by the Wilder's death, which I did not know.- Good bye, <u>dearest</u>.*

> *Yours*

> *P.*

*Jhelum (Punjab), November 13th, 1935*

*Lucile dear,*

*A few lines only, because I suspect strongly that this letter will never join you. — Anyhow, I will try my chance of telling you how I enjoyed your letter from Antwerp. — You are so much for me, Lucile; and I will be so happy to see you again.*

*We are working at present south of Rawalpindi. — Plans are always changing, so far as the time before December 15th is concerned. Possibly we shall go, de Terra and I, on the Narbada river (Central India) between December 1st and 15th — After the 15th, I go to Calcutta. And then the boat. Everything all right. — I think that you are now approaching India!*

> *Yours*

> *Pierre*

*Rawalpindi, Nov 19th, 1935*

*Lucile dear,*

*I wonder whether you will have received the few lines I have sent you from Jhalum to Singapore, — but I hope that my letter 18 was given to you at your arrival in Shanghai. - Anyhow, I wish that my deepest thought and feeling might reach you as soon as possible after your coming in Peiping. When I think that you are going to open this letter near the trees of your little chinese home, between the two dogs, and under the friendly eyes of old Wang, that gives me a thrill. If I could only slip myself in the envelopp! — Now, you have passed Ceylon, and you are approaching the green shallow water of Malacca. Very soon I am going to follow your track. — I am sure that you are going to find so much yourself in the shadow of the Imperial palace.*

*Personnally, I am all right, — and going on in researches which are for me more interesting every day, according to that I can grasp better every day the problems in a personal way. — But a few weeks only are left now for research. Tomorrow, we are leaving de Terra and I, for the Lower Indus, near Karachi. (24 hours by railway). Then we plan to come here a last time, for packing. Then, at* the beginning of December, we shall go to Central India, along the Narbada river. Short after Dec. 15th I have to be in Calcutta, in order to sail to Shanghai, — directly from Calcutta, or from Ceylon, I dont know. In anyway, the end of my Indian experiences is approaching fast. I will explain you how much this trip has been useful for me. Really, independently from the positive results we have reached, I have the feeling, to have acquired new eyes for understanding "the geology of China".

Your last letter (sent from Antwerp, and which I tried to answer by airmail to Singapore) made me an immense pleasure. It seems to me that by having so many friends in common in France now, you have become still more a part of mine. The Bégouëns wrote me how much they have appreciated you, and like you. "Quelle femme intéressante! Tant d'intelligence et de sensibilité harmonieusement réunies en elle". (Don't be vain). — I am sorry you could not see I. Treat. —

Hope you have found a sunny weather (and not too many Japanese) in Peiping. Here, the conditions are simply exquisite. Two days ago, in the bad lands, I had the most beautiful evenings of my time in India. The sun was gold over the yellow and pink clays of the dissected desert, — over the dry grass and the thorny trees of the bush; and, just like firm white clouds in the blue sky of the East, the snowy lofty Pir Panjal (the last born himalayan range) were floating above the landscape. And troops of green parrots were incessantly passing too. — I am anxious, now, to see a little more of central India.

I dont think that you can reach me now by any letter before I leave Calcutta (Archbishop's House, 32, Park Street). But I will write you regularly. — Give my best regards to Rose, to Mac, to Grabau, — and to Alice. I wrote her some 3 weeks ago. Tell her that the Bowles are here (she went with them to Choukoutien, with Don.), on a scientific trip. Unfortunately, Dr. Bowles has become sick, a fortnight ago. He has lost much weight, and one does not know exactly what is the matter with him. Rawalpindi does not seem to have first class doctors.

Good by, dearest,

Yours ever

Pierre

Herewith a few flowers of the bush. They were so exquisitely fragant. But they lost their strange perfume. They are growing on a thorny liane, without any leaves on it.

Rawalpindi, Nov 29th, 1935

Lucile dear,

Just before leaving North India, I wish to answer your dear letter of Nov 3 (Port Said) which I found here two days ago, when coming back from the Karachi area. I have greatly admired and appreciated your typewriting (the handsratching was also there for establishing your individuality). But chiefly I was so happy to be sure that everything was all right, in you, and around you. Now I am *only afraid that you will have to reach Tientsin by boat: the papers of this morning are full of bad news concerning the Japanses moves in the North. That makes me ever more anxious to be back as soon as possible. And yet (you will forgive me dearest?) I am afraid not to arrive but a week later on my scheme. A letter from Java (von Koenigswald), received yesterday, urges me to stop a few days in Bandoeng, - and for serious reasons. They have been many finds, there, during the last year. That would be a "fault" of mine not to take the opportunity of criticizing personally the facts, and of tightening the collaboration between Peiping and Java. I had the idea to go there with Weidenreich during the Spring. Following the Koenigswald's suggestion will save me time (in Peiping), and money. — My first thought was for you, dearest. But I thought also that you would tell me to do the best, — just as I want to be the best for you, too. So I have answered to Koenigswald that I was coming. Maybe I will find the way, in Calcutta, to start earlier from India, so that my final "retard" will be very slight. I will let you know as soon as I can. —*

*Last week, we went, de Terra and I, to Sukkur, on the lower Indus, not far from the Beluchistan border. Professionally the trip was successful, since we found a large area simply littered with old stony implements. But, from the picturesque side also, we have been fully rewarded. The Sind is much more like Egypt or, I suppose, Mesopotamia than anything else — Along the majestic Indus, high and triangular white sails move slowly, between dense patches of date-palms. On both sides, with the exception of a few low hills of white limestone, the country is absolutely flat, sandy or silty: an endless tamaris-bush which a powerful irrigation scheme (started fifteen years ago) turns slowly into cotton-fields. And, above that, a perpetually clean, blue sky. Weather pretty hot; but I like it. We spared a day for visiting the famous Mohendjo-Daro,[*] the center of the "Indus civilization", discovered and partly excavated since the war. The city (3,000 B.C. or more), partly unearthed, looks amazingly modern: rectangular streets, houses built in red bricks with an elaborated irrigation system, etc. I will tell you more about that, in a few weeks.*

*This night we are leaving for Lahore (1 day), then Delhi (1 day), then Central India, where we plan to work some twelve days. Then I go to Calcutta, — from where I will write you again.*

*Nothing specially new, besides. Yet, à mesure que le temps passe, I realize curiously how deep is the change which, in a year, has darkened for me "the Past", and illuminated "the Future". I still work my science steadily, and with pleasure: but the real interest of my life has shifted away elsewhere, definitely. — My next paper will probably be: "The personal Universe". I shall talk it over with you. ——*

*Good bye, dearest.*

*P.*

---

[*]A pre-historic "copper" city and the first known site of Aryan civilization, it is northeast of Karachi, in Pakistan.

*Lucile dear,*

*Yesterday, arriving in the Archbishop's house (!) I found your dear letter from Singapore (so well typed!), which I liked so much. I got also a number of our solemn review "Les Etudes", with "La Découverte du Passé" printed without any suppression. Just a bit of concealed dynamite in this wise periodic. Almost 15 years I had published nothing there . . . I am so glad you like "Comment je crois". We shall have to improve it, during this winter. By the way, when I say that Christ saves Evolution, I mean that, in its present human state and stage (that is dealing with rational beings) Evolution can not go further without the perception of some Personal Center of the Universe ahead; and Christ is the present expression (or approximation of such a Center. Now, I would admit that, for animating (without checking) further progress, the figure of Christ has to evolve itself: this is the whole modern problem of Christianity. For my part, I confess that often I am conscious that my position induces me too much to force the new Universe to the conservative figure of Christ, instead of reshaping a New Christ in conformity with a new Universe. But I hope that things will gradually adjust themselves. — Some progress, I hope, will be realized if my plan of writing "A personal Universe" materializes, in 1936.*

*So I am now in Calcutta, — for a short time. I have booked on a steamer (Dec. 22) for Singapore and Batavia, via Rangoon, — arriving in Batavia Jan. 4th. If I find a boat in Java before the Jan. 15th, I will reach Shanghai approximately in time for being in Peiping before the 25th. I will write you in the meantime. You can address me a letter for Jan. 20 in Shanghai "Eglise St. Joseph, Rue Montauban".*

*My last letter was from Rawalpindi. This last fortnight, was probably the most delightful period of my time in India. We spent it in Central India, along the sacred Narbada River, in small towns known as Hoshangabad and Narsinghpur. A wonderful, scarcely hot, bright weather. A golden light was spread over a lovely country, thickly spotted with huge ever-green trees: mango-trees, banyans, etc. On both sides of the valley, the tabular masses of the Penninsular India's ranges, covered with dense jungle (A Tigers jungle!). You could see peacocks flying in the woods, a few crocodiles in the river, and lot of dark-faced, white-bearded, long-tailed monkeys everywhere in the bush and along the roads. Native people exceedingly clean and amiable, the men with white clothes and turbans, the women all in pink or scarlet veils, — much better-looking than in Punjab. No European faces, practically. — Geologically, we had a grand time, exploring formations which had been left untouched since 1850! — Lot of beautiful old paleolithic implements (a single one had been found 80 years ago), and interesting stratigraphy. It is a real delight to make good finds in a perfect landscape.*

*Here, in Calcutta, I am most cordially received by my colleagues, and also by the people of the Geological Survey of India. Much to work, there.*

*More than ever, I am anxious to be soon back in Peiping in order to see personally what the conditions are, for the Survey. - (and to see you). I found here a long letter from Alice [Cosme]. There are some bright prospects in front of her,*

*— but many clouds, also. And the sympathy did not improve much for Dr. G.! If you see her, tell her that I will answer her, — and was extremely glad she wrote me. - My most friendly regards to Rose. And to you, dearest, the best of my heart.*

*Be happy! A bientôt.*

*Pierre*

*I have received <u>all</u> your letters since America.*

*Singapore, Dec 31st, 1935*

*Lucile dear,*

> *Last year, I remember, at this very time, you were dressed as a restaurant-maid, and we were organizing together your New-year's party. And, the day after, we were going to have our private evening. And, the day after, I was leaving for the Kwangsi. — Today, I am far from you. But I am coming, very soon. And, in the meantime, I don't think that ever I have wished for you more deeply, more fervently, any kind of happiness than today. Yes, God bless your new year, dearest, with all the most precious blessings of Earth and Heaven. — I know that now, at the present minute, you are also making for me the same "prayer"; — and I receive with my whole heart this loving message of you, — comme une bénédiction.-*

> *My last letter was written in Calcutta (Dec. 17).[*] On the 22nd I have left India, — and, by Rangoon (a very pretty place, all shining with gold pagodas!), and by Penang, I took slowly my way to Singapore, where I have arrived today, — almost on your track, this time. — Here, unfortunately, I have to wait three days almost, the Batavia boat leaving only on the Jan. 3d. Yet, after that, I shall make good time. My ticket is already booked on a Dutch steamer leaving Batavia on Jan. 15th for Shanghai: so that, you see, I shall be scarcely a few days late on my first scheme. And that will be such an advantage for me to have seen the people working, and the Pithecanthropus material collected, in Java! — I have to make myself such as you can be proud of me, Lucile.*

> *Nothing much to tell you about the last fortnight. Life on the steamer was perfectly monotonous, — and I did not make any particularly interesting acquaintance. Luckily, I was alone in a decent cabin. So that I decided, in leaving Calcutta, to use these days for making the "spiritual retraite" for which I had found no time since the one I made when you were in Mongolia (August 34). — This is a social rule [a rule of the Society of Jesus]; but, as you know, I need positively, periodically, this kind of contact with the spiritual world. — So I am, once more "remonté" - wound up (is it the proper word? I have no lexicon here). And, in addition these are 8 days which I shall not have to spend in Tientsin this winter. A double gain, for you, I hope.*

---

[*]The "Dec. 17" date for the Calcutta letter seems to be a simple calendar error on Teilhard's part. Only the letters of the 16th and the 31st were among Lucile's papers.

*I wonder whether I shall find any opportunity for sending you a letter no. 22. Anyhow, I hope to find news of you, short after the Jan. 20th in Shanghai (Eglise St. Joseph, Rue Montauban, pour attendre).*

*Yours, so much*

*P.*

*January 27, '36 (!!), S.S. Tjineyara*

Lucile dear,

*The twelfth day since we have left Batavia! I did not expect that would take so long. We have lost a full day by the bad weather. — Still, here we are. In a few hours, I shall be ashore in Shanghai, and send you a telegramm.*

*Everything all right. My stay in Java was delightful, and chiefly full of unexpected results. Real discoveries, — linking so beautifully with the results in India. I shall explain you everything. Such a pity if I had not gone there. So you forgive me, sure? —*

*Now, I will lose no time for reaching Peiping. Yet, I must spent 48 hours in Shanghai, — perhaps (I hope not) stay a few hours in Nanking, — and finally give a short time (a day, or two) in Tientsin: for decency, - and because I need to pick up there some fur-coats. — I hate these protractations, and would a hundred times prefer to jump in the Blue Express straight to Peiping and Ta Tien Shui Ching Hutung (what a name!). But you will understand.*

*Anyhow, we are very close now. Such a full and solid joy, dearest!*

*Be patient, and believe me yours deeply*

*Pierre*

---

Teilhard, working with von Koenigswald in Java as he had with de Terra in India, helped establish the connection between the Pithecanthropus and Sinanthropus hominids. See *Letters from a Traveller*, p. 218; and Cuénot's *Teilhard de Chardin*, pp. 191-93.

---

*[Telegram] Shanghai, Jan 28. 1936*

*Well arrived come soon love Pierre*

*Tientsin, Feb 1. 1936 (Saturday)*

Dearest,

*I have arrived in Tientsin today, morning, only, - after a day spent in Nanking. Impossible to leave Tientsin before next Tuesday (Feb. 4). — But Tuesday, I will take the morning train, and come to you for tiffin. At last! ——*

*Thank you so much for your two letters, found in Shanghai!*

*A très bientôt*

*Pierre*

---

On May 4, 1936, Teilhard finished "Esquisse d'un univers personnel"—later translated as Sketch of a Personalistic Universe (See *Human Energy*, New York: Harcourt Brace Jovanovich, 1969; pp. 53-92). He began writing it during the Batavia-Shanghai trip and re-worked it in the Spring of 1936. The essay considers the mutual attraction of the sexes in the development of life. "In its initial form, and up to a very high stage of in life, sexuality seems identified with propagation." But with the appearance of human beings this attraction serves rather to bring about the mutual development of their personalities.

"Through woman and woman alone, man can escape from the isolation" in which he could find himself enclosed. Yet the man and woman should not absorb one another, nor "should the two lose themselves in the enjoyment of physical possession." Rather, "the only right love is that between couples whose passion leads them both, one through the other, to a higher possession of their being." For love is "a three-termed function: man, woman, and God." In such a love the human passion is sublimated; this means "not an elimination but a concentration of the sap of the earth." Thus, "without ceasing to be physical, in order to remain physical, love will make itself spiritual. Sexuality for the man will be satisfied by pure womanliness. Is not this the dream of chastity translated into reality?"

[Journal — Peking]

*May 6 — 1936 — My whole world seems to have tumbled down — I suppose nothing has changed — I only see more — perhaps it is as well — I have been living in a fool's paradise —— and I've been awakened — no it wont change everything — only my point of view - there isn't anything perfectly beautiful on this earth — I suppose that is why religion has always had a place —— Probably I shall see clearer in a few days — the hurt is too new, too raw to be forgotten just now — it is out of perspective — I can't see anything clearly or correctly — I suppose a lot of the things I have been living on were built by my own imagination — that is not his fault — He is sincere in his desire to make me happy — It was I who built that happiness on blocks of ideals — now I must try to build it over on realities — If I can know what they are —— His birthday was so perfect — I thought we were really so close — and yet the next morning there was that feeling that it was not real —— I suppose I realized inside of me that much of it was my working.*

*May 7th, 1936*
[Peking]

**Dearest,**

*Since yesterday, I suffered much (more, I think than ever in my life) because I have realized that you were still more dear to me than I knew, — and that, at the same time, I might be a danger for you. — When, years ago, I began to see you, Lucile, I had (so far I can understand my instinctive attitude of that time) the feeling and the hope that you would (as you did) enlighten my life, — and that in turn I could give you a new energy for becoming more yourself, an energy, Lucile. And now I realize that I have become for you a center, which has not, I am afraid, the material consistency which would be required for a safe support of your life. — To be an energy, and yet not a center. Is that a mere utopia? — Think of that, Lucile, — and tell me what you think. — What is born between us is for ever: I know it. — But if you see something which could help your happiness and your peace, in any possible way, tell me, I pray you. My dream is to make you gloriously happy.*

*Pierre.*

*Dearest,*

*I hope that in spite of the grey weather they are no clouds on your soul, today. — Once more, with all my heart, I have been thinking of you and me, since yesterday. And I come always to this same conclusions that, if you don't find <u>me</u> as you would, the reason is not any petty foreign intrusion between both of us, — but the presence of God <u>whom I love as a Person</u>, and to whom I have to give the final activity of my life. For me, the whole problem is there, and the reason for which you find me somewhat elusive or reluctant. You, you are searching an equilibrium "à deux"; and for me, this is a question "à trois". — My conviction, I told you already, is that the third element is not a barrier, nor a sort of "rival". I hold (and I experiment) that he brings me, on the contrary, a sort of new dimension, in which love expands more freely, and reaches an incredible degree of consistency. But, at the same time, I am still "inhabile" in moving in this new atmosphere, — and, for many reasons, you can not perceive it clearly. Hence, a lack of adjustment. Yet, I think we can fly, both together. In the meantime, let us forget the weakening analysis and hesitations, — and concentrate on the joy of the creation and of the discovery. I am not a preacher, you know it, Lucile, but a desperate searcher. And you come to me as a light. — On another hand, any time you will need to collect yourself, — to be alone (materially) with yourself, just tell me. You are too much for me pour que rien puisse me coûter, me lasser, ou me détacher de vous ——*

P.

*A demain 5h.*

About two months later, while Teilhard was starting out on a survey trip based at Tsingtao in Shantung, he wrote her a short letter about his current geological interests. He wanted eventually to develop a comprehensive map of the eruptive rocks of China, hence his keen interest in the Laoshan hill country.

*Tsingtao, July 16th, 1936*

*Lucile dear,*

*We arrived here in excellent conditions, Tuesday, 10½p.m., and found immediately a decent and inexpensive place in a very clean small Chinese hotel, close to the station and to the sea. Everything all right. Tsingtao is a much nicer place than I remembered, - and the breeze is so cool! I wish you have been with me yesterday morning along the sea-shore: a bright rain-bow circling exactly the beach eastward, and westward, closing the deep-blue bay, a dark storm-cloud hanging over a rugged granitic range. The whole landscape was an overhelming beauty. And I thought of you, of course. That was approximately the time when I cross the marble-bridge, reintegrating the Peitang.*

*We have immediately started the work, — and we face a much more complicated problem than I thought. A very attractive solution of the geological con-*

*ditions found here has been recently published by two men of J.S. Lee; and my idea was to accept and develop it eastwards. But now, my impression (and that of Yang Kieh) is that the two Nanking's geologists have made a serious mistake, so that the matter has to be taken over, afresh. I do not like it, — but that is interesting, too. Since enormous masses of granite and porphyries are involved in the problem, it is worth reaching a definite solution. — Tomorrow we are going by car to the Laoshan. — Nothing yet very clear, concerning our progresses eastwards. I suspect that we shall decide for a few number of stations along the coast, with branch-trips around these places. — I will write you before we leave, and give you our definite plan*

*In the meantimes, I hope that you are busy, quiet, and happy. — After all, we have been so much together during the past months that we need perhaps those days for assimilating the treasures accumulated by the physical presence. So far the spiritual presence is concerned (and this is something essentially physical, too!), you know that I never get out of it, —— because you have become a part of my deepest own life.*

*Yours ever, dearest*

*Pierre*

*I am afraid I am developping an "anti-Chinese-food-complex"!. Still, I am not starving.*

*Tsingtao, July 19th, 1936*

*Lucile dear,*

*Finally, due partly to the fact that today is Sunday (Banks closed, etc.), we cannot leave Tsingtao but tomorrow. This is a much longer stop than I was planning. But, as I told you in my last letter, we found here, geologically speaking, conditions which we did not expect; — and we could not move eastwards without a safe base. Now, I believe that we are on the right track. — For material reasons (impossibility to follow the cliffs but by foot), I am obliged to alter somewhat my plans. We shall use mainly moto-cars road, following roughly the coast, — and we will stop in a few selected places: 3 or 4 before Weihawei. — Evidently, I was more than ambitious when I hoped to cover the area in two weeks. But I don't think that we shall travel, on the whole, much more than three weeks. Things may go faster and faster, for our survey and we are limited by the money. Anyhow, I am sorry not to have given you the name of our Tsingtao hotel, in my last letter: your answer would have caught me here.*

*I am still impressed by the nice side of Tsingtao. But for enjoying them fully, — I miss some "white people" society, — or some old friend as Bien. Y.K. is a charming man (just a bit rough) and a wonderful worker but that is all. I did not expect of him anything more, of course, — at least for a first trip. — Our most interesting and picturesque day was spent along the sea, at the very foot of the Laoshan, near a beautiful Taoist temple, surrounded by forests, - precisely at the contact between the Laoshan impressive granite and a formation which I was anxious to visit since 1926! (when I saw it from the boat at my first return in China). The site can be approached by car. But they are four or five miles to walk,* along a new track, including several hundred of steep steps, up and down. I still feel my legs somewhat broken. But the scenery is perfect: the temple, hidden behind a thick screen of bamboos, is sheltered by beautiful gingko-trees. In the court-yard were the fragant white flowers which you brought back, some day, from the Drummond's. I did not need that for having you present, — to my enjoyment, and to my work. — The weather keeps bright and cool, — with some fog. The next days, far from the seashore, we shall regret it. —

Nothing new, besides. — On the whole, I feel satisfied to have decided this trip in Shantung. — In a few days, we have already succeeded in making good observations. And, in addition, I need (you know it) to keep directly in touch with "mother Earth". Yet, I shall be happy to see Peiping again.

I hope that everything is for the best with you, dearest, —— and that the camel is in full progress.

Yours deeply

Pierre

I will write you again after a few days.

Haiyang, July 25th, 1936

Lucile dear,

We are progressing, - but <u>slowly</u> - because, in Shantung as elsewhere in China, motocars in summer are "un mythe". There is always some "hsia-yü"* breaking the trafic. As a consequence of which, we are obliged to force our way by the old Chinese types of transportation, under the habitual and uncomfortable feeling to be stopped and trapped somewhere by the conditions of the roads. — Still, we are progressing. I write you (when is this letter going to reach you?) from a most picturesque city, about half-way between Tsingtao and the eastern end of the Shantung: something like Aigues-Mortes in S. France. Haiyang is an half-dead, but typical, Chinese city, built on a small promontory, amongst the swamp, near the sea; a square tower, with nice strong walls, without any suburbs, geo-metrically planned. One temple, north of the town, on the slopes of the moun-tains; another one, south, on the sea-shore. The whole just so regular as a diminutive Peking. — I nearly thought that we should never reach the place, two days ago, when, half-way from the precedent town, we found, at 7 p.m., a flooded swampy river. We had to spend the night in one of the most awful inns (smell, mosquitos, food) I have ever met. Finally, the next morning, we crossed (ourselves and our pekinese cart) the flood in a small boat. And it was all right, because we found on the other side, the very geological features we were searching for. — Yes-terday, rain again. We decide to make the next stage in three days by mule (instead of the supposed 5 hours with motocar). The good side of this handicap is that we can do a much better work. Yes, — but my fortnight absence might well turn to be a month's trip. — Anyhow, I think that I am not loosing my time, —

---

*Literally translated "hsia-yü" means "falling" water. The term was used to identify the heavy rainfall that often made the roads impassable.

*chiefly if the japanese geologists have not too much "défloré" the problems here, — a fact which I must ascertain on my way back. What I see interests me <u>plenty,</u> and will have an important bearing of my famous map of the eruptives in China (you know: the map "with the spots"). - As for the pleasures of the trip, there is naturally absolutely no trace of comfort, — but the country is extremely nice: a background of barren, rugged, serrated ranges, — and, in the plains, a rich country covered with beautiful crop (millet, kaolian, etc.). The villages are clean, well built, and surrounded by large trees, much bigger, and much more diverse than in the Hopei: chestnut-leaved oak, sophora, pine-trees, etc. Thousands of noisy cycads [locusts]. Beautiful fruits also (chiefly peaches) but invariable sold green. As Yang-Kieh observed, Chinese enjoy fruits when they break under the teeth as carots. Lot of Chinese melons and other types of "gwa": I can not see the fields without thinking of the "monastery" in your garden.*

*And that's all for today. — I hope that my next letter will be very soon, and not too far from Weihawei so that I can tell you "à bientôt", dearest.*

*Be happy.*

*Yours*

*Pierre*

[Telegram] *Hankow 17.9.1936*

*Arriving Tuesday evening seven. Teilhard*

*Peking, September 24 - 36*

*Lucile, dear,*

*At this very time (6 p.m.) when you are probably moving towards a glorious sunset, in the middle of the Hankow plain, I write you from the table of Jacques, where I have searched for a shelter when leaving the P.U.M.C. - (I have a dinner with the french attaché de l'air, at 8.30). On my right, a picture of A.M. Wang. On my left, a fragrant bunch of flowers. In my soul, your presence, dearest, - so vivid in spite of the miles between us. -May you be happy during this journey, Lucile, and fill your eyes, your mind, your heart, with visible and invisible light! -*

*Sept. 25*

*I could not finish this letter yesterday evening. - Now I am in my room of the Petang: a fine cool morning. Camels, with a nice fresh hair are passing in the courtyard, carrying coal or something else; 6.30 a.m. You are probably still asleep in your cabin, somewhere along the complicated loops of the Yangzte . . . -Today, at last, I am leaving for Tientsin. Finally Dr. Wong did <u>not</u> come to Peking (the "quorum" of the PUMC trustees being reached without him) so that I might have left since Monday. Yet, I do not regret this "retard" which allowed me to finish my paper on the Chinese fossil lakes and to advance my maps-business. But now I am glad to go to the Hautes-Etudes (in spite of the fascinating golden light on the pearl-coloured water and the yellowish lotus leaves of the Peihai), - because I want (and I need) to make this retreat, - and because Peking looks so empty without you. - Since Monday, I felt perfectly lost, at 5 p.m. The first evening, I went to* see Grabau, who did not seem too astonished to see me two days consecutively. The second evening (I had a 8.30 dinner in the Grand Hotel), I did not discover any other escape than the house of Apostolic Délégué, Mgr. Zanin. And then a funny thing happened. I was in the room, not of Mgr. Zanin of course, but of his secretary, Monsignor Commisso (a good friend of mine, since years), - smoking, and chatting about Church, Europe, etc., - when, at the end of the talk, Commisso asked me whether I could not write for him a confidential report which he would send privately to some high officials, "at the heart of Rome". - Well, I was startled by the idea, - and I think I will write the thing, - very shortly, and with the appropriate tune, - but very frankly. My idea is to choose, as a title, "Réflexions sur la Conversion du Monde" (because the pages should be sent first to the "Commission de la Propagande"), - and then to expose why (and how) we need to propose a new side of the "old" God, and a new type of worship (based on adventure and discovery). - The substance would be the same as in "Christ & Evolution", but with a slightly subdued expression (and yet perhaps a clearer and more direct focusing of the question). I hope to show you this "exposé" when you come back, - as a new result of our "spiritual union". -

Nothing new, besides. I have met Mayo yesterday in a Bardac's lunch: he seems busy with a new theatrical production, and was very gay and hungry. - Wednesday, I had a pleasant chinese dinner with Grabau and a bunch of Chinese (= the geological department of the Peita University) in a restaurant of the West-City. Exquisite Szechuanese food, I must confess; lot of Kampei ["bottoms up" toasts] and an extremely hearty atmosphere. Grabau was at his best. I have the impression that he prefers the Chinese to the foreigners, just now. - The social event of today is a stag-party given by the french Ambassador, - in honour of the French admiral (another determined bachelor): ten males pickniking in the Mings Tombs. Jack, who is one of the guests, was amused, but also perfectly amazed by this conception of a pleasure-party.

Now, I must pack. - My next letter will be in ten days; - but you know that these days will be full of you. I know that the more I will love God, the more I will love you.

P.T.

Peking, October 6th, 1936

Lucile dear,
I thank you _so_ much for your two letters, - from Hankow and from Chungking. I found the 2nd one half an hour ago, when collecting my mail in the Survey. (I have come back today, 12 o.c., from Tientsin). I am so happy that you have enjoyed your trip, and that there is sun shining in your soul! - I hope you will find in Hankow my first letter, sent from Peking the day I left. - From Tientsin I found uneasy to send you a word by airmail to Chungking. But you know that I was with you. - Presumably, I had a good time (or at least, I hope, an useful time) in Tientsin. I believe to see more clearly the meaning and the line of life in front of me. And, I too I realize how really you have become a part and a strength of myself. - Do you not feel that the next talks and meeting, will be even more rich and sweet than before? - To grow in and by love . . . - I have finished the

*redaction of the paper I told you in my last letter (for Rome? . . .). Nothing new, - but more organized, concentrate and focused, I hope. -Very short, evidently. You will have a copy, of course.*

*I stop here. Trassaert is waiting for me, - and the first hours in Peiping are always somewhat hectic. -*

*Yours more than ever, dearest*

*P.*

*Dec. 24, 1936*

*Dearest,*

*Naturellement, I forgot to give you, yesterday morning, the name of the French gentleman to whom you could send a copy of both "How I believe", "The spirit of the Earth".*

*Prof. Le Bras      Grand Hotel de Peking.*

*Thank you again so deeply for what you give me so richly. God help us to conquer the fire! -*

*Yours*

*P.*

*[Tientsin] December 30, 1936*

*Dearest,*

*Just a few lines, - with my best wishes of happy new year! - May 1937 (I am sure, it will do . . .) find us closer together, & higher!-*

*I have received with a great joy your letter of Sunday. So many things to talk about, next Saturday! — Here, I got no letter so far, except a long one from my brother in Paris, — rather bitter for the internal situation in France. — No news from the Review to which I sent my last paper. Is that a good sign? or not?. .*

*Here I have a quiet time, — working most of the time with Trassaert a puzzling group of Antelopes (with straight, curved, twisted, spiraled, round, oval, or triangular horns), by which Nature seems to have enjoyed the game of perplexing paleontologists.*

*I still plan to leave Tientsin Saturday morning. I will come to Ta Tien Shui Ching at about 3.30.*

*Yours, so much*

*P.*

*Peiping Jan. 25, 1937*

*Dear Friend, -*

*Whether it should have a sequence or not, it seems to me that our conversation of the other day has brought us to a point where for my interest as well as yours, I owe an explanation. I sensed (and besides you said) that both my interior and my exterior situation seems to you illogical, - or even to use the word, not frank. I will attempt in these few lines to make you understand, in all sincerity, my position, in its strength and in its weakness.*

1) *Above all, have no doubt, that I do all I can to be loyally a "priest" in the full meaning of the word. I say my mass and I follow to the best of my ability the rules of my Order. In the interior of which I am considered as a "good religieux" and even perhaps a bit more. And I hope that what follows will help you to see that I conform to its frame (though many of its elements seem to me of a very contestable value) for reasons which prevent my acts from being a pretence.*

2) *From what does the appearance of being a bit complex in my attitude come? The origin I find (if I analyse myself well) is the co-existance in me of two "passions" neither of which I can sacrifice, and which therefore I must attempt to synthesize.*

*The first of these two passions is a fundamental belief in the grandeur and the value of the World (understood as the totality of the real energies which surround us). I am first and essentially a "born-pantheist". And all the developement of my scientific carreer has been animated by this initial sentiment, which all my studies have reciprocally systamitised, rationalised and nourished.*

*Therefore I love the World passionately, as a "pagen" say those narrow ones who have never understood the profound mystic of the Universe. But (and here is where the difficulty starts) I love equally passionately the God who expresses Himself in the Christian Christ. Originally, no doubt, this second love was less natural than the first; it was largely implanted in me by the influence of my education. Never the less I think it awakened in me another profound native disposition. Left to itself my initial pantheism would have without doubt, evolved in the direction of some vague "immanentism". Initiated by Christianity to an incomparable taste for "adoration of a Person", I quickly realized that the Universe to which I had always been devoted would remain structurally uncrowned unless it was possible for me to discover a sort of heart and face for it which I could love.*

*It would be too long and useless, to detail for you the interior steps which lead me to a synthesis which was working in me between the two passions of the Universe and the Person. The only interesting point for the end which I propose here is the following: I find myself at the present time in an equal impossibility (vital) to pass either the Universe (conceived as an organic All in evolution), or Christ (who appears to me, in the experimental domain, the only existing center and the only positive sign of a "universal Person"). If I do not believe in the World, I can no longer believe in Christ: and if I do not believe in Christ I can no longer love the World. All my interior equilibrium is therefore tied to a possible conjuction of these two supreme realities in a unique Reality, seizable in the same and unique act of adoration.*

*The problem of this synthesis between Christ and the Universe has naturally two faces: a theoretical face (or "theologie"), and a practical face (or "moral").*

*The theological solution has seemed to me relatively easy. Taken in its most authentic definitions (particularly in St. Paul) Christ is endowed with a mass of properties which, transported into the Universe such as we know it today, inevitably take on "cosmic" dimensions. If the "theologians" as a whole*

*Teilhard explains himself*

*still refuse to see it at this time, it is simply because they do not yet realize what
the experimental World has become for us.*

*The moral solution is more delicate, because it tends to express itself
externally in attitudes which run against an equilibrium (a routine) of a social
order. I have analized at length in several essays, the transformations which the
idea of Christian "saintliness" undergoes when Christ is envisaged, no longer as
a Restorer of a damaged World, but as the Animator of a Universe in progress.
These transformations are profound. But one thing seems to me sure: if they gen-
eralize the evangelical moral code, and make it dynamic, they do not deform it.
After the transformation the love of God above all, expresses itself in a continual
effort of universal "going beyond", it lives and and affirms itself always as a law
of perfecton. And is that not the very essence of the Gospel?*

*It remains (to the near reserves, - and they are important, -which I will
make further on) that the religious transformations of which I have just spoken
are still only at their beginnings. They still effect but a minority. Those who are
conscious of them find themselves therefore, in the situation of having to live
what I call by convention their "hyper-Christianity" in the social forms (still
dominant) of the "ancient-Christianity", -and without having the right nor the
power to break with them, in which their roots still are deeply immersed. In this
duality lies exactly the reason which could give you the impression of an equivocal attitude in me. But I believe that this duality has nothing of a "duplicity". If I
continue to give way to many gests and formulas which are empty for me, it is
not by simple formality, approaching hypocrasy: but it is because I believe passionately of sensing the circulation of a sap under the old dead shell, of which I
have an essential need, and which I cannot yet attain without my holding to the
entire tree. After all my situation is no different from all the men who have new
ideas on the value and the future of the social body to which they belong (nation,
army etc.).*

*And now two questions to finish: How much of the Hyper-Christianity of
which I speak is special to me? and in what degree can it flatter itself to be the
true Christianity?*

*My reply to the first question is the following: No, the new Christianity
which I defend is not personal to me, and it is just this that gives it value. I am
conscious in the matter of being only a voice expressing that which rises like a
cloud around us. In France, Belgium, America and England I can give you a list of
names (religious, and laymen, philosophers and even teaching theologians) which
are those of men thinking in exactly the same direction as myself and who have
the conviction in doing so of not diminishing but of emphasizing their Christianity (exactly because their effort goes to magnify the reality of Christ which is necessarily the very essence of Christianity). These men have never ceased to
encourage me. They have read everything that I have written. Why, you may ask,
then continue to work below board and not in the open. Simply once again,
because the proportion of men who see is still too small, and have not yet pene-
trated far enough ahead (as it yet does) in the governing spheres to be able to
impose ifself. And also because a premature "decortication" could do dangerous*

*harm to the organization it attempts to enlarge and save.*

*But then, and this is the second question, supposing that the future proves us right we the "innovators", and that in place of the Gospel of "Separation and resignation" we see a Gospel of immersion in the World and of "sublimation" succeed, - how will we be able to still say that Christianity has not been suppressed and replaced by a new religion? We can say it for the good reason that, under a grander and more liberated form, it will be the same current of living love for the same living reality (the Christ) which will continue over us. How, some years hence, can we say we are the same selves, each of us, if not by the continuance of a current of consciousness? The same for the Church. The change is no doubt no greater between the Christ Universal (of which I dream) with many others) and the "Christ-King" (proposed for adoration to the faithful by the official church) than between this Christ-King and the Man encountered by the fishermen of Galilee. And besides, in reality, of what importance is this largely theoretical question from the connections with the Past? The reality of God without which human effort (lacking a common ideal) would fall to dust must be found every moment for us in the direction of the most achieved image which humanity has been able to make of the Divinity: The most true Christ can only be objectively the one who appears to us subjectively as the most perfect and the greatest Saviour. It is in this sense that I believe to be still sincerely a christian.*

*I hope that these pages, necessarily brief, do not appear to you too incoherent. In any case believe in my profound sympathy. And be assured that you have in no way hurt me by your frankness. I doubt that you could say to me anything of religious matters more hard than those that I have expressed a hundred times to myself.*

*Yours*

*Teilhard.*

---

Lucile tried to accomodate herself to what she found unreal in this real situation, and she read and re-read his January "position" statement. She continued also to translate and type his papers; and she joined him in his search for God.

In February of 1937 Teilhard left China for the United States. There, together with old friends, he attended a scientific conference in Philadelphia. Later (in April) he went to Paris. — In June he left his Jesuit confreres and journeyed south to visit with his brother Joseph in Auvergne. He left France and returned to China by boat in September.

*Nanking, 24 Febr, 1937*

*Dearest,*

*I have open and read your precious letter yesterday, when passing before the Taishan. I had kept it so long, unopen, so that I might be more quiet, better prepared for your message. And surely, Lucile, this was a precious part of yourself that you have enclosed in those pages, - the deepest expression of what we have been gradually improving and building in and with both ourselves in the course*

*of a long and happy year. - Yes, dearest, I will, during these six months, bring with
me your impulsion, your light, and the consciousness of what you have tried so
much to impress on me: that whatever of truth I believe to see should not be
wasted, nor kept in some unduly shadow, but used at the utmost for freeing the
"spirit of the world". - Really your work, Lucile, as well as mine. -*

*In the meantimes, I hope that we shall not miss each other in a depress-
ing way, - but that the unavoidable feeling of physical absence will be ultra-com-
pensated by the thought that this very absence will work into making us more
deeply present to each other. You and I, during this spring, we shall expand the
surface on which we construct, and by which we can join. - You and I, hand in
hand, facing some rising sun, - your last sculpture, Lucile. - Might this feeling
make richer for you the coming blossoms of the Central Park and of the Western
Hills. No regrets, and no retreat . . . I like so much the picture you have sent me.
But Göring ought to have pictured us as Peter and Delia, over the top of a rock,
with the light on our face.*

*N'est-ce pas?*

*Je quitte Nanking dans deux heures.
Bon voyage jusqu'ici. J'ai eu le temps de
penser à bien des choses: à la "lecture" de
Philadelphie (j'ai trouvé mon sujet), - et
aussi au "Phénomène spirituel". Je suis
décidé à rédiger quelque chose là-dessus
en mer. Il me semble que je vois bien clair,
maintenant. J'ai causé assez longuement
avec Bob Lynn, qui m'a dit bien des choses sur ses recherches: quel mystère que
l'organisation d'un système nerveux
humain: vraiment on touche là la "structure de l'Esprit". - Bob s'est chargé de
transporter lui-même à l'hôtel de Shanghai ma caisse en fer, - de sorte que l'erreur
de Wang a tourné au mieux.*

*Ici, gris et un peu de neige. J'ai vu ce
matin Dr. Wong, si surchargé et toujours
si souriant et si désintéressé. Nous avons
longuement causé. J'ai bien fait de m'arrêter ici pour le voir.*

*Demain, je vous enverrai quelques
lignes au moins de Shanghai. La journée
sera sans doute chargée. - Maintenant
que j'ai quitté Peking, j'ai hâte d'être
tout à fait parti: je me sentirai plus près
de revenir.*

Don't you think?

I am leaving Nanking in two hours.
Good trip so far. I have had time to think
of many things: the "lecture" in Philadelphia (I have found my subject), - and also
"The Phenomenon of Spirituality". I have
decided to write something about this
while at sea. I feel that I see quite clearly
now. I spoke at length with Bob Lynn
who told me many things about his
research: what a mystery the structure of
the human neural system is: really one
gets there into contact with "the Structure
of the Spirit". - Bob undertook the transportation of my iron box to the Shanghai
Hotel, thus Wang's mistake turned out
for the best.

Here the sky is grey and we have a little snow. I saw Dr. Wong this morning, so
overworked and always so smiling and
so unselfish. We talked for a long time. I
was right to stop here to see him.

To-morrow I shall send you a few lines
at least from Shanghai. The day will
probably be very busy. Now that I have
left Peking, I am eager to be completely
gone: I shall feel nearer to coming back.

*In your letter, Lucile, the most wonderful thing you tell me is that I may
help you to be closer to God and to all that is good. Now be sure that you do the
same for me, - and that is the everlasting reason for which so much I love you.*

P.

*Dearest,*

 *I am leaving the Hotel for the boat. Everything ready. Just these few lines for repeating my last letter, from Nanking: that I am leaving under <u>your star</u>, - for the best!*

 *Very busy day. I have seen my colleague Leroy (with great pleasure), - and Mrs. Walen (a very complex case . . ., but still hopeful), - and Camille (no more blond but brown, - and so full of life): she is ashamed not to have written you: address lost. -Breuil is in Japan: so I could not see him.*

 *Adieu, Lucile, ou plutôt à bientôt. I believe in you.*

  *P.*

*R.M.S. Empress of Japan, Febr. 27, 1937*

*Lucile dear,*

 *We are due tomorrow to Kobe. - Just a few lignes, to bring you the deepest of my thought, - and to tell you that everything is all right. -*

*Le temps est gris, et assez mauvais. Mais le bateau est si grand qu'on ne se doute pas des vagues. Je suis seul dans une cabine très convenable (je crains qu'il ne monte pas beaucoup de monde à Yokohama!). Compagnons de route "ordinaires". Plusieurs missionnaires américains, - gentils. Je commence à les initier à mon Christianisme, qui les surprend un peu, - mais les attire plutôt, - sans trop les effrayer. Il faut dire que j'y vais prudemment.*

The sky is grey and the weather is pretty bad. But the ship is so big that we don't even know there are waves. I am alone in a quite suitable cabin (I am afraid that lots of people will come aboard at Yokohama!). My travelling companions are "ordinary". Several American missionnaries, - nice people. I have started introducing them to my Christianity, which surprises them a little, - but rather attracts them, - without scaring them too much. I must say I am moving prudently.

*Après vous avoir écrit, de Shanghai, j'ai été dîner avec Mrs. Walen au Cathay. Conversation très émouvante, qui a vite débordé la question 2. - Cette dernière est du reste bien compliquée. In many ways, she is bigger than he, - and cannot admitt to be absorbed by him. Hope he will understand. - Par ailleurs, l'amie de Mrs. Walen, Mrs. Ames, est à bord (en 1$^{re}$ classe évidemment). J'ai aussi eu une conversation avec elle, - et me suis aperçu qu'elle est très supérieure à ce que je pensais. Que de magnifiques énergies spirituelles qui cherchent leur voie, et un Objet! . . .*

After writing to you from Shanghai, I had dinner with Mrs. Walen at the Cathay. A very moving conversation which quickly went beyond the question 2. - The latter is really quite complicated. By the way, Mrs. Walen's friend, Mrs. Ames, also is on board (first class of course). I also had a conversation with her, - and realized that she is very superior to what I thought. How many magnificent spiritual energies are searching for their way, and an Object! . . .

 *I have started "Le Phénomène Spirituel". Good or not good, I will try to finish it. Other ideas are already coming to take the place. I will explain that to you from Honolulu. Be happy, dearest, - as you make me full and happy.*

  *P.*

Yokohama, R.M.S. Empress of Japan.
March 1, 1937

**Dearest,**

*Nous arrivons ce matin à Yoko-hama. Hier, à Kobe, il faisait beau et bleu. Ce matin, nous nous sommes réveillés dans le gris et le vent. Mais qu'importe le temps sur les grands navires?*

We are arriving in the morning in Yokohama. Yesterday in Kobe the weather was fine and the sky blue. This morning we woke up in dullness and wind. But what does the weather matter on these big ships?

*What I wish and want to tell you this morning, Lucile, is that, when our ship will leave Asia, this night, the best of my soul will go to you, - westwards, - or rather eastwards, in the direction where the sun rises, and where the water and the rail bring me slowly back to Peiping. - I shall be richer for you, at that time, Lucile; - and you for me; - and that time will be very soon ours. -*

*Not much to tell you since yesterday. In Kobe, I went a short time ashore, just for a walk, - and also for meeting, in the Mission, a colleague of mine (the brother of one of my best friends, Auguste Valensin) who is touring the Far-East for "spiritual" purposes. This rather "important" man was extremely kind with me, but I realized that we were, each for the other, in the depth of our souls, perfect strangers (and that he did not see it!). Without understanding, he believes that he understands,- and that is worse than everything.*

*(handwritten: who only thinks he understands so true)*

*Hier au soir j'ai reçu un radio très aimable de Mrs. Grew, m'invitant à venir à un lunch à Tokyo: je vais y aller si l'auto promise m'attend au quai (et si nous n'arrivons pas trop tard à Yokohama). Je vous raconterai cela. J'espère que Bill Drummond aussi sera là, aujourd'hui, - et je sais qu'il m'apportera une lettre de vous ...*

Last night I received a very kind radio message from Mrs. Grew inviting me to lunch in Tokyo: I will go if the promised car is waiting for me on the quay (and if we don't arrive too late in Yokohama). I will tell you about it. I hope Bill Drummond also will be there today, - and I know that he will bring a letter from you ...

*Entre temps, I am struggling on the "Phénomène Spirituel": something is coming slowly out. - The features of the child will probably be recognizable in Honolulu. -*

*So much yours, Lucile*

*P.T.*

R.M.S. Empress of Japan.
March 5 (Meridian day) 1937

**Dearest,**

*A few minutes ago, I was on the deck, looking at the sun sinking in the direction of Peking; and I felt so deeply that my life is there, that I wished the boat could turn backward, - to west. And yet, which other way might bring me closer to you, Lucile, than the road* forward *... The more I think it over, dearest, the clearer I see that I need to go through what is awaiting me in America and Europe for being more yours, and more what you like and search in me. -*

*It was a joy for me to receive your letter in Yokohama, - and to hear from you about everything in your life: about the symbolic couple in your studio, about your last party, - about Tarnowsky (!), - about your prospects going to the Hills. And above all, Lucile, I feel so happy each time you tell me that I can help you to be yourself, - more gloriously.*

*My last letter was posted the day before we came in Yokohama. A few minutes later I received a radio from Mrs. Grew, asking me to spend the following day at the Embassy in Tokyo. A car was waiting for me at the boat, and brought me back at 10 p.m. The weather was grey and rainy. But I had a very interesting afternoon, - and "interesting" is a very poor word, in the case. After a short drive in Tokyo, we went back to the quiet salon of the Embassy, - and there, for my great surprise, Mrs. Grew opened me a part of her soul, - such a beautiful soul: she seems to read or to hear directly what I am striving to reach by the dark paths of Matter. It is a great experience to meet, from time to time, a child of heaven! - After that, we had a charming dinner at four: Mr.& Mrs. Grew, myself, and the young Dane with whom we discussed politics a few weeks ago, at the Lyon's. - By the way, I found Mrs Grew still much disturbed by the news that the little girl, in Peiping, had the scarlet fever. Hope that she is completely well, now. -*

*When I came back to the Empress, in Yokohama, I found the boat occupied by a large new crowd, including a group of French and Canadian congressists of Manilla. The first impression was rather depressing. But after all, I was left alone in my cabin, - and gradually I discovered in the pious group a reasonable number of really pleasant people. - But Bill Drummond was the real relief. He is located downstairs "next to the right propeller", but we meet frequently, and had with the Captain and a number of important wealthy people, (including the Ranee of Sarawak, in Borneo) a regular series of evening cocktails. Bill, on the whole, has a grand time, - chiefly since he has discovered on board a very cute little girl whom you have probably seen at the Merrell's the day I left Peking. - He and I we have also seen many times Mrs. Ames, who is decidedly a most interesting type of woman. I regret that she did not meet you in Peking, rather than other people who could not understand and help her. She asks for "our books", which she has seen in the hands of Mrs. Walen. -Would you send her both of them:*

*Mrs. Robert Ames*
*c/o L. A. Greene*
*5504 Hollywood Blvd   Hollywood (Cal.)*

*She leaves tomorrow in Honolulu. - On board I met also a certain Mr. Penrose, who is the brother of the famous Penrose who recently made the geological Soc. of America the wealthiest scientific society of the world. And also an english lady who is a friend of Mrs. Garrod. Etc. - World is very small.*

Penrose

*In the meantime, I have advanced the "Phénomène spirituel", of which I am writing the Part III (Moralisation). Sincerely, I don't know whether the essay is as good and clear as he could be. Anyhow, I had to write it down before I could see something ahead. At the least, these new pages are a good preliminary study for a further work. - I plan to write, next, something on the experimental evidences we have of an actual progress, movement of the human mind, now: "Le vent d'esprit"...*

*Excuse this letter and its handwriting. - Je vous l'ai écrite par morceaux,*

"Le vent d'esprit"

*sur un coin de table dans ma cabine. Tomorrow you will be for me the light and the fragance of Honolulu.*

*Yours P.T.*

*Please give a cake from my part to Spotty (and, if he likes it, to Dungshi). I suppose I will still discover some of its hair on my clothes in Paris . . .*

*R.M.S. Empress of Japan, March 12, 1937*

*Dearest,*

*Tomorrow morning we arrive in Victoria, [British Columbia], - and I will have, with Bill, to fight my way to Seattle in time for taking the night train to Chicago. This is the end of the calmest part of the journey to Europe. Yet I will be happy, I think, to meet the circle of congenial friends gathered in Philadelphia. Anyhow, before leaving the Empress (which will sail back to China in four or five days) I want to tell you once more how, during this important time in America, your presence will be with me as a light and a strength, - your presence, precious Lucile. - I will do my best for visiting your family in Chicago. And, in any case, I will write you soon after my arrival in Philadelphia.*

*So generally, the few hours spent in Honolulu have been most charming. I went round a part of the island with Bill, and we had together a very amusing farewell-lunch at the Moana Hotel with Mrs. Ames and another Canadian friend of the boat. The next days have been rainy and rough, - but this morning the sea is smooth and the sun shining. Very convenient for packing. - In the meantime I have written the 30th and the last page of my Essay, which I will send you when typed (in France, I suppose). I don't think it is perfect, - but this is at least a good advanced sketch for further developments. And I feel more free now for opening my mind to new ideas and new impressions.*

*As generally, also, I have discovered at the last minute interesting people on the boat. One is a certain Lady Hozy (daughter of a British General Consul in China), a highly scholar type of old lady, which knows well Dr. Wong, Hu-shih, etc., and was a friend of V.K. Ting. Another one is a certain Mr. McKenzie, in charge of Education, etc. in the Cook Islands: he has fascinating talks on the beliefs and the traditions of the Polynesian peoples, - how, by jumps, they spanned the great Blue from Java to Hawaii and New Zealand. - Sorry not to have spotted this man earlier. - World is surely full of marvelous things: what a subject for a collection of books it would be to describe the successive "conquests" of the world by Man, in the course of ages. I wonder that no editor seems to have got or realized this idea.*

*Now I have to pack my things, and to fill the applications for the Customs. How difficult it has become to enter any country in the world. It would seem that you have to fight at each frontier! . .*

*God bless you, dearest*

*P.T.*

*Dearest,*

*Voici plus d'une semaine que je suis en Amérique, - et je ne vous ai pas encore écrit. Ne m'en veuillez pas: Dès mon arrivée à Philadelphie, j'ai été pris dans un tel tourbillon que je viens seulement, il y a un instant, de lire les dernières des lettres que j'ai trouvées en arrivant! - Mais vous savez que votre pensée m'a suivi, parmi tout cela. Et j'ai été si content quand le jeune White, rencontré au symposium m'a donné une photo (prise à Liou-hi-ho, avec les Stephenson), où tous les deux, nous sommes très bien: je vous l'enverrai quand j'aurai le courage de m'en séparer.*

*Voici maintenant un résumé des événements depuis ma dernière lettre de l'Empress of Japan. - L'arrivée à Seattle a été laborieuse, parce que nous étions trop nombreux: la journée s'est passée à faire la queue, pour les passeports, pour la douane, d'abord à Victoria puis à Seattle (dans l'intervalle, il m'a fallu rédiger un télégramme de 300 mots pour l'Associated Press). Finalement, j'ai manqué mon train à Seattle, ce qui m'a obligé à rester un jour là-bas, en compagnie de Bill; journée très amusante du reste grâce aux Griffith's qui nous ont reçus d'une manière charmante dans leur jolie maison sur le Washington Lake. Nous avons tout juste échappé aux cocktails pour ne pas manquer notre train une fois de plus. Mais, de l'affaire je me trouvais si en retard pour le Symposium que je n'ai passé qu'une heure et demie à Chicago; impossible d'aller voir votre père et votre mère, ni Mrs. Wood. J'espère que Bill l'aura fait.*

*Je suis donc tombé en plein congrès: reporters, flashes, etc. C'était plutôt ahurissant. Enfin je crois que ma com-*

I have been in America for more than a week now and I haven't written to you yet. Don't be cross with me: When I arrived in Philadelphia I was immediately caught in such a whirlwind that I only just read the last of the letters I found on my arrival here! - But you know that your thought followed me all the time. I was so happy when young White, whom I met at the symposium, gave me a photo (taken in Liou-li-ho with the Stephensons) in which we both look so nice: I will send it to you when I have the courage to part with it.

Now I will give you a summary of what happened since my last letter written on the Empress of Japan. - The arrival in Seattle was strenuous because there were so many people: the day was spent in line - for the passports and customs first in Victoria, then in Seattle (in the meantime I had to write a 300 word telegram for Associated Press). Finally, I missed my train to Seattle and I had to spend one day there in the company of Bill; a very pleasant day thanks to the Griffiths who welcomed us most charmingly in their pretty house on Washington lake. We just escaped the cocktail party, otherwise we would have missed the train once more. But, because of all the rush, I was so late for the symposium that I only spent one hour and a half in Chicago, and there was no time left to visit your father and mother, nor Mrs. Wood. I hope Bill will have seen them.

So I arrived in the middle of the convention: reporters, flashes, etc. It was rather astounding. However, I think

*munication a intéressé: je l'ai faite oralement, sans texte écrit, et c'est apparemment ce qui a plu. Par exemple je me demande si je ne vais pas susciter quelques plaintes dans le monde religieux conservateur: par la force des choses, j'ai pris nettement et publiquement la position évolutionniste, - et la presse a comme de juste "emphasized the thing". Peut-être est-ce "providentiel". - A la remise de la fameuse "Mendel medal" (qui est considérée ici comme une chose plus importante que je ne pensais)*

people found my presentation interesting; I did it orally, without a written text, and apparently this is what people liked. Although I wonder if this will not bring some complaints from the conservative religious milieu: By necessity I had to clearly and openly take the evolutionary position. Naturally, the press "emphasized the thing". Perhaps this is providential. During the presentation of the famous Mendel medal (which is considered here as something much more important than I thought)

*my little speech (written) has also been an explicit expression of belief in evolution, and the mostly catholic audience seems to have been pleased. I told essentially the same things to a reporter of the main newspaper of Toronto (he had come right from Toronto in order to interview me! . . .): I am a bit curious to read the result of the long talk I have had with him. - On the whole, something has perhaps been launched: I had never had so far such an opportunity for expressing openly my thought. - Another and perhaps more important thing is that yesterday I have met here, in Washington, a really intelligent and influential colleague of mine (F. Walsh)* [Father Edmund Walsh, S.J., at the School of Foreign Service, in Georgetown University], *who told me that he had just had a long talk with Dr. Carrel* [Alexis Carrell, French surgeon and Nobelist]: *he thinks of starting a kind of "Institute of Man", in order to study Man "as a whole", and is searching for specialists who could attack the problem from different and wide angles. Exactly what de Terra, I, etc. were dreaming! Walsh will write to Carrel about me (Carrel knows probably me also by the Rockefeller Foundation), - and I will try to have a talk with him in New-York, next week. - You see, everything seems to take a favourable way, ahead.*

*I have seen a number of friends here: de Terra, von Koenigswald, Miss Garrod* [Dorothy Garrod, English prehistorian], *Chaney, Granger, etc. De Terra shelters me in his nice little home, in the charming suburbs of Philadelphia, - and I have found, a second time, with him, his wife Rhoda, and the little Noëlle, the family life of Rawalpindi in India. We have long talks together on any possible subject, included those on which we don't agree so much, you and me: and Rhoda is so amusingly and definitely on your side. - I found here an english translation of "Sauvons l'Humanité"; I will keep a copy for you. - I had also several interesting talks with Miss Garrod: I hope to see more of her during the crossing of the Atlantic, - since she takes the same boat (Normandie) in the same class.*

*Nothing very clear concerning the plans of the next year. De Terra is still uncertain whether he will stay in Philadelphia, or go to Harvard: from both sides he has propositions, - but nothing is settled. The famous Institute of Man in Philadelphia is still somewhat in the clouds, because the financial decisions will not be taken before the summer. Yet, I believe that something will materialize. In the meantimes, de Terra is afraid that the Hundes-basin (Himalaya) will be difficult* to reach (for practical reasons), and we have made therefore another possible plan for exploring the Irawady valley (Burmah). No date fixed. Perhaps (?) next winter. In any way, I foresee vaguely that I will be surely in Peiping the next autumn, and have a trip somewhere in the south during the winter (1938) with de Terra, or v. Koenigswald, or Pei. -

On the 29th of March, I go to Boston, in order to receive an honorary Doctorate in the Boston College (held by my jesuit colleagues) together with Miss Garrod! The 31, I shall give a lecture in Harvard. Then I come back and stay in New-York up to my departure (April 14), - with a trip in Princeton University. -In Boston, I hope to see Alice [Cosme] and miss Tucker. - Found here a very good and long letter from Ida (which I will send you in a few days), and another one from Max which I had not yet time for reading decently: he seems hopeful, on the whole, for his african business.

Pardon me this hasty letter. I am still half-drowned in the number of things to do, and, this morning, I take the train back to Philadelphia. - At least, you will find here the substance of what I have done, and of what I think, - the whole thing being illuminated by your spiritual, but so real, presence, my dearest Lucile.

So deeply <u>yours</u>

P.T.

In the 1937 letters they exchanged (he in the States, she in China), they often referred to the many walks they had taken in the beautiful parks of the city. Lucile recalled an afternoon when they went to Central Park, a part of the Forbidden City where bowls of remarkable goldfish were exhibited. She remembered Teilhard explaining how the fish were bred — some to have tails longer than their bodies, some to have pompoms over their eyes. On these occasions he often discussed his philosophical and religious thoughts. As his thinking became more and more familiar to her, his ideas were more comprehensible and took on greater and greater importance. She listened intently and from his conviction that "what she did was important because it was God's work", Lucile found affirmation and felt herself to be a part of it all; that "God would be always with me and that we were building something - always, all the time". — from Lucile Swan's unpublished autobiography.

The following letter is the earliest text of her letter to him.

1 Ta Tien Sui Ching
Peiping, March 31, 1937

Pierre dear,

One of the six months is all gone. For the first time since you left, I gave myself the luxury today of thinking concretely about the time when you would be back here again! Because it <u>will</u> happen one of these days and that will be so wonderful.

I have read your letter from Honolulu many times. I agree dear that it was very important for you to go to America and Europe just now, and I hope you realize how really glad I am that you are there. Bob Drummond read me some of Bill's letter which gave many more details of your life; and it certainly sounded as if you all were having a very good time. I loved the picture of you two rushing through dinner to go up and join a cock-tail party! And apparently Mrs. Ames is still telling the world how much she "adores" you! However I sent her the books! But all that must seem so very far away now, because *you will have crossed another ocean when you read this. And then you will seem so much nearer.*

*Am so eager to get your letters from Philadelphia etc. and to hear how things went there; though I could well understand if you did not have anything absolutely definite to report. And what have I to tell! Am still working on the head of Tarnowski which I think is going very well, though he is difficult to do. And the two figures is almost done; people seem to really like it and find it one of my best things. I hope it is for it was so marvelously inspired! Otherwise life is pretty quiet. Very often go to a movie with Tarnowski after work. He comes in the afternoon. I have seen more pictures these last few weeks than in <u>months</u> before. Have been to a few neighborhood dinners, but have also had many dinners with a good book for company. Have gone to the country the last few Sundays so have not seen Grabau, but Germaine said he was <u>terribly</u> depressed the last time she saw him. I must try to get there this week, but when? it is so far.*

*Today was really rather spring-like, Central Park was full; the goldfish are out again and they have taken the winter coats off the peonies! So maybe spring really is near. I felt so depressed last week but I think it was mostly due to the endless dull cold windy days. The proofs of <u>Personalistic Universe</u> have gone back for the last time. I do hope I did not overlook too many mistakes! They will be ready in about two weeks. I told him not to hurry but to print them well. I'll send some to Simone as soon as they are finished. You will be seeing her soon! and is Max back yet and was he successful? what a lot of things you will have to write about! Do give them my love and how I wish I could join some of your talks! I hope my last letter was not too -insistent! But I guess after some of the talks we have had it would not shock you. Have not yet finished typing <u>Christology and Evolution</u>; that too I'll send to Simone. I gave her a very badly done copy when I was in France.*

*It seems to me I have not much news for you today, but I haven't been doing much. Spotty was very surprised and delighted when he received cakes the other day without even begging for them. I told him you had sent them but he did not properly appreciate that and I have to confess begged just as much as ever. Even Tungshi enjoyed them. His puppies are the cutest things I ever saw - am sorry I decided not to take one, but 3 would be a bit too much.*

*I wonder if you finished the Phenomenon Spiritual; it was probably much better than you thought at the time. The new paper sounds fascinating and I can see how it might try to crowd the other one out of your mind.*

*It will be so good to think of you in France and what a relief it will be when your letters can come regularly. And I do so hope that you will see clearly there - Life is not so simple as one can think it or talk it. But still some of the really important things do stand out - and I hope there will not be unexpected complications for you.*

*As you know dearest my thoughts are always with you and you are always the best and most beautiful of life to me.*

*Yours always*
*Lucile*

---

In New York Teilhard had his first word from Lucile in over a month. Shortly afterwards he received from her a long chatty letter about their mutual friends and her ongoing copy work for his paper, *Christology and Evolution*.

---

*Dearest,*

    *Day before yesterday, at the American Museum, I found, with a deep joy, your precious letters 2 and 3, - the first ones since Yokohama; and, reading them, I felt like a seaweed when the tide comes back to it and shelters it anew under its flow of life. I knew it when I left Peiping, Lucile: this parting would only give me a better perspective of the great strength and happiness which you have become for me, - a kind of wide, and living, and personal atmosphere in which the best of myself expands so totally and so naturally! God bless you, dearest, for what you give me so abundantly! - and may He help me to be always more the same for you! - I have enjoyed also reading all the small news you give me on the Peiping's life: those are little things, but which help me so much in living with you. Tell me all these details, when you write me, - specially those concerning your work, - and the people you see, - and your thoughts on the wall or in the Tai Miao. - By the way, there is surely a larger part of truth in your observation that "love of God" may be compared with the love one has for one's parents. But I do not think that this comparison reaches the very essence of the phenomenon. God seems to present itself to our being as the final center of our achievement by union (or by communion): and this is in the direct prolongation of the very attraction which brings each to the other two lovers. In fact, any kind of love can be recognized in the love of God: but true love gives to the whole thing its final hue or flavour. I will probably have to analyze these facts in a next Essay on the "Prolongations of Evolution".-*

    *My last letter (7) was sent from Washington. Since that time, I have been back to Philadelphia (where I have spent Easter with de Terra); - then to Boston and Harvard. I am here since two days.*

    *(1) In Philadelphia, I had the most pleasant time, and we talked for hours with "Hellmuth and Rhoda" on any possible subject (religion, philosophy, ethics and practical life). It would be difficult to find two people more deeply fond of each other, and yet more different from each other than those two. Rhoda has almost no conscious need of organizing her life under any philosophical nor religious conception; and Hellmuth is almost "douloureusement" craving for it. She is full of an happy possession of the present; - and he is full of an anxious anticipation of the future. He therefore is closer to me; but she obliges me to think more, - being given the fact, in addition, that she is terribly intuitive in psychological matters. I hope you will meet them, someday. The saturday, eve of Easter, we decided to enjoy our time: lunch in a swedish restaurant, movies in the afternoon, and music in the evening (the 9th symphony of Beethoven in the Philadelphia Orchestra). -*

    *(2) In Boston, I spent three days, and I saw a lot of people, either in the magnificent college belonging to my order, or in Harvard, and in town. - As I told you, perhaps, I have been invited by the College to receive an honorary Doctorate, together with Miss Garrod, - on the occasion of the opening of an anthropological department. Several "catholic anthropologists" were there. I was perfectly received by my colleagues, - but I found the position somewhat delicate. From*

*Boston to Seattle, I have been pictured by the press as "the Jesuit who believes that Man descends from Apes"; and this crude translation of my scientific statements has resulted into a shock for the irish-catholic opinion in this part of the world. My confrères, who are supposed to lead the roman orthodoxy, have been flooded with anxious letters (I have personally received a few of them, together with several others expressing relief) - And finally, very kindly and most embarrassed, the President of Boston College let me understand that it would be difficult for him to confer on me the famous Doctorate, by fear that this honour would induce the american catholics to believe that Boston College was endorsing my views: a rather funny and a bit dangerous situation. Since however I have met, very friendly, the most important representatives of my order in Washington, Boston and New-York, I hope that things are not going to become more serious for me. On the whole, I am rather disgusted by the press, - but not absolutely disatisfied to have found an occasion for expressing what I think. (In Boston, as in Washington, I had several private talks, perfectly frank, with several of my younger colleagues).*

*In Harvard, I found the most charming and refreshing welcome, and my lecture seems to have been appreciated. This time, helped by the Harvard's professors, I kept the newspapermen in almost decent limits.*

*Finally, in Boston, I have seen Alice and Miss Tucker. - Alice and Frank met me the first day, and brought me to their home for lunch. I found them in the most extatic conditions of the youngest couple of the world. She is in the sky, - and he is beaming on her. And yet there is no excitation in the matter: they have a rather difficult life, - not many prospects. Simply they enjoy to be and to struggle together. In a month, they will leave the Dr. Grabau's brother's house and settle in their new home, - a positively charming spot, with a few acres of ground, in the woods, some 8 miles from the town. Frank is really a lovable young man, energetic, clever, and affectionate. Alice is a different woman, much more steady and optimistical, under the same childish enthusiasm for a poem or a flower. She does not regret China, - but she does not forget her friends of Peking, and you are one of the best. Her feelings for Dr. Grabau have also settled or evolved in a right way. I could easily feel that she likes now to talk of him. She writes to him, from time to time. The old man does not write her, but recently he sent her all his books on gardening. - With Miss Tucker I spent the morning and the noon of the last day. She is really a nice girl, so frank et so alive. We had lunch together in the "Country Club", at the expenses of Daddy, - and we talked philosophy, Bégouëns, Ida, etc. She hopes to spend a few weeks in France this summer, - and she told me several times how much she likes you. -*

*Here, in New-York, I have so far spent all my time in the American Museum, mostly with Granger. Roy had me at lunch with Granger in his impressive office (planned and under the control of "Billy", who has wisely insisted for a small liquors-cabinet): we had a gay time. - Tomorrow, I am invited by the President of the Rockefeller Foundation (Dr. Fosdick); I hope to meet there Dr. Carrel. - Before the 14 (date of my sailing to Europe) I will write you my impressions in these lines. - By the way, nothing more has been decided with de Terra concerning next year: all depends on the further decisions of Merriam concerning the position of de Terra in Philadelphia. The Burmah trip might be therefore post-poned up to the winter 1939. In such case, I would probably have to spend in South China a part of the next winter 1938. - In any way, the next autunm will be a calm period in Peiping, for me. -*

    *This letter, I observe, is very badly written, dearest. I hope you can read me. Something at least which you will understand easily is how much I belong to you and I hope in you. - So far, in spite of the confusion of too many various impressions, I feel that this journey has come in the right time for pushing me more clearly forward. - I suppose that the three next months will give me still more, which I soon will bring back to you. -*

    *yours*

    *P.*

*I was much interested by your impressions in reading the Translation of a Per-sonalistic Universe. -*

    *Toutes sortes d'amitiés à Nirgidma: Williams n'était malheureusement pas à Washington (on m'a dit qu'il voyage actuellement en Malaisie!).*

    *Souvenirs à Tarnowski!*

---

At the beginning of April, Lucile had just received Teilhard's March 12 shipboard letter written as he had prepared to disembark at Victoria.

---

*1 Ta Tien Shui Ching, April 7, 1937*

*Pierre dearest,*

    *Your precious letter from Victoria came a couple of days ago and as always was a great joy to me. You seem to have met a lot of really interesting people on the boat which is rather unusual; or perhaps not, maybe it is you who bring them out. It was good of you to write and I am even more anxious to get your next letter from Philadelphia.*

    *Life goes on much the same here, spring seems to have really arrived lately and some of the earliest fruit trees are in blossom, and the lilacs in my front court will be out in a few days. They have dug up the grape vine and all together it is beginning to have a more festive look. The wisteria is always late so I do not yet know how it is going to behave, but I hope that it is going to bloom this year. It will in my heart if not on the vine!!!!*

    *Pierre dearest I have been so full of you lately, not that I am not always so, but it seems that you have been especially close lately. I wonder where your are now, probably in N.Y. and will soon be leaving for France.*

    *Last Friday I had had a beautiful day in the country with Hedime Gage and John Tarnowski. I came in a bit late and who should I find having tea here but Nirjidma and Tressard!!* **[Trassaert, misspelled by Lucile]** *I got such a thrill out of seeing him because it felt as if you must be some where near. I hope I did not startle him by the warmth of my greeting. I was glad to see him for himself but the extra enthusiasm was all for you dear. He was also dressed for the field, which was quite a relief, was leaving that night for Shansi. He said that he had heard from you so he has also probably written to you. Last night Nirjidma came and had dinner with me alone and told me a lot about*

*Brael. She is leaving in a few days to live with him in Shanghai, also taking her son with her. She told me a lot about his life, why is it that we nearly all must go through such a terrible fire? Also she has seen Quintini several times lately. From what she said, it seems that his affairs are not going any better. She said she spoke very straight and frankly to him; which may have seemed hard, but also may have been rather good for him. But probably you have heard directly from them all.*

*Today I went to a cocktail party at the Gages, she is leaving for Europe on Saturday. I have seen quite a lot of her lately and like her so much, am so sorry she is leaving. Tomorrow the Gages, Tillie and Tarnowski are coming for dinner and then we are going to an amateur play at the P.U.M.C. Saturday I am going to the Hills for a few days with Nathalie Merrell and Tillie. I have only been out for Sunday up to now. It has really been too cold to want to stay longer, but shall be glad of a few days; it is always such a delight to wake up out in the country. Remember the delightful week end we had at Chou Kou Tien last year? Which makes me think of the Camps. I had the announcement of the birth of a daughter of Feb 16, from them, perhaps you heard too.*

*I am glad you finished your essay before leaving the boat and I await most impatiently the copy of it. I suppose in America you will be too busy with scientific things to have too much time to write. But I do so hope you talked with a lot of people and got the "feeling" of things and of people of TODAY; Oh dearest it is so hard some times when you are away for me to reconcile certain things, your ideas which are so completely modern, with certain other things, which are so a part of the Moyen age!!! Is it part of the whole scheme of things that we should not understand things?? And we talk about love, but always with so many restraints and restrictions that it has no natural or free expression!! The same old subject, you say? But I really don't understand nor feel the rightness of some of your views any more than I did the first time we talked!! That is, if we are REALLY honest. Sometimes I wonder if I place honesty too high? It has always seemed to me the one sure "free will" that we have, and that it is the most important instrument we have for making progress. At least I know that for myself it is not only important but absolutely necessary. Even if it hurts and seems to do harm sometimes, I can't see any other way to get ahead. Oh I probably just don't understand or else my view point is not long enough!!! But I know that you are much wiser than I am and also that I love you more than anything in the world . . so it will all be alright. . . .*

*Good night precious, at least I feel so sure that you have not changed . . and that is much.*

*All the strength and goodness that is in me is yours. Oh dearest I want so much to say all sorts of foolish but beautiful things to you - and the "rain" is falling so fast I can't see the letters!*

*Normandie, à bord, le April 17, 37*

*Dearest,*

*We are now half-way of the atlantic, and I wish to have this letter catching the next Transsiberian. In two days, I will feel the hot of Paris: a new period in my journey. Here I must try to summarize, in a talk with you, my last impressions of America.*

*My last (8) was written, I believe, just after my passage in Boston and Harvard. Since then, I have been in New York; then, for the last week-end, in Philadelphia (and Princeton) with de Terra, and then I have left. - On the whole, from*

Lucille
on
Honesty

*the scientific side, I have been "comblé". Awfully nice people, and most interesting talks, suggestions, and observations. Every day, I had lunch or dinner with some friends, - either in a small New York appartement, where we cooked in the "minuscule" and neat kitchens, between the electric stove and the frigidaire, - either (once) in the princière résidence of Mr. Frick at Roselyn, Long Island, - either (once also) at the 65th floor of the Rockefeller Center, or in the Rockefeller Institution, en tête à tête avec Carrel et son bonnet blanc. This month in America seems to me a perpetual talk with an incredible variety of different people: on science and ethics or religion. During the last fortnight, the reporters did no more care of me, - and I have the impression that the "fundamentalist reaction" has greatly settled down. Nobody, I suppose, will complain to Rome.*

*At the Rockefeller Foundation, I was treated by a big bunch of some 20 people: Dr. Fosdick (the President), Dr. Weaver (the head of the department in charge of C.K.T.), and all the available officers of the Foundation were there. Most cordial meeting. - and (still more important) most frank and pleasant private talk with Dr. Weaver. Mr. Gun was there, - and I remember the last cocktail given by Magdalen.*

*Dr. Carrel is just like his picture and his book: cheerful, clear- and strong-minded, - very objective in his views. I had him talking on his dream of an organisation for the study of "Man as a whole". So far I can focuss and interpret it for myself (without distorting it, I am sure) the Carrel's idea would be to start a "Science of human Energy", covering the following points: 1) physico-medical preservation and improvement of the best races; 2) preservation and development of human interest and zest for life by discovery of appropriate aims or ends, - and consequently by elaboration of a true Religion of effort; 3) special study of various psychical forces, such as sexual attraction, telepathy, collective energies, etc. - I feel that I will soon try to fix these views in some personal Essay on "L'énergie humaine", which seems to me, just now, the best way for concentrating and expressing the ideas on the "still moving world", and on a new Morality (based on the increase of Energy) which we have been so much discussing during the last months. By flashes, road discovers itself so clear and straight, in front of me... - When in France, I will type the pages I have written on the Pacific concerning the "Spiritual Phenomenon". But I think they are only a sketch of what I perceive now from a better point of vantage. - I have left to Carrel a Memorandum of de Terra on Human Geology, and my pages on "le front humain". We shall possibly meet in Paris in June.*

*From de Terra's side, it seems that the Burma plan becomes more consistant. The trip is decided, and its strategic importance appears now overwhelming. But the date cannot be fixed so far, so long as the work of Paterson in England (on the Indian material) is not finished. We hope to have the thing made next winter, however. The Pinkleys [from the American Museum in New York] would probably come.*

*On the eve of my departure, I had a call from Bill Drummond, back in New York. First, strong cocktail and pekinese gossips in the strange appartment of strange H. Priest, strangely dressed in white silk kimono. Then, dinner and long chat (both of us) in a german restaurant near Lexington. As you know, Bill has been dropped by his girl: not depressed but growing suspicious towards the female of the species. Hope that he will emerge of the thing wiser, but not defiant nor cynical. You may help him. He plans to come back to China next fall, if the curios business proves satisfactory.-*

*And finally, on the morning of the 7th, I stepped on the deck of the huge Normandie, leaving in N.Y. several things undone. (positively no time for reaching your friends; I have even forgotten to telephone to de Grive, a friend of the Bégouën and of Betty Tucker! . . .). Miss Garrod is on board, in the same class, - and the french "garçons" address us ceremoniously "Monsieur et Madame". She is a fine girl, and an extremely congenial friend, - in the same exactly religious position as myself. - You have probably been amused to see our pictures in Life. - The crossing is so short that I do not make any acquaintance outside of her. -At the same table, in the dining-room, a young and rather green patriote-catholique-Alsacien is a bit scared of my pink political color. In New York (amongst my religious colleagues) I had also a short, but rather sharp talk in support of the Spanish leftists: more expects me probably in France. Miss Garrod told me that a grand-grandson of Darwin has just been killed with the loyalists, in Madrid. - I don't know whether I am with the communists; - but I am sure that I am with the moving wing of mankind; - the left one, by definition.*

*Now I must tell you the great and deep joy which has been for me your letter of March 13, - when you try to analyze "what has happened to us" this year. I know, Lucile, that you will probably not see <u>so clear</u> all the time. By periods, the feeling of being separated will perhaps submerge the consciousness of our fundamental and growing union. But I am so happy that, from time to time, (when your perception of things is at its <u>best</u>), you become aware of the consistance, the value, and the increase of "what is happening". - You have never been more precious, nor so close, to me. - Your presence will help me in France, whatever good or bitter may be there waiting for me. - I will write you again as soon as I am a little "installé". - God bless you, dearest.*

*P.*

*P.S.- I scarcely saw Roy [Chapman Andrews], very busy. We had, with him and Granger, a most charming lunch in his impressive office, nicely arranged under the supervision of "Billy", who has wisely insisted for a closet full of material for cocktails. - But perhaps I have already told you that.*

*"Good Earth" was going on in the movies, with a wonderful advertisement in Broadway: a green dragon, with a red tongue, and puffing vapour through its nose!*

*- De Terra gave me the last book of Whitehead: "Religion on making"* [Alfred North Whitehead's "Religion in the Making"]. *Full of interesting statements.*

*- Roy sends me as a representative of the N.Y. Museum to Moskow.*

*Paris, April 24, 37*

*Lucile dear,*

*I answer here your two letters of March 31 and April 7, the first one found here à mon arrivée, the second one received two days ago, - two very precious let-*

*ters, dearest, which made me deeply happy, because you are so comprehensive, so active, so close to me. Still, evidently, remains this question of "honesty" which you move at the end of your last letter: honest you are, from your point of view, - and honest I am, from my side, because I go as far as I can to remain fair to my truth, and not to ruin myself in the minds of those who, I hope, will gradually follow the same path as myself. You must forgive me, Lucile, for this apparently unnatural situation where I drove you (perhaps too much unconsiderably) by my fault. God knows that I would like to have the whole burden on myself, - and that there is nothing which I do not do for compensating, on the possible grounds, the things which, for higher reasons, I cannot give you (and it is hard for me not to give you). Sometimes I think that this very privation I must impose you makes me ten times more devoted to you . . . Anyhow, something seems <u>sure</u> to me: even admitted that I am materially wrong, and that, someday, "chastity" will definitely prove not to be connected with a higher spirituality, it remains that love needs presently a deep transformation in order to become the great human energy, and that we are working and praying for this transformation. Let us find, in the consciousness of this task, the strength and the joy for going ahead. This letter will reach you very close to May 10 [Lucile's birthday]. That whole day, especially, I will be present to you. God bless you, dearest, for what you are, and for what you are for me!*

*In your letters, I enjoy immensely all the small details you give me on your life, and on your work. Hope the glycine (wisteria) is going to grow! - Here, since six days, I have been caught in the whirl I expected (and I was afraid of): a queer feeling to find oneself immerged in something which was formerly so tense and so alive, and to which one is no more adjusted, at the depth of oneself. A mixture of exaltation and anguish . . . . - I try to cling to faith in life, and to go on, - without understanding much what is happening to me on the whole. - So far, nothing especially interesting to tell you: a number of hasty contacts with various friends, without reaching the vital points. The dominant thing now, in France, is the universal feeling of discomfort and anxiety amongst the obscure movements of the social masses. In the course of a year, apparently, the "syndical" spirit has intensely increased. An isolated individual is a dead man. And, unfortunately, the lower parts of the mass exhibit the worst parts of themselves: instead of justifying their rights by working better, the workmen become more impossible each time they are accorded something more. They can not accept any more to work "for a boss" (pour un patron); but they do not realize yet what kind of brain is required for carrying on the direction of any kind of business. That leads to impossible situations. A favourable circumstance is that, now, the engineers (ingénieurs) have started their own unions, and have eventually decided their own strikes against the striking workman, - a great and unpleasant surprise for these latter ones. - Evidently, something is changing fast at the depth of the civilized world. But an increase of ideal is absolutely necessary for avoiding that a <u>necessary</u> dissolution should turn into a "décomposition": hatred, and bestial sensuality, are rampant in the "peuple". - Anyhow, there is no doubt that the new world "est en train de naître à gauche", - and therefore I feel myself more and more on the left side, - in spite of the fact that, just now, the leftists are often just* *as disagreable as the rightists. I do not think that it is possible to guess already what is going to be the shape of the world ahead. But that would be a first serious improvement if more people were fighting today with the idea that we are constructing something, - and not only trying to escape a "catastrophe". - As we have already told together, the present crisis, and its solution, are a matter of Hope (or Faith).-*

*Here I am provisonally living at the place where the Review "Les Etudes" is edited (where I was planning to have my article on the Front Humain published): the most intellectual center of Paris so far my Order is concerned. Two types of men here, belonging to two intellectual sides and generations, but all of them very friendly to me. I could not yet make clear why my paper has been so unanimously held as "impubliable", and I suspect some mistake in understanding which perhaps can be corrected. Anyhow, I feel that my thoughts are centering more and more intensely on the theoretical and practical problem of Human Energy. I will do my best for typing as soon as I can "le Phénomène Spirituel". - No indication, so far, that my "evolutive statements" in America have stirred the Roman authority. But, on this point, I do not worry: if I am asked for some explanations, my position on the problem [of evolution] is perfectly simple, strong and definitive. - Probably I shall see the Cardinal of Paris and give him myself "La Conversion du Monde".*

*Since this letter is started writing, I have seen (yesterday) Simone and Max (just arrived from Africa). Max looks all right, tanned, enthusiastic, - almost a new man. His fight in and on the Colonies have hardened his will and made his mind clearer. Apparently he has really started a change in the relationships between Whites and Negroes. The final battle is going to be fighted here, au Ministère des Colonies. Simone is still more marvelous than before, if possible. Both talked of you with such admiration and sympathy! . . . I was proud, of course. The photo of my "buste" was there, - much prised (as a piece of art). After a real "drama" which I will tell you in Peiping, everything is all right with Ida. She has succeeded in transforming the mind and the soul of André, who is now for her a son, as much as a lover. André is now writing with her, and more than her: a surprising awakening, according to Simone. And Ida is so happy to watch her own work and success on this young man. "Paul" in the meantimes becomes an important political man (I hope to see him), at the risk of losing his fine and clear idealism. —*

*Goodbye for this time, dearest. I will write you again very soon, when things have a little more developed.*

*yours*

*P.T.*

*I have seen Pei, with great mutual joy. His thesis is ready. He will come back to Peiping this summer, probably with me.*

Coincidentally, Lucile wrote to Teilhard asking about Alexis Carrel while his long letter about that meeting was en route. In fact, he had written again — from France before she wrote from Peking.

*Your visit in America was a grand success, I am so glad, but not at all surprised! I suppose in your next letter you will tell something of your meeting with Dr. Carrel. That sounds MOST interesting. Getting in touch will all those people was of course one of the most important parts of your trip . . All the medals, etc. are rather gratifying, I should think, but they are for PAST works; and these meetings etc. are all for the future!! Your picture of life with the De Terra family sounded so delightful — and I am so glad Mrs. de T. was so strongly on my side!!! Perhaps the women will have to come out more for the next important steps in progress to take place!!!!!! I told you a friend had sent me a clipping about you from a Florida paper: heading "Man is descended from apes, say Jesuit scientist". Have you had reverbrations from the conservatists yet? I suppose it is bound to come; but it must have been rather a relief to you to SAY what you so strongly believe — and out loud!!*

*And now you have been in France for a long time, or more than a week anyway. And what do you find there. Are conditions as bad as they sound? Your letters will be coming more regularly soon and that will be good. Yesterday I saw Jacques at a cocktail. He was glad to have news of you, he looked more bird-like than ever!*

*This afternoon I have my last meeting of my class for this year. I have finished the head of Tarnowski which everyone seems to be quite enthusiastic about and "our" couple are really most done, though there are a few details that do not yet wholly satisfy me . . . I do so want that to be good!! And another small figure which I started a few days ago is quite successful, at least it has a certain "sculptural" quality which I was trying so hard to get. And I have made a few drawings that rather please me!!*

*The week-end in the country was lovely, we had a lot of long walks, the bright small green leaves on the willows and the fruit blossoms made it quite enchanting. It was just about a year ago that we went to Ta Chieh Ssu with Rose and Michael — which was such a happy day in spite of the dust. I have just returned from a walk in the Nan Hai, every place is so beautiful just now..and it is all so much more beautiful because every thing has so much more meaning than it ever had before, which as you know, is due to you.*

*This morning I met Mrs. Bien, who said that Eddie is still in Yunnan. Andersson is here now but I have not met him . . I heard he gave a most interesting talk at the Natural History dinner last Saturday. And dear old Grabau, I see him so seldom . . . I am going to the country again this weekend with Bob Drummond and two house guests of his. We are going to a prince's tomb up near the "Eagle's Nest" — where we had that picture and the grand picnic with the Tyrwhitts and Goehring. You remember it? That was one of the most perfect days of my experience!*

*Yesterday I sent Simone 36 copies of <u>Personalistic Universe</u> (could only have 18 in a package). If ever she wants more tell her to let me know. Also sent separate copies to B. Tucker, Mrs. Ames, Mrs. Wood, Rose, Francis Carter and another two friends of mine. Be sure to tell me if there are others you want sent. And I shall be hoping to receive a copy of the last paper before very long . . Am glad you told me about the translation of "<u>Savons l'Humanite</u>" . . I should love to have a copy of it . . I don't know about sending to de Terra!!!! but I think I shall do so anyway. Im sure it can't do any harm and he might like it in English, or at least she.*

*Nothing much else my dear..The wisteria has put out a few feeble leaves, but at least I know it is not dead, it always takes several years for them to get started. And it will soon be your birthday. You can be sure I'll be thinking of you most of both days — and even some others too!!!!!!*

*Your letter was so full of exciting news, this seems very quiet in comparison — and I do so hope the good things will continue in France — and I feel so sure they will.*

*My deepest love to you, always and all the time — I have said to you so often how you make life rich and full for me. But almost every day something happens that makes me always more conscious of this fact - and I am so grateful to you for all you give me —*

*Yours always — Lucile*

*Paris, May 5th, 1937*

*Lucile dear,*

*This is my second letter from Paris. Since the last one, I received your no.5 (18 March!), forwarded from America: not much "up to date", of course, but so precious too, because there is no "date" for what you send me of <u>you</u>. And preciously, also, I have received, and I keep in myself, your warning, not to let me influence unduly by anybody. I do, and will do, my best in that line, for me, and for <u>you</u>. — In the meantime, I enjoy so much to know something of the detail of your life, — and of the development of your work. - I wonder whether you will decide a trip in the Shansi.*

*Here, I am still in the whirl, although I succeed so far in saving most of my evenings, and consequently of my nights. Finally, I am glad to stay here (15, rue Monsieur): the house is quiet, — and I have more opportunity than everywhere else for talking with the best of my colleagues. Gradually, the social contacts become more definite. This afternoon, for instance, I have a lecture (on Sinanthropus) à l'Institut d'Ethnologie. Private talks, on another hand, help me in the task of acquiring a better consciousness of my own views or aspirations. I suppose that my next Essay will be positively a sketch (or programm) of the new Science, "qui est partout dans l'air", the Science of Human Energy. — We need terribly a constructive and optimistic soul, today, in France. Here as elsewhere, "la masse" is awakening, for never going to sleep again. But here there is no strong hand for keeping it forcibly at its proper place. France is making an experiment for self-education of the "mass". Will the workmen prove themselves able to keep the "sense of the work" above the pure enjoyment (?) of their success? The whole question is there. I have seen recently one of the leaders of the Front Populaire, — hopeful. One thing at least is sure: people are decided to break "les pouvoi<u>r</u>s d'argent" (without breaking, for that, "le pouvoir de l'argent"). A new world is surely coming to birth. A matter of stronger hope, as we have told so often.*

*I have somewhat retouched my paper on Le Front Humain ("Sauvons l'Humanité"), <u>without</u> weakening it: maybe it will be accepted (my colleagues wish its publication). Slowly, also, page by page, I type "Le Phénomène Spirituel"), which I will send you as soon as it is ready. A few days ago, Simone [Bégouën] showed me the supply she has now ready of my papers: a real clandestine shop!*

*Talking of the Bégouëns, I must tell you that things are not going well there, just now. Last week (on the very day of his return) Max got new and serious trouble in his poor arm; and he is now in the hospital, with a strong fever. Yester-*

*day, the surgeons (amongst the best of Paris) were still undecided to perform an operation. Poor Max! — Simone is simply wonderful, — always with her quiet, angelic smile, — never showing how tired she is. — Life is so strange and so hard. And yet I see less and less how we can do anything else but to adore what is going on through it. — Nothing new, so far Ida is concerned. I hope she will come to Paris from Marseilles, before I leave.*

*Next Monday (May 10) I go to Lyon, in order to meet several friends, — and also my "Superior". Apparently, Rome (my Order, I mean) is a bit angry for the comments of the press on my talk in Philadelphia. But I do not think that anything serious will arise from the situation. I am rather strongly supported by my colleagues, and it was impossible for me to talk in a more moderate way than I did in America. — Anyhow, I am glad, at the bottom of my soul, to have found this opportunity for being frank; and I am sure that a number of good christians thank me for it. — I plan to go to Cambridge on May 31. —*

*Goodby, dearest. — I will write you very soon a letter n.12, — probably on my return from Lyon. I feel so light and so strong because you are <u>with me.</u>*

*My best regards to the friends (Bob Drummond, Tarnowsky, etc.)!*

*Yours*

*P.T.*

*les Hoppenots are here: I did not see them, so far.*
*Dr. Wong is expected in Paris at the end of May.*

---

Some personal comments and news about friends, colleagues, and mutual concerns are omitted in the following paragraphs from a very long letter that Lucile wrote to Teilhard on her birthday.

---

*1 Ta Tien Shui Ching Hutung*
*Peiping*
*May 10, 1937*

*Dearest,*

*And now it is my birthday!! and how I wish you were here to celebrate it with me as you were last year. I remember we went to Central Park to see the peonies and then sat on a bench near the water and you talked . . so beautifully and so inspiringly . . .*

. . . . . . . . . . . . . . . . . . . . . . . . . . . . . . . . . . . . . . . . . . . . . . . . . . . . . . . . . . . . . . . . . . . . . .

*Your blessed letter of April 17 written on the Normandie came a few days ago and as always most welcome, and this one was of particular interest as it told of your last days in America. I am so excited about the proposed Institute for the Science of Human Energy - and it seems to me <u>you</u> would have such a tremendous amount to contribute to such an institution. Have those people seen any of your other papers? I hope you will meet in Paris again in June. And I am so glad the trip with de Terra is definitely going to be. I have a feeling that you will be tying up the threads of your scientific work more and more the next few years and then spend more and more time on the study of and help for the man of today and tomorrow!! And with these few trips that you feel are necessary for you to round out your special work done, this new institute will come just at the time when* you will be most ready to contribute to it — It may be your great chance to present and help to save and expound your idea of a Personal God — which is in danger of being put aside by the scientists. It looks as if things are working out so well for you . . . and how true and how assuring are those times when one sees the road so clearly ahead — I hope the light will always be there to guide you. There are times of course when it is not so clear, but you have your ideas so definitely in hand now that they can only be momentarily (if at all) confused —I suppose, dearest, that you may not yet be through with what the newspapers started in the States..things travel around the world so quickly these days; I only hope that there will not be anything very disturbing or depressing for you to face.. Pierre dear it makes me so very happy to think that my love and belief in you may be of some strength to you —

Am so glad that Roy is sending you as the representative of the N.Y. museum to Russia. The Life with your picture has not yet arrived here, shall be most interested to see it —

You forgot to send on the letter of Ida Treat . . . but maybe after you are settled down a bit there you will have time to give me news of all the people there. And dearest I do so hope that things are going well for you, be sure to tell me.

*Paris, May 19th, 1937*

Lucile dear,

I am very late in my letters, this time! Three letters of you (the 2 last ones from April 22 & 28) since I sent you my no. 11. But, as you shall see, this is not my fault. First, I had to go to Lyon, last week. — Then, the very day I came back to Paris, I got a rather strong fever (nothing serious finally), — and I am still in the Hospital! (a very good house, "l'Hôpital Pasteur", where I am perfectly attended, — visited by friends, — and somewhat spoiled). — Finally, the doctors could find nothing serious, — nor very clear, in my case. The fever is over, — and I am just recuperating, now.

This small illness has been evidently rather disturbing for all my plans and various appointments. Hope that everything will be settled the next week. — In Lyon, I had three busy days. Finally the American complaints will have <u>no</u> practical results for me, so far Rome is concerned: the question seems settled "pacifiquement". — On another hand, I have received, from Rome, "la défense formelle" to go to Moskow. without any explanation. — Possibly, this is a mere misunderstanding, which will be cleared up these very days. — But, if I am forbidden to go there "en défiance de Moscow", then, la défense sera maintenue; — and I will have to plan my way back to China by a simpler way, for instance via Siberia, directly, at the beginning of August (?) — I will write you longer when I am out of the hospital.

Good bye, dearest. — Your presence helps me now more than ever! — Thanks for your long letters! — Max is much better, and at home, now. Simone has received "the Personalistic Universe" (I did not see it, so far).

Saluez Ida.

Yours

PT

*Lucile Dear,*

*I have received yesterday your long letter of May 4, in which you give me so many details on your life and on your work. Such a joy for me. Yes, dearest, you care "a lot" for developing whatever I may have in myself useful for the world around us.*

*In the meantimes, I am rather experiencing the less strong and glorious sides of myself — which, after all, is also a useful experience, since life is together increase and decrease. I am still in the hospital — although so much better (no more fever since several days that I wonder why I am still kept here. Apparently, I did not have anything else but a "banale infection intestinale". But it seems as if the doctors had taken this opportunity for giving me rest and cure. — I must say that I begin to find the time a bit long, in my bed. Hope that after two or three days they will let me out.*

*This small illness has just come in time for preventing me from giving a few lectures. All my plans are somewhat disturbed! Probably, I will go to see my brother, in Auvergne, at the end of the month, — and later to Cambridge. As for Moskow, I have no answer from Rome, so far. After all, if they insist for my not going to the Congress, many things will be simpler: I will take quietly and smoothly the life up to the end of July, — and then come back to China directly. —*

*Good bye, dearest. — Evidently the typing of "Le Phénomène Spirituel" has made no progress; since a fortnight! On the other hand, after a talk with Monsignor de Solages (an influential friend from Toulouse), I see more and more positively that I should write, for publication, a kind of summary on "Man", — in which the main and surer lines of my other Essays would be selected and recasted into a whole. Better than to try to mend and to re-adjust the old things.*

*Good bye, again.*

*Yours*

*PT*

---

Teilhard spent the summer in France. He was ill and Europe was certainly in crisis when he wrote from Paris in the spring. (The German Army was occupying the Rhineland, civil war was tearing Spain apart, Portugal's dictator continued in power, the Rome-Berlin axis was flourishing, and France seemed to be wavering in its committments to Czechoslovakia.)

---

*Paris, May 29, 1937*

*Lucile dear,*

*I hope you have not been anxious when receiving my two last letters from an hospital! . . . Now, I am back to my Paris home, since three days already, — and I feel stronger very fast, every day. Finally, although I have been in care of the best doctors and of the best institution in town for any kind of colonial disease, nobody knows exactly what I got during these few days of fever. Probably a very banal type of infection, by which I have possibly got rid of slowly accumulated "germs". I can not say that I have particularly enjoyed this time of confinement in a small room and in bed. But, after all, this is an experience, and an useful one for getting a real conviction that the success of our lives is in the hands of a Greater than ourselves.*

*Just for my return here, I got your precious letter of May 10 (your birthday!), and I enjoyed so deeply each line of your two long pages. So glad that you had such a fine day, and so many flowers, and so encouraging appreciations for your work. This work of yours interests me just so much as anything I can do myself in my own lines . . . And, in addition, it is such a pleasure for me to have by you "the Peking's chronicle". The scientific side of the life, there, I got yesterday by a letter (long and methodical) from Weidenreich, and a few (much more funny) lines from Mrs. Hempel. Everything seems to be going OK. in the Lab. Weidenreich complains to be short of money for trips in South China: but I know that the Geological Survey will back us for this purpose if Rockefeller turns to be insufficiently generous.I will send you a copy as soon as it is ready.*

*Rien de très nouveau, comme de juste, dans mon expérience. Ce séjour en chambre m'a fait manquer une série de conférences que je devais donner. Tant pis. Je suis juste sorti à temps pour assister en partie à la remise solennelle d'une médaille à mon vieux maître et ami, le Prof. Boule. Réunion à la fois solennelle, familiale et amusante, où j'ai revu beaucoup d'amis. Pei est apparu avec un bel habit neuf, où il avait du faire passer toutes ses économies (moi aussi, je me fais faire des habits neufs.). Breuil était là aussi, naturellement. Je l'ai revu plusieurs fois, depuis une dizaine de jours. — Ce matin, coup de téléphone de Hoppenot, qui me demande à déjeuner la semaine prochaine. Ce soir, j'attends Le Fèvre, que je reverrai avec grande joie. Vous ai-je dit qu'il s'est fait baptiser catholique, il y a deux mois? J'ai été très surpris de la nouvelle, et je voudrais beaucoup savoir ses impressions (que je vous dirai). J'avais toujours remarqué son intérêt pour les questions religieuses; mais je ne pensais pas qu'il évoluerait si vite. Je soupçonne que les événements politiques ont eu une certaine influence sur sa décision. Vous ne vous doutez pas de la tension "spirituelle" en Europe, et spécialement en France, en ce moment. J'avais laissé la France vague et inerte, il y a deux ans.*

Nothing very new in my experience of course. This stay in my bedroom made me miss a series of lectures which I was supposed to give. Never mind. I had just left in time to attend part of the solemn presentation of a medal to my old master and friend, Prof. Boule. This reunion was at the same time solemn, friendly and amusing, and I saw many of my old friends. Pei arrived wearing a handsome new suit for which he had probably spent all his savings (I, too, am having new suits made.). Breuil was there also, naturally. I have seen him again several times these past ten days. Hoppenot called me this morning: he wants me to come for lunch next week. This evening I am expecting Le Fèvre; I'll be very happy to see him again. Have I told you that he asked to be baptized as a Catholic two months ago? I was most surprised by this news and I really want to know about his impressions (I'll tell you about them). I had noticed, a long time ago, how interested he was in religion, but I didn't think he would evolve so quickly. I suspect that the political events have had some influence on his decision. You have no idea of the "spiritual" tension in Europe, and especially in France right now. Two years ago I left a France which was passive and lifeless. Now under the pres-

*Maintenant, sous la pression des menaces et des aspirations sociales, tout le monde pense et cherche <u>un point d'appui et de direction</u> dans la vie. C'est passionnant et pathétique. Deux questions dominent toutes les autres: d'abord (et toujours!) la question de l'organisation des énergies humaines, débordantes dans tous les domaines. Et puis, plus encore peut-être, l'angoisse de sauver la personnalité humaine au milieu des organisations dites "totalitaires" (communisme, fascisme). On ne peut pas ouvrir une revue sans trouver ces problèmes mis en avant (ceux dont nous avons si souvent parlé ensemble). A moi il parait de plus en plus évident que toute la solution dépend de la reconnaissance du fait qu'il doit y avoir un terme <u>personnel</u> au monde. <u>Si</u> l'on accepte l'hypothèse (communiste ou fasciste) d'une Humanité allant vers un achèvement collectif-impersonnel, il est forcé que les personnalités individuelles soient absorbées et détruites en chemin . . . Je continue à espérer que mon Essai sur le Front Humain passera: il vient encore de trouver une approbation enthousiaste d'un côté (dans mon Ordre) où je ne m'y attendais pas. Entre temps, je continue à taper "Le Phénomène spirituel".*

sure of threats and social aspirations, everybody thinks about, and looks for <u>support and direction</u> in life. It is fascinationg and pathetic at the same time. Two questions outweigh all the others: first (and always) the question of the organization of human energies overflowing in all other fields. And also, perhaps even more, the anguish of saving the human personality in the midst of the so-called "totalitarian" organizations (communism, fascism). We cannot open a magazine in which these problems aren't brought up (the problems you and I have discussed so often). It seems more and more evident to me that the very solution depends on the fact that we admit there must be a <u>personal</u> goal for the world. If we accept the hypothesis (communist or fascist) of a Humanity moving toward a collective-impersonal achievement, it is inevitable that the individual personalities will be absorbed and destroyed on the way . . . I continue hoping that my Essay on le Front Humain will pass: it has just found another enthusiastic approval from a side (in my Order) where I did not expect it. In the meantime, I continue typing "The Phenomenon of Spirituality".

*un terme personel au monde*

*My plans for June and July are still unsettled. I am not yet decided to go to Cambridge (where I should have to go before June 13th), and I am still waiting for an answer of Rome concerning Moskow. No doubt that this answer will be here very soon. After all, if they insist for my <u>not</u> going, I will not feel too much sorry for it. Very few people, finally, will be present at the Congress (no Italians, no Germans, a few British, very few French), and I wonder what are the excursions going to be in such conditions. If I do not go myself, I will spend quietly July in France (talking, writing) and come back quietly to China for September. After a few days (or in a fortnight) I plan to visit my brother in Auvergne, amongst the meadows and the old oaks, in his old family house.*

*Yesterday, I had the good surprise to meet Dr. W. H. Wong at my door. He had just arrived in Paris, and his first visit was for me. I was very "touché". Pei was with him, beaming. Wong himself is always the same: marvelously kind, simple, and smiling. I wonder what is his inner philosophy.*

*Max is much better now, and Simone not too much tired. Tomorrow (Sunday) I plan to go with him (in the car of his friend Gradys) for a picknick in St.*

Germain. *Everything is so richly green around Paris, just now. Yet, I would prefer
to be with you in the Western Hills. — Ida Treat was in Paris for a few days: but
I saw her only in the hospital, too shortly. I enclose here the letter she wrote me
in America. (No, it is too big: so I send it to you under a separate envelopp).*

*Good by, dearest; and thank you, always more, for the light, the strength,
and the riches you are for me. ——*

*Be happy, — and God bless you! ——*

*P.T.*

*Peking
June 9, 1937*

Dearest —

Your precious letter of May 18 just came yesterday. I am so very sorry that you
have been sick and trust that you were telling me the truth when you said the fever was
over and that you were recuperating. I do hope it has long since been finished and that it
did not leave you in a weakened condition, but that you were able to go to Cambridge the
end of May. I heard from the Richards that they were making great preparations to honor
you there. But eventually you will tell me, and also I hope more of what happened in Lyon.
I am desperately disappointed at the outcome. I did not realize until your letter came how
much I hoped that something would happen so that you could face the world with a <u>united</u>
front with your ideas. I just wrote you a long letter about it, but I shall not send it now —
but I cannot help mentioning my great disappointment. and about Moscow too, I shall be
simply SICK if you cannot go — all these thoughts I will try to hold in check until I hear
more fully from you — but my heart has been heavy ever since your letter came. I will save
this other letter and if after I hear again it seems good, will send it then.

Last night I had dinner with Mme Raphael, just we two, which was so nice, we
went to a cinema and then to the Peking hotel roof, which opened last night . . There was a
great crowd and very gay, Raphael seemed quite satisfied. Tonight I am dining there with
Tarnowski — he is still waiting for his money to get away . . Then there is a big dance at
the American Embassy on Friday, with several cocktail parties in between. Having lunch
tomarrow with George Merell, she left last week. Jacques gives a big cocktail on the 15th
etc etc . . As to work? I have been drawing lately, with a model every morning . . nothing
very exciting but it is such good discipline and I enjoy it too . . "The couple" is rather disappointing in plaster . . . but most everything is!!!!!

Dearest I wont try to write more now . . I do so hope you are well . . what caused
the fever? and is it really completely gone?

That you may be home earlier than you thought is too wonderful . . . but I am
Still hoping that you will be able to go to Moscow.

All my love, no not ALL, but all that is best —

Oh Pierre I want so much — <u>not</u> for me dearest, you must believe that — just as
in the famous "honesty" letter — chastity was the very heart of what was in my mind — I
answered as I did because I was <u>waiting</u>. but I was thinking of <u>so much more</u> than our personal relations.

I hope you have written again — I shall be so anxious about your health — and I
want to know so much more too - but perhaps some of the things will have to wait to be
told —

*God bless you dearest ——*
*Lucile.*

Paris, June 13th, 1937

*Dearest,*

*I answer here your two precious letters of May 18 and 26, which have brought me their ordinary supply of strength and joy. I feel so happy when I see that you are happy, and expanding in your spiritual activity. It makes my own life brighter to hear about your thoughts, your work, and even your daily life. So glad that Mrs. Clubb is back, when so many others are leaving!*

*So far I am concerned, things are not yet perfectly satisfactory (although distinctly better). Last week, I got another (much slighter) period of fever. I did not leave the house, and everything is OK again. But finally, all my plans of summer have been much upset. I had to cut several lectures. I could not go to Cambridge (and now it is too late for going there since Paterson is leaving for Greenland tomorrow . . .). And, with some disappointment, I have decided to cancel my trip to Russia, the prospect of being even slightly sick in the middle of the Siberian excursion being positively uncomfortable. After all, what I am going to miss is perhaps not so much. Very few people seem to go to the Congress, so few that I wonder whether the Siberian excursion is not going to be suppressed at the last minute. At the same time, political conditions in Russia are apparently critical just now. Well, in any case, I have to follow my own life, and to trust it in love, even if, this time, it leads me along an apparently less successful path. A spiritual "philosophy" would be fundamentally uncomplete which could not help us in facing the troublesome, as well as the pleasing, sides of life. My next plans are still a bit cloudy. Essentially, I will spend in Paris and in Auvergne a quiet period (nothing much to do, here, in July), and come back directly to China (via Siberia?) in August. I will let you know, as soon as I can. -Besides, don't worry for my health. The doctors could not find a single weak point in my constitution. Did I get some malaria (no positive indications of that have been recognised!) or some accidental intoxication? Probably I shall never know, and it does not matter.*

*In fact, I feel quite alive, just now, even spiritually. And it may be that this small physical handicap will turn to have been more useful for my real well-fare than more satisfactory conditions under which I would have had lesser opportunities for thinking. By better realizing (in a personal and actual experience) how much we are dependant on the divine harmonization of life, I felt as if my familiar views on the world grew deeper, and chiefly were passing a little more from the theoretical to the practical plan: which of course is the greatest trial for any theory! Crowning my growing convictions and "admiration" for Human Energy, I discover more clearly, just now, the tremendous value and "fonction" of the "Love of God" (well understood, of course) for building the human world; "Love of God", which has been chiefly studied so far as an individual relation between Man and the Summit of the world, - but which has now to be understood as the highest and most universal form of spiritual activity. By this wonderful type of psychical energy, every single other form of activity is* *increased and overanimated; a natural agreement becomes possible between the totalitarian tendencies of human society and the achievement of personality (love is the <u>only</u> strength which makes things one without destroying them); and finally, a possibility is open for controlling (without diminishing) the fundamental power of human love. A chapter on these considerations will surely be the end of my next Essay on Human Energy, unless it turns to be (in addition) the matter of a subsequent and special Essay. - In spite of my confinement, I could spread lot of my papers, during the last weeks, even inmost "laïc" circles interested in Social Economy. Everybody is thinking of Totalitarism and Personality, just now. I will send you very soon a copy of "Le Phénomène spirituel". "Sauvons l'Humanité" is much praised amongst my "confrères" here, and will probably be printed, with very slight modifications.*

*Politically, Europe (and even France) is just a volcano. And in some way there is something excellent in this condition. Everybody is now awaken to the urgency and to <u>the size</u> of the human problems: and the necessity of finding a practical solution to the difficulties <u>obliges</u> the most conservative people to face a thorough recasting of the ancient conceptions of the world. Something is obviously coming to birth. On the other hand, "impersonnal" totalitarisms (Communism, Fascism . . .) prove to go to a failure. Positively, I do not see any natural escape but in the direction of a Personalistic Universe. My faith in a Neo-Christianity is growing stronger every day. So, you see, I am not losing absolutely my time. A degree more of contact with the Center of things is more important than any progress in the knowledge of past Geology.*

*Max is much better now, and Simone is every day more an angel: so gay, so strong and so pure. — Dr. Wong was here the last week. He gave me his first and his last visit: two hours before leaving, he came with Pei to see me in my bed (I had my second fit of fever). I have been extremely touché by this frank and kind friendship. In a lunch given aux Affaires Etrangères in the honour of the chinese delegation, I have seen Pelliot. Two days earlier I had also a lunch with the Hoppenots, extremely nice; Mme Hoppenot longs for Peking; and so does Plessen, they told me, in Colombo. Colonel Newham (spelling?) and wife (not the boy) are staying in Jacques house here, I heard. Met twice Mme Bonnet, still rather lost in her life. If I was more free, I could spend all my life with friends here. A pity to have cut so much, in life.*

*And now good bye, dearest and precious; I will write you again very soon — perhaps from under the oaks in Auvergne. In the meantimes, may you be happy — and progress in your internal and external work. — Two days ago, a colleague of mine, here (a friend of Max, and very clever) told me that he had such an admiration for the profile of the bust you made of me! — I was so pleased!*

*Yours*

*P.T.*

*My best souvenirs, if you meet them,
to Jacques and the Raphaël's.*

---

Before leaving France, Teilhard returned briefly to his native Auvergne where he stayed at

*[handwritten marginal note: This sounds frighteningly like what we are saying today]*

his brother's country house. He wrote to Lucile from there at the end of June and then again in July from Paris.

*Murols (Puy-de-Dôme), June 27th, 1937*

*Dearest,*

*Maybe tomorrow I will receive a letter of you, forwarded from Paris. In the meantimes I wish to send you, in due times, my own [letter] number 16. Since three days, already, I am in my native Auvergne, amongst the deep green trees of the small estate belonging to my "holy" brother and to his so vivacious wife. I feel quite at home here — perfectly all right physically — and I enjoy thoroughly the silence, the quietness, and the simplicity of my country-life, with so congenial people. In this restful environment, I have the impression to "expand" internally; and I become more conscious of a kind of new light which has been dimming in myself in the course of the apparently somewhat disappointing weeks of this last staying in France. Never before, perhaps, did I perceive so clearly* the possible meaning of the deep evolution of my internal life: *the dark purple of the universal Matter, first passing for me into the gold of Spirit, -then into the white incandescence of Personality, - then finally (and this is the present stage) into the immaterial (or rather super-material) ardour of Love. — And never before, too, did I realize in such a tangible way how much people, around me, are starving for the same light, which perhaps I can transmit to them. — For several reasons (including the simple fact that younger generations are gradually emerging over the older ones, — and also the marvelous and critical conditions of a world which is facing for the first time the real dimensions and risks of its destiny) I was never received before by my friends with such a frank sympathy, — and almost "expectancy". — Maybe something will come out, of the seeds which* you *help me to spread, some day, not too far ahead? — As I told you, in my last letters, I had to miss apparently a lot of opportunities, these past weeks: and yet, as a final result of this kind of failure, I* feel myself *more than ever. Is it that I needed to be somewhat cut from Science and Past in order to perceive more distinctly the higher precincts of the coming Universe? Before long, I shall try to focuss these things at* your *light. And I suppose you too will find me more and better myself. The sweet price of absence... —*

*So far my external life is concerned, I plan to leave Paris, at the middle of August, — travelling via Siberia with a colleague of mine. — Now that I am physically OK., I feel appreciably the regret of missing the Moskow congress. But it is late now for changing my decision. And, in addition, one wonders which kind of congress the meeting is going to be. Is even the Siberian Excursion not subject to shortening or cancellation? . . . Nobody knows it, exactly. Anyhow, July and early August will be for me a period of rest — mostly in Paris — the right time, perhaps, for starting my next Essay on "L'Energie Humaine", which I feel almost ripe in my mind, already.*

*Besides, not much to tell you about. An article by me on the Sinanthrope (essentially what I have expressed in Philadelphia) is going to come out in the next number of the Review "Les Etudes" (a rather conservative, but much read paper — edited by my colleagues in the place where I am staying in Paris). I was*

*positively asked and congratulated for it; and I think that "Sauvons l'Univers"
will follow, shortly, later. — Pei has successfully got his degree (Docteur de
l'Université de Paris) the day before I left Paris — and he was so proud and
happy! — He too will be back to Peiping in September. — Max and Simone I left
in good conditions (as good as possible, I mean). — Yesterday, a long letter from
Ida (André had just left for a two month journey). Again she urges me: "I can't
imagine you standing aloof, with a holier-than-thou feeling, while the world
stews...". But what can I do more than I do? Descend in the street? . . . The more I
look around, the less I see any group which I would like to join. "In these days,
only action counts", says Ida. Of course, I would bless and seize any opportunity
for <u>materializing</u> my faith. But living ideas are, finally, the blood of action (think
only of Marx — and Christ). And just now I don't see what I could do outside of
promoting the birth of a new consciousness in the World. — Tell me what you
think. — You would like, I know, to see my papers more openly defended and
spread. — But they are spreading, I assure you, at an unexpected rate — and
along the most efficient way: as a shot in the main arteries of the body. - Let us
have patience, and faith.*

*From a nice letter of Lt. Quintini, which has reached me yesterday, I send
you herewith two amusing pictures (taken in Paomachang, the day before I left).
— Keep them. You will give them me back in September if you like. (I wish to keep
the face of Quintini). — Mrs. Walen is in Peiping. I wish you could see her.*

*I am just now reading the last novel of Ch. Morgan "Sparkenbroke". Try
to find it: a bit intricated, and the same lack (as in "Fountain") of a clear interpretation of pantheistic aspirations and Love; - but a wonderful spiritualistic
move through Matter. - You will like it, and find in it a lot to discuss. - Anyhow, I
will bring you my copy.*

*A vous,*

*precious and dearest,*

*P.T.*

*Paris, July 14th, 1937*

*Dearest,*

*I am somewhat late this time, and I have to answer two of your letters
(June 14 and 24), each of them has been so precious and sweet and so "new" to me.
I enjoy to see you so alive, so well surrounded by many friends, and at the same
time so much the same interiorly. Funny and pleasant that we should have the
same eyes, you and I!.*

*The reason of my being a bit late with you is that, just on my return from
Auvergne, a week ago (you have received my letter 16 from Murols, I suppose), I
have got a third small attack of fever. More and more likely a kind of malaria,
although the germs do not show. That brings a new trouble in my plans. I had
practically decided to leave Paris via Siberia at the middle of August. Now, I feel
that it would not be wise to risk another fever in Moskow or Manchouli. And I
am inclined to book a comfortable first class cabin on some french mail, also in
August. That would make me two or three weeks later in China . . . But what to*

*do else? Do not worry. You did the best, by far, in deciding your American journey.*
*Let us trust life. Life has brought us each to the other: it will make us always*
*closer, provided we follow it steadily and lovingly. Of course, I am a little anx-*
*ious about the political conditions in Peiping just now, - and I am glad you are in*
*Peitaho. Let us hope that once more the trouble will be settled humorously, in the*
*Far-Eastern way.*

*Not much to tell you, this time. I met very few people you know, lately,*
*with the exception of Ella Maillart [Dutch travelogue author], who has suddenly*
*decided, last week, to fly to Afghanistan and Persia: such a courageous girl, and*
*not in a very strong health, this year. I scarcely know her; and yet she seems to*
*hope something from me, and asked some of my papers. This evening I have din-*
*ner with Max, Simone and their "daughter" Betty (you have seen her) who is in*
*Paris for a holidays trip. Lately, Simone has made a great printing work for me*
*(including the "Phénomène spirituel"). I had to spread a number of copies, spe-*
*cially in a new group: "Centre d'Etudes humaines", including amongst the mem-*
*bers of the directing board Carrel and A. Huxley (!). As I told you in my last letter,*
*my mind has perhaps never been so clear and so tense as during these last (some-*
*what disappointing) weeks. I really think that something is moving, inside and*
*outside of myself, which drives me slowly towards the type of activity which you*
*dream for me: after the study of the past Man, the discovery of the coming Man. If*
*I come back by boat, that will be the right time to write "L'Energie humaine".* L'Energie
*May be the following step would be to try a first sketch of the famous book:* humaine
*"L'Homme". A friend and colleague of mine was just saying to me this morning* in the
*that my Essays are each time approaching more the conditions for being "publi-* making
*ables". And yet I do not weaken my position, but I learn and I see how to say* soon
*things in an unquestionable way. My article on Sinanthropus is out (a very popu-*
*lar one, but clear). I still hope for the Front Humain.*

*So many thanks for your translation of Christology and Evolution. I am*
*so much interested in it that I retouch it. I will send or bring you the corrected*
*copy.*

*Politically, we are going through hard times, in France, and still more*
*financially. One must confess that the Front Populaire has not been sufficiently*
*practical in its idealism. For instance, the "semaine de 40 heures" turns to be*
*extremely difficult in its applicaton, which would require a better industrial*
*equipment, and chiefly the will in the workmen to work better in a shorter time.*
*Such transformation can hardly be tried by a country* alone. *Just as if a country*
*alone decided to disarm. Anyhow, as I told you already, people are ten times more*
*awake and eager to do something now in France than a few years ago. This is the*
*brightest side of the present situation. So far as communism is concerned, it is*
*surely still growing in the country. But I have some feeling that the Russian*
*"mirage" is gradually fading. To save human personality turns to be a banal slo-*
*gan, these days: everybody realizes that something has to be done in that line.*

*And now, dearest, nothing much to add, but to tell you, once more, how*
*strong and sweet it is for me to think that you are with me. To grow towards*
*Light, each in the other, - and each by the other! This is the future in front of us,*
*through space and time. —*

*May this letter reach you without too much delay! — Be happy!*

*Yours*

*P.T.*

*If you happen to see the Raphaëls, tell them my best regards. I never forget them, in spite of not writing them.*

*I send you, by the same mail, the last letter of Ida. Just destroy it after reading. —*

*De Terra plans to be in Burmah at the end of November next. — I hope I will be in good conditions, and in position to join him in December.*

*Paris, July 25, 1937*

*Dearest,*

*I hope that in spite of the political troubles you have received safely my last letters. As you understand easely, the new developments of the political situation in Peiping have been somewhat worrying me, the past week. And in spite of the fact that I know what to take and what to drop in the newspapers reports concerning China, it was a kind of relief for me to think that you were at that time swimming at Peitaho. Now, it seems that the worst of the crisis is over. The whole quesiton for me is to be sure that the Survey will not be scared by the new conditions to the point of reducing still more its basis in Ping Ma Ssu. I still hope that nothing will be changed in that line.*

*Your two precious letters of June 30 and July 4 have reached me safely, and without any delay. As usually, they were full of light, strength and interesting news. And I was so glad specially to hear of the last successes in your work. You know that nothing makes me more happy than to feel that you are living fully by the best of yourself. And, so far I am concerned personnally, you know also how your deep sympathy and "encouragements" have a special power for driving me ahead along the path leading to the discovery of Spirit in the world. I am surprised not to have told you my pleasure and proud surprise in seeing the english edition of the Personalistic Universe. A few "fautes d'impressions" (but very easy to correct for the reader). Simone reproached me to have had my name printed on the booklet, and perhaps she is right. We shall see the next time. In the meantime I have finished the last retouchés on your translation of Christology and Evolution: a few critical places are now much clearer, so that this english text is distinctly lighter and better than my original text. On account of the unsafe conditions of the mail just now, I will bring with me your manuscript, rather than to send it via Siberia. On the whole, as I have already told you, I have a distinct feeling and many objective proofs that the time is coming when I will be in good position for publishing more than in the past. And perhaps that was the best thing of me to have to mature my ideas in "private" essays before I could reach "la pleine possession" of what I want to say. I believe to see more and more distinctly what has to be my next paper on Human Energy and its highest form, Love.*

*And, slowly, days are passing, and I approach the end of my staying in France. Without being yet perfectly strong, I feel much better. And, if nothing hap-*

the
Personalistic
Universe

*pens, I plan to leave Marseille on August 6, by s.s. D'Artagnan (Messageries Maritimes), in a comfortable first class cabin (alone). I. Treat will be there for seeing me off. She is still dreaming of the Far East. I will naturally try to write "L'Energie humaine" during the journey [about four weeks].*

*Nothing much to tell you about my life here. One by one, people are leaving Paris for the holidays, so that the town looks rather empty. Max, Simone and Betty have left yesterday, by car, for the Pyrénées. I am glad they are going to have a little rest: Simone is working too much (she even learns Russian!). Politically, we are in a lull: but the financial side is just so dark. It seems that Communism has lost its chance (people are distinctly "cooled" by the way things are turning in Spain and Russia); and even the workmen seem to resent the tyranny of the Unions (C.G.T.). My impressions is that, as a result of the short leadership of Blum with the Front Populaire, a deep impulse has been given in the country towards social changes; but that the Front Populaire has proved to be unable to materialize these changes. Curiously enough, a growing number of people are looking towards Christianity. A week ago, Cardinal Pacelli had a really "triomphante" reception in the streets of Paris, and his picture is cheered in the movies. May Christianity understand that this sympathy does not mean any tendency of Man to go backwards to the old forms of life, but some desperate hope of a new World!*

*Last Sunday, I have seen Good Earth [from the Pearl Buck story] in a movie of les Champs Elysées. Not bad at all. The wife (O Lan) plays very well. And I longed for China.*

*And now, good bye, dearest. I will surely write you at least once more, before I leave Marseilles. — God bless you! — and be happy!*

*Yours*

*P.T.*

---

Lucile was vacationing at Peitaho, a summer resort on the Gulf of Po Ha in northern China when the Japanese began their undeclared war in 1937 by invading southern China. Eventually they reached Nanking (about 150 miles northwest of Shanghai) and in December captured it. Meanwhile, Teilhard, en route from Marseille in August, became increasingly alarmed by the news from the south of China. He was particularly concerned for the safety of the P.U.M.C. staff and for the work at the Cenozoic laboratory in Tientsin — about 80 miles southeast of Peking.

---

*Marseilles, August 6, 1937*

*Dearest,*

*Just a few lines, in order to make you sure that I am leaving today for Shanghai by the S.S. d'Artagnan (Messageries Maritimes). I wonder what I am going to find in China. Did you receive my last letter? — I have received your first letter from Peitaho.*

*In any case, what is between us is bigger than any war and any change.*

*Good bye, - et à bientôt.*

*P.T.*

*[P.S.] Yesterday I spent a good day with I. Treat*

Teilhard avoided Shanghai and the possibility of being trapped there because of the war by traveling instead via Kobe. From there he was able to make his way to Taku and then to Tientsin in northeast China.

*Kobe, A bord S.S. D'Artagnan Sept. 10, 1937*

*Dearest,*

*I wonder whether this letter will reach you, or at least reach you before my own arrival. But I will try the chance, by a few lines. —*

*So, I am really coming back — and already so close to you! To receive your letter of August 23 in Hong-Kong was an unexpected joy. Are you in Peiping now?*

*Personnally, as you see, I am trying my way by Japan. In Shanghai, I was afraid to get trapped: we did not go further than Woosung, — the passengers to Shanghai being transferred in a battleship. The river was full of Japanese ships, and the bombing of the suburbs very distinct. — My hope is to find in Kobe a steamer to Taku, and to reach Tientsin in a week. Three people, on board, are trying the same way. — Useless to tell you that, as soon I am in Tientsin, I will do my best for reaching Peiping. Maybe I will find a letter of you aux Hautes-Etudes (Race Course Road). — By the way, did you receive the few lines I sent you from Marseilles, the day of my departure?*

*On the whole, the journey was a bit hot — but pleasant. Mme de Champeaux (do you remember her?) was on the boat, going to Saïgon; and I made several new friends. I worked a little — and, in Woosung, I wrote the last line of a new Essay (L'Energie Humaine) — rather long: 75 pages.*

*But now I am only anxious to reach China — and to find you. — No news from anywhere since I have left France.*

*A très bientôt, j'espère*

*Yours*

*P.T.*

*Tientsin, Sept. 18th, Saturday, 1937*

*D'st,*

*This morning I tried, unsuccessfully, to send you a wire. I have arrived Tientsin yesterday night, via Kobe. No trouble at all. — Got your letters in Hong Kong, and here (letter of Sept. 4). — I wrote you from Marseilles, and from Kobe (to Peita ho!). — I will go to Peiping next week, as soon as possible — no later than Wednesday — and right to you. ——*

*A bientôt*

*P.T.*

In October 1937 Teilhard completed "Human Energy" (see *Human Energy*, Harcourt Brace Jovanovich: New York, 1969, pp. 113-62), in which he again considered the meaning of love: "Between man and woman a specific and mutual power of spiritual sensitization and fertilization is probably still slumbering. It demands to be released, so that it may flow irresistably towards the true and beautiful."

The Japanese presence was growing in Peking. War was threatening the whole of Europe. In these last years as the foreign population diminished and the social life lost verve, Lucile and Teilhard saw each other more frequently. Both of them refer to this time as a deepening of their friendship. In early December Teilhard left for Burma. (He would not return to China until May 1938.)

*Tientsin, 7 December 1937*

*Dearest,*

*Apparently, I am leaving today, afternoon! — But that still seems to me scarcely credible. Anyhow, I will write you on the way. — As I told you, you can send me letters: c/o Dr. de Terra, Thos. Cook & Son, Rangoon, Burma. — I still do not feel the thrill of departure. But it is so clear that I have to go, — that I find in this feeling the strength I need — as well as in your last smile. ——*

*A bientôt, dearest.*

*P.T.*

*My boat is the Hoihow (Butterfield s.s.)*

*s.s. Hoihow (before Tsingtao), December 10, 1937*

*Dearest,*

*So, finally, I have left Tientsin, on the 7 — The departure was somewhat a hectic one. But I am glad not to have missed a single chance to meet de Terra before it should be too late; and, on the whole I feel happy to follow a positive track, instead of hanging in a mist of hesitations, as it was the case during the last weeks. I thank you again for having been, during that time, such a sweet comfort. Whatever might be the result of the present journey, I see clearly now that I had to undertake it. -*

*As you know, embarking in Tangku is not a pleasure-party. First, the Moukden train (not crowded however, and not late). Then, the smaller train to the docks. Then the lighter [a flat bottomed river barge]: two hours on the muddy water, charged with blocks of ice. (But no wind, luckily!) — Finally, the Hoihow, a rather large boat, but with very few accomodations for passengers. Three "saloon-rooms", very modest, are occupied by unknown ladies. The place I got at the last minute is in ordinary "first-class", not bad at all, I must say. Only chinese people. But in the case I was lucky too. I share my cabin with two chinese doctors, educated abroad, — one of them being Dr. C. V. Lee from the P.U.M.C., going to Hongkong! — Both are very cheerful, and talk mostly a very good english, the doctor number two being a Seattle man who speaks only cantonese, — whilst Dr. Lee speaks only pekinese. — So, everything is all right — and the food is good. — But, so far, we are rather snailing on the way: 24 hours in Chefoo, 12 hours in Weihawei — taking cargo. I would never have believed that they were so many sacks, nor so many soja-beans in China. — At last, we have passed a few hours ago the land's-end of Shantung (a familiar landscape, where I was amused to spot the places I visited a year ago with Yang-Kieh) — and we are due tomorrow morning in Tsingtao, where I will post this letter. Hope that tomorrow, by this time, we shall be sailing to Swatow.*

*Hours do not seem too long. Since I have decided to use this first part of the journey (up to Hong Kong) for making my "retraite", a part of the day is spent in trials for seeing more clearly things in myself, and ahead. For this purpose I miss somewhat my notes and the familiar surroundings of Tientsin. And yet, to be practically alone on the sea, and bound for action, is a favorable atmosphere for perceiving the best of God. Many points seem to appear more simply and more distinctly in my mind. And, incidentally, I add, every day, a few touches more to my scheme about "L'Homme". — You, probably, do the same with the Lady and the Hound. - And so are we going, you and I, so close in spite of the growing distance —*

*I will miss, and much, your letters, for a long time. But your life, when I left, was sufficiently stable for making easy to me to imagine approximately what you do. - And I shall be so soon on my way back! — In the meantimes, dearest, be happy! — I shall be always with you. ——*

*My next letter will be from Hong Kong*

*Yours*

*P.T.*

*St. Lucia's Day - 1937*
*Peking China -*

*Dearest -*

*You have been gone more than a week and I wonder where you are now. And so deeply hope that you have escaped the storms that put the S.S. Pres. Hoover on the rocks - It will be so good when I know that you are safely in Burma and have met up with de Terra - but I suppose it will be a long time before I can hear - I have such a feeling about this letter - as if I were going to send it off to the blue void!!*

*Nothing much new since you left. I went over to see Grabau yesterday - Peggy Boyden - who has just returned - was there too — Then Pai came in — He seems happy now that he has gotten into the work — I went to the P.U.M.C. (wanted to ask Mr. Ho about getting some plaster - it is difficult now to get good plaster). and old Weidenreich told me, with much glee, all about how he had sent that telegram to Dr. Wong! He was much pleased with himself! Is busy writing <u>another</u> lecture - so the work of reconstruction is still postponed - But I do not mind for I am busy.*

*Am casting the head of Romola, which the sculptress from Harbin liked the best, or one of the best of my things - The figure is going well - <u>up to now</u> it has gone better than they usually go -and this morning I started another head - an American girl - Mrs. Griffith - quite nice - and completely different from Romola - So you see I am busy -*

*Friday I went to a small cocktail at Cecil Lyon's and Saturday to one of Jacques - Today there is a big one at the British Officers mess - Tomorrow Peggy Boyden is coming for lunch and I've asked Jacques - etc etc - Nothing exciting, but all very nice and I like seeing people late in the afternoon - especially as I feel quite lost at 5 o'clock - It is just that time now and I'm having tea with Spotty and Tung Hsi!!*

*Lucile dear,*

*My last letter was from Tsingtao — and I did not write you from HongKong, for the simple reason that I did not stop there. When we arrived Swatow, I discovered another Butterfield steamer just about to leave for Singapore, direct, with a cargo of several hundred chinese emigrants; and I jumped on this chance. And here I am, very comfortably in a good cabin, alone "white" passenger, with a staff of cheerful scotch officers who grumble a kind of hardly understandable english. Very good crossing. It is pretty hot, already, and I wonder at my old fur-coat, hanging in a corner of my berth, as the witness of some strange age of the world. We are due in Singapore this night. And tomorrow I shall know definitely at which date I can reach Rangoon — before January, I hope. That would be a pretty good time. I will wire de Terra, anyhow. Hope that he did not leave for the Thibetan border, so far —*

*So, everything is all right, presently. Putting the things at the worst, I have enough friends and scientific interests in Singapore for spending there a few pleasant days. I will let you know what happens. A pity, only, that you should have to wait so long for this letter 2 — But you know that I did not forget you.*

*Very litle to tell you about the two past weeks. I was sufficiently busy — making my "retraite" (!) — and thinking about Man, — for not minding the monotony of the days, and the emptiness of the sea. We had, by the way, almost a perfect weather, with the wind mostly from the rear. On the Hoihow, I enjoyed rather the company of Dr. C.V.Lee, whom I gradually spotted as a very familiar figure, and an old friend of Alice Woodland. He told me many things about her former husband — and also about V.K.Ting, who was very close to him. — I discovered also that the two british ladies were more interesting than I first thought: Mrs. Herbert (her husband is in the British Consular Service) and her young sister, Miss Romer. Did you hear of them? - Mrs. Herbert was apparently a good friend of Roy C. Andrews, when he came first in Peking. — Here, on the Anhui, there is nobody to talk with but the merry Scotchmen. One of them remembers me of Granger. The finest type is the first officer, Keyworth, one of the three who had this strong experience to be kidnapped, six months, by bandits, near Niuchuang, some two years ago (maybe you remember it in the papers). He has a radio, a good library (did you read "The gap in the curtain", by John Buchan, a very clever book?). He just took me down today inspecting the three decks occupied by the chinese emigrants: a most picturesque accumulation of sleeping, opium-smoking, washing and eating people, with a good exposure of fresh-looking baby flesh. —*

*As I told you, I have reflected a good deal, these days. — Essentially, I feel mentally alert, with a fundamental satisfaction to have taken the step which assures me that, whatever will result from this new experience, I have not failed de Terra, — nor my luck. In spite of my good reasons (and they were) I had the impression that I would lack courage or decision if I was staying in my Peking's slippers. I needed to prove to myself that I can keep young. And, at the same time, I experience more and more distinctly that the deep of my life is no more with ter-*

*races, gravels, and fossil Man. The <u>future</u> of the World and Life drives me decidedly to itself. — Burma attracts me chiefly as a step to that. Let us wait hopefully for the developments. In any case, you can help me more and more, — and I hope so much to do the same with you: since the progress has to be from <u>both</u> sides, - not only you for me, but I for you, dearest.*

*By the fact, "Man" did not make much progress. But I have the impression that the whole thing begins to be better grasped in my mind. I just still lack the blaze which will illuminate the subject when the mass is sufficiently concentrated. Just the final spark, you know: But that can make all the difference.*

*I will write you very soon — as soon as I know something concerning my journey. — In the meantime, be happy. — I think of your Xmas parties. — Ta Tien Shui Ching is a sweet place to think of ——*

*your*

*P.T*

*P.S. — Singapore 21.*
*I am leaving day after tomorrow, due to Rangoon the 28! — I will read your Xmas letter in Penang. Yours P.T.*

---

During the fall when the two friends were in Peking, they had had a talk both regarded as important. In fact, Teilhard described it as one of their "coeur à coeur" talks. On leaving lower Burma he wrote reassuringly of his return, also explaining the reasons for starting out early on the trip. Teilhard, Helmut de Terra, Ralph von Koenigswald, and the other scientists in the Carnegie-sponsored expedition subsequently spent three months in Indo-China — making geological-archaeological finds that are fundamental to understanding the prehistory of man.

---

*Rangoon, Dec. 28, 1937*

*Dearest,*

*I hope you have received my letter from Singapore. This one will tell you that I arrived today in Rangoon, by an unusually bad weather: wind and rain — a real calamity, people say, for the country, since the rice was just lying, cut, in the fields. However, the sky seems to improve — and, as a compensation, we enjoy a very cool air. — This morning, I found news from de Terra. He will be at Mandalay day after tomorrow. And myself, I am leaving this night for Mandalay, arriving tomorrow at noon. So, the meeting will be much more easy than I thought — and apparently I am here on time for the work: so that everything seems all right. Now I see more clearly how I have been right to leave Peking at once, three weeks ago: "Providence" has smoothed the way it had apparently chosen for me; and <u>you</u> are a most dear and tangible aspect of this Providence, Lucile!*

*From Singapore, the journey has been short and easy — on a very good boat — on which I discovered, the last day, that two american ladies, from Chicago (Miss Muller and Miss Buchanan — they did not know you) were, in November, in Peking, and had been shown Nelly by Mrs. Hempel!) — We spent Christmas in Penang — and there I opened your letter, which was such a joy for me: a joy, Lucile, because I felt that what is borne between us is growing — and growing in such a way that nothing in the world can be a danger for its growth. I feel sure that when I am back to you, in a few weeks, we will discover that we are still closer to each other than we thought when I left. — I was glad too, Lucile, to talk with you, the day you mean. And you must be sure that I will always bless the opportunities for those "coeur à coeur" talks. Have a happy new year, dearest. It will not be a long time now, before I see you again. You will tell me, in your next letter, what you think — and what you did achieve in your dear little studio. — It is so easy for me to see all these things — when I close my eyes.*

*Since Singapore, I did not work much (I felt to close to the end of the journey) — and I read novels, or even detective stories. Yet, I have tentatively modified the fundamental plan of my Essay sur l'Homme. I found some way for dividing the subject in a more "thrilling" way. That I will explain you, if it works. But, during the next weeks, I will probably have very little time to spare for anything which is not a gravel, or a fissure. I think that this change will be most useful for my mind, and that the things will slowly mature in the meantime.*

*I forgot to tell you that the two days spent in Singapore were very pleasant. I have a good friend there, young Dr. Collings, of the Raffles Museum. We had a pleasant dinner in his bungalow, amongst the dark trees and the flowers; — and a most interesting talk went on, up to 11 p.m., on the meaning of Life and God. This was completely unexpected! In Singapore too I met a well known archaeologist, Dutch Dr. Stein-Callenfels, surely one of the biggest men and of the strongest beer-drinkers presently alive. I should like to see him meeting Dr. Grabau: They would both sympathize immediately. — Stein-Callenfels explained me that he does not smoke but Manilla-cigarettes – so that he had to prepare a convenient supply of them for his next 6 months tour in Europe: 15 thousands, only! — He is surely a grand man! — And such a beard! You would make a fine bust of him! — —*

*I will write you before long, after I have met de Terra, and started the work on the field. — God bless you, dearest!*

*Yours*

*P. T.*

*1 Ta Tien Shui Ching*
*January 5, 1938*

*Dearest, -*
*Your precious letter from Singapore came last evening, which was remarkably good time — just 14 days!! And it was simply splendid how quickly you got through..I am sure that is a good sign that your luck is holding out and that you are going to have a very successful trip. By this time you are probably already off in the wilds. And how delighted de Terra must have been to see you. Your trip did not sound bad at all and I only hope that the trip back will be as quick. And dear DON'T hurry any of it on account of me..not that you are apt to, but still, I know you do think of me; and so for the Survey, well it will get along alright, and now that you are there it is more important that you should finish things there than that you should be here a few days or weeks sooner or later. You had to wait for Pai, so if he should have to wait a bit for you . . . well . naturally I am hoping that*

*your work will be finished, but don't leave there until you are ready, on account of things here.*

*Life generally is very quiet and orderly, I have not seen much of your people but New Year's day I went out to see Grabau. He said that he was the only one that was doing any work; Pai a little, but the people in the South, except those in the field, are doing absolutely nothing . . Since they have taken Nanking, the Japs are rather quiet, but no one knows when or where things will start next, so naturally they can't settle down to any sort of work. I havent done too much these last two weeks with all the parties and gaiety. Tomorrow night is the big charity ball, which seems to finish the big events. [Tho I just got an invitation for a Cocktail at the Raphaels on the 10th.] The 9th is Grabau's birthday and several of us are having a cocktail party at his house. Weidenriches, Fortyns Hoepplie, etc. and then Peggy Boyden, the Kullgrens and I will stay on for dinner, all of which we will take; so it ought to be fairly gay for him. He looks well as usual.*

*Saw McDonald Sunday. He had just returned from Shanghai. He was on that U.S. gunboat when she was sunk, had pretty dreadful experiences, but seems to have been somewhat of a hero and really it has done wonders for Mac, he has so much assurance when he becomes a father soon, goodness knows what he will do!! Bosshard is also back, but did not have such exciting experiences. Lichnowsky came and had lunch with me yesterday, I always enjoy talking to her, she expects to leave in a few weeks. I must see her again, in talking of some one she said "He is a Jew" with such contempt!! I must get that sort of idea out of her head before she gets to Germany — on the whole she is very fair, is mostly interested just now in modern questions from the woman's standpoint. Which is natural, because all her countrymen keep telling her the only place for a woman is to be married and have children. And as she says they are the very men who want the freedom of bachelorhood for themselves. If Western man were forced to get married at an early age as the Chinese are they would have some ground to talk from. She is really worried as to what she will be able to do in Germany and the place of women there. I insisted that although things may have a temporary standstill, they can't go backwards, which seemed to give her some comfort . . Was that correct, Maître?*

*Dearest, your letter made me so very happy and proud when you say that I can help you more and more!! But you also say you <u>hope</u> you can do as much for me..It always seems to me so evident how much you give to me that it never occurs to me there could be any question about it . . Dear, just because I sometimes want the whole moon and cry because I cannot have it . . don't ever have any doubts about it, you help me so much and have made life so rich and full . . and with things, or ideas, that can never, never leave me. You must know this and the fact that after your "retraite" and contemplation you still feel that you want and need my help, that is enough, I pray and work to have more and more to give to you. (Yes, and to give Him) but that seems so <u>necessarily</u> to follow the other, that one does not need to <u>say</u> it. Yes I feel that your interest is more and more towards Man and the future and I wonder what you mean exactly, when you say that was one reason that Burma attracted you . . any how, dearest, whatever it is you want from Burma, I hope with all my heart you will get, I suppose it isn't exactly <u>Burma</u> but somehow the whole thing . . well you will be telling me about it before too long . . Pierre, to know that you <u>are</u> is a grand thought . . and that you will be coming back to me soon!! oh dear, you do make life very rich and full and happy.*

*In spite of parties etc. the Lady and the Hound are progressing. Also another portrait of an American woman which I started a short time ago. Perhaps that final spark for "Man" will come after you have finished that work down there, or maybe before. One never knows when it is going to hit.*

*I think this is the fourth!! letter I have sent to Burma, the last was Xmas eve — have not written since as I kept thinking everyday there would be a letter from you, but it was grand that you did not have to go to Hongkong .. your old fur coat must look out of place .. It is cold and a North wind today, so I am glad to think of you there in the warm sunshine, but take care .. Good bye for today,*

*Irrawady Valley, January 6, 1938*

*Lucile dear,*

*I write you from a small steamer, along the Irrawady. Blue sky, cool air. And the dark green jungle on both side, - creeping, eastward on the high shoulders of the Shan plateau, the end of China. De Terra and his wife, and our several boys are on board. We are going down to Mandalay, after a stage in Mogok the famous "rubis [rubies] district", high upon the Shan plateau; and, tomorrow, we start for the Arakan Yoma, the mountains west of the Irrawady valley. So, you see, things have been progressing well since my letter 3, from Rangoon. — In short, a wire from de Terra asked me to join him, not in Mandalay, but further on, in Mogok, after a stage in Mogok, which was easily managed. I was in our camp on December 31. And I have immediately started in an interesting work.*

*So far, nothing "sensational" has been found. But we have already reached a number of substantial conclusions, supporting exactly the views which I had in mind when planning this Burma expedition. I think it is a positive blessing of God that I have been allowed to leave Peking. I have come here still in time. And de Terra wanted me badly for helping him in his work. Conditions, here, cannot be properly understood unless you know China. And, in addition, Dr. "Movius", who has been selected by Harvard as an associate for de Terra, is a pure archaeologist, practically hopeless in the type of researches we are doing in this country (by the way, I did not see so far Movius, who is trying his chances presently somewhere in the south-east). — So, everything sounds well, and I feel fine (excuse the handwriting: the boat is vibrating frightfully).*

*Mogok is a most interesting place: high mountains, covered with a thick jungle, swarming of monkeys, deer, jungle fowl, civet cats, — with tigers, also, elephants and rhino, which, of course, I did not see. The days were warm, — but it was just freezing during the night under the tent, and we had to get padded blankets and even water-bottles! Mrs. de Terra manages the domestic side of the expedition in a most efficient way; and we are all very gay. — As I have told you — Mogok is a famous center for rubies and saphires, which are mined everywhere in this district, — under the careful supervision of very elegant burmese ladies, who use to come to the places, under their enormously broad hats and always attended by a "suivante", whilst the husband stays home and smokes his cigars (everybody here seems to have constantly a big cylindrical cigar in his mouth). —*

*By the way, I bring you back a ruby, if it not of the best deep colour, at least it is certainly genuine. —*

*So far I have seen, the country in Upper Burma, is mostly jungle. — And everywhere an incredible number of monasteries with yellow monks, who live as perfect parasites on the country: somewhat as the mongolian lamas. In Mandalay the palace is rather pleasant, but it looks as a ridiculous reduction of the Peking's palace: rectangular too, with broad moats, and miniature-towers at each angles.*

*Maybe I will soon receive a letter from you. I am anxious to know that everything is all right, to you. Tell me everything about the detail of your life, — and about your work.*

*I will very soon send you more news.*

*Yours, dearest*

*P.T.*

*P.S. — Coming to Mandalay, I find your first letter, so full of good things! — Thanks! — Yes I had* <u>*plenty*</u> *of over-thought for the day of St. Lucia. — I am so sorry for the Laroux! —Received also a letter from my cousin in Paris (23 Dec.): she tells me that Simone Bégouën has just had to undergo an operation. I am anxious to have more explicit news. — I write to Max.*

*Your*

*P.T.*

*We are leaving this evening for "Minbu", along the Irrawady.*

*Magwe (Burma), Jan. 23, 1938*

*Lucile dear,*

*My last letter was from Mandalay, down from Mogok. - Today I write you in a most charming place. Since a week, our camp is pitched in a grove of old mimosas, next to a gold and white pagoda, on the very shore of the Irrawaddy. Opposite to us, westward, the skyline is formed by the jungly Arakan Yoma (the range running between the Irrawaddy and the golfe of Bengale). If you add that the days are not yet very hot, the nights cool, the sky of a pekinese blue, and the mosquitoes absent (but not the white ants, which have started several night-attacks), you will conclude that my expedition has much to do with a pleasure trip. And this is true. I am thoroughly enjoying this new period of field-life — and I feel curiously strong and younger — somewhat like in India two years ago. Really, even as far I am physically concerned, it seems that the Burma business is something like a blessing of God. And I thank you too.*

*Scientifically, our progresses are satisfactory. After almost giving up the hope of good results in archeology, it seems that we have finally hit a good "old Paleolithic" stuff in the Irrawaddy gravels — something approaching the old implements of India and Java. If true (as I seriously believe) this find would greatly substantialize our stratigraphic results. — We are presently at two days by boat south of Mandalay. Tomorrow, we shall move a day northward — and work there a week or two. — By that time, the heat will probably have increased.*

*So we plan to come back on the Shan Plateau, for sometime. The end would be a short exploration in the Mitkyina area, the northernmost part of the Irrawaddy basin. — If completed, this programm would keep me here up to the end of March(!), and I wonder whether Weidenreich is not going to object. But, unless something very serious requires my presence in Peking, I feel that it should be unwise for me to cut my work and my chance here. The success of the work depends on my collaboration much more than I realized — which means, incidentally a much closer connection between me and the american institutions (Carnegie Institution and Harvard). I like more and more de Terra. But I have very often to cheery him up, and I had my time in smoothing the situation between him and his collaborator, archaeologist Movius (and wife) — a delightful young man, but rather unfit for a pioneer-work. Everything is O.K. now, since the discovery of the old implements. — As you can easily think, the only thing which worries me, if I stay longer, is to be longer away from Ta Tien Shui Ching. But I am so sure that you understand, and that, if I could talk with you, you would approve me.*

*I expect very soon a letter from you — and also from Max. Nothing from Paris since I left Mandalay. But, the airmail is so fast, with Europe: 7-10 days only! — Something will arrive before long, no doubt. As far as I can guess from the papers, situation is awful on the Yangtze. Poor China! — and what will be left of the Geological Survey? It seems that we are witnessing a complete recasting of the far-East. — And what about Bosshart? We speak very often of him with de Terra.*

*Be happy, dearest. — I like so much to think of you. — God bless you, a hundred times!*

*Yours*

*P.T.*

*I bring you a ruby from Mogok. Did I tell you? ——*

*Chank (Burma), Feb. 13, 1938*

*Lucile dear,*
*I have received yesterday your letter of Jan.16, and a week ago the one of Jan.5 (the letter of Xmas did not arrive!) I hope that my letter did reach you, in spite of the fact that the mail, in Burma, is simply helpless! Those two letters of yours were simply precious to me, bringing me, as usually, so much of light, strength, and sweetness. — But what did you discover, in re-reading me, which might have given you the feeling that I was, even slightly, "discouraged" with you! — I cannot remember writing anything like that. And that would be so far from what I ever felt, dearest. Never, on the contrary, since this last fall, did I so much realize how much we are, for each other, a mutual and everlasting comfort. — In your letter of Jan.5 I was so happy to read that you would approve me if I tried to get the utmost from the present expedition. What I wrote you in my letter 5 is still the most probable plan: that I should go to Java with de Terra at the end of March, postponing my return to Peking up to the end of April. A joint meeting in Java with de Terra & Koenigswald may have some important result for my personal "carrière". I wrote to the PUMC. asking a wire if they feel that I must*

*come back earlier. Not a single word from Weidenreich since I left. I suspect that a number of letters were lost, either from China, either from Europe. No answer from Max, so far. From a letter of my cousin, I caught vaguely that Simone is better but still pretty weak. — Nothing on that in a short letter of Breuil (Jan. 18) received yesterday (he had received your letter). — Nothing from my Order, either. Mail is pretty discouraging, here. — I wrote, three weeks ago, to Jacques and to the Raphaëls: glad for them, sorry for you and me, that they have left, and Eleanor too. Where are the Lyon's going to? — By the way, I heard from my cousin that my article of October (mutilated as it was) has apparently been appreciated: the number of the review was exhausted before January.*

*Here, everything develops all right. Since we left our pretty Magwe camp, we went first to Pagan, the most picturesque burmese site of Burma — then to the jungle along the Arakan Yoma — then back to Pagan. Now we are camping near an oil-field, still along the Irrawaddy. Our work in the low lands is almost finished, and we have now a beautiful and rich old Palaeolithic industry from the Irrawaddy grounds — which probably should have been overlooked if I had not strongly taken the side of de Terra against the discouraged archaeologist Dr. Movius who had already sent to Harvard a cable announcing the failure of his researches. Now, Movius is beaming and collects perfectly. So, you see, I had to come and to stay. — In a week, we leave for the Shan Plateau. - Weather is still almost cool here; and I feel perfectly strong. Also, I like this country where the simplest man or woman in the fields is just so bright as a flower. - I forgot to tell you about Pagan, the old capital of the burmese kings. The place, now is nothing more than a native village buried amongst the palms; but the country is covered with hundreds of old pagodas, several of them as old as 1200 A.C.\* Nothing very artistic nor very great about them (everything was built with bricks): but the whole thing, chiefly at sunset, has something irreal and fantastic. You would like the sight — and the life here, too. —*

*I am so interested by everything you tell me about your life and your work. — Nothing can make me more happy than to realize that you live more by me, as I by you. ——*

*I will write you from the Shan Plateau.*

*Deeply yours, dearest*

*your*

*P.T.*

*I realize that this letter is terribly hasty. — But I have a complete mail to write today.*

---

\*Usually B.C. in standard American English.

---

Lucile sent him a picture of herself and her dogs — probably in February. Teilhard responded enthusiastically to it and to her plan to go to the States later in the year. He speculated on the possibility of their meeting there.

*Lucile dear,*

    *Since my last letter, I have well received your precious news, and the lovely picture of you and the two dogs, which I enjoyed so much. — To look at it makes me a little sick to be soon back to Ta Tien Shui Ching. The next month we shall meet again! Your plan for the summer in California looks very wise and promising. We shall have a long time together, before, in old Peking. - And maybe, also, I will pay you a visit in your American resort: if I have to go to France next fall, I think seriously that, for several reasons, I should have to take the Pacific way. Would not it be wonderful?!*

    *Since I wrote you, the work has been going on in a satisfactory way. Many more implements collected along the Irrawaddy. But now, after a few days spent near a very majestic volcano in the plain (Mt. Popa) we have migrated to the Shan Plateau — Very cool weather, and such a magnificent scenery: huge green forest, on which spring spreads creamy and pinky touches, and eventually flame-coloured patches. Two days ago, we motored along a precipitous road to the deep valley where the Salween river runs parallely with the Mekong. A few miles further were the first slopes of the Yunnan. Chinese everywhere on the tracks, with their blue dresses and their mules, just as in Peking! — You would enjoy to observe the people of the hills, here: black-turbaned Shans, — Kachins women, in broad "décolleté", with a coloured kilt, — wild Wans, almost naked [a tribe of headhunters], and just so shy as jungle animals: a complete ethnological collection. The country is so densely forested, or so much covered with red clays that geology is not easy. Yet, we get a good number of interesting facts. Presently, we are camped at Lashio, the head of the main road to China [800 miles long to Kunming; later called the Burma Road]. I have been surprised to hear from the British official that Peter Fleming had just passed (with his wife) going to the Yangtze, and also Mr. Gage (!) coming from Hankow. I should have liked to meet him here. All that makes me closer to you, it seems.*

    *I have received several letters: one from Weidenreich, before his departure, — one from Breuil, — one from Max. Simone is better now, but still lying in her bed, at home. Max was rather enthusiastic concerning the spiritual developments of his Company (I will show you the letter); but he tells me that my Essay "L'Energie Humaine" has been regarded by my colleagues as "impubliable"! I was really surprised (but not really disapointed) — and I have written today a rather strong statement to my best and most influential friend and colleague in Paris (F. d'Ouince), in which I tell him that the critized paper being of a scientific, not a religious, turn, I did not recognize the right to anybody to interfere with its publication. We shall see. — On the other hand, it seems that my short (and somewhat truncated) article of October has met with a sufficient success. — Did you see the last book of A. Huxley; "Ends and Means". Insufficiently constructed, but stimulating.*

    *My plans keep the same. We leave Rangoon on next 24. At that time, if nothing has come from Peking urging me to hurry back, I will travel via Java — an important trip for me, as I told you. Then, straight to Peking. The next month, as I told you, we shall be together again.*

*In the meantime, dearest, I hope that everything is all right for you. When I am back, and when we shall talk of so many things accumulated in our mind and in our heart during these months of separation, I am sure you will forgive me completely for having been away so long. — I hope you will find me "grown up", for you.*

*Your*

*P.*

*After March 24, address: c/o Thos. Cook, Batavia*

---

After making no Journal entry for two years, Lucile wrote a brief summary of the evolution of her friendship with Teilhard.

Meanwhile, throughout 1936 and 1937, he had kept her informed of his fieldwork in Chou-Kou-Tien, Java, and Burma. Often he also "talked over" his evolving ideas on the philosophical and mystical significance of matter.

---

[Journal] *March 12, 1938, Peking*

*So much has happened since that last writing — and yet between P and me — so little — I mean so little change — just everything deeper and stronger and surer — I remember how that misunderstanding — the greatest we have ever had — was cleared up and brought us closer together than ever — we had a whole marvelous year together — most of '36 — with much talk and work and a constant <u>growing</u> in depth and breadth — — Then in Feb 22, 1937 he went to America and France — I know I had hoped there might be some definite break with his order — but it did not come — in fact I had subconsciously counted on it more than I realized and it was almost hard to realize and accept things as they were — that we were more and closer to each other I am sure — but how to live and express this love is still a problem that sometimes brought up difficulties — I suppose it always will —our whole lives have been so very different.*

*Penang, March 27, 1938*

*Lucile dear,*

*We have left Rangoon two days ago, and we pass Penang tomorrow. Perfect sky and sea. I enjoy the feeling to be on my way back. For, in spite of the branch trip to Java, I am really on the <u>way back</u>. And, in fact, now that the real work is over, I am positively in a hurry to see again the walls of Peking. Very soon, dearest, I will be there; and it seems to me that, after these months, I can bring you something better and new — as well as I know that something still better will be given me by you. — Your last letter (Feb. 26) was so clear, so courageous, and so sweet. I got it in Rangoon the eve of the departure. And I enjoyed greatly the new face of Nelly — but still more the studio with the living Buddha (not the living Buddha, of course, — although he will be a good addition to your exposition). So many things you will show me. And so many things we will have to say. —*

*The last two weeks in Burma have been interesting and useful, — entirely spent on the Shan Plateau, amongst the trees, the flowers, and the strange people which I described you in my last letter. Our last stay was in the Ruby [gem] district of Mogok, the very place where I had met de Terra at the end of December. The country looked just so attractive — but a little funny: some trees are getting their news leaves and blossom, as for the regular spring; — and a larger number were loosing their leaves, on account of the dry season, just as in autumn. I think that I felt a positive kind of regret, when leaving these places which I had, for several months, regarded as "mine". But, so attractive as it may be, Burma is not much more than a National Park in Asia. In spite of all its deep charms, this last expedition has brought me the final evidence that the interest of my life is no longer in past rocks, but in modern world. This is the sea on which you must help me to sail, henceforth, more and more.*

*Practically no news, neither from Europe, nor from Tientsin: nothing from the P.U.M.C., nor from Pei, nor from Trassaert. Everything I know, concerning this side of the world, I got by you, — which, at some extent, is the most precious way. — As I told you, I believe, in my last letter, I have written to my friend d'Ouince in Paris, insisting for a publication of L'Energie Humaine, which I hold as a purely <u>scientific</u> paper. In any case, I am decided to write "L'Homme", which, I believe, I see now more distinctly. We shall talk of that. — You would have enjoyed the way in which I have been "sermonné" by Rhoda de Terra: exactly as by you! I am sure you would like to see her in America. — Received a letter from Mme Raphaël: she seems to enjoy Dalat and Saïgon.*

*A bientôt, dearest. I will write you from Singapore or Batavia, as soon as I have fixed the boat which will bring me to Tientsin — via Kobe, I suppose.*

*your*

*P.*

*Singapore, April 20. 1938*

Lucile dear,

*Hope this letter will arrive to Peking before me! - These few lines to let you know that I am leaving today Singapore by S.S. Felix-Roussel (French Line), due to Shanghai on the 29. I was told here that there is no difficulty for getting there another steamer to Tientsin. — In any case, you know that I will not loose any possiblity for gaining a single day, in order to meet you earlier!. So sweet to go, now, straight toward you! -*

*Useless to tell you, in this letter, details on my journey which I will very soon <u>talk</u> with you. On the whole, the trip to Java was extremely interesting, — and I regretted somewhat to leave the party before the end: but I could not delay longer my return to China. I wonder what they are thinking, Pei and the other ones, in the P.U.M.C.! — Coming here, day before yesterday, I found that Collings, my friend of Malaya, has just made an important discovery, linking the finds of Burma and Java — just what I was hoping when we decided the expedition. All right! — On another hand, I received in Batavia two letters from Paris, rather comforting, so far the progress of "our ideas" is concerned. I will tell you.*

*A bientôt, dearest. I know that, when we meet, we shall feel still closer.
— I love you so much ——*

*yours*

*P.*

*If this letter reaches you, let Mrs. Hempel [secretary at the P.U.M.C.] know that I
am on my way back.*

T.S.S. "Patroclus", May 2, 1938

*Dearest,*

*Hope you have well received my air-mail letter from Singapore. - These
few lines, which I send you by MacDonald are to tell you that I am <u>really arriv-
ing</u>. — We are due tomorrow morning to Taku. — I will probably stay two days
in Tientsin. Before the end of the week (probably Friday) I shall, at last!, be back
to your dear little home. — Such a joy, Lucile! And such a lot to hear and to tell! I
am so glad not to miss your birthday. —*

*The journey back was quite easy; - and it was such a luck that I found the
Patroclus. I did not wait more than half a day in Shanghai. — On the french mail
[boat], between Hong Kong and Shanghai, I met Nagiar (the french ambassador)
and Dr. Andersson. And, on the Patroclus, I travel with Mac and his secretary
(formerly secretary of Jameson). — In Saïgon, I have seen the de Champeaux and
Mme Raphaël. — Peking everywhere.*

*If you can, would you <u>let Mrs. Hempel know</u> of my arrival? Thanks. ——
A très bientôt*

*your*

*P.*

---

In June Teilhard had begun writing l'Homme, later entitled *Le Phénomène Humain*. In the
middle of August Lucile left Peking to visit friends and relatives in the United States and to
exhibit her recent works — particularly the sculptures she had done in China.

Peking, Aug 15, '38

*Precious Lucile,*

*When you read these lines, Peking will be already behind you; — but
once more, we must regard forward, not only to the next meeting (so soon!) in
New-York, but to the increase, under any conditions, of our marvelous friendship.
I told you that, already, several times, - and several times, too, we have experienced it: momentary separations (although unpleasant they are) are a useful part
in the process of what is growing between us. You have to be more yourself — and
I also — in order to bring a new supply to the common growth. Now, it seems evident that the next ten months are, for both of us, a "providential" opportunity to
become richer. Let this feeling of hope and conquest overcome, in our heart, the
impression (false, in a true respect) that, up to the next spring, our boats are drift-
ing apart. Fundamentally, we shall be just so close as in Peking — since we will
discover the same world together.*

*From Lucile Swan's 1938 exhibition: "Mother and Child" and "Chinese Wrestlers."*

*This year, Lucile, you gave me still more, if possible, than the preceding years — first because we were, by the depth of our lives, still closer — and secondly, also, because, as I become "less young", I feel deeper the need of a full comprehension and support. To begin is much more easy than to achieve. Keep this point very strong in your mind and your heart: You can and you must help me to go on straight ahead, by giving me light and warmth. Keep me alive on Earth, whilst I try to bring you closer to God. This seems to me to be the meaning and the definition of our mutual union. Make me more myself, as I dream to make you reaching the best of yourself. Along this road, there is no danger to get tired, nor to find an end. — And thank you, <u>so much</u>, for forgetting as you do, for me, what you might, naturally, expect, but what, for higher reasons, I cannot give you. I love you so much the more for this "renoncement". And there is nothing I will not do for you, in order to repay you.*

*I am <u>glad</u> to think that you are travelling with good friends — and also that you leave <u>first</u>. I should hate to leave you behind, in China. Don't worry for me. I will try not to feel too sad at 5 p.m. Besides, these last weeks will be busy, and partly spent, probably, in Tientsin. — Anyhow, I don't think I will risk myself to the Tai Miao ——*

*Yours more than ever!*

*God bless you!*

*Pierre*

*Addresses:*
*— Victoria (Canada), Empress of Japan, October 6.*
*— c/o Dr. W. Granger, American Museum of Natural History,*
*Central Park West (N.Y.) and: Campion House, 329. West 108 str.*

*Peking, Aug. 29th, '38*

*Dearest,*
*Excuse me to use this awful paper. I write you on the corner of a table, at the Raphaël's, so that you should have surely, for your arrival in New-York, my answer to your first <u>three</u> letters (the one from Kobe reached me this morning). I was so happy to have these news on your journey — and so happy, specially, that, in spite of the growing distance, you should still feel the substance of what has grown between us. Yes, spirit (the true one, so different of "abstraction") is the most consistant of things, - if only we try to build on it. — As you say, there will always be a lot of things to debate between us: but the great things is that we should find a way which <u>works</u>.*

*Since you left, I have been rather busy. First, I made this famous "retreat", which is over since yesterday. Finally, being in Shih-hu hutung [the Jesuit residence on Rue Chabanel in the North City] was not too bad; - and I hope to have a bit better focussed the aim of my life. In fact, I have the feeling that my life has to be more and more devoted to the discovery (for me and the others) of the wonderful association of Universality and Personality which is the God we need for being thoroughly human. And I think that for this work of dis-*

Universality & Personality

covery we are associated, Lucile. — Did you notice, at the end of "My way of Faith", the analysis Miss Petre gives of her friendship (and more —) with Tyrrel. I thought a lot of you, when reading it. Conditions are so closely similar, in a way. — Well, I am now ready to start for the new trial and conquest (?) of Paris, in a few months. But we shall meet before!

Physically, I feel all right. Blanc\*, however, goes on giving me the full series of shot: not tiring at all, because he has found for it a special method, suppressing the depressing influence of emetime. Each time I meet him, we have long talks on a lot of sujets (medical, social, religious —). I appreciate him more and more, and I forget completely his charming accent de Marseille.

In fact, due to the retreat, I have seen extremely few people, since your departure, except the Raphaël's where I took several lunches when I could not come back to the North City. They are leaving at the end of the month, by their danish boat. — Today, I go to Tientsin for two days. I will come back with Trassaert and Leroy. So far, no decision from France concerning Trassaert: I still hope. — I did not yet find the time (nor the heart.) to enter Ta Tien Shui Ching, so that I can give you no news of the Drummond's, nor of the figs. — Mrs. Hempel has come back today from her second staying in Peitaoho: she looks like a little Redskin! — Finally, Weidenreich had a successfull Copenhagen meeting, and is on his way back: he does not seem even to suspect what was on the point to come on him! — From the de Terra's, rather sad news (confidential): they have, at least for the time being, separated — and both are suffering. The whole thing is so absurd. We shall talk of it in N.Y., and perhaps see them. — I think you could help her. — I went twice to Grabau's: we missed you, and received your card from Kobe. Olga [Hempel] will be back in a few days. Grabau has now a huge police-dog, very like Mowgli, but young, and impossible, because he finds the courtyard too small — which is true. — Met once Nirgidma. Bréal should be here very soon. ——

I will write you again in a few days.

Yours so much

Pierre

*Peking, Sept. 12, 1938*

Dearest,
I have received, with such a joy, your letters from Kobe and Yokohama. They were so true, and so sweet. — I try to send you these few lines via Siberia, in case they should arrive before me. I am leaving this afternoon for Tientsin, — and to-morrow from Tientsin to Kobe (with Trassaert and Leroy, up to Tokyo! they take a trip to Japan). The Empress of Japan is supposed to leave Yokohama on Sept. 24. I will probably have time to see the Grews in Tokyo. She is surely a remarkable person. —

This last weeks have been sufficiently busy for not allowing me to think *too* much of Ta Tien Shui Ching — where I did not risk me since you left. I suppose

---

\*A French physician, not his scientist colleague, Alberto Carlo Blanc.

the Drummonds are in Peitaho. — Mrs. Clubb is back, - but I did not meet her — I have seen a good deal Jacques, the Raphaëls (they leave the next week, by the boat you know), and also Peggy Boyden. Peggy gave me, last thursday, a very nice small farewell dinner: we were only four, Peggy, Helen Burton, Grabau (!) and myself. The Mayo's dog died at the hospital! The boys have managed to get another one, of the same race (Peggy hopes that it has not been stolen!). - Dr. Blanc gave me a full series of shots (<u>not</u> because I was sick, but in order to clean me from any germ) — and that was an opportunity for me to have a succession of long talks with him. I appreciate him more and more — and his wife, too. –

Since you left, I did not advance much "Man" because (on account of memoirs to correct or to print) I had absolutely no time. But the end of the first part (the most delicate section in the Essay) is definitely clear in my head. I hope to make a serious step ahead during the journey.

Hope you have a nice time on the sea, with a lot of ideas germinating, and even blossoming. — These last days, I have received two different letters from Paris from editors, asking to publish my large Essay, written 10 years ago(!), "Le Milieu Divin". I will probably try to start again the matter in Paris. So many things to do! —

Good bye, dearest — et à bientôt! I write you these lines "en hâte". Excuse the hand-writing — and be always "my light"!

Yours so much

P.

New York, Oct. 28, 1938

Lucile dear,

Once more, we are parting — <u>in order to</u> meet and to be united deeper and higher. — God bless you for all what you have given me these days — still more perhaps than in the past! — As you told yesterday, the special value of these three weeks is that we have put in common, in a new environment, our work and our friends, as if it were in a single and common activity. Art and science, your friends and mine friends, are so closely mixed in my last experiences, that I can hardly separate them in my feelings and my memory. — This is, I suppose, the way to the future of what is between us — always growing. —

More and more, I count upon you, for animating me, and directing me, ahead. Life must and will be for both of us a continual discovery — of ourselves, and of the true face of God who is the deepest bond between us.

Yours for ever

P.

Paris, Nov. 7, 1938

Dearest,

Just a few lines to give you the first news of Paris. This letter will be brought to you by the same Ile-de-France which took me away from dear New-York. Positively, I felt sore when I could see, for the last time, the sky-scrapers *above 55th street — And yet it was such a fullness, inside, to have with me these last three weeks, and your sweet letter. Well — by living only we shall gradually find how to adapt our two lives, for the highest, the closest, and the best. —*

*The journey was quiet, but a little monotonous — and I felt a little "blue" also. I never like to come back to France; and this time, I had been so spoiled and so happy in America. When I came back to my cabin, after leaving you, I found a luxurious basket of fruits, sent by Frick! — Such a nice man. — During these days, I had several long talks with Gilbert, and I liked him: another one who, after a period of hopeful youth, feels pessimistical, and inclined to retire from a fighting life, because he has lost his faith in the world. I saw also a great deal of Lecomte du Noüy; we developed an immediate mutual sympathy — although we differ in this point that he is more inclined to criticize the narrow sides of modern science than to emphasize and correct its hopes (the immediate consequence of this turn of mind being that he missed a year ago his chance to become a colleague of Breuil au Collège de France). His wife [an American] is really attractive, but utterly different from Nathaly: completely "francisée", and working in the Lab. with her husband. — In Tourist class, I found a rather important priest from Paris, whom I could not avoid since the chief-steward had decided to put us together in the dining-room — but who turned to be an interesting man (I will send him a choice of my papers).*

*Finally, the boat-train reached Paris at midnight! — The following morning, I was heartily received [at] Rue Monsieur, where I am, on the whole, happy. I have already met here an extremely interesting representative of the young generation emerging from the "Ecole polytechnique": apparently, a movement is just borne there, aiming to develop this very type of "spiritual scientist" of which we have so often dreamt together: a man for whom research and discovery mean adoration. At the end of the month, I will see the group, and give there a short talk. — Before long also I am going to start the question de "L'Energie Humaine".* -

*In the course of two days, I met a lot of friends. Prof. Boule, unchanged; Breuil, looking a bit older, but cheerful (we talked of you). Yesterday, I spent the day with the Bégouëns. Max was delighted with the seal, and Simone with the silk: first she thought of a pyjama, and later of a chinese dress (when she discovered that the silk was "à jours"!). Both look very well — but she had such a dreadful experience last winter.). We planned a lot of things, together. Later, in the evening, I went to see my brother, whom I found almost fat (relatively!). Camille was there, smarter than ever, with the cutest possible hat. She has spent three weeks in Auvergne, at my brother's place, and is simply regarded as the second daughter of the family* [Camille was married to one of Teilhard's nephews].-

*Politically, things are somewhat gloomy, but not too much. I have the impression that, in spite of many "récriminations", the public feeling has improved in Europe, because the Munich agreement, in spite of betraying some weakness in France, has chiefly been a manifestation of good will and human repulsion from war. Spontaneous expressions of sympathy for France have been noted in Berlin and Munich, in the german people. I am decidedly optimistic.*

"spiritual scientist"

*Yesterday I saw Licent. He is decidedly leaving Tientsin — and there are serious possibilities for the coming of Trassaert. Licent will probably go to Shanghai — the best solution by far.*

*I think of the opening of your exhibition — and I hope for your success — so deeply. — Let me know everything about it, and about your life in N.Y. I can so well understand it, now.*

*Yours, — dearest.*

*Pierre*

---

Teilhard's impressions and hopes proved to be unduly optimistic — German troops were already in the Sudetenland and Hungary had been "given" southern Slovakia by Hitler's Germany. But France was to be free of war for nearly another year.

---

*Paris, 20 Nov, 1938*

*Dearest,*

*I have been delighted, yesterday, when I received your so long and so good letter of Nov. 9 (!). Your lines were so full of life, si compréhensives, et si affectueuses! I found there what I love and need the most of you. Now I know so well your surroundings that I had, for some minutes (and even now) the real feeling to be still with you, in New York. And, in fact, do I not belong just so much to America that to France? I am deeply happy to think that you get from the big city the very enrichment for which we have, both of us, left for a few months dear Peking. I am waiting now the next letter in which you will tell me the end of your first experiences. I am quite surprised by the attitude of Malvina H[offman], and I can not believe that it means anything. She may have queer reactions. But it seems impossible to me that she should not like to show you her work [sculptures] and her "institute of art". She is such a "prosélyte", and she knows how much you are dear to me. — Tell me your impression about Rhoda, too.*

*I hope you have well received my letter (1) (7 Nov.). Since that time, I had a busy and interesting time — and yet not too hectic, because I keep my rule to stay home every morning — with the result that I do not feel tired at all — and that I can think. My paper on Man did not progress, as far as the number of the written pages is concerned. But I have the impression to mature it constantly, — which is the most important thing. A number of people make me almost ashamed of myself by the way they appreciate "L'Energie Humaine", and go on saying that I may become the center of momentous things. I do not believe them. Yet I feel my responsibility just the same. "L'Energie Humaine" is now under new "révision". I have discovered that the people in charge of the first révision (last winter) did not take the matter in hand with sufficient energy. This time, I am decided to go as far as possible. Maybe I will also try to publish "Le Milieu Divin", for which I have a most positive offer from a well known editor in Paris. But I wonder whether it would be wise to start the two things at the same time.*

*I wrote you already about the Bégouëns. I have seen them several times — and we meet again next Sunday, in a real meeting, with some 10 other peoples (a little too much). They were just so delighted as children by your silk and the* seal. Simone looks better than Max, who got too many "migraines" recently: he could not rest enough, last summer. — I have received very good letters from Miss Garrod, from Miss Petre, etc. — By and by, I come in contact with a lot of friends, old and new. — Pray God, dearest, that I should be really able to give something _real_ to so many, to whom I am so anxious to give the best.

Scientifically, I make also some distinct progresses. — I am now settled in my office, à l'Institut de Paléontologie Humaine, and I had already several illuminating talks: I see more clearly the work ahead. But, evidently, work on ideas will absorb me much more than work on fossils, this winter. I will have several public lectures to give — but no regular "cours" — which suits me perfectly. — I foresee a week in Toulouse, at the end of January, — and a 3-weeks trip in North-Italy after Easter. Otherwise I will not move from Paris. —

Day after tomorrow I have to go to Lyon (2 days) for a formal visit to the Superior there. A rather uninteresting trip, except that I will make the journey, go and back, with a good friend, and that I hope to meet in Lyon a group of progressive minds. —

Politically, things are still gloomy. Yet, I believe more and more that the Munich agreement has a much deeper meaning than what the politicians think: "Mankind" has expressed itself in refusing war, and this instinctive choice will evolve, I think, into far reaching consequences. In the meantimes, the world (and more specially the working mass) suffers of a strange incapacity to perceive anything above individual interest. A bright ray of hope, in France, is the fast increase of several important Christian groups (workers _and_ "intelligenzia") which try to place in human development the base of their religion. I know several young men who have decided to give their life to research, just as they would have decided to join a religious order a few years ago! . . . So many things I have already collected which I would like to talk with you. -

The next time, I will write you in Chicago.

Be happy and God bless you!

Your

P.T.

I have received a letter from Béchamp (rather depressed, physically), containing a nice letter from Barbara: she is still in Chentu — apparently happy.

---

Teilhard had returned to work in the Laboratory of the Institute of Paleontology in Paris where he had served under Marcellin Boule (its director) in the 1920s. His old superior and research associates apparently managed to find office space for him during this period.

---

Paris, Dec. 7, 1938

Dearest,

Such a long time since my last letter! - Your number 3 came here three days ago — and I was so happy to read it, as well as the precedent one. I am deeply glad that your exhibition was a success — even, at some extent, finan-

*cially. The most important is that you should feel, at the end of it, a new "impetus", as Grabau says, to think, to imagine, and to create. After all, this is the fundamental reason for which we happen to be, just now, you in America, and myself in France.*

*So far I am concerned, everything is remarkably O.K., except that, in Lyon, I discovered that my Roman General is (one time more!) pretty scared of me. A copy of "Le Phénomène Spirituel" came to his hands — which of course was a perfectly bad trick for me of Fortune — and, in addition, he heard that I was disturbing the mind of my young colleagues in China — which is positively unfair. Finally, I hope to go on sufficiently un-hampered. But I have to be somewhat cautious provisionally in the line of <u>public</u> lectures and so, if I want not to break something which (I see it more and more clearly in France) <u>must not</u> be broken by my own fault or initiative. Don't be afraid. I have <u>never</u> felt so clearly how many people (even in my Order) stick to me, support me, and expect something from me. Something deep and broad is obviously moving in the world, and in France specially (far behind the ridiculous political stage). Since a fortnight, I spend hours, almost every day, with the most extraordinary diversity of people, ranging from the boundary of the working class up to the most refined, agnostic or sophisticated parts of the society. Everywhere I find the birth, or at least the expectation, of the new creed of Man in a spiritual evolution of the world. Don't be afraid, I tell you. I will do (and I do) my best to get printed, sometimes. But mere diffusion of ideas by private circulations are astonishingly powerful: after all, in such a way Christianity was born. Practically, "L'Energie humaine" has been recently read and approved by a colleague of mine (a professor of Theology at the Catholic University of Paris). But Paris is not Rome. I wonder whether, in the present state of my affairs, the best plan is not to postpone the real fight, and to start it on "L'Homme", when it will be finished. In this book, my views, because more developed, have a better chance to defeat the critics. So far, I have not yet made my mind up; but I watch the development of the situation. Just now, I am writing a short paper on "La Mystique de la Science", for a lecture, and most probably for an article to be published in "Les Etudes": this short Essai is more or less an undevelopped chapter of "L'Homme", and a preliminary trial.*

*So, you see, I am pretty busy. But my plan to keep my mornings spent quietly at my table still holds strong, - and is remarkably efficient and restful. In the afternoon, I use to go to the Institut de Paléontologie Humaine, where I do <u>not</u> find so far, I must confess, a real field of scientific activity. In this line things will perhaps improve, gradually. - As often as possible, I go rue Raynouard. Max and Simone will perhaps go to Morocco in January — in which case Ida Treat would come here and keep the Bégouën's appartment during their absence. Ida wrote me, two weeks ago. She had well received your letter (from Peking). She is writing slowly, for an american publisher, her "Mémoires". The first chapters, I was told by Simone, have been tested by the publisher with several types of readers, and prove to be a real success. But, for Ida, it is a painful and depressing task to live again, and to re-make alive, all this past. — I am extremely glad of the Nirgidma's marriage [to Michel Bréal]. She might perhaps have reached a higher*

*yes!*

*La Mystique de la Science*

*and broader sphere of activity in Asia, would she not have been so utterly "fémi-nine". Still, I am sure she will be happy, - and Michel too. –*

*Good bye, dearest. — It is such a comfort and a strength to write you! — Hope this letter will reach you in Chicago.*

*Yours*

*P.T.*

*I was very pleased that you liked Rhoda. —*

[Paris] *Xmas, 1938*

*Dearest,*

*I have been so pleased to receive your letter 4, and so happy to feel that you are going on rather successfully and with plenty of courage along your amer-ican life! I feel it particularly sweet to write you on the very Xmas morning. I still remember your message of the last year, on the same day, when I was on my way to Burma. Each new year finds us closer to each other, is it not true, dearest? The same will be true, I know it, in 39. In the meantimes, let us go straight ahead, each of us, along our own converging paths. May you be stronger by me, as I feel stronger by you! —*

*I hope you have not been disturbed by my last letter 3, written after my journey to Lyon. In fact, I don't think I have been ever so active and so busy in my life as during the past two or three weeks. Either during the morning, when people come to see me at home, either during the afternoons, when I use to go in town, I meet an astonishing number of colleagues and laymen who are equally on their quest for a new meaning to life. Indeed poor France, in some way so weakened in her external energies, seems to be tremendously alive inside, much more so per-haps than any other country in the world. I had the most unexpected meetings with the most influential, and sometimes you would say the most incredulous, people in Paris. And each time I realised that I could give them, at some extent, the thing they are craving for. — Why should I tell you all these things? — Because we are working together. — And also because I want you to believe that my method (to yield as far it is necessary not to break) is not so bad. On this point, which I can appreciate better than you, trust me: to break in a premature way, by my fault, would be a disaster for what I want to develop and to spread. — I have written what I think to be a good article on "La Mystique de la Sci-ence", to be published after january (after a lecture on the subject): the readers (critics) seem to be frankly enthusiastic about it. On another hand, I have devel-oped, in the course of a month of conversations, the matter of an interesting Essay on the internal dispositions required for the modern research-man. May be I will try to write it this winter. These side-works do not really interfere with, but prepare the completion of "Man". By these new shorter studies, I prepare the ground and the ideas of the book. In fact, they are sketches (des esquisses) of what I try to fix more definitely in the book. -*

*Just now, they are many friends in Paris. I see regularly Breuil and the Bégouëns, - just the same. Ida Treat has come rue Raynouard, for 3 weeks. She is very busy with her book, which is going to be an inside story of the Communisme in France between the war and 1930. The first 7 chapters are excellent, I was told; but, for her, to live amongst the "dead" is painful and depressing. She and I, we are very close spiritually; yet, her "mystic" is much more a "mystique de sympathie et pitié" than a "mystique de construction". I have never met anybody so able to résonner à la souffrance des autres: she positively feels in herself the pain of the world . . . For publication, she is helped and coached by a friend of yours, Mrs. Evans (Ernestine?), whom I could not yet meet. Simone likes Mrs. Evans extremely. - Met the Hoppenot's: they have a wonderful appartment near Notre-Dame, at the western end of "l'Ile", full of Peking's souvenirs.*

*And I just receive your letter of December 11 (Chicago) exactly for Xmas! Is that not marvelous and sweet. - I am deeply interested by your impressions of Washington. The need of a change in the heart of politics, an <u>ideal</u> for Democracy: you are absolutely <u>right</u>. I am just having a series of talks on this subject with a group of young influential men in Paris. So far Catholicism and its anti-progressism are concerned. well, we are changing that in France. If we succeed, something new will come in the world. This is the very fight of my life. — Art and Idea: I have met the problem already three times since I am in Paris. This is a great question: we shall discuss it, because I need an answer.*

*Tomorrow I go to Auvergne: a few days with my "holy" brother. — Weather is pretty cold — but there is plenty of wood to burn in the country. —*

*A happy new year, —— <u>dearest</u>*

*P.T.*

*Mrs. Hempel had to undergo an operation in the German Hospital (abdominal tumour?) Hope that there is nothing serious in the case. -*

*45 rue Monsieur*
*Jan. 10, 1939*

*Dearest,*

*I have received three days ago your sweet Xmas letter. So, we were just writing to each other at the same time. No wonder. Are our two lives not "synchronised" since a long time? And are we not, in a true sense living the same life? I enjoy this feeling that, each of us in his own environment, we are developing the same effort, and consequently becoming nearer and nearer by the whole and the deepest of our experiences. To become one by the whole world. Is that not the true expression of love and God?*

*Since my last letter, I have spent a week in Auvergne, and some ten days again in Paris. My staying in Auvergne was very pleasant and restful. The country was somewhat bleak and white with snow, - and the old family house bitterly cold. But it was so pleasant to spend the day at the corner of a country fire, looking at burning logs of which my brother could say: "This piece of wood comes from such or such tree you know, at such place of the estate"; or to walk "en sabots" along the frozen river, - or to listen at some distant radio. Three of my young nephews or nieces were there, for the holidays, making the house very gay; and I* *enjoyed as usually chatting with my holy brother and his witted* wife. She is very busy grouping the country girls in one of those new christian associations which swarm presently in France; and she gets surprising results in the line of restoring in these peasant people the pride of the earth and a positive spirit of conquest. An amazing metamorphose! Something like the changes observed by Snow[†] in Western China. — Life was simple and comfortable. Even my brother used to come in my room every morning to light the fire before I got up. Is not that sweet? —*

*And now I am once more in the deep of my parisian life. Meetings and meetings. I had seldom to talk so much about my ideas in the course of my existence. A proof of it is that I have been interrupted here, and had to spend almost five hours in discussions with five more or less influential people. You can easily understand that, in the course of such meetings, I get just so much as I give — because I have to go continuously further in the process of deepening and clarifying my views. One becomes so better aware of the importance of such or such point or topic when it happens to recur, just the same, in a whole series of intellectual contacts. — So, <u>don't be</u> anxious or impatient concerning my work. As I told you so many times, as long as things are progressing, no use to force them ahead: there is a natural rhythm everywhere in nature. Besides, I have several positive evidences that Rome becomes more favourable towards me, and that I am going through. Just like a shy horse: you must not bewilder it. I have got full allowance to make the Nancy lecture at the end of january, and the text, rather suggestive, will be published in the "Etudes" ("La mystique de la Science"). Besides, I plan to write another Essay during the next weeks ("La grande option", meaning a new universalistic attitude born in Man). Of course, such things delay the writing of "Man" — but prepare it directly. —*

*Coming to external news: 1) I expect Trassaert in a fortnight; he comes here via Rome; apparently poor Licent is not agreed by Shanghai, so that he is excluded from China altogether: I do <u>not</u> approve the decision, which seems to me unfair and inhuman. I shall be delighted of course to see Trassaert. 2) Mrs. Hempel was very weak after her operation (three "tumeurs"! . . .), but the conditions were sufficiently hopeful by the middle of December. 3) Nirgidma wrote me a nice letter: she is married, and expects a baby. Address: 10/1273, avenue Joffre. Shanghaï. - 4) I see often the Bégouën's. Ida Treat is there, with them, so full of life and so practically idealistic!. I met twice "Ernestine", who has become an "habituée" of rue Raynouard. She is a grand person. 5) Camille is in Paris for two months more, — and more and more a daughter of my brother Joseph; she discovers, each time I see her, a more wonderful hat. Very difficult to marry! 6) By lack of time, I did not join so far the Raphaël's nor the Walen's. Maybe they are not in Paris, just now.*

---

* Teilhard's "English" for witty.
[†] Edgar Snow, an American journalist who wrote, *Red Star Over China*, the seminal account of Mao.

*I must stop here, because today is again a busy day. — Such a pleasure and a comfort to have had this talk with you. — God bless you, dearest*

*Your*

*P.T.*

---

After almost three years without an entry, Lucile wrote briefly about their friendship.

---

[Journal] *Jan 14 - 1939 - Chicago*

*And I've just gone through horrid days of <u>doubt</u> again - Shall I never get rid of this thing - must I always be so earthly and feminine? Thank goodness it is better now - but it seems so long before we will be together again - you left New York Oct 28 - and what a talk we had the night before you left - So terrible to me in some ways and yet so marvelously sweet - it is often a misunderstanding of words - but it is more than that too - It seems sometimes that I have to accept so <u>many</u> things - But you are such a wonderful such an unusual person that our friendship is worth anything - It is my fault for being too - well feminine! I love you so much - but I must love you more - then all will be well —*

---

No copies remain of Lucile's two Chicago letters that are mentioned in the following letter from Teilhard. It appears that she reopened one of their "pet discussions" — the physical aspect of their friendship.

---

*45 rue Monsieur*
*Paris, VII, February 1, 1939*

*Dearest,*

*I answer here your two letters from Chicago, 3 and 15 Jan. I answer you a little late; but I have been specially busy, these two last weeks; so many people use to come, now, even during the morning, in my room. Well, I liked very much your letters — even that one which you did not like yourself — because it was so frank and so true. You know it, Lucile. I am fully aware of your difficulties inside, —— and sometimes anxious about my own responsibilities. The root of the whole thing, we have discussed it often. I do not belong to myself, —— and consequently I cannot give me entirely and exclusively to anybody. In some way, any love in my life must keep and make me (as well as those who love me), not only more alive, but free and freer, in an ever growing intimacy. Such things seem rather contradictory. Yet, I still believe (and specially from our own experience) that they are possible in a sufficiently rich and high atmosphere. So that my conclusion would remain the same: let us go on, trying and building, more than analysing and criticizing. Things are true when they are working. Whatever may happen in the material part of our existence, something is born between us, which is stronger than any external conditions. Joy and union are in a continuous common discovery. Is that not true, dearest?*

*I am glad, and deeply, because your exhibitions have been successful. But I understand so well that you feel the need for some rest and solitary work. I hope that you have already found both of them. — Here, my life is essentially the same.*

*I meet more and more people, mostly interesting; and I believe to see more and more clearly in my own mind: it would be impossible, of course, to have so many contacts without receiving a lot, and without understanding better the deep meaning and the deep internal connections of the truth which one tries to make understandable and attractive. - Last week, I went to Nancy [in northeast France], for three lectures (one on Geology, the two others on "ideas"). One of them ("La Mystique de la Science") will probably be printed this month in Les Etudes: rather well written, and with a few interesting ideas in it. Just now, I am writing another short Essay on some fundamental attitudes of Man towards Life. And maybe I will try also an article on the Racial questions (I have been asked for, by my colleagues here).*

*Two days ago, I was very happy to meet Trassaert — who has left already for a short time, but will soon be back. He came by Rome, where he had long talks with the higher superiors of my Order; and apparently he has succeeded in changing a lot their views concerning many things in China, - and specially concerning myself. It would seem that, provided I can avoid some external or premature manifestations, I will be at some extent approved, and even positively backed. The wish of Rome is that I would succeed in giving some general exposition of my views in a way which could be accepted and recognised more or less officially. — Maybe. - Otherwise, not many news from China. Yet, I was delighted to receive a good letter from Mrs. Hempel, back in the Lab. She confesses that the Doctors were afraid before the operation. She urged to be operated. And now she seems to be O.K. Probably she will have to be careful, and not to work too much for some time. But to know that she is still there as before is a great relief. —*

*As usually, I have seen several times the Bégouëns. Ernestine has become a regular pillar of the house. — We talk often of you.*

*This month, I have several lectures to give (on Choukoutien and on my trips). At the end of the month, I must go to Toulouse (several talks and lectures). —— Concerning the further future, I still plan to be in New-York at the end of June, — leaving the West-Coast (Vancouver?) between July 20 and 30. But I cannot be absolutely sure. My return-ticket is by the Canadian-Pacific: I don't know whether I could change for the Dollar Line?*

*Good bye, dearest. —— God bless you!*

*Your*

*P.T.*

*Paris, Febr. 13, 1939*

*Dearest,*
*I forgot to inscribe on my note-book the date of my last letter 6, so that I am not sure not to repeat a few things in the present one. Anyhow, I have received a few days ago your sweet message of Jan. 24. I am so happy to feel that you are active, interested in your art, and sufficiently busy. It is such a grand thing to be alive by both of us!*

*Personally, I go on approximately along the same path. Not much time left to scientific work. But I do not care much about it. After all, these months were to be devoted mostly to personal contracts and thought; and both are developing in a satisfactory way. The trouble (?) is only that, so far as external activity is concerned, I do not find any clear <u>object</u> on which any positive constructive work might materialize. I just succeed (more or less) in creating, or at least in developing, a spiritual climate or <u>atmosphere</u>. But, after all, maybe this, is the best and very thing I can do. - Did I tell you that I went to Nancy at the end of January? Three lectures, one on the geology of China, one on "La Mystique de la Science" (<u>to be published</u> very soon in our Review, here), and a third one delivered, most unexpectedly, before a large audience of young priests (on "the place of Man in Nature"). I left too soon for having any idea of the reaction amongst these young men. — Next week (between Feb. 22 and 28) I must go to Toulouse for another series of lectures. — And, in the meantimes, I will have given four more lectures or semi-private talks here, two of them to various groups of students (Sorbonne, and Ecole Normale Supérieure). The best results of these talks is perhaps for myself, since they oblige and help me to go deeper in the organisation of my "gospel". — I feel inclined to write on those new ideas immediately, - so that the writing on "Man" is somewhat postponed. But, at the same time, everything I do is precisely a preparation to give, in "Man", a better synthesis of what I believe. -*

*Finally (did I tell you?) Trassaert has arrived, and I was very happy to see him. Presently, he is away from Paris. But he will stay here — up to the summer — instead of Strasbourg; so that we shall be together several months. He came via Rome, where he had long and friendly talks with the highest superiors — the conclusion being apparently that I am in a much better position, and in a higher consideration there. — When I began to be friend with Trassaert in Tientsin, some 6 years ago, I never suspected that he could help me this way.*

*Three days ago, I have received a short letter from Malvina Hoffman, answering a few papers I had sent her. She sounded courageous as usually, but deeply affected by the fact that young Miss Branch, whom she tried to save, had finally fallen back down (dope?), and deserted her. Maybe she will rescue her another time. Terribly pathetic to see how so many of the finest men and women waste their life in a wild quest for more life ——*

*In my last letter I told you the best I can foresee for the date of my departure (end of June from Paris, end of July from Vancouver, unless I can commutate my ticket for San Francisco). At some extent <u>I can adjust me</u> to your plans. — If you cannot come to Paris, do not worry. My plans for Northern Italy keep uncertain (political tension). But, in any case, April will be for me a busy period; and Max (and perhaps Simone) will probably be in Morocco. (I think they still think going to America). - So, we shall not loose much, probably, - if you decide not to come.*

*Last week, I had a lunch at Passy, with [Charles] Lindbergh and his wife, in the perfectly pretty house of Mr. and Mrs. Miller (friends of Dr. Carrel). I discovered that the Miller's are great friends of your friend the painter (Johnson?), the one who brought you in Touraine when you passed here the last time. Is it not funny to meet each other in this way! Lin-yu-Tang (is that the correct name? — I mean the writer of "My country and my people") is living in the same street as the Millers, and they know him very well.*

*You will enjoy the two enclosed pictures taken at the Bégouën's, on Xmas day: Ernestine, Ida Treat, Simone, Max. — We were talking of you.*

*Deeply yours*

*P.T.*

*Received last week a letter from Mrs. Hempel, vivacious and teasing as before. She has returned her work at the P.U.M.C. Weidenreich goes to the States in May, for a year, in order to get an american citizenship. —*

*Paris, March 6, 1939*

*Dearest,*

*I found here your letter of Feb. 9 on my return from a small journey to Toulouse — the gay pink-bricks-built, southern city. It made me a little miserable to think that you had flu — and I understand so well that you should have felt a bit depressed. In such and other similar circumstances, nothing much to do, but to wait patiently and optimistically for the next rays of sun. I think that you are now back in busy New-York — such a pleasant town in my memory! —*

*I hope you have well received my last letters. My plans, for which you ask, keep substantially the same. But I feel so difficult to fix them in a definite way. A few days ago, I received a letter from Ralph Chaney urging me to be present at a scientific meeting, end of July, at San Francisco. That would delay my departure from Vancouver or San Francisco up to the middle of August. I really do not see and know where is the best for me and for us. Anyhow, I plan firmly to be in New-York the very first days of July. I am afraid these perpetual changes in my schemes will be a trouble for you. Maybe the best would be that you take your own decision; and I will try to adjust me to you as much as I can. — For the spring too, I go on without being able to build my plans much ahead. The possibility of a trip to Italy seems to decrease, now — partly on account of the french-italian feelings — partly because young baron Blanc is apparently less free to direct me on the field. — Unless Miss Garrod suggests another date, I intend to go to Cambridge-London between next 20-30 of march. — Rose wrote me a very kind letter a week ago (she is still living at the same address). I would surely see her.*

*In the meantimes, I am so busy in Paris that I do not feel specially anxious to go abroad. I gave a lot of lectures, since three weeks — two in Paris, and four in Toulouse, mostly on scientific subjects, but also on more philosohical things; — and this week I have still to address the students of the "Ecole Normale Supérieure" — first the men, and then the girls. — My article on "La Mystique de la Science" will be published on March 20; — and I am in the actual preparation of another article on Races, which interests me deeply. — Another short paper is finished (not yet typed): interesting, but perhaps not sufficiently focussed. Maybe*

*I will try to publish it somewhere (no intrinsical difficulties — but I do not see where to publish). On the whole, I believe to progress in my views — and to smooth appreciably the way for the book on Man, - which I am more and more decided (and asked) to finish, in a year if I can. - As far as Rome is concerned, I have (and many others of my friends have too) the strong feeling that sympathy towards my work is really improving. — Let us go ahead, Lucile. I feel so much stronger, and everything is so much sweeter for me, because your influence is on me.*

*Yesterday, I went to see the Bégouën's. Max is in West-Africa, since a few days. Simone was just finishing a very cute chinese dress with your pink silk, which proved large enough to provide the material for a complete "robe", and a chinese "veste" to be used with blue trousers! — We paid a visit to Ernestine who had a bad cough for two weeks, but looks much better now. — Jacques should be here — but I could not spot him so far. The same with the Raphaël's. — Such is the life in big Paris. — Everything is so much more easy and cosy in old Peking.*

*Trassaert is here, already working hard, and distinctly happy. — News from N. China prove that Japanese feel more and more uncomfortable in the midst of the Chinese hornet, and begin to grow nervous, with some unpleasant reactions on foreign institutions. Everything is quiet in the P.U.M.C. Mrs. Hempel is busy as before her operation; and Dr.Weidenreich plans to spend the next year in New York (for an american citizenship). Von Koenigswald is in Peking. He brought his Pithecanthropus material, including a fine upper-jaw, discovered two days before he left Java. Very exciting.*

*Good bye, dearest. — Be happy, and God may give you the inside view and feeling of the birth of a Loving World!*

*Your*

*P.T.*

*Paris, March 19, 1939*

*Dearest,*

*I have well received your long and precious letter of Febr. 26 — from the Gorham Hotel. And it is so sweet to think of you in the familiar New York sur-roundings. I hope that you will find some ways to develop there your thoughts and activity — with many friends, and perhaps along some definite lines of work. — To converge towards each other by the deepest of the life: I do not know any warmer feeling than that.*

*Here, my own life is rather the same, interesting, and rather busy. More contacts with different people, each week. I still keep the same routines: at home, and mostly writing in the morning; doing some scientific work afternoon. — Writing is going on regularly. My article on "La Mystique de la Science" will be out tomorrow (I will send you a separate). Another one (on some fundamental attitudes of Man) is finished, but perhaps a bit complicated; I am not decided to use it — unless Simone makes a special edition for it. And now I have started an Essay on Races, to be published here. I am rather interested by the subject, which leads me to unexpected and new conclusions. A very useful preliminary sketch for* a chapter of "Man", in any case. — In the line of Sciences, I am busy with an old material from Abyssinia, collected by Breuil and myself years ago, and still waiting for publication. The subject is not exactly exciting. But it has to be worked out; and if I do not take it in my hands, nobody will do it.

Besides, I had many semi-public talks, since the beginning of the month, - one specially which will amuse you: to some sixty "artists" (sculptors, painters, writers, musicians) forming a new section in the group for the study and improvement of Man organised by the french ingénieur Coutrot (in association with Aldous Huxley!). I had to address this selected crowd at the end of a lunch, and my subject was: "how to understand and use Art in the line of Human Energy". I expressed the idea that Art was the expression of the "exubérance" of human energy — so that its function was to give a kind of consistency, an intuitive and almost instinctive shape, and a _personal_ character to this ever growing supply and excess of spiritual forces gradually freed from material ties: just like science and philosophy, but in a much more spontaneous and personalistic way. — People seem to have been satisfied.

Besides, I have met several friends, including the Raphaël's, a week ago. They look perfectly happy in Paris, he witty, and she pretty, as ever. She has dropped (relatively speaking) shop and theater, to become a student of l'Ecole du Louvre, where she enjoys the mystery of pre-Corean [Korean] tombs and such things. Facing this new hobby of her, he keeps sceptical and obviously proud. — Jacques is on his way back to France. — I understood that Quintini is in Paris, and Mrs. Walen in South Africa. I did not see either of them — and I feel a little ashamed. -

And this is practically all. Max is in Guinea, somewhat tired, it seems. Too much to do in a short time. — Ida was supposed to go through Paris with "André" — but she was delayed in Marseille with a slight flu. Next thursday I go to Cambridge and London, for a week, to see Miss Garrod, Patterson, and others. I will meet Rose [Jameson] in London; in april, she will have to enter hospital for appendicites: a nuisance! — My plan seems to be definitely to leave Le Havre to New York on June 23. (_Champlain_). — Impossible practically to move earlier. — Two days ago, I got a letter from de Terra: he had just arrived Genoa, rather depressed morally and physically (intestinal trouble and nervous breakdown); he has left Boston to search rest and medical care in Italy, near Tyrol; the only good news is that he has got support from the Carnegie Foundation to publish the Burma memoir. —

Well, you know the critical position of Europe. "Anti-münichois" are satisfied, — since Hitler proves impossible to be trusted. I still hope blindly that there will be no war. But everybody is anxious. France will _never_ give a bit of Tunis to Italy: this is the only sure thing. — Under such political conditions, my trip to Italy seems to be impossible.

Good bye. I have a heap of letters to answer on my table; and yours, of course, went first.

Ever yours

P T.

132    *Dearest,*

*I am awfully late in writing you this time, both because I have been merged in the writing of a paper, these days, and because of my trip to England. And yet I have well received your two letters from New-York (March 10 and 23), the first of which reached me in London. You were so full of feelings and ideas, Lucile. That made me so happy!*

*My stay in England was simple and satisfactory. When I reached London, Président Lebrun was still there. But I took the underground straight to Liverpool str. sta., and went directly to Cambridge, where Dorothy Garrod was waiting for me on the platform. She is living with her mother in a highly english cottage, attended by a highly british maid, and protected by a most amusing little fox-like welsh sheep-dog. And we decided that we could live altogether in perfect association. Weather was rather bad, even snowy — a pity, because the grass was green, spread with crocus and daffodils, and the almond-trees in full bloom. I saw Patterson (the one who was in India with de Terra and myself) and his new norwegian wife — and also Burkitt [Miles C.], the high-bred prehistorian who is presently living in the most charming house of a village, 2 miles outside of Cambridge: we had not seen each other since 27 years(!) in Spain, but the reconnaissance was easy and cheerful. Dr. Lindgreen was in Lapland. — Dorothy, the Patterson's and myself spent an interesting day motoring to the gravel-pits north-east of the town. And, the last evening I was a guest of the Trinity College usual dinner, - not so different from those in my own houses — with the "master" at the head of the table, everybody in gown — and the large, dignified, Elizabethan room. — In London, I settled in the extremely fashionable house of my Order, Farmstreet, near Hyde Park — a very convenient location to reach the South Kensington Museum (Natural History). I enjoyed really meeting the people there, and I saw a lot of interesting things. But everybody was more or less wasting time in "anti-air raids preparations". I spent the most part of a day in a pleasant visit to Rose, who has found a nice little flat, some 45 minutes from the center of town. I found her a little the reverse of reduced, but otherwise just the same. You know that she has had rhumatisms, and will have this month her appendix removed. She is very courageous, and on the whole she looks happy (largely because Michael has developed in a tall strong, laborious and affectionate boy). But she is terribly short of money, because she is not allowed by the law to teach regularly, and because Jim does not earn much this year. She had received recently a long letter of Mr. Bennett, which sounded rather unpleasant, as far as the condition of un-protected foreigners (e.g. Russians) is concerned in China.*

*And now I am back since a week in Paris. My article (Mystique de la Science) of march seems to have been appreciated. (I will send you a separate). And now I am writing the last paragraphs of an Essai sur les Races, where I believe to tell a few rather new things. This Essay should be published. The precedent one*

*("La grande Option"), written in January and February, is perhaps less focussed, and not so easy to be printed, because of the lack of a convenient Revue. — When the paper on the Races is finished, I will probably turn back to Man. But then my time in France will approach its end. — I have made a reservation on the Champlain (leaving Le Havre on June 23). <u>Any boat</u> leaving the West Coast after August 1 would suit me. Make your choice, and let me know. —*

*As usually, I keep seeing many people here. And I enjoy greatly to discover that Trassaert is quietly following my track. Two days ago, he was asked by a friend of him to speak to some 30 working-girls (the acting representatives of a huge association, the J.O.C.F., Jeunes ouvrières catholiques, born in France some 10 years ago). He talked about spiritual evolution in the world, and the girls were tremendously enthusiastic. Now you must remember that the JOCF includes some hundred thousands members in France only (they are spreading in 22 nations) and that they spread in an astounding way — exclusively by mutual love and devotion. The way these girls approach and win the other ones by genuine, intelligent\* and indefatigable help and friendship is simply amazing. The same is true with the young men together. I am convinced that we are unconsciously witnessing one of the most startling human movements in history, — with <u>no trace</u> of hardness nor hatred whatsoever in its progression. Simply love, — but love based on the faith that the World "is converging into <u>somebody</u>" also loving and definite. And this is the point where my poor intellectual efforts come in: because, to these working boys and girls (as well as for the other classes of people), my "views" supply a perspective where the past, the present and the future meet in an atmosphere of material progress and progressing love. Once more, maybe, a new life is expanding from the mass, below. — Anyhow, I was just a bit surprised, and so happy to discover that Trassaert, whom I knew mostly by collaborating on dry bones, was just another myself on the deeper ground!*

*Besides, I have seen, this week, Ida Treat, and the Raphaëls. — I.T. is just finishing with André the book (on the Far East) to be printed in New-York by the Pearl-Buck's new husband. Several chapters have been published in "Asia" latterly under the name of Marc Aven. — Her own autobiographical book should be ready by the fall. — From the Franco-chinese bank I heard a rather amusing (or pathetic) news. Because they do not have sufficient gaz for their trucks along the Burma-Yunnan road, the Chinese have ordered a thousand kilometers of narrow-gauge rail: and the transportation will be made by small wagons pushed by thousands and thousands of coolies. It is so courageous — and <u>so</u> chinese! — In the meantimes, Japanese get nervous. Peking is quiet — but Tientsin not so. A month ago, some 3,000 "ash boxes" (Japanese soldiers) were passing weekly from N. China to Japan. In addition, suicides seem to be positively more and more common in the japanese army. — Two days ago, I have paid a visit to Mr. Gunn, at the Rockefeller Foundation here. I tried once more to get the fellowship in America for Eddy Bien; but the thing is not easy, being given the present policy of the Foundation (to help organisation of China <u>in</u> China). Dr. Grant is now in Yunnan and Szechwan; — but is already appointed to Calcutta, for an important work.*

*Good bye, dearest — Day after tomorrow is Easter. May you feel happy! — My deepest thought and affection will be, as usually, with you.*

*Your*

*P.T.*

*In fact, although sticking jealously to their "classe", they develop personalities much above the supposed level of this classe.* [Footnote written by Teilhard. EDITORS]
*(This is the first time I use this new letter-paper!) — Max is still in Africa. Simone with her mother in Normandie, and she has the flu.*

> *Laboratoire de Géologie Appliquée*
> *aux Origines de l'Homme*
> *Paris, April 26, 1939*

*Dearest,*

*I am so sorry to be late in answering your sweet letter of April 6! But I have been somewhat drowned in my life, here, since Easter: papers to finish, people talk with, etc. Anyhow, the first thing I wish to tell you is that I have booked this morning on the Empress of Japan (aug.5). I hope that the schedule of the French Line will not be too much disturbed by the disparition of the s.s. Paris, so that the "Champlain" will sail at the right time to New York. — So, everything is settled for my departure. unless we should have an European war. But this last eventuality seems to be less and less probable. The Roosevelt's speech has apparently more impressed (nobody can stop radio diffusion) german and Italian masses than the dictators would have liked or expected. I am convinced that every month of protraction of peace is a won time; not only because England and France have time to prepare — but chiefly because the spirit of peoples is changing in the meantime. — Let us be optimist.*

*Since my return from England, I did not move from Paris. Weather was glorious, at Easter time — but now we have a grey and rather cold sky. Yet, Paris is magnificent, in his chestnut-trees glory. Everything green; and so beautiful flowers between Le Louvre and les Champs-Elysées. — As I told you, I have been busy. First, I have finished my article on Races, which seems to be accepted by Les Etudes — and even rather enthusiastically. In fact, the thing is rather clever. — Now I have started a short study on Education (observed from a biological point of view), to be printed as a Conclusion of a book prepared by a colleague of mine. To have got more precise ideas on both Races and Education will help me a lot in the question of Man. — So, I do not wander so much as you could suppose. On the other hand, it is more than useful for me to write "printable" things just now. Everything is approximately settled, and OK, with my order; but I had something like a narrow escape. I will explain it to you orally, in a few weeks. The trouble of course was a misunderstanding between me and Rome. Here, my colleagues are awfully nice, and devoted to me and my cause. So, do not worry.*

*A more serious trouble, last week, was with Simone, who got seriously ill, when she was in her family home, in Normandie. She got a broncho-pneumonia, "staphylocoques" (a nasty germ, this year, they say, all over the world) —*

*and we were seriously anxious. At the same time she lost her father (for the same cause?), and also an aunt. Now she is safe, but not yet back in Paris. Max was in Guinée! — He flew back. — Ida Treat kept the Rue Raynouard home, and was in charge of the young American girls, in the meantimes. A rather bad period, as you see.*

*From Peking, Pei has just written me that the Japanese (this little snake of Akabori, I suppose) are doing some work at CKT [Chou Kou Tien]. The P.U.M.C. tries to stop the thing. But will they succeed? We just wait for subsequent developments. I have written to Wong, asking for personal direction, in case the Japanese would interfere more seriously. One reason more for which I should like to be already back in China. But I cannot leave earlier than June, — unless something very serious should happen.*

*Nothing much to tell you about the political situation. People talk and talk. But nobody is able to do more than express personal wishes or impressions. The common feeling, as I told you above, is that, in any case, war is not absolutely imminent. But we spend a terrific lot of money in military preparations of all kinds: the situation can not last more than a few months.*

*Good bye, dearest. It seems so sweet to think of you. I am glad that you can work a little, and that your mind is active — and your heart deep and —— wise. ——*

*Your*

*P.T.*

*Les meilleurs et plus affectueux souvenirs d'Ida Treat!*

*Paris, May 10th, 1939*

*Dearest,*

*Your precious letter from Southborough was still unanswered when I received the not less precious one from Milton. Don't scold me too much for being so slow. My time is pretty full up — so much so that I wonder whether I could do any scientific work more, should I stay in Paris. So many people to talk at, to answer, to help! On the whole, a most interesting period, during which I have continually to test and to improve my "Gospel". But that will be a good thing for me too to escape for a while, in America et in China — in order to assimilate the mass of these experiences. — As I told you in my last letter, I have booked on the Champlain (Le Havre, June 24) and the Empress of Japan (Aug.5). I plan to spend the end of July in San Francisco, where they have a Pacific Congress [of geologists]. - In some way, I wish I should have already left St.Lazare station. The last weeks in Paris, with so many people clinging to you, are sometimes a real trial — chiefly this time when I stayed longer. Well, God will help me, — and you are waiting for me.*

*On the whole, everything is all right with me. My paper on Races has been accepted, rather enthusiastically, by the Etudes, and will possibly come out at the end of the month. Of course, Les Etudes are not an exceptionally glorious place where to be printed. But they have many readers. And to be accepted there*

*for a second time will surely do a lot for my good reputation. — I have just fin-*
*ished also another short paper on the "biological" meaning of education, to be*
*printed as a conclusion of a book edited by a colleague of mine — which will*
*work along the same line. Both these Essays are perfectly sincere, rather clever;*
*and they will help me a lot for the redaction of* Man. *So many things grow clearer*
*in my mind.*

*These last days, I met a good number of Chinese or ex-Chinese friends: the*
*Raphaëls. Lagarde (now an important man, just as Hoppenot, at the Foreign*
*Affairs), Jacques — and even the Velloso's, by mere chance, in an Hotel (they were*
*on their way to the Rome embassy). The Raphaëls expect to be sent back to*
*Peking in a few weeks, and do not like it, since they feel thoroughly happy in*
*Paris. Jacques is already lost amongst his friends and lady-friends. He brought*
*with him his number-one boy, who has immediately discovered the Hoppenot's*
*boy, and the de Martel's boy — all pekinese. Going to the Jacques flat, a few days*
*ago, it was such a fun to be greeted by the same Chinese smile, the same proposal*
*for a drink, and the same Anna-May Wong's pictures. — Ella Maillart went*
*through Paris a few days ago. She plans to go back to Afghanistan — motoring*
*there with a Swiss lady. —*

*Finally, Simone is back Rue Raynouard, — not very strong yet, — but so*
*sweet and gay. She complains not to feel the need of working, - which of course is*
*a sure indication that she is not yet just like herself. I still feel a little anxious for*
*her health. — And Max is unfortunately obliged to go, this very week, to*
*Morocco, — only a fortnight after arriving from Guinea. The Morocco visit was*
*cut on account of the illness of Simone. —Ernestine has become a regular friend*
*and visitor of the house. — Ida Treat has left a few days ago, to Britanny, with*
*André. — Did you hear that Nirgidma had a dead-child, and was very sick!..*
*Jacques told me that she has recovered. But how sad! You ought to write her. I*
*don't know how to do it myself, since I know nothing about her reactions.*

*Good bye, dearest. — Only two or three letters more!*

*God bless you*

*P.T.*

*Paris, May 28th, 1939*

*Dearest,*

*Your last letter (May 7) came here short after I sent you my Number 12.*
*And I am sorry not to have answered it earlier. But I have been more busy than*
*ever. And now the day of my sailing is approaching so fast that I begin to feel as*
*if I could never finish what I have still to do. In fact, I hate these last weeks*
*before a departure: I could not stay here for full eight months without getting a*
*lot of people accustomed to have me, and without getting myself accustomed to*
*them and to the places. This periodical breaking of my life is possibly useful.*
*Still, it is a little hard. Fortunately, you are waiting for me in sunny California,*
*dearest! Most probably my cousine Marguerite (I told you often about her) will*
*come with me as far as New-York: she needs to see America and Washington,*

before writing a book on Lincoln (an aunt of her, formerly Miss Lamon, is the granddaughter of the secretary and friend of Lincoln). If the plan materializes, crossing Atlantic will be a pleasure-trip! — I have sent to Chaney (California University) an abstract for two "communications" at the Pacific Congress of San Francisco. Most probably, I will not stay very long in New-York, — but move to San Francisco as early as possible, — on about July 20 probably.

Here, I have practically stopped lectures and writing, — and I try only to finish a short scientific paper before my departure. My article on Races (a rather long one) will come out on June 20: I have already corrected the proofs. And the paper on Education is accepted too. These last days, I have come back a little to the manuscript of Man. My ideas have decidedly improved, during the last months, I think. We shall talk them over, on the Pacific! A week ago, I understood, from a letter of my french Superior, that Rome has very much relaxed, so far I am concerned. They wish positively, down there, to see me writing more and more "possible" papers. A good omen for Man! Anyhow, I will try to make a good use of this favourable mood.

Just now, during the feasts (Pentecôte), Paris is almost empty. Max is in Morocco — and Simone in Bréhat Island (Brittany), with Ida Treat. She was better when she left, but not yet very strong. — I will probably myself spend a few days with my holy brother in Auvergne, next week. — After a very cold month, we have now a fine spring; and Paris is so green and wonderful. They keep digging shelters (against air-raids) everywhere. But nobody seems to care any more of the war. And yet the danger is still there; and the whole life is more or less paralysed by this constant threat. Something has to be done for reorganizing internationally economic life!

Did you hear of the election of Dorothy Garrod as a professor in Cambridge? She is amazed herself by this unexpected success. Being the first woman in this situation, a whole code of étiquette has to be elaborated in the University, on account of her! — Hellmut de Terra is in München, in good physical conditions again. I do not think he will come back to America.

Good bye, dearest. My next letter will be the last written in France.

Yours

P.T.

S.S. Champlain, June 29, '39

Dearest,
We are due tomorrow in New-York, and I wish to let you know immediately that I am really back to the states. Finally, I did not write you a "last" letter from France. My time has been crowded, the last days. And chiefly, I got a kind of cold or flu, two weeks ago; and I was wondering whether I should not have to postpone my departure. So I did not feel like sending you a letter at that time. But now, everything is practically over; and I am glad not to have altered my plans. — I expect to find a letter of you at the Museum! — So far I know, I will stay in New-York ten days or a fortnight (at the most) — and then proceed to

*San Francisco (Berkeley), where I plan to arrive on about July 20. — But I will write you something more precise from New-York.*

*Since Le Havre, the journey is quiet, but the weather grey and rainy. I am travelling with my cousine Marguerite (I told you about her), who plans to spend a few weeks in Philadelphia, Washington, and other places, in order to get a personal impression on the country of Lincoln (an aunt of her was formerly Miss Lamon, daughter of the friend of Lincoln; she will write a book on Lincoln for the french public). In addition, I had the great joy, in Southampton, to meet my friend and colleague, Pierre Charles (from Louvain), en route to New-York, too. Charles is one of the men I like the most, inside of my order: extraordinarily intelligent and witty. And, for years, I had not seen him.*

*Besides, the boat is half-empty (not the same, when she comes back), and very comfortable. — I had a lunch, two days ago, with some friends in first class, and Stokowski, the great musician was one of the guests.*

*The whole situation in N. China is a puzzle. Well, the best, I think, is to go and see.*

*A <u>bientôt</u>, dearest.*

*Yours*

*P.T.*

*N.Y., July 15, 39*

*Dearest,*

*I have well received your last letter from Chicago. - These few lines to tell you that I am arriving in <u>Berkeley</u> on July 23, by the train reaching San Francisco at 8.25 <u>a.m.</u> - I have no answer from Dr. Chaney; so that I have no idea so far where I will stay. - But that does not matter. -*

*A très bientôt!*

*Yours*

*P.T.*

*Everything O.K. here.*

---

Teilhard spent almost three weeks in July working at the American Museum in New York. Then he visited Henry Field in Chicago, before hurrying on to a geological convention at the University of California — Berkeley. In the San Francisco area he gave two talks. Then he went on to Vancouver to meet Lucile where they boarded the *SS Empress*, sailing from Vancouver on August 5, 1939. They arrived in China in September, just as Europe was becoming engulfed in the Second World War.

Once back at the Jesuit house in Peking, Teilhard settled into thinking and writing. He also resumed his regular visits to Lucile's house where they discussed what he was writing — *The Phenomenon of Man*. They reviewed it together, and she retyped the pages he had reworked.

Sometime in October she wrote a long letter to him. She did not send the letter; the unsigned original was among her papers. Her own later note (early in 1940?) on the last page records only "Written some weeks ago — in October 1939."

What happens to cause this deep feeling of depression and outbursts like yester-day? It is true that things have not changed, at least your attitude has not changed. It is just that I understand it better, perhaps not "understand" but at least I know more about it. And I *am* convinced that the root of the whole thing is that you really do live on a differ-ent, a higher, plane than do most of us - and I have always considered you as a regular man - superior, yes, but nevertheless with the same needs as other men. And now I don't believe that is true - I have thought that there was a certain aloofness or coldness about you which I would help by giving without reserve a deep warm love. But I wonder if you either want or understand it. You love, yes, but on a different plane. I have been able to get glimpses of that plane, so that I can understand you, but it is very difficult for me to maintain that level - and then is when the difficulty comes. You just don't experience jealousy or some of the other less admirable emotions and so cannot understand them. They are quite normal in the "average" person - but anyhow it is all mixed up because I can't keep up to your plane and I ask for things that you do not want to give because you really don't under-stand them - and then that causes an inequality that is ugly. And then these things happen and then I feel like hell -and what's it all about anyway.

And I THINK I now understand better your writings too. Mankind is so unhappy, so miserable, that most people are trying to find some way of changing this and of making it possible for man to live more happily on this earth — but you are really want-ing to establish a RELIGION — I mean the existence and the kind of God — and trying to prove that He does really exist - and you use modern scientific methods to prove what the old boys more or less took on Faith. That is why it is sometimes difficult to understand you, because I have been looking for something that is really only of secondary consider-ation. Yes, if Man believes in God and the Universality of Him, they will discover the means of making life more beautiful and full, etc. But Pierre, your God seems so cold, so far away. Am I all wrong in thinking that I could help you to feel Him more warmly by giving you a deep and constant human love? You are hampered at every turn by that Order - but surely it can't hamper what you FEEL! It is rather difficult - I honestly want so much to help you - and I know that you do need me too - but how? What can I do. And when I become so damned HUMAN (?) is it really very UGLY? It seems that I can go for just about so long and then the dikes burst. Am I making any progress? It seems to me that I really do understand the whole thing better — and the thing to keep in mind always is that you do operate on a higher plane — when I judge you, and US by ordinary stan-dards, they just don't make sense - NICE men don't do things like that — and so we always come back to the same thing and that's the answer — you are so superior that I can't always keep up with you.

But Pierre, I do appreciate you and I do believe that you have something really important to give man and if there is any way that I can help I really do want to do it - that I have even slight visions of your needs is something and I will try to keep those visions before me more and more. Because you mustn't get too far away. The people right here need you so much. You see I have probably idealized human love and thought that it could be the highest expression of love on this earth - but will you not get impatient, and help me to see and to understand what you see and feel? Which I know is much higher and better than anything that I can imagine. It is when I want some human, some warm response *from you and day after day it does not come - then that terrible feeling of aloneness and of losing you gets more than I can stand - and then I realize that I am not losing anything - because I never had it! And that doesn't help much either.*

*I suppose for the first time, I mean since our talk on the boat, I have really realized and accepted this. At least at times I have accepted it and then your behavior all seems so contradictory that I don't know what to think and then the explosion comes -and I will, I will try to remember that the mix-up is all because the plane is not the same. You are not wrong, and I am not wrong, but you are living on a higher plane and I must try to see that and feel it and be a PART of it. And you will help me I know.*

---

In the coming year Peking's foreign population diminished steadily. Families of government officials and businessmen left for home. The French who remained in the city met as frequently as possible to sustain themselves through the long anxious winter that would finally end with the despoliation of their far-away country. New arrivals were greeted eagerly for news more recent than that reported by six-week old magazines and papers. But except for the more and more conspicuous Japanese presence, life continued in much the same way. Both Teilhard and Lucile were in Peking from September 1939 to August 1941 — the two-year period when he was completing the "famous book." Lucile wrote briefly about the manuscript.

---

[Journal]

*"In my 'Line a Day' I note that it was June 18, 1940 that he first brought me the manuscript of L'Homme which was soon changed to Le Phénomène Humain. He was very happy about the book. It took me a long time to read it. So we discussed it a great deal, and we read aloud, especially the Gospel of St. John."*

---

Teilhard had finished *Le Phénomène* just as France was about to surrender. Friends tell of Teilhard the Frenchman weeping quietly and saying, "I don't understand". (German troops occupied Paris on June 14, Marshal Pétain sued for peace on June 17, France surrendered on June 22.) A month later Lucile received a brief letter from Teilhard. She had just written to him from the seashore resort where she was vacationing.

*Institut de Géo-Biologie*
*Rue Labrousse*
*Peking, July 17, 1940*

*Dearest,*

*I have well received yesterday afternoon, your precious letter of July 13 — and with much joy. A kind of compensation for the much missing 5 o.c! I am so glad that you have such a good time, with so many good friends. In fact, Peking is practically empty, these days.*

*Our large vans have finally reached Rue Labrousse the day after you left: three monstrous things, which may have been mistaken for elephants-cages. A few policemen were so scared that they tried to stop them. And Vargassov took a full set of pictures! So, I have plenty of work, rather amusing, to sort the speci-*

*mens in my cases. — Besides, I go on, typing my palaeontological memoir, and completing the granites of China. — Miss Barbier was more busy, these last days, so that the progress was slower. Yet, notebook 5 (the largest) is soon finished. I have improved a few things in my manuscript.*

*Besides, I went to Grabau last Sunday, as usually. On Monday, very amusing lunch at the Raphaël's, with Leroy. Jeanne Mollard was at her best, and Raphaël, teasing her, at his best too. — Do you know that the Peking's Hotel is now sold to the Japanese, — in very good conditions apparently. Possibly very little will be changed externally. I hope so for Vetch and Helen Burton! —*

*Half an hour ago I passed by your house to take the sketches for my book. The boys were quietly playing Majong — and the dogs were delirious when they saw me. Evidently they expected you next. The sitting-room was clean — but of course the couche not yet back.*

*I have received a letter from my cousin (end of may). She is decidedly better, — and nothing at the lungs. Such a relief. — But how are the french people living, just now? Nobody has received any letter so far, later than the armistice.*

*You are right when warning me not to accept to get "old". As you know, the year was not specially good physically for me; and probably also I lack a definite object of work or conquest ahead. Not so much a "right" as an incentive to live. — On this point, particularly, you can do a lot for me, and I need you — and I wish so much to do something in turn for you.*

*Already wednesday afternoon. The week is almost finished. And you come after the next one.*

*Yours, so much*

*P.T.*

*Tomorrow I have tea with Tilly*
*My best regards to J. Smythe*

---

As the international social circle grew smaller in Peking, the two friends were together more often — on excursions to the Hills with friends, in meetings with others interested in talking over philosophical ideas, and at the small cocktail and garden parties that continued as before, but now were also a way to maintain morale. They kept their established rhythm — tea at 5 o'clock, often preceded by walks. And, when the Institut de Géo-Biologie moved within a short distance of Lucile's house, Teilhard no longer had to hurry off shortly after six to be in the Jesuit quarters before the gates were closed.

On looking back, Lucile admitted that she stayed on in Peking long after she was warned to leave, because it was such a happy time for her, even though open hostilities with the Japanese seemed immanent. At last she decided that she must go back to the U.S.

# The Letters of the Long Separation: from 1941 to 1948

Lucile Swan's friends gathered on August 8, 1941, at the Peking railway station to bid her farewell sadly as she began the long trip back to the States. Many of the British and American nationals had already departed, leaving behind a coterie of mainly Europeans whose countries were either neutral or occupied by the Axis powers. Both Teilhard and Lucile expected to meet again soon, if he could get a U.S. visa.

In September, Teilhard's colleague and friend, Pierre Leroy, returned from Indo-China where he had been working. The two Jesuits lived together and worked together in Peking throughout the war years, mostly on fossils and information from Chou Kuo Tien. During this period, Teilhard also met regularly at the Wilhelms to discuss religions East and West. He also met with other friends to talk over ideas and current events.

*Peking, 8 août, 1941.*

*Lucile, dearest,*

*I scarcely can realize that you are leaving today. And I still less realize that tomorrow Peking will be for me without you. But I want you to know that, above any sense of loneliness, I will feel stronger, in all directions, than when we landed here two years ago. — These two precious years of constant presence and uninterrupted mutual confidence have certainly achieved and sealed our friendship. This friendship is now strong enough to face everything, and to grow through. — As I told you these last days, I think that our dominant disposition has to be a stubborn and loving "confiance" in the Future. New experience and new environment are a universal condition of progress. — Thanks to you, I see more definitely what I believe, and what I have to fight for. I am convinced that your going to America is just a providential and necessary step in the constructive convergency of our lives. Go ahead in full peace, joy and hope.*

*Herewith I enclose a copy of the only "pious" object left, since years, on my working table. Hope you will not think it too much "roman-catholic". For me this quite simple illustration is a vague representation of the universal "foyer" of attraction which we are aiming for. In this atmosphere we can always love each other more and better. ——*

*Ever yours (et au <u>revoir</u>)!*

*P.T.*

---

The "pious" object was a postcard-size picture of the Sacred Heart of Jesus that Teilhard had brought from his home in the Auvergne.

---

*Institut de Géo-Biologie / Rue Labrousse / Peking, August 11 1941*

*Lucile dear,*

*May these few lines reach Shanghai before you leave China, to bring you something of the deep of my heart! God bless you again and again for what you gave me since twelve years, and more specially during these last months! - And may we be together again — very soon. —*

*Here, I am still a little "ahuri" [bewildered] to be without you. Fortunately, I have been quite nicely entertained by friends, during these two days. After you left, Friday, Tillie and Eleanor took me with them for tea. On Saturday evening, I went to Raphaël. And yesterday I had lunch with the d'Anjou at Pao Ma Chang (Mme d'Anjou invited me, when you left, on the platform; she is certainly a sweet person). — I went to Pao Ma Chang in the Houghton's car. The whole d'Anjou family was there: they are so fond of each other that one forgets, or even likes, in them everything. — Today, the week begins without you. I do not mind any more to see the days passing too fast, now. — Just now I have to go to Vetch for the question of publications. Such a luck to have them to keep me busy! — As soon as the rush is over, I am decided to begin "L'atomisme de l'Esprit". — The "egg" is ripe by now, I think. — To write it will [make] me feel closer to you.*

*Be happy — dearest —*

*Everything is all right, — but I miss you.*

*P.T.*

*P.S. - Address your letters as before to the <u>PUMC (anatomy)</u>*

*Nirgidima of Torhout, princess of Mongolia.
Portrait sculpture made by Lucile Swan in China.*

Institut de Géo-Biologie
Rue Labrousse
Peking, August 27, 1941

THEIR
1941–48
LETTERS

145

Lucile dear,

It seems that a President [a Dollar ship] is going to leave Shanghai by Sept.1. So I must try my chance to answer your two precious letters, sent before the departure of the Coolidge. I had sent a few lines by air-mail to you on the Coolidge. Did you receive them?

And now begins seriously for me the period of an "isolated" life. You were right, and I experience it. The difficult time is not so much the first two weeks after the separation. After a while, one accumulates the need of being together again — to exchange and fecundate life. We had two years so completely for ourselves! —Well, it will be still better and "vitalizing" to be together again.

Since your departure, Peking has still succeeded in getting more empty than it was. Two days ago Tillie has left, almost abruptly, by the Kaiping (Colonel Mayer was anxious to get her [out] as soon as possible), — and Eleanor went by the same train to Peitaho. Mrs Margetts takes the house. But this is another trace, which disappears, of your presence. Billy Christian was often there, the last days — and he gave me direct news of you, in Shanghai. — Besides I have seen a good deal the Burcharts when Otto was in the P.U.M.C. (in the very room occupied this winter by Col. Mayer) — and I have quite appreciated them (although rather egoistic, the way he worships her is touching). Now Otto is back home; it seems that Loucks found how to handle him. — Raphaël is expecting his wife back on Sept. 1. In spite of the restrictions, he seems to have gazoline; but I could not persuade him lately to go to the Hills — which I miss (although I know perfectly that they will seem empty to me when I see them again). One reason he did not like to go to the country on Sunday, last weeks, is that he feels tired by his double work at the Tramcars Co. and in the Bank. — Jacques, luckily, is due back in a few days (according to Tillie, he will keep the same house, east of Hatamen, as the last year). — The Embassy is rather empty. Two days ago I had a lunch there with an interesting french colonel of aviation, who has fought the whole Battle of France, last year. A fine man — and somebody so different from what one hears from Vichy. He told me that during the french retreat, the number of the germans airplanes sent down by french fighters were three against one! This idea that we were defeated much less easily than generally thought is also expressed in a letter of my brother Joseph (28 may) received last week. He is, as usually, terribly conservative and anti-British in his appreciations — but this was before the russian war. On the whole, and although he confesses the loss of several pounds, the "ton" [tone] of the letter is not depressed at all, - and he seems especially proud and hopeful as far as the development of his fields in Auvergne is concerned.

By the same mail I received a very nice letter of Nirgidma (15 June), who had well received our letters, sent this spring. Very few details on her life, in fact (on purpose, I think). Michel is somewhere, I understand, on British ground. — She sees the Bégouën, who are all right, she says, except that Max exhausts himself on bicycle. And that is practically all. But she was happy, clearly, that we did not forget her. Try to write her again. From America it is so simple. —

Besides, and except for 5-8 p.m., the routine of my life is the same. Work helps time to go fast. Dr. de Terra's paper is now practically out — and the printing of my own paper on Early Man in China is going to start these very days. On the other hand, the memoir on Choukoutien (Deer and Rodents) is already printed for a third, and going fast. Proofs are pouring from everywhere; — and at the same time I am deep in the Beavers world (a new memoir started at the Lockart Hall). — I have also begun, shortly after you left, writing "L'atomisme de l'Esprit" — an "egg" it will be of normal size. By the end of September, probably, I will send you a copy.

Leroy too wrote me (middle of July). He was in very good shape — but without any marked scientific results. I expect him before october, unless he gets in some trouble with the boats. — I am afraid he will find the life of Peking dull; but I shall be glad to see him back. —

At Grabau's, the house is more and more, it seems, under the domination of the Flying Angel. Mother India had to leave (it seems?) — and Truda is searching hard for another job (did you know that she has in hands a written guarantee of Dr. Grabau that he will take care of her as long as she is in China?). Now that the Tillie's house is closed, I will probably go to the Z'ou ya t'sai Hutung next Sunday. But I have some feeling that I am not "persona grata" there any more.

Good bye, dearest. — The gossips are exhausted, pour cette fois. — But it remains me to tell you how happy I was that you liked my last letter, and even the picture contained in this letter. — Let us go on closer and closer together in a better discovery of the light and the hearth of God, at the deep centre of everything is beauty and truth.

Your

P.T.

Hope you have found everything all right in your family!

Institut de Géo-Biologie
Rue Labrousse
Peking, 9 sept. 1941

Dearest,

My last letter was written on Aug. 26. I hope you have received it. This new one I send you in the hope that it will catch a President in the middle of the month. By this time, you must be safely and pleasantly settled in Berkeley. Have a good time! I am sure that the physical and moral atmosphere of the States is just acting on you as the rising tide on the sea-weeds along the shore.

So far I am concerned, not much to say. I still miss you — and in some way still more. And at the same time, I feel as if your presence was expanding steadily in my life, because I realize better (and enjoy) the place you have taken, and hold for ever, in me. An expanding and deepening presence, — and animating, too for further progress: I am sure you experience the same thing also. And I bless God for the two years he gave us for achieving that.

*Externally, life is essentially the same here. Leroy reappeared, a week ago (quite all right, and well relaxed), and Mrs. R. too. In fact, the boats are so rare with Saïgon that they were practically forced to the happy condition to come back together. She looks almost fat, and had a grand time (in spite of the invaders) with the Corsican colony of Indo-China. I am glad to have Leroy here again. We have started immediately the usual talks. We are planning new publications. And in the meantimes we hope (in spite of the reduction of gazoline) to go to the Hills next Sunday. The weather is splendid: a beautiful autumn has begun since the middle of august. You would enjoy it. —*

*Work is going on. The de Terra's paper is out, well printed; — and I got today the <u>last</u> proofs of my Memoir on the Deers. On the other hand, the printing of "Early Man" is started, or practically so. These last days, I was simply merged in the proofs! - During the first morning hours, I proceed also in the redaction of "l'atomisme de l'Esprit", almost finished now. I hope it is good. But I must first type it before I can really appreciate it (40-50 pp., approximately). At the Lockart Hall, I am, as usually, busy with various types of Rodents. — The difference is that I stay longer now in the office (up to 6 p.m., often). — After that, I go to the Grand Hotel to talk with Vetch, — or, if possible, I call on some friends: the Bardac, or the Burchart (more or less once the week). — Jacques keeps his house, fortunately. With Otto B. we are great friends now. He still has fever and "tommy's" troubles, and today he felt low, and Poney was a little depressed. He has finally started writing a book, with a secretary: a good thing for him. — Last Sunday, I went to Grabau. The "angel" flew at my first appearance, so that the visit was quite normal. In fact, Truda is nothing more in the house now except a continously scolded "servante" — a situation which makes Pei himself angry. Truda is searching a way to get out — but to find a shelter and a job is not easy, now. In the meantimes nobody can turn her out of the house, since she has (in a safe place) a paper signed by Grabau. An impossible situation.*

*People will soon come back from Peitaho. Mme Cosme and Eleanor this week, and probably many more. — I told you that I had received a good answer from Nirgidma. A few days ago came a long letter of Ella Maillart, from South India. She is deep in her initiation to India wisdom — and so serious in her efforts to find God! "Je sens qu'il n'y a que Dieu qui existe réellement, que je suis en lui autant qu'il est en moi (quoique je ne l'ai pas encore vu)". The last sentence is so charmingly candid, do you not think? I was quite moved. —*

*Good bye, dearest. I go to bed. - A bientôt the next letter.*

*Your P.T.*

*Institut de Géo-Biologie*
*Rue Labrousse*
*Peking, Sept. 27, 1941*

Dearest,

*I have received, two days ago, your precious letter from Honolulu (but not yet the one sent by Clipper). It was so good to read you, - and almost to hear you again. Now I suppose that you are in Chicago, - facing a new life. Today,*

*Eleanor told me that she had heard that the famous transport was leaving Ching-wantao these very days. So, you may hope for your boxes. I hope so much that you have found your family all right, and that you can make interesting plans for yourself.*

*Here, things are going on approximately the same way; — but that makes such a difference for me not to have you, dearest, to tell and divide <u>everything</u>. So many things I have to keep for myself, now; and so many things, probably, which do not get born in my mind because you are not there to give me (as Grabau would say) the "internal impetus"! — And yet your influence is still with me, and the most essential part of the impetus too. — I hope to be worth of you, Lucile, and of so much you gave me. This thought makes me stronger, and gives me a great sweetness, also.*

*Publications are going on normally. The Memoir on CKT will soon be out; — and I am typing the last pages of "L'atomisme de l'Esprit" (some 40 pages). Rather good, I think; — but not so "final", perhaps, as I hoped. You know this feeling. I will probably ask Mlle. Barbier to retype 3 or four copies — and send you one. — The paper on Early Man is in the Peit'ang press since 3 weeks — but they are so slow there. Not a single proof, so far! - Next week I will advance steadily (with Leroy) the famous "List of Chinese Fossil Mammals", which has improved a lot since the first "ébauches" [draft or rough cast] we had made of it a year ago. — As a result of some letters and cables recently arrived from N.Y., Houghton seems quite optimistic about the future of the Cenozoic Lab. — I think we are practically sure, now, to be kept alive, and eventually to come back to full life, - as soon as the political events will make it possible.*

*In town, life has been more active recently, on account of the end of the Peitaho season, and because several people (french) came from Shangai to enjoy the Pekinese autumn. The Guillaume are leaving for Chunking next week (<u>she</u> will be back after a month); but the Lagos have to postpone their trip because <u>she</u> has got a pleuritis when leaving Peitaho. — She is better now. — Mme Baudet leaves tomorrow, with the little girl (to Chunking, too). Jeanne Mollart writes pitiful letters from Hankow: she dislikes the place, and gets nervous about the conditions, on account of her expected baby: no good doctors, no pharmaceutical supplies of any kind. I am sorry for her. — Eleanor is now settled in the Bob's house, — quiet and quite nicely transformed. The big yellow cat ("Brother") and the little dog are excellent friends. — Eleanor seems to be, as before, quite popular with the american colony. Today she had lunch with Brice (who leaves tomorrow, with H. Cruchfield), and Billy Christian, still fighting for his factories. — But you will get directly all these news from Arthur Ringwalt who proposed me kindly to take this letter, and plans to see you in Chicago. He will tell you everything about the kidnapping of Mrs. Clark (in your very Hutung, near Agnes Black) — and the tragic death of the "Erica"'s husband, burnt by an explosion of ether, when preparing dope. — Claire Hirschberg was quite "shaked" morally by this misfortune of her friend; she is a good and practical girl. — At Grabau's, the Angel is definitely the mistress of the house. It seems that Truda will continue her secretary work, but have an appartment in town (this was decided by Grabau himself, in a* *written message to Truda, who jumped on the opportunity. The appartment was found by Germaine, whom I did not yet see). —*

*Rue Labrousse, everything is peaceful (but not broader!). Roi has left for Tientsin and Shanghai. With Leroy, we are making the same good team, — and, as before, we see much of the Raphäel. In spite of the scarcity of gazoline, I went several times to the Hills: once with the Raphaël (to the Bishop's Mine, you remember the cold?); another time in a hired car, with Leroy, F. Matthews, Pei and Truda (!). We were searching (and we found) a site of fossil Plants behind the 2d Patachu temple. Now, Matthews has something to work on. — Next Sunday (tomorrow, in fact), we are invited to the Tillie's temple, by Mme Cosme. That makes me a little "blue" to see the place again without Tillie and without you. —*

*Good bye, dearest. - It is late in the night, — and I must bring this to Arthur [Ringwalt] tomorrow.*

*Be happy, and God bless you*

*Your*

*P.T.*

*Institut de Géo-Biologie*
*Rue Labrousse*
*Peking, October 17 1941*

*Dearest,*

*I have received with great joy, a few days ago, your sweet letter from Berkeley. Now, you must be in Chicago, busy and "domestic". I hope that, very soon, you will be free again to be "yourself". I am much interested about what you are experiencing and thinking. Don't forget that, for the time being, you are my connection with the western (that is with the real world). Nous vivons toujours "à deux", n'est-ce pas?*

*Here, life is going on, rather the same. And, tomorrow, I am beginning my "retraite" (do you remember the wall, just a year ago?). During these eight days, because I will try to be closer to the great Center of Love, you will be closer of me, too. You gave, and you give me, so much — and so much of life, Lucile. God bless you, and make you strong and happy, dear! — I would like, this week, to discover how to concentrate, better and more efficiently, my life on the only aim which counts for me, more and more: the awakening in our world, of a better understanding of Matter and Spirit, as they pass in each other in the brain and the heart of Man. We had long talks with Leroy on these things, lately. And the famous paper on Chasteté was unearthed from your leather-box for thorough discussion. Really, I believe that, deeper than the political convulsions of today, a thorough revolution is fermentating in the religious zones of our Universe. How to help it for the best? — In a week, I will send you a copy of the "Atomisme de l'Esprit". I must have it typed once more in order to have a sufficient number of copies. —*

*From the scientific point of view, things are proceding slowly, but favorably. I have received, at last, the first proofs of Early Man in China; and the "Catalogue of Fossil Chinese Mammals" reaches its final stage of preparation.*

*Besides, in spite of the scarcity of gazoline, I have been every Sunday to the Hills, mostly with the Raphaël's, who prove more and more to be delightful friends. Once, we went to Papaoshan (yellow leaves, instead of pink flowers), and I took (alone!) a part of the walk we made together in the spring; — and, somewhat, you still walked with me. — A week ago (a friday), we borrowed ourselves a car, took along Eleanor and Mr. Wright (a newcomer, student of Harvard, quite pleasing — speaking exactly like Movius, and we went to Fahaissu; then I made the section between Fahaissu and Patachu, following the foot of the Hills — along the path you know well (as you told me). — And you were there, too. -*

*In town, I go from time to time to the Burchart and to Eleanor. Otto is on his bed, as before, most of the time — but he seems to buy a good number of beautiful pieces (partly for Komor, it seems — who did not yet get his boxes, detained in Japan). Poney told me to send you her most affectuous regards. — Eleanor has quite metamorphosed the Bob's interior — very nicely, I think. She seems to have a good number of admiring friends, and looks well "entrain". She plans to work for herself this winter (perhaps translating in english the book of her father on Thibet). — The Raphaël's had finally to leave their house, and are now (since today!) located Nan-ho-yen, in the northern-most house of the Schuhmaker's, just opposite Ta Tien Shui Ching. They had already a lot of discussion with Mrs. Schuhmaker, but take it with a full sense of humour. Mrs. Raphaël has decided that she liked extremely to "déménager" from time to time, — and she is fond of the new appartment. It seems that, after a few months, they will move again to the former house of the Mayer's (Rue Labrousse); Garrido has decided to leave the place. Paul Doncoeur is still in Kunming. The wound left by his operation seems to be long to heal. He is expected here, for rest. —*

*Tou-ya-ts'ai hutung is definitely under the rule of the Flying Angel. Truda goes there every morning to do secretary work — and has her evening free. She has found a small, provisional, appartment East of Hatamen str., not far from Nystrom. She looks like a free bird. I must say that since weeks, I did not pay myself any visit to Amadeus. I must go there the next free Sunday. -*

*So far, I did not start the "démarches" for the American Visa. You will scold me, I know. - The trouble is that, when I come to the facts, I do not know finally whom I shall trouble to be my "sponsors". - Immediately after my retreat, however, I will go to the American Embassy, and try to reach a decision.*

*Now, I go to Vetch to discuss publications matter, - and I will mail this letter in the Hotel.*

*Good bye, dearest.*

*Your*

*P.T.*

*I have well received the letter sent by Clipper.*

---

Sometime in late October or early November of 1941, Lucile wrote a long letter to Teilhard. It did not reach him. Apparently their friend, Arthur Ringwalt, was not able to pick it up in Chicago for hand delivery in China, as originally planned. The uncorrected, undated carbon was among Lucile's papers.

*Dearest, -*

*Arthur Ringwalt has offered to take this, he is soon returning to Chungking, so I feel as if this letter may really reach you and there is so much to say I don't know where to start!! I wrote to you in October and again in December, but of course I have no idea if you rec'd them . . I repeat that I received your precious letter sent by Grimpsholm and have read and reread it until it is almost worn out!! It was written almost 8 months ago, but I believe the things it says are still true, I hope so. . . . and that you are able to go on working . . I wonder what material you have for scientific work . . and if there have not been some more "eggs" by this time . . You must have a great deal of time to THINK . . and with the conditions of the world what they are, surely it has also made you question the methods of the church etc. The TRUTH is there and Christ is just the same . . . but the way his follow-ers have allowed his teaching to be interpreted and taught!!!!! At least that seems to me where the trouble is . . . I have just been reading an interesting book "Ten Great Religions" . . . and he compares them . . and it is so fascinating to see how MUCH they are alike. At least the feelings which prompted them were so much the same . . All of which should make the establishment of a Universal Religion so much easier!!*

*Well well how serious I am at the very start!!! when there are thousands of less "universal" but also very important things that I want to say to you . . If I don't write in detail I'm sure you understand that it is very difficult to write freely when I have no idea how many people are going to read this before it gets to you!! So for the more personal things, you must try to remember things said in the past . . . and then multiply them by all the hundreds of days that we have been separated. Precious Teilhard . . Precious Pierre. You are with me so strongly all the time . . and you make life always more beautiful.*

*My life goes on much the same . . My family needs me so much, so here I am and with world conditions what they are, I'm really very well off . . I told you of my nice little studio right back of the house . . . which is my life saver for there I can be myself . . I work every morning, usually go for a walk in the afternoon and read in the evening . . some-thing like Peking . . . only the high point of five O'clock, is not here . . I go out some, tho not much . . I really have few friends in Chicago . . Young Mary Wood is drawing with me 3 mornings a week and that is a great joy . . she is so alive and intelligent and sweet and is doing VERY well with her work. My own work is moving . . I've almost finished my "Temptation of the Lord" . . have spent weeks working on the face of Christ . . and of course it really does not satisfy me yet . . but the whole is not bad . . . now I'm doing a life sized head in Mahogany . . . Mary posed for the sketch . . . but it isn't really a portrait of her . . . I may go down to the Art Institute next month to do some work in stone . . an old friend has charge of that department and he can help me a lot. My New York exhibit has not materialized . . . I have not pushed the thing as the times are so bad for exhibitions . . however things are still "open" in several directions . . . We have had such a bad winter . . so much dull dark days and snow . . It has been snowing all day . . However I shall proba-bly go out as I'm invited to a small cocktail party at a young painter and wife . . and I want to get to know them better . . . Maybe if the weather clears up I'll be more enthusastic about exhibits. But it is expensive, so I would just as soon wait until the times are a bit more propitious. and the actual work I'm doing, is growing better. . . . . I think?? and hope.*

*Now for gossip . . Tillie is in Washington living in a small room!!! not a big house with a temple in the Hills . . and working hard, but she seems very cheerful. Bosshard is now in Washington, trying to find an apartment . . the Baudets are there . . .*

*so many old friends . . the Petros also . . Petro is an officer in the British army doing liaison work. The Col Mayers have just bought a house there . . Isabel was here for the day recently and gave me lots of news. Ida Treat was busy with passports the last I heard, finally going to England . . I've not heard if she was successful . . . I hear now and then from Ernestine Evans . . whom I saw in NY last spring . . Nathalie is living in Los Angeles where her husband is doing work for one of the big airplane works . . she sent me some photos of that picnic we had with them in New Hampshire . . remember? they are so good. I would send one but I don't think it would ever get there . . . Mayo has had two parts in movies!! I do not know what the last picture is but he has the part of Henry 8th which should suit him fine!!! I think he is very happy . . Poor Rose and Michael have been on tenter hooks lately as he is due for the draft . . He is now in Washington where Jim lives, and will probably something settled . . Jim is now with the Red Cross. Mlle Saizeau is still here . . she has sent a lot of her things to Komor who is selling them on commission . . and has had some success . . Mlle is now trying to get a job here . . it is not so simple as she has no training. I do hope she will find something . . I see her every week or two; I am her connection with Peking and also with les pères!!! she is a curious person and I'm afraid life is not very easy for her . . . but she really has a philosophy or religion that helps her . . and I am very glad that Père Leroy has been a great help and inspiration for her. He is her "model".*

*So many of the things I've been reading lately, Hooton, Carrel etc make me think more and more of the Institute of Man . . a short time ago I wrote to Ralph Linton and asked him to let me know if he hears anything at all definite about such a project . . He should be in a position to hear if there is anything doing . . He is now head of Anthropology at Columbia. Boaz died recently. So my dear I will certainly advise you if I get any news and I'll always manage to get in touch somehow with the people here, just to find out what is what . . maybe not directly MYSELF, but through some friend . . for I do so want you to work with such an institution . . and I am quite sure that that is also where your own interest lies . . The war is bringing out many interesting things . . and one of them is our great NEED for religion and to a certain extent the churchs have surely failed . . How terribly they need a renaissance . . especially yours . . The most interesting things, ideas, schemes, hopes, have come out of the Church of England . . The new Archbishop of Cantebury is really awake to the PRESENT world and I'm sure would agree with the final sentence of your last letter re. doing away with ALL barriers. There are lots of people and organizations who are really working in that direction. I keep a lot of clippings for you!! afraid they will be a bit out of date before you ever get them. But the idea of WORLD organizations is surely alive and I think, growing. I won't go into more detail, but be sure I am doing my best to be alive to all this and that am always thinking of how and where your teaching can be used . . for Pierre I am more and more sure that your ideas are what we need. (I hope this does not sound stupid or as if I were putting myself up, but I'm sure you understand and know how completely I believe in you.) Your scientific work gives the rest such a solid background . . well be sure that you are not forgotten and that when the time comes there will be a place for you . . and the time IS coming . . of that I am more and more sure.*

*I've been reading Petro's Life of G.T. which is most interesting . . . and makes you seem more and more of a miracle!! Oh I do wish I could know how life is with you now . . I imagine more or less the same, tho more difficult, expensive and probably not much of any social life, that is not MANY cocktail parties!! Tillie wrote . . "Oh what would I not give for a tea with les bons Pères" . . and wouldn't we all . . . well it will happen somewhere and I hope before VERY VERY long. .*

*I do wonder how much news you get there, I suppose you are in touch with things . . and must have been very excited with all that has been happening to your own countrymen . . I can imagine Raphael being especially interested . . and Francoise . . do give them my warm greetings . . also to all the other old friends . . Burchards, Truda, Germaine, Grabau(?) Helen Burton, Ruth Kunkle, Prentice!!! et al!!*

*I wrote you that Nirjidma is in London with her husband . . I have had no further news from her. People here send their letters around to other friends, so I had news of Bob Drummond who is in Kunming and well. I just had a telegram from Nathalie inviting me out to stay a month or two with her . . It sounds tempting as we have had a beastly winter and there is a regular blizzard now . . but I can't get away . . My parents are about the same, up every day . . but my maid does not come Thursday dinner nor Sunday, so I have to be here, and I am very fortunate to have any maid, and mine is good . . . Father is decidedly much more feeble but pretty well . . It is so fortunate that I am here. I am getting more used to the place and have worked out a pretty good life for myself . . as long as I have this place where I can be alone to work, it is O.K. I go to the Symphony concert often and tell Leroy I think of how much he would enjoy it and wish he could be there too . . I do miss my friends who are mostly in the east, either Washington or New York . . however I can work here and am really happy . . and I read a lot and <u>try</u> to think!! and some very good things have happened to me . . I mean I FEEL the love of God . . it has become something very real, especially as manifested in Christ very passionately a vital part of me . . and I got so much from Saizeau Yoga books!! Most of the church books are so complicated and seem to be so much more interested in dogma than in love . . they give me almost nothing . . perhaps they help, if you do not NEED help . . but they are very unsatisfactory if you are seeking . . Just as your talks have given me so much more than any thing else . . oh how grateful I am to you. . .*

*And PT I am also so grateful to you for being you . . how much we laughed!! and the long walks we had, how MUCH I do miss it all . . but I also feel sure that we will be together again . . if you ever have any plans for the future, or even desires I wish you would tell me. . . . if possible!!! Of course that is difficult, but still you probably know what you would like to do and where you want to be . . I feel pretty sure you will want to be in this part of the world . . and this is where you will be most needed. .*

*It makes me feel so close to you just writing and I long to say lots of things which I suppose I better not . . but you must be able to read my heart and see how full it is of love and how completely that love is full of you, my dear precious friend.*

[Stamped RETURN TO SENDER / SERVICE SUSPENDED,
this letter was later returned to Lucile.]

*2430 Orchard Street
Chicago, Illinois
November 26, 1941.*

*Pierre dearest, -*

*It is hard to know whether to write or not? If your plans have gone on as they were when I left, you should soon be on your way to America!! But if something has happened to change them, then I do want to have a letter on the way to you . . so here goes anyway . . . Also these days when it seems as if there might be more war any day, it is a* *problem to know if letters will ever get anywhere . . I know just how you feel about writing to France . . But the strange thing is, that letters DO get through and <u>eventually</u> reach their destination . . . and Pierre if my letters are as welcome to you as yours are to me . . then it is more than worth trying. .*

*Well I have been out in Iowa since I last wrote to you . . and it surely was a very good thing to do . . I only stayed a few days . . but I made a speech to the ladies who had sponsored the exhibit . . and I was invited out all the time . . and everyone was very enthusiastic about the things . . I've sold some drawings, but as yet I've not heard of any sculpture!! But the exhibit will last two weeks more . . The gallery is a government affair . . and the young man who runs it was So enthusiastic about my things . . said my show had done so much to raise the standard of the place etc. etc . . all of which was very pleasing AND stimulating to me . . I found it gave me a great deal of pleasure to feel that I had been able to help along that little project . . funny, I always said I did not have a bit of missionary about me . . and yet I always get a great kick out of some thing which is definitely missionary!!!! Anyway it gave me a lift . . which I sorely needed as things here were beginning to get on my nerves terribly . .*

*When I got home the maid had to go to bed sick . . then Dad went to the hospital . . - nothing serious, just for a rest and check up . . so I was on the job all the time . . but now that is OK . . the cook is back and I have really gotten to work again . . the ivory is progressing well . . but it is very slow . . and I like it so much that I don't mind taking lots of time to it . . I've also started that other piece of wood . . "<u>Brotherhood of Man</u>" idea . . With a few hours work every morning, it does not matter so much what I do the rest of the day . . I see very few people, as I have to take Mother to the Dr. 3 times a week etc. etc . . but all this won't last for ever . . and I really don't mind . . But, oh Pierre, I do so miss your talks!! and I DO DO DO miss you! I talked to Rose over the phone yesterday . . she has finished going over that translation and I am going down there in a few days, so we can go over it together . . she said there were not many places to change . . just a few where the English was too French in construction . . Last evening I felt the need of you very much . . so I read some of Julian Huxley . . and Pierre, that paper of yours "<u>Man from a Paleontologist, etc</u>" is SO SO much better . . clearer, and of course you go so much further than he does . . Oh we really MUST publish that . . I hope "<u>L'atomisme de l"esprit</u>" is on the way to me . . and what are you doing now? and is some new egg stiring around in your mind? I wonder when we will be able to <u>talk</u> these things again.*

*Sure we shall . . but we are two of many millions of people who are not doing just what they want to do these days . . and it simply can't last for ever!!! But I do so wonder what you have decided to do about coming over here . . I am waiting to make my plans for going East until I hear from you, so I do hope you have told me . . and, dearest, you know I will understand, what ever you decide to do . . It would be SO marvelous to see you . . but I don't allow myself to dwell on that — yet.*

*Pierre, these last two years really did do a very great deal for us, I realize it more all the time . . There is so much more calm sureness within me . . and yet always the light of your presence which stimulates me to do and to try to do always more . . and at the same time to get much out of whatever I HAVE to do at the time . . dearest you are SO precious . . You don't know what JOY it gives me when you tell me that I have helped you!! Precious Teilhard!!*

I don't say a word about the war, etc . . what is there to say? And conditions may all be changed before this gets over there to you!!

I was so disappointed not to see Arthur Ringwalt . . either he could not find us (some of the clerks at the hotel are very stupid) or he did not stay over here . . He probably could have told me so much about your plans . . but maybe not!!

It must be quite a blow to Eleanor that the Marines are going to leave . . I do wonder what life is like there now . . it must be rather quiet . . Mariann Clubb had just heard from Edmond that he has been transferred, at least for the winter, to Hanoi . . prices in Shanghai sounded AWFUL . . coal $800. a ton . . how are things with you? and are you having any trouble getting stuff? DO you still go to the Hills?. I bought a pair of shoes for Hill climbing . . I use them sometimes for a long walk in the Park!! It gave me a kick just to buy them.

Pierre, if you are going to be there for sometime more, please don't wait until you hear about a boat, they DO come . . unless by that time we are at war with Japan . . I STILL don't think we will be, but I may be wrong . . The world seems to be mad enough to do anything nowadays . .

Tonight Im going down to have dinner with young Mary Wood Erskine . . she was so interested to have news of Jacques . . am glad he is there, as long as you enjoy him!!!! But It must be very good to have Leroy there, and I can imagine that you are working well together . . is he more satisfied . . or still restless? and have you any more news of Trassaert?

The last letter from you was of Sept 27 that Arthur brought . . they seem to come only once a month . . so here's hoping for something in a short time.

Thank you, dearest, for everything that you are and that you give to me . .

My deepest love to you dear

Lucile

And greetings to Leroy - Raphaels - Eleanore - also Truda, Pei etc - and how is the Grabau Ménage?

*November 26, 1942*

Dearest,

Just a year ago we went to the Hills to Tillie's temple with her and Eleanore, Bob Arthur and Paul Boncoeur!!! It seems so close and at the same time as if it belongs to another life . . and it almost does, perhaps things don't seem to have changed much to you who are still there doing much the same things, but I really do think a great change has started . . of course it started ages ago, but the present war conditions are steaming everything up . . . and oh my dear how I do wish you were here to be a part of it . . . perhaps you can get a perspective by being there . . but I think you need to _feel_ what the people are feeling HERE and I can't even write it to you with any sureness that you will ever receive my letter . . .

And even if I could what to say? I agree with your last precious letter which came just a week ago, that of Oct. 17. where you say that the religious revolution is even greater than the political one today . . Everywhere you meet it . . BUT I do not think that the churches are going to be the ones to give the solution . . The fresh impetus is coming from

OUTSIDE *the church . . Oh how I would like to see you, not as the religious timidly (because of pressure) defending your religion through science . . . but as the scientist who proclaims his religion BECAUSE of science!! Oh how much stronger and how much more influential would be your position in the world. And if the church couldn't take it, it would be too bad, she is going to have to take a great deal more than that before the upheaval is finished . . Your method of the SLOW evolution within the church MIGHT have worked 100 yrs ago, but not today . . we are living in a ruthless age, and in order to be heard so that you can help, in order to make your voice heard above the triumphant shouts of the destroyers, you too must shout, and NOT hide your LIGHT under a bushel!! Oh PT how I do want to talk to you, NOW. It is shortly after 5 PM.!! and here am I and there are you.!!*

*And how am I going to get this to you? and what is happening to you there in your safe and sheltered life?? what are your associates thinking (IF they think). But I always think of you as the most deeply spiritual scientist, a GREAT scientist . . But this has all been said before!! But it is still true and I believe in you so strongly that I'm sure a WAY will come where you can be fully your wise and beautiful and _influential_ self, who can help to show that way to _innumerable_ other searchers . . It must come, the present condition is too too wasteful!*

Only two of Teilhard's wartime letters eventually reached Lucile in the U.S. Both came from Peking, a year apart; the first in the spring of 1942. Meanwhile, Japanese troops were in Lashio (they had already seized Hong Kong) and had cut the Burma Road. The situation in China was tense — for the Chinese and for the stranded internationals.

*Institut de Géo-Biologie*
*Rue Labrousse*
*Peking, May 31, 1942*

*Lucile, dearest,*

*Will this letter ever reach you, and when? In any case, I must try my chance, and the "diplomatic boat". After these months of complete separation and silence, I must try to let you know that I remain yours, and that I do my best to remain exactly and entirely what you wish and want me to be. I am so sure, for my part, that you are still the same, and even more! — But I would like so much to know what you are doing and thinking in these extraordinary times. — I miss you in my heart, — and in my mind too. I was thinking in you, and through you — you know it. And, because you are not here, I have sometimes the feeling that my thoughts do not mature in the same way, as before, when I could search myself in you. — Well, on the whole, I am glad, nevertheless, that you have left Peking just in time. Life would not have been easy for you, these days. For myself (being not a national enemy — who knows what the French are, today?), existence remains somewhat dull, but possible. Since the famous 8th of December, the closure of the P.U.M.C. (I cannot pass its gates without a pang in my heart) has radically changed my life. By now, I am exclusively working Rue Labrousse — busy with the redaction of the last papers which I would like to finish as a closure of my work in China. Since you left, I have published a Memoir in Palaeontologia Sinica (in October) — and a rather good "Early Man in*

China", in our own publications. Another interesting book (Catalogue of the Fossil Mammals of China) is almost finished printing in Shanghai; — and another volume (on Chinese Rodents) will immediately follow, provided we find the money. In addition, four "eggs" more have appeared this winter, following "L'atomisme de l'Esprit", which I sent you in October, but which you probably never received. — Just now, I am writing nothing more in this line. I need some excitant — and you are not here. — In town, the circle of friends becomes more and more narrow. I see mostly the Raphaël (now established rue Labrousse) in the Colonel Meyers house, the Dorget, and the Burchart (now in the Russian Embassy compound: Otto is better since a few weeks; they are regular meetings there, with Dr. Loucks, the Kandel, etc.). Once the week, the Belgian and Brazilian diplomatic wives can go out — and there is a "thé des prisonnières". The Bardac's are living in the same house as before, — and their marriage is a complete success. Marie-Claire is decidedly charming, and the most homey and attentive of wives. — Here, rue Labrousse, no change. The old superior is like a "foreign body" in the house — but quite discret and understanding. Leroy is calmer, and our friendship is complete. F. Marin left us for Shanghai (à soulagement!), and the house of Shih-hu Hutung is practically empty. This is something. Because gazoline has become a luxury, the trips to the Hills are more difficult. Still, I find some opportunities. A fortnight ago, we went to the Miao fan shan, spending two nights at the Bussières; — and I saw again the place of our picnic with the Tyrrhit. You remember? — Eleanor is in Shanghai, with a job. Ruth Kunkel is living at the same place, — not depressed at all. Helen Burton was sick recently (slight pneumonia), but better now; — just the same as before. —

And I have no idea what I will do next. Communications are completely cut, even with Indochina. Nothing to do, except to make oneself ready for the great re-construction. I am more and more convinced that something big is coming — a "revolution for Unity", throwing away all the false political, racial, economic and religious barriers. This is the only thing worth fighting and dying for.——

Yours ever, de tout mon coeur

P.T.

Ci-joint une lettre de Leroy pour Miss Saizeau Can you forward?. Grabau is living apparently the same life, more and more solitary, closed in his dreams, and practically cut off from any friendly contacts by the presence of the new "Mrs. Grabau". One does not dare nor like to drop in, as before. Perhaps I am lacking of courage.

This is an absurd letter, too much superficial and short. - But how to write, in such times — when even talking should not be enough for telling you what I want.

During most of the war, Teilhard was confined to Peking. However, in November of 1942, he and Pierre Leroy were able to visit and lecture in Shanghai, thanks in large part to Mme. Claude Rivière, a French broadcaster. Teilhard and Leroy both spoke to large audiences; the one at Aurora University, on Man as the supreme achievement of evolution, the other at the Alliance, on the wonderful inventiveness of evolution in marine life. For both the reception was mixed: great enthusiasm given by some, great misgivings by others, especially by some of the Aurora Jesuits who were very wary of "evolution." The two Jesuit scientists returned to Peking before the end of the year. The following spring Lucile, then living in Chicago, "talked" to him in her first journal entry since January 14, 1939.

[Journal] *April 8, 1943*

*Dearest — I have just returned from a wonderful symphony concert — the best I've heard this year — and you were right there with me all the time — I wish I could tell you some of the things I felt and thought — I realized more concretely than ever before the dynamic, the cosmic possibilities of a friendship such as ours - Oh Pierre we must nourish it well for it really has such depth and such broad horizons — If only two people can really feel and think big enough surely that could be something real and fine and inspiring in this sorry world of today — I think I have grown a lot in this last year and 8 months since we parted, and I hope for great things for us in the years to come — I don't know if this tells you anything much but I assure you there is nothing petty or personally grasping in my feelings — it is something fine and constructive — and you are the other half of the potential which makes a whole and solid structure, a force that can "see" and realize the deep harmony of all things and help to bring them into being — and I remembered the day I left China when I read your parting letter, the one with the picture of C[hrist] enclosed in it — Remember? And your last letter too — written almost a year ago —— I have sent four letters to you, this is the fifth — I wonder if you have received any of them — It would help so much if we could communicate — I miss you so very very much, it doesn't get less, quite the contrary —— Oh how I would like to hear you talk and share all the little and big things with you again — but that will happen again and will be better than ever before — you will see — but I know I do not have to convince you of this — that is one of the marvelous things about it all — I'm so sure you are feeling and building in just the same way that I am — it is us but oh so much more —and the more beautifully we love each other the more richly we automatically love God. I can see no difficulty there at all — it just works that way in the very nature of life and love — and I love you very deeply —— and I feel so much closer to God.*

*Peking, April 13, 1943*

Dearest,

If this letter arrives to you, it will reach you across the Hills. There is just a chance that you will get it — but I must try!

I hope that you have well received the news I sent you, last June, by the Lago. De mon côté, I got in July, a short letter of you, written to (and forwarded by) Dick Smith. That is the last I heard of you. Evidently, communications are more and more difficult. But, I know, we are too close to each other for being really separated by that. You still deeper remain my Lucile. Your "walking Virgin" and your wooden Crucifix still are illuminating the house here.

Internally, I keep the same. Scientific interest survives (I have published three memoirs in a year — and more are coming, if we can print). And chiefly (although I miss you a lot) I am going on, thinking. During the last months I have developed a fine theory on "Conscience et Complexité", which I tried, as a lecture, in Shanghai last November. More and more, the two joint ideas of "Super-

*Humanity"* and *"Super-Christ"* keep my mind busy. And maybe this *"emprison-nement"* in Peking will have as a final result that I emerge out of it, after the war, with something definitely clear to propose to people, in Europe or in America.

*Physically, I feel perfectly all right — and I feel just as fit as before climbing the Hills — <u>when</u> I can go to the Hills. In this line, the restriction of gazoline makes everything more and more difficult. They are still, however, a few cars running, occasionally. — Recently, I went to Chieh Tai Tze, and also to Nan Chih Tze. Searching for rocks prevented me from being too much heart-sick, thinking of the old time.*

*Socially speaking, Peking is almost completely deflated. As you probably know, the national enemies have been concentrated, a few weeks ago, in Weih sien, near Tsingtao. Helen Burton is there, and Miss Bullington, and Ruth Kunkel, and Billy Christian, and Mrs. Cotman, Mrs. Margetts, etc. — not too badly set-tled, according to the last news. — But I was <u>so</u> glad that you have left in time. - As a result of this emigration, the circle of friends has become so narrow!. — In addition, Paul Raphaël suddenly died, last January, of heart-failure, exactly as Davidson Black, and almost in the same conditions. As you know, I had him as a real brother. — For Françoise, the shock was almost too much. Few people real-ized how much she was living "on him". After his disparition, she felt lost, and empty. By and by, she becomes again herself, as before. But she absolutely needs some interest and belief to fill her life. And here, closed in Peking, what can she find to be forced outside of herself? — Outside of her, my best friends remain the two Dorget, the Bardac's, the Schlemmer (you don't know them, I think; — he is an "apprenti-sinologue", with Dubosc and Dhormon). Jacques is just the same as before, — <u>very</u> happy with Marie-Claire, qui est le modèle des charmantes épouses. Everybody in town admires her and is fond of her. —*

*In the meantimes, Houghton, Leighton Stuart, and Bowen are still kept "au secret" in a house, in town [interned by the occupying Japanese forces]. They are well, — but nobody can see them — even Höppeli, who has become one of the most popular figures in Peking since he is acting as Swiss consul for the anglo-american interests. I told you, I think, in my last letter, that the Peking's Man skulls are lost (or rather mislaid), all of them, somewhere. I hope they will be found at the end. Fortunately they were all casted and described.*

*Practically, I have no news of France. The last letter I got was from my brother in Paris, to announce me the death of my poor dear Gabriel (the "coun-try"-brother), who has passed away, quite peacefully (as he had been living) in November 41. He had rather suddenly developped a kind of cancer near the stom-ach, which was discovered too late for being operated. Life must be hard, in France. But we practically know nothing about it — except the propaganda. — A few days ago, I saw the brother of Nirgidma, who told me that she and her hus-band were probably together again, somewhere in Africa. - What about Ida Treat? - and the Bégouëns? Maybe you know, - since you are on the right side, now. -*

*Puissent ces lignes vous arriver, - et vite! I hope you are as happy as pos-sible, dearest, - and more alive than ever for the astonishing changes of the present world. May the war come soon to its end, so that we can soon meet again, and work together for the great task ahead.*

*God bless you!*

*P.T.*

*P.S. Grabau is living as before at Tuyats'ai Hutung, — undisturbed, — and well
attended by the "flying Angel". I did not see him since a long time. - Leroy sends
you his best regards. Roi [another Jesuit] is in Shanghai now!*
*Amitiés de nous deux à Mlle Saizeau si elle est encore là!*

[Journal] *Easter Sunday. 1943 - Chicago - April 25.*

*I have been so terribly unhappy lately — Hating Chicago - which certainly is a
completely hard and commercial place —— which does something terrible to people —
and then my house situation, finding myself tied for how endlessly long to two old people
— they are so old because they no longer dream or hope for anything, except perhaps death
— and they unconsciously try to take me with them — so that I feel I must fight to keep
alive — (really inside alive) and every day I miss P.T. more and more and I do so wonder if
he is well and what he is doing all this long time — life must be pretty dull in Peking these
days — every where!! At least Peking is beautiful — here so much is ugly and there are no
hills no Tai Miao no nothing to soothe the soul —only the Art Institute and that is a great
joy — tho' somehow different. But last night again I could not sleep — and in thinking
about my life — There were 12 years with Jerry — the first of which were so happy and
full of life and work and love — mostly physical — but good — Then that broke and I felt
life for me was hard — I had 1 1/2 yrs in Chicago and 2 in New York — trying to find
happiness and looking for a mate! - then to China!! and in the early days I'd met P.T. —
As time went on he grew to mean more and more and more to me — This glorious love,
not physical, so much deeper and more lasting - He has given me so much so rich — well
that is a long and beautiful story — but with difficulties too. For that same old question of
loneliness was there — or rather — aloneness — and now the war and here am I in Chicago and he in Peking and not even letters to help out — why this separation, this desola-
tion again? Is there something I must learn - some truth I must grasp for myself - alone?
and then it seemed to me I realized the real hope and meaning of Easter — The real hope of
the world which is always there, so infinitely bigger than ourselves, if we will only take it
- or let it take us! Pierre always says — "You must have confidence in the future" - If I can
only remember all this I'll have patience and try to learn my lesson and then it will all be
so much easier - I'll work and read and try to really grow spiritually. I must have something fine to give to Pierre when we meet again - Chicago! What matter - I will remember
Easter and all it means -*

Nearly two years later Lucile wrote again to Teilhard at a time when she thought there was
a chance that a letter might get through. It did not, as Teilhard's August letter indicates. She
sent another during the summer. The two unsigned carbons in Lucile's files seem to be
complete.

*14 East 10th St New York 3*
*February 1945*

*Dear PT. -*

*After all this long long time, how to begin??? That the "internal" conditions are
just the same as when we parted . . that I am sure you know . . only that everything is*

_more_. *I don't know what I would have done these sad days if I did not have your teaching and faith to give me courage . . I have done much reading and some thinking and have so MANY things that I want to ask you about and to discuss with you!!!! but that will have to wait a bit longer . . but I thank you again and again for all you gave me . . and I repeat so often "You must have confidence in the future" . . . . "all life is progress" . . even if it is hard to follow at times!!!*

*But now for news . . I have been here since last October. My Father died Nov. '43 and recently Mother has been with her sister in Iowa . . she is not well and probably will not be with us long. So I came here to try to pick up some of the threads of my own life . . it is not easy, especially at this difficult time. However I am working every day . . and that is something. I see old friends  . . and that is much too.*

*I phoned Mrs. Rachel Nichols at the Museum . . she sends dearest love to you . . says the dept. is all reorganized and Simpson at the head. Probably you know that Roy is no longer at the Museum. They would all be MOST happy to see you!!!*

*I have seen Rhoda Terra, had dinner at her place . . she was looking very pretty and has a book coming out very soon about a priest!!!!! Noel is a BIG girl!! also very attractive. they seem well and happy . . de Terra is at a university in Ohio . . he does not sound so happy . . but I think that is his temperament. Ernestine Evans is fine . . also sends much love — says she does not get on so well without your guidance. Rose Jameson is here and I see her often . . Michael is in the Navy. In Washington I saw Nathalie, the Lyons, also the Baudets!! Tillie, Bosshard, etc etc and all spoke longing of you. Ida T is in England for the last year. Simone in south Morocco! I have written several times to Nirjidma . . but no answer for several years.*

*Harold Louchs has a good job in Chungking . . Robt Lim is here now. His daughter has been very ill here. I hear through the Fergussons . . Old Dr. F. is still quite spry and gave me news of you!!! Pretty old now . . but still I bless him.*

*There is a girl in the down stairs apt who plays a little French song that Leroy used to sing so much . . it just makes me so homesick for the hills!!! I see Delia Tyrwhitt often . . Peter was killed several years ago. Delia and Ida Pruitt are giving a cocktail party this afternoon . . hope to see more old friends. D. and I often speak of that day we all had in the Hills . . just about perfect!!*

*This letter seems very superficial . . but if it arrives it will give you some news and let you know that all your friends are thinking about you and wishing you were here. And as for personal messages . . well just get out almost any letter of the last 15 years . . and there would not be much change. Except that like a good wine, a real friendship gets richer and more beautiful as time goes on. And that I am your true and devoted friend, there can be no question. How I want to know what you are thinking and doing these days. It is so long since there has been any direct news from you. I hope you are able to write and form your thoughts more and more clearly and concretely all the time . . the world is going to need what you have to offer more than ever before . . and there must be some way for you to give your message . . there will be . . and you will not fail to take it because it is going to be so much louder than ever you knew before . . this will be no time for subterfuge . . Christ's teaching seems so simple  . . but man seems to have forgotten or never heard it. I have just made some more copies of "The Future of Man" and the logic and intellectual approach is JUST what is needed. For all this I do have confidence in the future . . . and are you well?? that I do wish I knew more about. I have heard that you are now living in Tientsin!! which seems logical.*

*So much that must please you has happened since we parted . . no reason to think it won't continue to do so . . and that we can have long talks again about it and about!! Pierre I do believe it and it makes me almost too happy to be able to write more!! Saizeau is still in Chicago . . well, I think and has heard from her family that they are all well!!*

*14 East 10th Street*
*New York, NY*
*July 28 '45*

Dearest P.T., —

*A possible chance to send a line to you . . so I try to write a few words always hoping that you will receive them. It is almost 4, FOUR, long years since we parted and everything I said to you that day is still true, only like good wine, it has grown richer with age! Little did we realize that August 8th that it would be years before we would meet again. But now one can see hope for a finish before too long.*

*As I have no idea when you last heard from me I will give you a brief summary of my news. I have only been in New York since last October. Having lost both of my parents, I was free again to try to make my own life. New York is very crowded and hard to find a good place to live - so I have recently <u>bought</u> a house in Washington - so many of my friends are living down there - and I think it will be a happy place to live and also perhaps easier to get established with my work. I stayed with Nathalie while there . . and we talked much of you and the wonderful picnic we had . . you remember? she is now married to Bob Proctor, who went with us that day. Of course I saw Tillie, looking So well . . also Barbara and Petro. Never saw Petro looking better, he was home on short leave from Ceylon . . promised to try to write to you . . A recent letter from Nirjidma from France . . the first I have had for several years . . her husband it still with the news agency. Ida Treat is still, I believe, in England . . Bosshard was in Washington . . but expects to leave shortly for Switzerland.*

*I have seen Rhoda de Terra several times this winter - she has had quite a successful book out - Are YOU the hero?????? We had some "philosophical" discussions - and of course we did not agree - Oh, how many things I want to discuss with you. I have read and thought so much since we parted - and how I want to know what you are thinking and feeling these days - so much is happening in the world!! Oh, how I long for the time to come when you will be able to take your place here - for I'm sure your thoughts and your philosophy will fit into the whole scheme of things so perfectly - and give that added touch of the Personal - which is so needed. For I feel sure that you have developed more and more in that direction. Well ONE of these days now you will be able to <u>tell</u> me about it and what life has been for you these last years.*

*Rose Jameson is living here now too and I see her very often. Saizeau is still in Chicago . . still on the same job . . not so very interesting but it gives her a living . . which is something . . she has had good news from her family in France. how often we talked of our good friends les pères . . . .*

*Your wise and beautiful teachings? well, discourses . . have been such a help to me . . and have been the foundation for a lot of good thinking and feeling. and I really believe we will be talking together again before very much longer. Best greetings to Leroy . . and all my deepest love to you.*

*My permanent address will be 1217 34th Street N.W. Washington, D.C.*

*Institut de Géo-Biologie*
*Rue Labrousse*
*Peking, August 31. 1945*

THEIR
1941–48
LETTERS

163

*Dearest,*

*Just a few lines to let you know that everything is all right here. I am five years older than when you left, — but approximately the same outside, and (I hope) still more the same inside, — especially for you. — In Peking, this long stretch of time was practically uneventful, and rather dull. Except for a trip to Shanghai and a short holiday in Shanhaikwan, I did not move. During the two last years even the Hills were not easily reached! I have printed a long series of scientific memoirs (mostly not yet distributed), and laid a considerable number of "eggs". On the whole, I went along the same groove of thoughts; but I think I went deeper. Also, I read a lot, so that I have almost become a "lettré" under the direction of de Margerie.*

*My plans are still very hazy, as it is natural. Contacts with Europe are not yet re-established. As soon as possible I plan to go to France where the atmosphere is favourable to me, I believe. And then we shall see. Much depends also on the possible developments (or non-developments) of the Geological Survey. I do not give up the idea of starting some new periods of staying in China.*

*And what about you? I am eager to know. Since a long letter of you which came through Chungking (in 1944) I know nothing of America. Did you see Bosshart, in July? Eleonore is here since a year. Through Bosshart she just heard that Faure is OK (in Washington?) waiting for her "fidélement". For her, un grand soulagement! Besides, a few friends are still here, among whom, in first line, Mme Raphaël. Claire Hirschberg has married Prof. Tadjan, of Fujen University.*

*Hope that this letter will reach you soon and safely. Evidently, if I have the choice, I will try to go to France via America.*

*Yours, as before! +++*

*P.T.*

---

Teilhard's end-of-August letter reached Lucile in the early autumn of 1945. It was her first news directly from him since the spring of 1943. Moreover, the next letter from him in October indicates that some of her early 1945 correspondence was reaching China.

---

*Lucile, dearest,*

*Inopinément, j'apprends qu'il y a ce soir une occasion pour l'Amérique. En hâte je vous envoie ces lignes pour vous dire d'abord que je viens de recevoir votre longue chère lettre du 23 septembre, qui m'apprend tant de choses sur vous. Je savais la mort de votre père.*

Unexpectedly I have heard that there is an opportunity to get a letter off to the U.S. this evening. Hastily I write these lines to tell you, first that I have just received your dear long letter of September 23 which tells me so many things about yourself. I knew

*Pauvre maman, que je me rappelle si bien, si douce, quand elle habitait votre maison . . . Petit à petit, la vie nous sèvre de bien de choses. Le tout est que ces vides se remplissent de la seule passion des réalités plus belles et plus grandes. Je suis si heureux de vous savoir settled à Washington, que je connais, où je puis me représenter votre environnement, et où il y a tant d'amis pour vous. - Au début de septembre, je vous ai envoyé une lettre directe par avion, mais à Chicago, de sorte que vous ne l'avez peut-être pas reçue. Par le second Gripsholm, je ne vous ai rien envoyé, Mary Ferguson m'ayant dit que le transport des lettres était interdit.*

*Ce que je vous disais en septembre, je vous le redis. Depuis cinq ans, j'ai pris de l'âge. Mais dans mes orientations de fond, je n'ai pas changé. C'est vous dire que je ne regarde les années àvenir que comme un temps à consacrer à la défense et à la propagation des idées que vous connaissez si bien, et qui tendent de plus en plus à se résumer dans cette attitude unique et incroyablement riche: l'amour de l'Evolution comprise comme la genèse d'un Centre personnel et vivant. Je n'ai encore aucune idée précise sur ce que je pourrai faire. Mais il est toujours sous-entendu que votre influence sera là pour me sensibiliser et m'encourager. You can so much — on me and for me, Lucile . . . Au début d'Octobre, j'ai été officiellement avisé qu'on désirait me voir reparaître à Paris. La difficulté est le voyage de retour, avec un peu de bagages. Je pense profiter d'un convoi ramenant (en décembre?) une partie des diplomates de Peking. Dans ce cas, il ne serait pas impossible que je passe par l'Améri-que!! Dans ce cas, je vous aviserais en temps utile, ne serait-ce que par un câble de San Francisco. Ce serait si beau . . . Que ferai-je exactement en France? Reviendrai-je en Chine? C'est possible, mais je*

that your father had died. Poor "maman" whom I remember so well from the time she lived at your house. She was so sweet . . . Little by little life takes away from us so many things . . . What counts is that these empty places be filled only with the passion of more beautiful and greater realities.I am very happy to know that you are "settled" in Washington that I know well - which means that I can imagine your environment - and where you have so many friends. Early in September I sent you an airmail letter, but to Chicago, so that you might not have received it yet. With the second Gripsholm I sent you nothing because Mary Ferguson told me it was forbidden to carry letters.

I repeat what I told you in September. I have grown older these past five years, but in my basic orientations I am the same. This means that I consider the years to come as a time to dedicate to the defense and propagation of the ideas you know so well and which tend more and more to be summarized in this unique and incredibly rich attitude: the love of Evolution being understood as the genesis of a personal and living Center. I still have no specific ideas about what I could do. But it goes without saying that your influence will always be present to make me sensitive and to help me. You can so much on me and for me, Lucile . . . Early in October I was officially advised that they wanted me to return to Paris. The difficulty is to go back with little luggage. I hope I can join a convoy bringing home (in December?) some of the diplomats returning from Peking. In this case it is not impossible that I return via America!! If this is the case I would let you know as soon as I can, possibly by a telegram from San Francisco. It would be so good . . . What will I do exactly in France? Will I return to China? It is possible, but I can forsee nothing in this restless world.

*ne puis rien prévoir, dans ce monde en pleine agitation.*

*Le Péking si calme de ces quatres dernières années se remue et se désagrège. Tout le monde pense plus ou moins à partir, et on prévoit de nouvelles arrivées. L'afflux Américain a été une résurrection. Le Colonel Mayer est ici (je vais le rencontrer chez les Burchart après-demain). Larry Sickman a passé ici, en brillant major. Rencontré plusieurs officiers (civils mobilisés) très intéressants. A part de gros réalistes (comme Billy Christian) qui ne voient dans la victoire qu'un succès capitaliste menacé par de nouveaux conflits, j'ai été heureux de trouver du côté américain le sens des renouvellements nécessaires et l'urgence d'un nouvel esprit, à une échelle vraiment terrestre. Il me semble que le prestige de la Russie décline, et que c'est l'Amérique qui tient dans ses mains l'avenir immédiat du monde: pourvu qu'elle sache développer le sens de la Terre parallèlement avec son sens de la liberté.*

*Eléonore est ici (chez les Wilhelm). Par Bosshard elle a su que Faure lui est toujours fidèle et l'attend. Mais rien de Faure lui-même, et nous ne savons pas où il est! J'imagine que de son côté il ne sait pas où se trouve Eléonore. En ce moment celle-ci est un peu inquiète car on recommence à parler de concentration pour les Allemands de Chine. Mais ma conviction est que rien de pareil ne lui arrivera: car son cas est trop clair et trop favorable. Je vous ai nommé les Burchart. Pony est toujours aussi délicieusement la même. Otto est toujours malade et fantasque, et si sympathique en même temps. Depuis trois ans ils vivent dans un charmant pavillon de l'Ambassade Russe.*

*Je termine en hâte, pour porter ma lettre. Puisse-t-elle vous arriver vite!*

*A vous, dearest, si, si affectueusement.*

Peking which was so calm these past four years starts moving and dispersing. Everybody thinks more or less about leaving, but we are expecting new arrivals. The American influx was like a resurrection. Colonel Mayer is here (I will meet him at the Burcharts the day after to-morrow). Larry Sickman passed through as a brilliant major. I have met several officers (called up civilians) who are most interesting. Apart from some over-realistic people (like Billy Christian) who see in victory only a capitalist success threatened by new conflicts, I was happy to find on the American side a feeling for necessary renewals and the urgency of a new spirit on a really earth-wide scale. It seems to me that the Russian prestige is declining and that America holds in its hands the immediate future of the world: as long as America knows how to develop the sense of the earth at the same time as her sense of liberty.

Eleonore is here (at the Wilhelms). Bosshard told her that Faure is still faithful to her and is waiting for her. But I haven't heard anything from Faure himself and we don't know where he is. I rather imagine that he doesn't know where Eleonore is. Right now she is a little worried because people are talking again about concentration camps for the Germans in China. But I am certain that nothing will happen to her: her situation is too clear and favorable. I told you I saw the Burcharts. Pony is still as deliciously herself, Otto is still ill and whimsical, but so likeable at the same time. For the past three years, they have lived in a charming little house at the Russian Embassy.

I hurry to finish and bring my letter. I hope it will reach you soon!

Yours, dearest, so, so affectionately.

*God bless you a thousand times, for the past and for the future!*

*yours always*

*P.T.*

Sometime before Teilhard's October letter reached Lucile, she wrote to him on November 18, from her home in Washington. Much of this "talk" with him reviewed their many Peking agreements and disagreements and mutual concerns. And when his October letter did get through, she wrote again, a week later.

*1217 34th Street N.W., Washington D.C.*
*November 18, 1945*

*Pierre dearest, -*

*A few days ago Isabel Mayer phoned me that she had just had a letter from Bill written in Peking Nov. 1st and he had just had tea with* you *and the Burchards!! and that you had just had a letter from me!!! I am so glad that at last you have heard . . that must be the one that Sabe Chase, American Consul, took out for me . . I have sent two more since then by the regular Air Mail, so they ought to be coming along soon . . I had said much the same things, as I did not know whether you had ever gotten any word of me . . especially since I have made such a definite move as to buy a house here!! I have not yet been here two months, but I feel so at home and so much happier than I have any place else in America!!! and as I wrote you, it is a very well located place and I know I can always rent it if I want to GO places again . . . and I have a feeling I will get restless one of these days . . . .*

*I am so terribly anxious to hear from you and to know what your plans are for the future?? do you know yet where you will want to be?? but I don't suppose you will know until you have been over here and looked over the ground, . . I have a feeling that you will not want to settle in France!!! but maybe that is only "wishful thinking?" . . .*

*I am enclosing a small clipping from an address that Prime Minister Attlee made here recently . . I thought it would interest you . . as it reflects your own thoughts . . and one hears this sort of thing a lot . . . "The atom bomb has made people (at least a few of them) realize that we have to take stock of ourselves and the Christian principle seems to be one great hope - but it really is sadly missing. The church dogma is so far behind the modern scientific discoveries - that man just can't reconcile the two -he KNOWS what science does - so naturally it seems so much more REAL to him. Oh Pierre, isn't that where YOU come in?? to show him that the Christian idea is REALLY the most scientific?? Oh I do so want to see your new papers (eggs) to follow what you have been thinking these long years . . . Pierre . . I'm almost through reading "La Dignité Humaine" by Lecomte du Nouy . . Isn't he a friend of yours . . I'm sure you must have talked together for he puts forth so many of the same ideas as yours. This was published just a year ago in America . . I'm reading it in French so may miss some of the nuances, but I find it MOST interesting . . Aldous Huxley has a new book out which I've not yet read . .* The Perennial Philosophy *. . "The Author has drawn upon the wisdom of the ages to find the common denominator of a faith for today" even an agnostic can read this book with joy . . perhaps Mr. Huxley has written the most needed book in the world" . . . . (from the advertisement!!) Huxley has gone more and more toward the mystic . . I must get this as he interests me . . Oh so much to talk over!! I've read quite a bit of the real Wisdom of the East . . and I think it is*

*SO interesting how very SCIENTIFIC their approach is . . their explanations of the stuff of the Universe . . . its so modern so like YOU!! I so often think of what you wrote in the "Gripsholm letter" that doing away with ALL barriers is the only thing worth fighting and dying for . . That is of course the great question before the world today . . the advanced religious thinkers as well as all others . . there is such a chance right now . . I mean such an opportunity to help put things on the right track . . . and EVERYones effort is so needed . . It is almost unthinkable but SO true, how many many want to go BACK . . and so many of those are the people who still have a great deal of power, for things do change so slowly . . "How often have I made myself remember what you have said so often - that we must take a LONG view!!! and how often in arguments I've put forth this idea which I so fortunately learned from you - I could go on endlessly, and even this very one-sided conversation is such a joy - so much more than we have had for so so long!! It is just shortly after five!!! perhaps that is why I find it so easy to talk to you. Oh darling how I have missed you and your talk and the beautiful alive and creative ideas that you were always giving me . . we WILL have it again???*

*Saturday evening I had dinner with Peggy Boyden!! Lt. Commander Boyden!!! we talked so much about Peking and we all love it so much . . probably you are so fed up with it right now that it is hard to realize what a GRAND place it is . . If one had to be stuck in one place for the war, you certainly were lucky to have been there . . and we looked through some of her photographs and suddenly there YOU were, out in Mayos courtyard, Oh Pierre what a thrill, to see your dear self and smiling and all . . of course we talked about you and wondered how long before we would all be together again . . in Peking!! I think Peggy will try to go back as soon as she can . . Just at the moment things do not look too good in North China, but maybe before this reaches you, things will have changed, I do so hope so.*

*Tillie was here for dinner with me a few nights ago, looking so young and SO pretty and so much the same . . I think she too hopes to be sent to China before long . . Delia Tyrwhitt was in . . she may go to England soon . . you know that Peter was killed at Singapore and she has to go over to see about some of his affairs . . I hear that Bob Drummond is to be in Peking about this time before he returns to the US . . . so you have no doubt seen him. Bill and Helen and their darling little boy are here. Bill just out of the army and does not yet know what he will do. Barbara Petro so near . . she just heard from Petro from India, New Delhi I think, that his release had been deferred so he did not know just when he would be home, saw him here last summer, looking so well and fine.*

*I had a letter yesterday from Nirjidma which did not sound too cheerful. I guess life is pretty difficult in Paris right now . . she said Michel has left the New Agency and joined the Foreign Office and he hopes to be sent to the Far East soon as a Consul-General!! She said she had gotten in touch with the Jesuits in Paris but they had no direct news from you but knew you were well. No news yet from her family, tho they had heard from people in Shanghai!! Letters MUST come soon. I look so hopefully everyday . . YOU HAVE written?? oh yes surely . . I don't know why you did not get letters from me . . every so often all during the war I sent them to friends in Chungking . . but I guess the Japs just made things tighter . .*

*I have had no news from the other friends . . Ida Treat . . who seldom writes but has been in England for a couple of years . . well I suppose recently she is in France . . the Bégouëns were in Morocco when I last heard . . and Breuil in South Africa . .*

*I hear they are going to reopen the PUMC!! Mary Fergusson is to go out there very soon and some of the others . . If they should start work again at Chou Ko Tien would that interest you . . but how can you know now . . Oh we have heard the wildest tales about Grabau . . that he has MARRIED the Flying Angel . . in spite of the fact that he has a wife here. Is she still with him? and what has happened to Truda, and Germaine . . How soon will you be able to leave there? etc etc . . Now that there is a possibility of writing, the questions [seem] endless . .*

*And the things I would like to say . . that you are more dear more close [to] me than ever before and that the thought of you has been more than ever a living inspiration all these years . . I feel a littly shy, a little reticent to say all that is in my heart. And yet I don't believe that you have changed . . I read and reread what you wrote so long ago. May 31st <u>42</u> to be exact . . "I must let you know that I remain yours" that I do my best to remain exactly and entirely what you wish and want me to be. I am so sure for my part that you are still the same, and even MORE. After all that was written 3 and 1/2 years ago . . . so dearest do please write me soon and [tell] me that it is still the same!! my whole heart is here for you if you want it . . . well it is still all yours anyway / ! / no matter what you think!! It is so wonderful about love, no one can stop you from loving . . Oh darling I hope you don't want to stop me, I think I have learned even more than ever how to make it a good love a creative love . . I hope so . . for I would like so much to give you such beauty, such happiness that it would make all you do more rich and strong and vital . . There is SO much work for YOU to do, and my greatest wish is that I shall be able to work with you again.*

*As for my sculpture!! I always work every day - and I am having an exhibition down in Palm Beach in January - and hope to go down for a couple of weeks - which ought to be pleasant. It is hard to keep at sculpture these days - but I still believe that it is important . . and besides that is the only training I have!!*

*Best Greetings to Leroy, Françoise Raphael, the Burchards etc etc . . . and my whole heart full to overflowing with love for you dearest,*

*1217 34th Street   Washington   Nov. 25, 45*

*Dearest,*

*Your precious letter of October 30 arrived yesterday; oh can you imagine how happy I was to receive it! The one sent to Chicago will be sent on to me, but it has not yet arrived . . Those letters seem to take a very long time . . so I am going to try to send this another way . . I've sent three other Air Mail letters which I suppose will eventually reach you . . All the communications seem fairly slow . . and the way things are going in North China now!! One wonders when you all will able to leave. I do so so so hope you will have to come by way of the U.S.! Does your call to Paris mean anything special? I sincerely hope it is nothing but routine.*

*Though of course I also hope that you are going to use your coming years to really put out BOLDLY your ideas. You say in your letter of the coming years as a time "à consacrer à la défense et à la propagation de vos idées". Pierre, I hope there is going to be a lot of propagation, a defensive attitude is not strong enough now! You will see and <u>feel</u> it I am sure just as soon as you are in the Western world again - and from all I hear of France - she needs it so much, so very much.*

*Pierre, I hope you do not mind when I write you this way - the way we always*

THEIR<br>1941–48<br>LETTERS

169

talked - I feel in your letter a certain _reserve_, a something that always happens when you had been in Paris for a long time - do you remember after '39 how long it took to be really at ease again?! So I am assuming that as you say, "Mais dans mes orientations de fond, je n'ai pas changé" and I shall write with that in mind, for I have not changed - my interest in you and your ideas, and my deep affection for you, have only grown deeper and stronger during these years - and the need for a POSITIVE attitude about LIFE is so very great now - we need each other more than ever - or so it seems to me. It is so thrilling to be able to communicate with you again, but the lines are so uncertain that I feel a bit constrained .. so my dear, in the letters that I have already sent to you please remember me at my BEST .. for I seem to remember that I wrote about a letter to Rhoda and was trying to be a bit facetious, and I thought it might amuse you to have me so much myself .. but please forget it, if it was a sour note .. I know how really UNimportant it is.

I can imagine how everyone there must be restless now, almost released, but not quite .. what of LeRoy, will he leave too? and Mme Raphael? I can well imagine that you are all very restless .. Do give my warm greetings to Eleanore, how strange of Faure not to write!! but he IS strange!! I understand that he is in Paris, surely the Foreign office there would reach him .. oh, how many many people are trying to reach other again .. and how many will never succeed, at least in this life .. three of my very good friends lost their only sons .. and are we going to learn? One gets so terribly discouraged sometimes. I KNOW that evolution is the law of life (and that it converges in a personal Center). But it does seem slow! And then I remember the Time elements of Paléontologie!! and try to be CONSTRUCTIVELY patient. But so many of the "World Planners" talk of Unions and Leagues, etc., but so few seem to be able to talk of the absolute NEED of belief in a Higher Power - which seems to me the only thing that will REALLY change man! Oh Pierre, how I do need to hear you talk! How terrifically I have missed your blessed words of wisdom. I've read a lot and tried to think things out - but for so many years I had the great benefit of your help that I feel very lost without it - and will I have it again some day? Who knows - but I feel so sure that I shall have it! I have great Faith that Life will work out right. I am so very keen to know what has happened to you INSIDE - what these years have really done to you - As I said, your letter disturbed me a bit - it sounded so very reserved - but probably that is not the REAL inner you that I'm sure burns with an even brighter flame. More intense and more determined to throw its Light just as far and to as many as possible - but REALLY possible - not warped and held back by a lot of people who are still thinking in the ideas of the Moyen Age!!

You say you hope America is developing a "sens de la terre" - I wish you would write me more of what you mean by that - I am afraid she is NOT. But do tell me more and what one could do to help it!!

God bless you dearest .. always and always and I love you and thank you from my heart for all the beauty you have given to me .. and thanks for mentioning in your letter "for the past and for the _future_"

all my love to you

Lucile

I have no special news of our friends — Ida or the Bégouëns — a card yesterday from Ernestine Evans with no news except she says "I need badly some of the people who knew the Père" — we all need you! Saizeau still in Chicago - things going well for her. She hopes to go to China this Spring ——

1217 34th St. N.W. Washington D.C.
Dec 3, 1945

Dearest, -

   The precious letter of Aug. 31 sent to Chicago has reached me two days ago, and I can't tell you how very very happy it makes me -For your other letter, the one in French was so very much more RESERVED - but perhaps the one of mine that it answered was also very reserved - and perhaps they were both that way for the same reason - I was not sure IF you would receive it and had no idea how many other people might read it first!! However this one is so precious so YOU and while it was written two months earlier, I'm sure it is all true today - I was so moved I laughed and I cried and I said a very deep heart-felt prayer of thanks . . Oh Pierre I feel so sure that we will be working together again, perhaps not immediately, but before too too long - I have complete Faith in that and I do SO SO hope that in the meantime you have been able to send me some "eggs". How I long to follow your thoughts. Naturally they are along the same line, but what new development?

   I am glad to know that at least one of my letters via Chungking did get to you . . It gave you a bit of news . . This morning Ernestine Evans phoned me . . She said the last she heard Simone was still in Morocco and that life was quite difficult . . Ida had been in Brittany . . but she had not heard from her in a long time . . Ida is not very good about answering letters!! Ernestine was SO happy to have some news of you and said, "we just MUST get the Père over here SOON" . . was this summons to Paris, anything special? I do hope not.

   Yes I saw Bosshard here in July when I came down to get my house. He was staying in the same house with Tillie, and went to Switzerland shortly after . . He met Faure in Paris where I believe he still is . . Tillie said she was writing more details and sending it through some Marine in Peking . . so I hope Eleanor has already received more news . . Tillie hopes to be sent back to China very soon!! So many are going now and some coming . . a young newspaper woman who met you right after the peace was here and told Jim Penfield of meeting you and how WONDERFUL you are!! Oh it is so good to know, dear, that the old charm is still working . . after all it is only four years, not five since we parted . . I hope I haven't changed too much, I don't know . . somedays it seems to me I look mighty ancient . . but my heart is just the same . . oh Boy and will it dance and sing when we meet again!! for we shall do that and fairly soon!! well maybe not SOON . . but one of these days . .

   Delighted to hear about Claire Hershberg . . hope she is happily married . . and what is Mme Raphael doing all this long time . . and what of LeRoy, you do not mention him in either letter. Saizeau is still in Chicago and recently her affairs have gone very well and she has made some good connections and hopes to be getting back to CHINA in a few months . . I am making no plans in that direction . . Peking would not be much without you and I want to see you more than anything else . . so I shall stay right here until somehow some place I can see you . .

   I am planning to have an exhibition of my work down in Palm Beach, Florida this winter, I may go down for a week in January to get it going. Have just sent a garden piece down there for a big show that opens in December - a sort of introduction. Nathalie has been taking drawing lessons!! and works very hard . . They will be going back to Boston very soon. Washington is a little like Peking in that people move about quite a lot.

*Ernestine said she was going to see what about getting you on a plane for US++!! more power to her . . Remember, dear, if you have to have friends here for a visa that Arthur Ringwalt is here, also John Carter Vincent in the State dept . . and they will do everything possible for you . . so DO NOT hesitate to use them . . beside Roy Andrews etc., etc. You have THOUSANDS of friends over here and everyone of them would be DELIGHTED to do anything they can for you . . don't forget this . . really . .*

*I am sending this letter again to Chungking, which seems a long way around, but it is still the fastest that I know of . . I think this is the 6th letter . . so I do hope that you have received more than the first one . . they surely ought to be coming through regularly soon . . and I hope you have written again . . there is SO much I want to know . . but that will take HOURS of talk!!*

*Peking, December 13, 1945*

*Dearest,*

*I have just received, in the course of a few days, your letters of November 5 and 12. And I am so disappointed that you did not yet receive the two I wrote you since August. The first one, of course, was addressed to Chicago. But the second one, sent to Washington, should have reached you . . . The present one I give to Bob Drummond: certainly you will get it safely.*

*Dans ces deux lettres (perdues?) je vous expliquais comment, par le deuxième Gripsholm, je n'ai pas pu faire passer de correspondance (Mary Ferguson m'a dit qu'elle n'osait rien prendre). Je vous disais aussi que, pour moi, la fin de la guerre s'est passée sans aucun changement matériel. Toujours à la rue Labrousse, avec Leroy. Toujours publiant des mémoires variés (à peine encore distribués). Et toujours écrivant une suite d'essais, non publiés, ou j'essaie de préciser et d'appronfondir les idées qui nous sont chères à tous deux, et que vous connaissez. Dans ce sens je crois avoir fait quelque progrès. Pour l'instant, je suis en instance de départ. On m'a redemandé de France: mais si peu clairement (malgré que le cable eût une note d'urgence) que je suis encore ici. Les communications sont encore très difficiles par mer; l'avion très cher, sans compter que je voudrais arriver à Paris avec plus de 25 kilos de bagage. Bref, je marque le pas. J'avais d'abord pensé passer par l'Amérique. Mais de ce côté-là les lignes sont si chargées (et chères) que je crains d'avoir à me con-*

In these two letters (lost?) I was explaining how, by the second Grispholm, I could not send any correspondance (Mary Ferguson told me that she was afraid to take anything). I was telling you also that, for me, the end of the war happened without any material change. I am still at rue Labrousse with Leroy. Still publishing various memoirs hardly yet distributed. And still writing a collection of essays unpublished in which I try to clarify and express more profoundly the thoughts which are so dear to both of us and which you know. I think I have made some progress in this direction. Right now I am getting ready to leave. I have been asked to return to France, but not really clearly (although the telegram had a note of urgency). So I am still here. Communications by boat continue to be very difficult; flying is expensive, not mentioning the fact that I would like to arrive in Paris with more than 50 pounds of luggage. In short I try my best. I had first thought of going via the U.S.A . . But in this direction the lines are so booked (and expensive) that I

*tenter de la route Suez, si je peux trouver un bateau. Au delà, je ne vois absolument rien de clair. J'avais renoué mes communications, très amicales, avec le Geological Survey, - et je ne renonce pas du tout à l'idée de revenir en Chine. Mais tout dépend tellement de ce que je trouverai et de ce qu'on me demandera à Paris. De ce côté-là, aucune nouvelle! Peut-être me croit-on déjà en chemin.*

*En tous cas, dearest, you know that I do not forget you, et que, d'une manière ou d'une autre, je compte toujours autant sur vous pour me soutenir et m' "inspirer". Avec les années qui ont passé, je ne me sens peut-être plus autant de jeunesse ou d'enthousiasme pour la Géologie ( et encore qui sait, si je me retrouvais sur le terrain?). En revanche, mon désir de découvrir à l'Homme la grandeur et l'avenir possible du Phénomène Humain n'a fait que grandir; et c'est cette passion-là qui finalement semble devoir absorber ma vie. Or cet effort, précisément, Lucile, vous savez que je ne le conçois guère sans vous. Alors, vous le voyez, tout demeure et demande à croître entre nous, sur un terrain solide. Vous remarquerez peut-être que je vous écris le propre jour de Ste Lucile. C'est si tendre et si fort de sentir que, même très loin, vous êtes si près de moi . . .*

*Ici depuis la paix, nous vivons dans un tourbillon d'amis américains. Vu Larry Sickman, Bill Meyer, et fait une masse de connaissances. Merci des nouvelles que vous me donnez sur les amis de Washington, sur Nirgidma, etc. Je sais en gros, indirectement, que ma famille va bien, en France. Mais je ne sais rien des Bégouën, qui devaient rentrer du Maroc. Ici, Mme Raphaël est encore ici, et aussi les Burchart, qui pensent partir avant le printemps pour l'Amérique. Les de Margerie aussi vont partir quand ils pourront (au Japon Mr. Cosme a été "révoqué"!). Grabau se*

probably will have to use the Suez route, if I can find a ship. Beyond this I see nothing clearly. I renewed my relationship (a very friendly one) with the Geological Survey, and I am not at all giving up the idea of coming back to China. But everything depends so much on what I shall find and what I shall be asked to do in Paris. I have heard nothing from there! Perhaps they think I am already on my way.

In any case, dearest, you know that I do not forget you and that, one way or another, I still count on you to support and inspire me. With the years that have passed, I may not feel as young or enthusiastic about Geology (and yet, who knows, if I were back in the field?) On the other hand, my desire to show to Man the greatness and possible future of the Human Phenomenon has only grown, and it is this passion that might very well take charge of my life. And you must know, Lucile, that I cannot conceive this search without you. So, you see, everything remains the same and wants to grow between us on a solid basis. You will perhaps have noticed that I am writing to you the very day of Saint Lucile. It is so sweet and so strong to know that in spite of the distance you are so close to me . . .

Since the peace we live in a whirlwind of American friends. I saw Larry Sickman, Bill Meyer, and I have met many new people. Thank you for telling me about our friends in Washington, about Nirgidma, etc. I have heard indirectly, on the whole, that my family in France is well. But I know nothing about the Bégouëns who were supposed to come back from Morocco. Mme Raphaël is still here, also the Burchart who plan to go back to the U.S. before Spring. The de Margeries also will leave when they can (in Japan Mr. Cosme has been "recalled"!). Grabau

considers himself married with the Flying Angel. It seems that he received his divorce papers just at the time of Pearl Harbor (1941) but there no longer was a consul here to regularize the situation. So he acted "as if". In fact I barely saw him during these past years (we were not allowed to visit those concentrated at the British Embassy). He is a good deal worse and it is getting more difficult to hold a conversation with him. The best that can be said in favor of Mrs. Volange is that she has been a good nurse for Amadeus, sometimes sour-tempered but extremely devoted. It seems that Grabau cannot do without her, neither physically nor morally. On the material side, the people of the Geological Survey are coping well with this new development. I often see Eleonore who lives with the Wilhelms. She hasn't changed. Faure is in Yugoslavia and, in spite of the assurances transmitted by Bosshart, he remains as silent as ever. Perhaps he doesn't know where to reach Eleonore who begins to find the time long. I urge her to write c/o the Foreign Affairs in Paris. I would very much like for those two to finally get together again. She is so nice and so lively. We often speak of you and Tillie. Claire Hirshberg; who is now Mrs. Tadjan, is expecting a baby in February (Tadjan is biology professor in Fujen - an Armenian by birth, of Italian nationality and from a family who are living in Vienna). Claire really seems secure and happy with her husband. The Bardacs continue to be popular and happy. They get along marvellously. Since the arrival of the marines, their house (they now live at the bank) is the meeting place of the American officers. But they might be transferred to Tientsin. If I must stay here, I should miss them.

Bob will bring you three copies of a lecture I gave here last winter (you can

*que j'ai faite ici l'hiver dernier. Vous y verrez combien je reste le même. Ce que je voudrais tant, c'est de bonnes heures passées avec vous, en particulier pour vous parler de la "mystique nouvelle" que j'entrevois sous forme d'une "communion avec l'Evolution". Je compte développer bientôt celadans une Note. - Mon livre sur le Phénomène Humain a été arrêté à Rome par la censure: mais sans beaucoup de sévérité, il semble. J'espère encore surmonter les obstacles quand je serai en France. Vous savez que j'en avais confié un exemplaire aux Wiley. Où peut-il être (J'en ai encore deux, ici).*

hand them out). You will see how much I remain the same. What I want most of all is to spend some wonderful hours with you, particularly to talk with you about the "new mysticism" which appears to me as a "communion with Evolution". I intend to develop this idea soon in a Note. My book, *The Phenomenon of Man*, has been stopped in Rome by the censors: but without much severity it seems. I keep on hoping that I can overcome the obstacles when I am in France. You know that I have entrusted a copy of my book to the Wileys. Where can it be? (I have two more copies here).

*Soon I will write you again. Grandes amitiés à Tillie! . . .*

*Yours, as ever*

*P.T.*

---

Actually not published formally until after his death in 1955, *The Phenomenon of Man* is considered his most important book. It is the one Teilhard had "talked out" most with Lucile during the Peking years, and one for which she had translated many draft passages.

---

[Peking] *December 20th, 1945*

*Dearest,*

    *Just a few lines, in this letter of Leroy to Miss Saizeau, to tell you that I have just received your letter of Nov. 26 (and two more, by air-mail, before), answering my letter of Oct. 30. - A few days ago I have given a letter to you (and a small pamphlet) to Bob Drummond, on his way to America. - I will write you again in a few days, plus longuement.- Don't be afraid, as far as ideas are concerned, that I should be too "réservé", in Europe. If I am going there, it is in order to talk, — and I suspect that I am expected there just for to do that. ——*

    *No immediate prospects so far for the date of my departure. Except by airplane (but then practically no luggage.) Travelling back to Europe is still difficult. - And yet I must leave before spring. - I will let you know any further development. -*

    *A bientôt une autre lettre.*

    *With much love*

    *P.T.*

*Met two days ago Mrs.S.T.Wang (P.U.M.C.) qui m'a chargé de mille choses pour vous.*

1217 34th Street N.W. Washington D.C.
Jan. 4 1946

THEIR
1941–48
LETTERS

175

*Dearest Pierre, -*

*Have just written to Jane Smythe so will enclose a short note to you, as it seems, from here, as if it were so easy to send things to Peking from Chungking . . Jane wrote that she had sent a letter by Harold Loucks . . It must be good for you to see all these old friends again . . I do wonder if you have been able to make any definite plans yet . . Are the boats going now and will you go direct to France or come by way of US . . . . of course I'm hoping so much for the latter . . Well, I'm sure I will hear from you as soon as you know . .*

*I had a letter from Nirjidma a few days ago, saying that Michel has had a sort of nervous breakdown and has gone to Morocco for several months complete rest . . I suppose we who have been more or less out of it, have no idea what the people in Europe have been through . . people seem to be divided into those who have been bombed and those who have not . . We can be sympathetic . . but we can't really FEEL it . .*

*I am finding more old China friends here . . they seem to find Washington nearer to Peking than any other place in America . . it really is a very pleasant place to live . . Tillie was here for dinner last evening . . Had just had a long letter from Bosshard from Switzerland . . I think he expects to go back to China before long . . so does Tillie, in fact she expects to leave about the first of March . . is SO in hopes you will be here before then. Had a Christmas cable from Mariann Clubb from Vladivostok saying they would soon be in Shanghai. More and more people will be going back there . . and eventually I'll want to go too . . but not now . .*

*My work has gone very badly lately . . can't seem to concentrate . . partly the holidays and partly because I'm all interested in my exhibition . . I'm leaving on Jan 9 for Palm Beach to be there a week or two . . here's hoping things go well . . I sure do feel the need of some inspiration . . This is surely NOT an age of ART . . I suppose this is really a great transition period . . is that why one is so restless so much? Oh Pierre, how I do want to talk to you . . how very much I need your goodness and wisdom . . and esprit!! My modelling went so badly this morning, perhaps I am feeling a bit depressed!!!! but I do so very much hope we will be able to talk together again . . and plan and work . . You will see how much the world needs YOU . . Things must work out so you can give your great Gift freely!!*

*Write to me please, even if you haven't any definite plans yet, I want so much to know more how you are feeling and thinking . . I am thinking a great deal of you and everything about you is of the greatest interest to me . . Oh Pierre I do hope we meet soon!!!*

*All my love dearest,*

1217 34th Street N.W.
Washington, Jan. 29 '46

*Dearest, -*

*Yesterday I returned from Palm Beach and got your letter brought by Bob. He had just gone to New York but will be back in a few days. I can hardly wait to see him to get all the details about everything there and especially about you. I talked to Helen Drummond yesterday . . she and Bill expect to return to Peking soon!! and Tillie expects* to leave for Shanghai about March 1st!! it sure does make me restless .. but knowing that you will be leaving any day now .. makes it all much less attractive to me. If you were going to be there, I should certainly come too .. I'd manage it somehow .. as it is, I shall stay right here for the time being ..

"My exhibition was quite successful. I sold several pieces of sculpture, among others that <u>Madonna</u> which I had cut out of that piece of ivory I brought back. I'm rather sorry she has gone as I think I really got something quite spiritual there. I find it very hard to work these restless days .. it is certainly not an age of ART .. and yet it is important to keep the tiny flame alight .. and also I seem to function better when I am working.

Bob did not leave your pamphlets, I am sorry as I can hardly wait to see them. They contain ideas that are really important .. I am so glad dear that you have been able to keep on .. but of course you always will .. Pierre, I had a letter yesterday from Simone!! well I think I shall enclose it to you .. that will be best .. I'll send her a copy of your new EGG just as soon as Bob delivers them to me .. Helen said he wanted to give them to me PERSONALLY .. I will write to Simone in a day or so .. she will be so happy to have this recent news of you .. The letter enclosed in Leroy's, reached me in Palm Beach .. I sent his on to Saizeau immediately via air mail .. it is always SO SO good to hear from you .. and I do feel so very close to you dear and somehow, some place we will talk and laugh and be together again. Your ideas have become such a very definite part of my life and the real you is so close to me. I feel that I love everyone more because I love you so much - and it is you more than any other influence that is helping me to love God as I would like to. I realize more and more that it is not enough to just suddenly decide to love God and your neighbor. I can never thank you enough for all you have done to help me on the Way, and I know you will be so pleased with the word in Simone's letter of the people you have helped so much. And dearest I thank you from my heart for the things you say in this letter. "Or cet effort, précisement, Lucile, vous savez que je le conçois guère sans vous". Do you know what that means to me? that you still find a definite place for me in your life and work!! These bits of "warmth" mean so very very much dear. I feel so terribly lonely at times - but when I know that you have need of me too - well that gives me not only happiness but great peace. Remember dearest that I'm still a novice .. and your words of tenderness help so very very much. So very much to keep me faithful to all that I know is the BEST.

I am so sorry about your book. I do hope there are not serious obstacles in the way .. I hope so MUCH that it will be published. The Wileys are now down in South America as Minister .. I forget which country .. I will write and ask her about the copy she had. It is undoubtedly here somewhere. I do so hope and pray that you are going to be free to express yourself in France. You will see how MUCH you are needed and how wicked it will be if you are not allowed to talk. The church seems to have done so VERY little -certainly in this country one does not feel any REAL modern vitality and "will to do" .. It seems all along the same old lines - and dear there has been a GREAT REVOLUTION in the world - and man needs God more than ever - with his diabolical new inventions - but he can't get to him REALLY through the old forms and formulas. The age of air and atomic energy is not the same as it was 2000 years ago, nor even what it was 100 years ago. The communists have so much more drive and force and HOPE for Brotherly love - but they don't have enough. How I do go on - and you know all this so well - but Pierre you will feel it so much more when you are in the west - after all you people have been *pretty much isolated for a long time. I'm so glad that this time has helped to further and clarify your ideas - but now to <u>present</u> them will be the next important step - and that is a VERY important one. You will find a way I am sure, you love man too much not to find it.*

*I was so interested in all your news and gossip . . poor old Grabeau . . probably the Flying Angel was a blessing . . She has been very faithful. I am so sorry for Eleanor that she does not hear from Faure. oh how long the time must be . . Yes she is such a fine person. do give her my love . . and Peking will surely seem not the same without the Bardacs . . I am so glad to hear that they are so happy. I have tried to call Tillie to give her your message but she must be home, her family live very near here . . I do hope you two will meet in Shanghai.*

*I am waiting now for Nathalie to come in for tea . . they will be leaving Washington in a few days . . so many are beginning to go now . . It is like Peking in that way, and especially now with the war finished, lots of bureaus are being closed up.*

*I hope you will soon find a good boat for France . . I shall be terribly disappointed if you do not go through the States . . but at the same time I will so well understand . . everything is SO expensive these days. but DO come this way if you can!!!*

*Thanks so much dearest for your precious letter and I will soon have your paper which will help again to make you even more close.*

*This is the interesting part of Simone's letter. "We haven't had letters from the P. but my husband just back from Paris, heard he was on board a ship, and was to land in France in a few days. It was very bitter news for him who had waited so long for a passage home, to miss him thus. Everybody is anxious to see him and hope to be able to read all he has written. Max was stranded 4 days at the Azores and his room mate, a Frenchman former prisoner of war, said that at his camp the P's theories had helped many men, himself included. He was an atheist and Max says he is now an apostle! This gentleman is the "Directeur" of Cartier and on his way to New York. Another man, the former "aumonier" of the Marquis du Vercors, now deputy, a priest quite overpowered by the Père's philosophy and who had copies of my impressions. So I think Lucile dear, the best one can do for the moment, is to spread his thot as much as possible. For the moment, until we can correspond it seems the only thing to do, but happier days are close and we shall hear from him."*

*Well Pierre I feel so sure that somehow the time has come for you to talk and the way will be opened — and I do pray from the bottom of my heart that everything will go the way you want it to. I mean that there will not be difficulties put in your way for free and wide expression —— France seems to need her best sons so very very much. I can so well understand that that is where your heart must be — for myself???? I cannot see my place in the picture for the time being, but somehow Pierre I do feel sure that some time some place we can work together again. I can't deny that I feel a great void in me. I suppose I was some how HOPING that you might be here in America - but I know that France is right and now is the time for you to give your great gift — as for the future? Perhaps later we will be back in China!! who knows — but that you will share some of your life with me, tho it be only letters — will help — and I still hope that I may see you on your way to France.*

*I am so sorry about your book. I know how much it means to you (and should be a part of the world's knowledge) - so I do hope you will be able to get it published when you are there - it is so much easier to TALK about it — gee but I will be glad when you are finally there — you must be just bursting with all the good that is stored up in you!! and NOW the time has come!! that is very exciting.*

With the end of World War II (summer, 1945) and the establishment of the United Nations (winter, 1946), more and more news came through from Peking. Indeed, Teilhard's March 5 letter (carried by hand to Washington) reached Lucile long before her March 4 letter reached him — if it did. Lucile's carbon is incomplete.

*1217 Thirty-Fourth Street N.W.*
*Washington, D.C.*
*March 4, 1946*

*Dearest, -*

*I have just been reading again and studying "Vie et Planètes" . . and it was so like talking to you and made you feel SO close . . and after some time I got up and made myself a cooling and stimulating drink . . and I almost felt as if you were sharing it with me!! I've had so many of these "mentally shared" things!! how long will it be before we will really share things again?? Some day I am so sure . . . and two days ago came a letter fram Jane Smythe telling me of her trip to Peking and her visit with you!! Oh Pierre Nothing has made you seem more close!! Bob Drummond told me things about this and that!! but with Jane you were so yourself and so my dear friend . . she didn't tell me much . . but somehow her long ringing of your bell and the coolie slowly coming and then you not recognizing her at first and the burst of enthusiasm when you did!!! I can even see the expression of your eyes when you realized who she was!! (no wonder you did not know immediately with her dropping in like that +++) and then when you said goodbye and said you felt almost as if you had seen me!! I can see it all so clearly and it is SO GOOD to know that you are still and even more YOU!!!*

*But to get back to your dear "egg" . . It is indeed along the same line of thought . . but so much deeper and it is so really exciting. Oh Pierre I do so hope you are going to teach these things in Paris. It is so absolutely MODERN in approach and so deeply thoughtful and STIMULATING!! I sent a copy to Simone . . I hope you have received my last letter with the one from her enclosed . . I had one two days ago from Nirjidma . . says Michel is not getting better "no illness, just nervously run down" . . also said she had just been to the Jesuit Mission but no word about your return!!*

*PT wouldn't it be easier to get passage from Shanghai? how did the Burcharts get theirs? of course it may be a matter of finance!! In which case, well, I don't know what . . but Tillie was saying that there are so many Navy boats of one sort or another that you could surely get on IF you were in Shanghai . . wouldn't it be a good idea to go down there? I realize that I don't know a thing about the circumstances . . but I am so anxious for you to be on your way . . I still do not give up hope that you can come this way . . but in any case for you to get going seems so important . . I know that even with all your wonderful control etc you DO get impatient!! and I should think you would now be just about at the end of the string . .*

*All of which does not say much . . perhaps that is why you do not write, the last I heard was the short note enclosed in the one of Leroy's to Mlle Saizeau of Dec. 20 . . there are ENDLESS*

*Dearest,*

*I give this letter to my dear friend Mme de Margerie (the wife of the bright diplomate) who is leaving tomorrow for America, and plans to spend a few weeks in Washington. She is an exceptionally charming and intelligent woman, and a great friend of John Carter Vincent, whom she met in Shanghai. You will like her, and eventually help her in discovering some accomodation in Wash. for her and her vivacious daughter Diane. Why is it not possible for me to join them for the trip to America! Places are still extremely difficult to get on military transports, and so far I did not succeed, — mostly probably because I am not in Shanghai. In fact, this constant "incertitude" how, and when, and by which way to leave is the very reason for which I kept so silent with you since the beginning of the year. I hoped every new day to be able to write you something positive about my plans. Presently, I have decided to go to Shanghai next week, — and from there to fly to France by India, <u>unless</u> (which is <u>still</u> <u>quite</u> possible) I succeed in finding a boat to America at the end of March (that would be glorious!). Don't hope too much; but there is a hope! — I begin to feel more in a hurry to leave since I have received, two weeks ago, a cable from my first superior in France (a true friend) asking me to come back to Paris (aux "Etudes") as soon as possible. Besides, everybody in the French Colony of Peking is packing and gradually disappearing. The time has arrived for departure.*

*I got all right your long letter of Jan. 29 (on your way back from Palm Beach) with the letter of Simone and the little photo. Such things make me realize in what kind of "twilight" I have been living during the last years in the Peking "fish-bowl": when reading you, I feel the re-approach of the sea. After all, the most stringent reason for me to travel via America n'est-elle pas d'aller reprendre conscience de moi auprès de vous, dearest. A bath of life, and a rejuvenation, before I reach the battlefield in Europe. I do <u>not</u> regret the last six months spent in Peking, at the hot point of treble contact between Communism, Democracy, and the rising Yellow Mass. I saw, I thought, and I learned a lot. But now I must try to talk and to act. You will give me the spark, — as you ever did.*

*Two weeks ago, I had the surprise and the joy to see Jane Smythe dropping in my room, rue Labrousse. It was so sweet of her, — and we had such a delightful talk about you, and the friends of Washington. — She expects to leave Chungking, with Bob, and to come to Tientsin rather soon. — Françoise Raphaël plans to cross America in April; most probably you would see her. — Eleonore is still here, at the Wilhelms. Obviously she approaches a final decision with Faure (no more news of him): pro or con? May be Tillie will bring the final elements for the solution of the problem.*

*Au revoir, pour cette fois, dearest. — I will let you know as fast as possible how my plans are evolving. - Eleonore will keep the books and papers you left me.*

*En grande affection*

*Your*

*P.T.*

*Herewith a snapshot: Leroy and myself.*

*S.S. Strathmore. March 29, 1946*

*Dearest,*

*Just a few lines to tell you that, unfortunately, I had to give up the hope to return via America! . . Following a friendly cable of my present superior in France (a dear and intelligent friend), urging my coming back to Paris (aux "Etudes", 15 rue Monsieur), I left Peking by plane a fortnight ago, to Shanghai. And there I discovered that places to America were so difficult to get that, in order not to be delayed too much, I decided to jump on a large British repatriation boat. Airplanes in fact are almost just so slow on account of the crowd waiting in Calcutta. As you understand, I did not take this step without much disappointment. But I feel that I must hurry up to France, for major reasons. If necessary, later, I might perhaps go to the States from France? Let us look forward optimistically. The boat, of course — a beautiful liner — is already crowded and we are sleeping in hamacs —— those being unfavourable conditions for writing. Anyways, there are several friends aboard, and I can keep alive. Already the work in France begins to appear to me as an approaching reality, — no more as a dream. As soon as I reach Paris (for the 1st of May, I suppose) I will write you about the conditions and the prospects. —— I will miss tremendously your contact before I start again. But I know that your loving spirit will be with me. -*

*Yours ever*

*P.T.*

*Paris, at last.*

*15 Rue Monsieur*
*Paris, May 8th, 1946*

*Dearest,*

*Arriving here three days ago, I have found your precious letter of April 26, and the lovely picture (which I kissed immediately). Oh Lucile I still feel almost sick to have missed this crossing through America. But, really, I felt lost, in Shanghai, between the urgent calls coming from Paris, and the risk to be delayed for weeks if I did not decide for the "Strathmore". In fact Françoise Raphaël, leaving a few days later to America by a boat (on which General Worton had succeeded in getting me a place, but I did not know!!) has been disembarked in Guam, because the boat was suddenly shifted to New-Zealand and England. On the other hand, the Dubosc's had been positively refused to join de Margerie on the military transport (in spite of very strong support), so that I wonder if Colonel Mayer would have succeeded in my case. So, let us hope that I did the best. One thing remains: I need, for scientific reasons, to see people in the States. When things are settled here, and if politico-financial conditions are not too adverse, I wonder if I could not manage to go to America, and to stay there sometimes, more at leisure than if I had crossed in a hurry the continent. Why not?. That would be really satisfactory and glorious.*

*Well, in the meantimes I have reached Paris after a non particularly com-*

fortable, but easy trip. The trouble of the journey was the crowd and the noise: very difficult to establish contacts, — and simply impossible to work. Une traversée sans plaisir. Finally I spent my time with a limited group of good friends (from Tientsin and Shanghai: les Vayron, of the Franco-Chinese Bank, and two ingénieurs). Some interesting and useful talks. But I could not write anything down, as I hoped. Some good books, too. I read with great pleasure the last novel of Aldous Huxley ("Time must have a stop"), in which the germ of "Perennial Philosphy" is conspicuous. I think you will like it.

And now I am here, since four days, still searching for my bearings. One thing is clear. I was warmly received, — and the atmosphere is much more favourable for me than it ever was. But then I feel a little anxious. People are hoping, expecting too much from me, Lucile. I am a poor, groping man, fighting too much for his own light and life. I am not a God. What can I do to help them? What comforts me is to think that this internal experience of my weakness is probably my best chance of success. After all, my "fonction" is not to bring life to Man, but to show him a little better where Life is coming from. Anyhow, I realize deeply how superfluous would be my intellectual work if, at the same time, I do not increase my internal contact with the Fire which I dream to spread on the world.

Naturally, my life in Paris is not yet organized. Aux Etudes, it is clear that I will have to meet a lot of people; and that my papers (articles) will be welcome. Along the scientific line, I will try to develop my small Lab (aux Hautes-Etudes) (Labor. de géologie appliquée à l'Homme). But I did not yet meet enough people to plan anything precise. — As far as France is concerned, I am still confused. My first general impression is that people here are lost in a maze of petty interests and petty preoccupations: they do not perceive the main lines of world-development outside France, nor the main psychological currents inside the country. — Judging from the "vote" of Sunday, rejecting the new Constitution, the Communists are loosing ground, and this is their fault (greedy, and selfish: Thorez turns to be a rich man, by now!). But I would hate a reaction. I must try to join Ida Treat (perhaps in Paris?) to get some inside lights on the Party. My best friends (in my order and around) seem to be somewhat prejudiced. In a confuse way, I feel that I would horrify the French if I tried to express clearly what I think about nations, races and collectivisation. I must proceed cautiously: but I will.

Leroy left Peking by plane two days after me, but did not arrive here much earlier than me! I was delighted to see him again. He will probably stay a year in France. The future of the Institute of Geobiology is quite hazy. In any case, I remain an adviser to the Geological Survey: I keep open the way back to China. — The Bégouëns are expected in France, this summer. I am so anxious to see them. —

I don't tell you but the half of the news. But I prefer to send you this letter fast. — More will follow. —

I am so glad of the pictures. You are just the same, and even better!.

Yours +++

P.T.

*TEILHARD*
*& LUCILE*
*CORRESPOND*

*1217 34th Street*
*Washington D.C.*
*May 10, 1946*

182

*And now today is my birthday!! and the last one we spent together was <u>five</u> years ago in 1941. Little did I know then how long it would be before there would be another one!! but it was SUCH a happy day. I wrote in my diary how you came early, then we went to a lecture at the PUMC and came home for tea when you were <u>very</u> sweet and said many wise and beautiful and wonderful things!!! I'm sorry I did not write them down just as they were said!! so often you <u>said</u> such wonderful things - it is a pity I did not write them immediately. I remember another of my birthdays when we went to Central Park\* and I remember just where we sat - facing that lagoon near the west front of the Park!! and that day too you were particularly eloquent . . . Precious friend. The first thing I did this morning was to ask God to bless you and to thank Him for giving me this wonderful and beautiful friendship - which years and miles cannot change - on the contrary they make it always more rich and beautiful. Thank you too Pierre for all that you have given me through many years. Let us go on as always -*

*I am sure you must be very busy . . and how marvelous to really BE THERE instead of thinking and dreaming about it . . Do you know yet just what your work is to be? and how do you find Paris and France . . the reports sound rather bad, but reports are often so "concentrated" they do not give a true picture.*

*I talked to Poney Burchard a few days ago, she was just here for a day, but expects to come back soon . . she told me much about you dear . . and I could see more clearly than ever what you all went through during the war . . Im sorry for some of those reasons that you did not get to America first . . well dear for EVERY reason!!!! I wonder if you have any special lacks in your diet now . . It would be such a pleasure to me to send things to you . . won't you please tell me if there is something you want . . ??*

*Many friends are planning to go back to China . . you and Tillie must have just missed each other in Shanghai . . I have been trying to get a Chinese visa for Mlle Saizeau . . which I am sure now will go through . . John Carter Vincent was able to help. I wish she could come to see me here before she returns to China . . but I imagine her funds are not too good.*

*I am sure you are going to be very busy there for some time and will probably not want to even think of coming here!! but still there just MIGHT be some opportunity . . and Pierre PLEASE take it . . If something should happen that might make it possible for you to come IF you had the cash . . won't you my dear let me do it? I know you do not like to do this . . but these are most extraordinary times when formulas do not hold so much . . I'm sure I could raise the money easily and as you know NOTHING would give me more pleasure . . Maybe you are very rich!!! but I write this just in case there might be an opportunity that you would not be able to avail yourself of, because of lack of finds . . .*

*I find several letters to you which I never sent as I did not know you would still be there . . one in regard to Jane Smythes visit to you . . she wrote me all about it . . I suppose they are not in Nanking . . . I wonder what has happened to Mme Raphael? M. de Margerie wrote her that I would love to have her visit me here but I've never heard a word*

---

\*One of the Imperial City's lovely parks and not far from the beautiful chain of urban waters called by the Pekinese the South, the Central, and the Northern lakes.

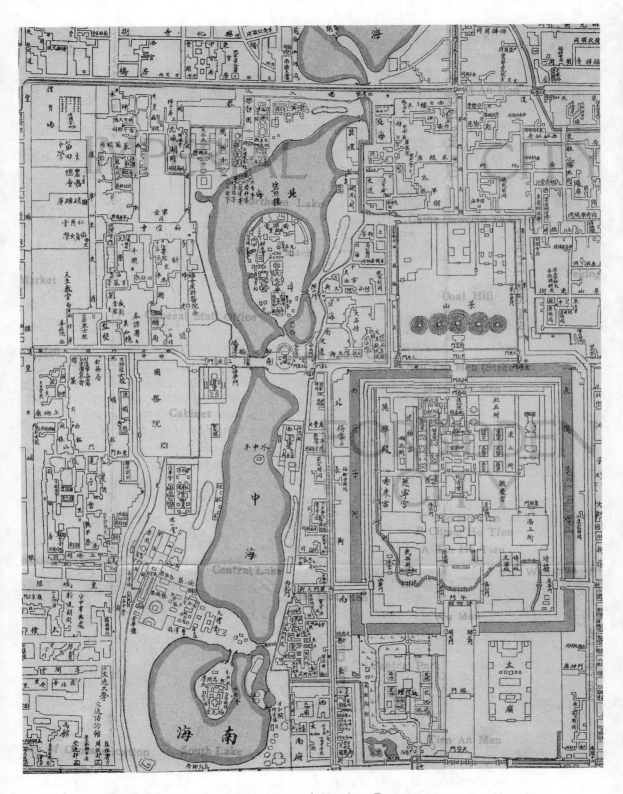

*Detail from map of Peking in the 1930s. Courtesy of American Express.*

*from her . . perhaps she went directly through . . The Burchards are looking for an apart-
ment in New York . . They say Otto is well and Pony FINE . . .*

*Pierre it is wonderful to think of you so close . . after all it took less than a week
now to get a letter!!! isn't that wonderful . . when one of yours from Peking took two and a
half years . .*

*I wonder so much how you find France and the morale of the people and what you
think can be done to give people FAITH again . . well some day I know you will write to
me and give me a few of your ideas . . and maybe <u>suggestions</u> too!! Until the time that we
can talk again . .*

*Yes my loving thoughts are always with you . . and I know that you are going to
give SO much to France and will be such an inspiration to your colleagues (not that that
interests me SO much) . . . there are SO many who want and need you so much more than
they do — as you know dear the lost sheep has great value!!*

*And now I must go . . It is so hard to stop . . sometimes you feel so close to me . .*

1217 34th Street N.W.
Washington D.C., May 21, '46

*Your precious letter from Paris came about a week ago . . it was so your old self
and you seem so close . . it made me very happy!! Pierre I'm sure that you did make a good
decision, even if my heart does not agree, for you might have been delayed here and now
you are there and soon you will know how things are and what may be your future moves
— It would, WILL, be so wonderful when you come here from there, when you have time
and your mind is more at ease. and in the meantime it must be very good to be making
contacts with your old friends there . . and I hope you will soon have your life more or less
organized!! I don't like to think of its getting TOO organized there!!!*

*Your trip sounds like so many these days. I had a note from Tillie just as she was
arriving in Shanghai, saying she shared a cabin with four women and five children!!! I
wonder what has happened to Mme Raphael? Mme de Margerie wrote her that I would be
so happy to have her stay with me here . . but I've never heard from her . . Mlle Saizeau is
still in Chicago, having difficulty getting her Chinese visa . . Through the Vincents I think
it is all fixed . . but now the news from China is so bad, it makes one hesitate to go there
just now. I was so pleased with the photograph you sent me, but I cut it in two and sent
the Leroy half to Saizeau!!! She has had some hard times, but I think on the whole it has
not been too bad . . I invited her to come here if she would like a look at Washington before
she goes back . . but she does not yet know what she will do . .*

*Just now I am waiting for Betty Vincent; she is bringing a man from the best Art
Gallery here to see my stuff . . do hope he likes it well enough to give me an exhibit this
fall. I am quite sure I can get one in New York if not here . . but I'd rather make contacts
here . . I've just finished the portrait head of a darling little boy of a friend . . and I so hope
to get some commissions . . it is very hard to constantly work for "Arts Sake"!!! but it
also takes time to get established in a new place . . I get discouraged, but after all I've only
been here 7 months . . and NO ONE any place is very interested in Art these days. Well
they are pretty terrible days . . and I do wonder what you think of France now . . what you
say about being absorbed in petty interests is what every one reports . . it is understandable . . but sad . . I hope you have found Ida Treat and heard from that side of the fence . . . .*

*It seems to me the Russians are being most difficult and arbitrary just now . . I am so sorry, because they can give so much . . so can we all!!! when will people stop trying to grab things and stop to think of how much they can give and how much they can learn from each other!! I'm sure we agree very well about these things . . I hope you may have some influence on your crowd - they seem to be just about the most conservative and reactionary influence in the world. I don't mean your immediate gang, but the organization as a whole which is a pity because they could do so much - and it seems to the outsider as if they are doing nothing constructive, which brings me to what you say about . . what can you do?? oh darling I do so know how you feel . . so many expect so much of you!! and just how to do it!! well just by BEING yourself you do so much . . !! If somehow your Light can dispel the DOUBT and FEAR . . so predominant in everyone, or nearly all . . and Pierre I know how much people want to feel that it matters what they do individually, in their own little lives - that it counts. I know you stress this in your writings and your philosophy (as I understand it) NEEDS the effort of every single soul to succeed - therefore we each do matter and it is important what we do - but everything is so big and there is so much that people feel lost and finally it doesn't seem to matter anyhow, each one can do so little etc. etc. - a terrible long and strong chain that wrecks so many. You can give them courage and that is so very much - and your Light is so strong, so sure, it will be seen and give warmth to so many, who will eventually revive and start to BUILD. Oh Pierre how I wish I could talk to you - and there are several things I regret so much that we never talked about very much - things which seem simple to you probably but in which seem so difficult to me!! for instance, I think meditation would be SO useful these days - not just prayer, but the kind of thing you do on your retreats - and I don't know quite how!!! does that seem dumb to you? it is really true. I mean certain kinds of exercises which would help so much to make one FEEL, to REALIZE the things that your mind accepts very easily ——— the nearness of Christ, the oneness of Life etc . .*

*Have you read Wilkies "One World"? there is a newer book out, "One World or None"!! how long before man is going to accept this and live accordingly?? there is still VERY much greed in the world - and I'm afraid Evolution has not yet reached the place where men are going to live by the Golden Rule!! You probably read about all the strikes here - sometimes it is hard to know just who is right, but mostly the employers have not wanted to be fair . . . Well all this is hard to write . . but Pierre it is so wonderful to know that you are THERE and that this will reach you in a few days . . Oh I'm SO happy that you are out of China!! it seems SO far away now, in spite of the many friends who are returning . . I wrote you a letter there about your latest pamphlet that Bob Drummond brought but think it was not sent!! so I will leave that until next time . . I was SO glad to have it and to realize how you progress so deeply in the same lines.*

*All my love dearest, it is wonderful to have you so near!!!*

*Paris, June 18, 46*

**Dearest,**
        ***Pardon me if I did not answer earlier your precious letter of May 21. I am still simply submerged in the Parisian life, — people (every kind of people) calling, telephoning, asking for papers or for lectures all day long. The whole thing is extraordinarily interesting and exciting. But no time is left for writing; and letters, unanswered, are piling up on my table. A good thing, indeed, that July is***

*coming when most people will leave town for the summer vacations. Just now, I am burning the coal which I have accumulated during the seven past years in quiet Peking. But, at the same time, I get a lot of new material from my present experiences, and very soon I must start writing some new Essays, or even another book (for instance on the "Noosphere"). It is only when talking with human beings that one can realize what is exactly important to select and to say in what one thinks. - My old papers are spreading everywhere, at the most unexpected places. Several of the new ones (L'Esprit nouveau, La Planétisation humaine) are going to be published before the fall. "Vie et Planètes" was re-published in the "Etudes" in May, and made somewhat a "sensation". On the other hand, I will try during the summer, to push for a second time the publication of my book on the Phénomène Humain. And maybe I will succeed. Obviously, in the midst of the present political chaos, there are plenty of evidences of a kind of religious revolution: the re-birth of God. In the roman-catholic clergy the disgust is obvious for the old, claustrated, type of priesthood: not to be separated anymore from, but to <u>participate</u> at the utmost with human anxieties and hopes, has become now the dream and the ideal of our best young men. - So, I feel hopeful for the future, - and so happy to have got my chance for helping the metamorphose, - and so "tenderly" aware of what you did for keeping me alive. Because you really have been, — and are, — life for me, Lucile. And you know it pretty well, — and I too.*

*In such a turmoil, days are passing too fast. In fact I am still just camped as the first day of my arrival in Paris. No time for looking at my things. The mornings I usually spend in my room, — mostly seeing a continuous chain of people. Afternoon, I go to various places in town to see friends. Every week I have one or two or three evening talks in philosophical circles. That is really life!*

*Plenty of old friends here. Leroy has embarked in a series of biological studies, and will remain in Paris the next year. Guy and Laurette Dorget are staying in the nice appartment of pretty mother, à Passy (Guy is working aux Affaires Etrangères, in a section of UNESCO), surrounded by a circle of young people and old ambassadors or Academicians. At a dinner they gave me, I met Ambassador and Mrs. Guillaume (ambassador in Paris). Baronne Jules (as poor Raphaël used to call her) was charming, but clearly showed me that she resented I should not have called to her earlier, — and unfortunately I have <u>not</u> yet paid to her any call (no time!), a fact which makes me feel a bit uncomfortable, now. — I have met Baudet (an important man, now, au Quai d'Orsay), but not yet Jacqueline. Les de Margerie have also settled here. Roland has left for a while active service (one of the many blunders of the so-called épuration) and seems to enjoy thoroughly the life in Paris. Yesterday we have visited together a marvelous exhibition of all the Gobelin tapestries preserved in the French collections. — Ida Treat (Bergeret) is back from her Bréhat island, — full of life, as usually. She looks happy, and her husband is now in a rather high position, which he really earned. The two Bégouëns are still in Casablanca, somewhat tired physically, it seems. The business of Max is prosperous. But both of them need France. We hope they will come back this summer. Nirgidma has turned into a really impressive and dignified person. According to the last news, Michel Bréal (who was made "conseiller d'ambassade") is going to Peking (!!) this fall, - so that Nirgidma will be the mis-*

*tress and the hostess of the French Embassy, in dear Legations Quarters! — Life is so strange, sometimes!*

*Good bye, dearest. I hope material life is not too hard for you. And still more I hope your work keeps you busy and interested inside. We are very little, and so powerless as far as politics are concerned. But at least we can do our best so that the spiritual "temperature" of the Earth might be as high as possible: and finally this is the most important thing for Life.*

*With best love*

*P.T.*

*I will probably spend a few weeks in the south during summer (August). I will let you know. In any case, write me <u>here</u>.*

---

The following incomplete letter (right-hand edge missing on the carbon) may be either the June 15 or the June 30 letter that Teilhard mentions in his letter to Lucile from Paris on July 16.

---

—— *June 1946*

*that so much more completely . . It is SO good that your thoughts are developing along this same direction . . well of course they really could not do otherwise!! The fundamental TRUTHS are always the same . . but your presentation and development are SO of TODAY which is so very very necessary . . oh how I do want to talk to you! I had a long good letter from Simone recently written May 11 and they had not yet had direct news from you . . but of course communications must be fairly simple now and how happy she and Max will be to be in close touch with you again . . Poor girl was in the hospital . . she does SO much and has not too good health . . one of the REALLY beautiful people in this world . . and how fortunate I was to know her . . thanks to you!! and Pierre what a treasure are those years of our close association . . Simone also said Max had seen close friends of yours, Père? who said they had at last awakened to what a fine fellow you are!! (only she did not express it quite that way) . . but I'm SO SO glad dearest for you . . and for the OTHERS . . it is especially THEY who will benefit if at last you are going to be allowed to talk!! and now maybe your precious book can be published . . oh how I do hope so . . Have you heard anything more about it?*

*I am expecting Mlle Saizeau next week for a visit with me . . She has at last gotten her Chinese Visa, with the help of the Vincents . . and so I suppose she will soon be going back to China . . It will be good for her to see something more of USA before she goes back . . she has not had an easy time of it in Chicago so I hope she can have some fun here before she goes back, and Washington is so beautiful now, it will give her a better view of America . . Chicago is really pretty TERRIBLE . .*

*Did you hear that de Terra was down in Mexico looking for remains of early man? I saw it in a magazine early this spring . . I've not heard from Rhoda and have not been to New York except for a very few days, since I left there . . I'll be up there early July . . but she will probably be away by then . .*

*Do you remember the little house of Nathalie's where we went for a picnic when we were staying with her? she has loaned it to me for the summer . . and Betty and John*

*Carter are going up too early in July and then when John has to come back Betty and I will stay on until September . . Rose Jameson will come up for a few weeks and probably other friends . . Oh Michael Jameson was married last week!!! can you believe he is old enough? a lovely girl and Rose is very happy about it . . Erika von den Steinen and family are going to occupy my house while I am away . . He is teaching in the Navy school and has just been transferred here . . It will be nice to have them here this winter . . I do hope they will be able to find some place to live . . EVERYwhere housing is so difficult . .*

*Pierre I sent a box to you about 10 days ago which should arrive early in July . . I sent chocolates, toffee, soap, shaving things etc . . I do so hope they will be some of the things you want and do so hope you will tell me WHAT to send . . it is a really great pleasure for me to send things to you . . but it would be so much easier if I knew WHAT you want and need . . so many send dried fruit, tinned meat, cheese . . but living the way you do, I'm not sure what to do . . PLEASE tell me . . and what about socks? or such things . . .*

*A friend had a long letter from Tillie, but she did not say anything about Eleanor Tafel and her problems . . I wonder if you have had any news of Faure? Tillie is now in Nanking and seems very happy to be back in China . . but life seems to be very expensive and since you have left there, it seems SO far away and for the time being I am not making any plans at all about returning. I saw the Burchards here a few weeks ago . . Otto still looks very thin and in a short time he told me a great deal of gossip!!! Especially about Jacques Bardac and Hart(?) . . I suppose you have heard of the latter's death . . it occurred on the trip to the USA and they do not know if it was accident, violence or suicide . . There was evidentally some scandal but I forget the details!! Bob Drummond is back in Peking . . The Bill Drummonds are still here . . Helen is having another baby in a few weeks so now they will have to wait until she can travel again before they go out. Petro and Barbara expect to return to Hong Kong this fall. Did Grabau die before you left China? Poor old dear, I wonder how many volumes of his great opus he had finished . . and what will become of the "*Pulsation *The y . . . . Well all that must seem very far away to you now.*

*I am still working at sculpture nearly every day, but my time has been some what interrupted lately by so many guests, but after all people are VERY important . . My "Spirit of the Earth*

---

Since it was now five years since the war had separated them, their hopes to meet seemed increasingly ephemeral, perhaps more to Lucile than to Teilhard.

---

*Paris, July 16th, 1946*

*Read this letter on a sheet of white paper. My ink is too weak!*

**Dearest,**

*So many thanks for your two letters of June 15 (with the clipping (excellent) of W. Lippmann) and June 30. Lucile, I am so afraid you should think that I think less of you because my letters are so scarce. But it is* not true. *The truth is that you are always more the same for me, — but that I can scarcely find the time to seat quietly a few minutes at my table in order to scribble the more urgent answers to business letters which constantly arrive when I hope to have a quiet hour. — Well, I do not complain too much, since I am sure that you would approve, and tell me that I must go on, and follow the wind, when it blows. —*

*And it is still blowing. - Since my last letter, I still had to deliver several speeches (on "Personnalisation et Collectivisation"; on"L'amour de l'Evolution", — to 80 young new priests of Paris, — perhaps I told you already); and I wrote a rather good short article on "Les retentissements spirituels de la bombe atomique", — to be published in "La Revue de Paris", probably. — Due to innumerable talks, ideas are pouring in my brain, and there are many "eggs" I would like to lay. The first work should be to readjust someway the famous book, you know on "Le Phénomène Humain". I will try to do it during the summer, with the help of a few wise friends. — Just now, people are leaving town. My own plan is to join, on about August the 5th, a group of friends near Besançon, for a holidays-symposium. Later, I would go to Auvergne, - for the wedding of a niece (the daughter of my dear late brother, in the country). I will be back here, in Paris, on Sept. 20. In the meantimes, you can always write me here: letters will be forwarded. I am glad that you should enjoy your own vacations.*

*Here, I remain in contact with several "chinese" friends. Roland de Margerie will remain sometimes "en disponibilité" — but most probably will rise again, someday. The two Dorget are just the same delightful, enthusiastic children. Laurence Castellet has found national funds to rebuild the family castle, burnt by the Germans the last days of the war. A fortnight ago, I was invited by the Guillaumes to an impressive lunch, where I met (and had an 1/2 hour of private talk) with Queen-mother Elisabeth, — certainly a most remarkable person. - Leroy is not living in the same house as myself; but I see him often. We remain extremely close friends. — I was so pleased that you could see Françoise Raphaël. Did she mention to you the death of her mother? —*

*Well, I stop here — after several interruptions. I will write you again, before leaving for vacation. — So far, I do not need any support for food, etc. — Cigarettes would be appreciated: but taxes are so heavy that I would be soon broken if you started sending me any. — If I need something, I will let you know, sure.*

*Yours so much +++*

*P.T.*

*— I have received a letter from Weidenreich. The Rockefeller Foundat. elected me "associated Professor": one link more with America!*

*Les Moulins (Auvergne), Sept. 8th, '46*

*Dearest,*
*I am so sorry to be so late in my letters (yesterday I got your wonderful letter of Aug. 31, — the one of July 30 I received just at the time of my departure from Paris). Since six weeks, I am moving almost continously, most of the time in places where sending an air-mail letter to America seems to be an "affaire". Hence my "retard", which is no proof that I did not think of you: your letter was always there to remind me of you.*

*Just now, and since a week, I am in the old and comfortable house of my Parisian brother, in the heart of Auvergne. The house lies in the deep of the fields and of the woods, facing a marvelous landscape: first, a series of rolling hills, —*

*then the plain (la Limagne), — then, right on the west sky, the full series of the volcanoes; — and the lofty Mont Dore, in full also, at the right. Yesterday, the sunset was marvelous. I am planning to stay here up to the 18, day on which I will perform the marriage of a niece a few miles away (the daughter of the dear brother I lost in 1941). Then, on about the 20, I shall be back in Paris. And the real life will start again.*

*Here, I am really resting, physically and mentally (although I have a few things to write). In August, I met a lot of friends, mostly of my Order, first near Dôle, — then in Besançon (a funny old town: was not your dear French grandmother from somewhere there?), — then in Lyon, near which I made my "retraite". - Everywhere I had a busy, but interesting time. Two of my most influential friends took the time of reading the manuscript of my book (Le Phénomène humain) and agreed that the critics made in Rome were nonsense, so that the thing should be published. Much depends on the type of "Général" we are going to get. Elections will be finished before a week. Everybody seems to be hopeful. — Several articles of mine (4) were supposed to be published this summer, or this fall, - two written in Peking, and two last June in Paris. I did not yet see them. Two more are ready in my head. I will send you what I can.*

*I deeply realize, dearest, what you say about personal contact. And I long myself for America. Be sure that I will do my best in order to go there at the first chance. But, just now, I am not in the position to decide. So much depends on the political and financial conditions of the world! In case China would not settle the next year, I am trying to organize a short trip to South-Africa, with the help of President Smuts and Breuil. De Terra might perhaps come. We hope vaguely a support from the Rockefeller Foundation. This might be reason for me to cross the sea, to New-York??!*

*Good bye, dear, — I give this letter to my brother who is going to Paris for a few days. When I left Paris, your "free-of-tax" cigarettes had not yet arrived. And they <u>may</u> be there by now. I will let you know. They would be highly appreciated! But already I enjoy the thought that you had the idea to try to send them to me. So sweet of you.*

*Yours ever*

*P.T.*

*I enjoy every bit of news you send me on the friends of America. Of course, I remember the picnic with you and Nathalie: I can still visualize almost every detail! Do tell her, and Betty, etc., my deep regards.*

*Paris, November the 7th, '46*

*Dearest,*

*Your two letters of October 20 and 29 have come to me almost at the same time. And I feel somewhat "desperate" to have kept you waiting so long. At the root of the silence don't search anything else but the true fact (which you will understand, knowing me as you do) that I was busy writing feverishly a paper to be ready before the end of October, — a work to which I could only devote a short time every morning, between telephone calls and people coming to talk in my* room. But, in spite of all, my letter of August 15, 1938, remains true. By the deepest of me I am still leaning on you and I rely on you. Only and simply life is going on along its logical, and yet lovable way: less and less I belong to myself. Such you took me, and such you must keep me and bring me forward ahead of me. and such you will find me, or rather we will find each other at the heart and core of ourselves. Yes. And yet I feel that a real contact, a real talk would bring and give so much to me. Let us hope that the marvel will become true, soon.

Here, since my return from Auvergne, life goes on the same way, rather hectic, but interesting, or even exciting. New contacts and new possibilities are pouring every day. The difficulty is to select and to build something coherent using all this material. On the other hand, the sky is not perfectly clear in the direction of Rome. The fundamentalists are trying to counter-attack, down there. And although there is no serious danger in the air, I am friendly requested by my Order to refrain from being too openly conspicuous. For instance I had to give up a lecture to be given in Bruxelles last week, and for which I had prepared the paper which kept me silent with you last month. But, be quiet: the paper will be published in January, in a scientific review, just the same; and there is no difficulty for the case of several talks which I am going to deliver at two "superior" schools in Paris. On the whole more things remain to be done than I can handle. So everything is all right. I still hope to be able to publish the Phénomène Humain (which I wrote in Peking in 1940, you remember). My ideas have somewhat advanced since six years; but I could make use of this progress in a sort of Summary at the end of the book without recasting the whole thing, which seems to me an impossible task. I was going to have a small symposium in Toulouse with a few influential friends, to decide the matter, next week. But I heard this morning that the meeting was somewhat postponed (perhaps only for a few days).

I get more and more friendly here with Dr. Needham (English) one of the heads of UNESCO. Last week, he brought me, near Boulevard St. Michel, to a Persian restaurant, together with a certain Mrs. Weltfish (of the Department of Anthropology, Columbia University) on her way back from a Women Congress in Moskow. Everything was so exotic and so strange in this place that I had the feeling to be hundreds miles from Paris, - at large again. The spirit of wandering is not yet dead. During October I had also a dinner with Julian Huxley (executive secretary of UNESCO), but with Breuil and a few others, so that I could not contact him on the vital points. But I sent him a monthly with a recent article of mine (also about "planetisation" and he answered me that we were very close. The same day I had had lunch with Marshal Smuts (the author of Holism, you know), and we felt very close too. This last meeting with Smuts was motived by possible going to South Africa next summer (for two or three months) in order to study the fissures containing Australopithecus remains, a South African Choukoutien. If things materialize (it seems that money is coming) I should go there with de Terra. But nothing is definitely settled so far. Apparently, Johannesburg is not exactly in the dreamed line of Washington. But the reverse remains possible, because the money would come from the Vikings Foundation in New York, which means that I may have to go there for some sort of reporting, after the trip.

*I envy you for meeting so many old Pekinese friends. If you happen to see them, tell my best regards to the Lyons, to Mrs. Grew, and others. I forget none of them. Here, the Chinese friends belong mostly to more recent formations, of the de Margerie's time. Yet several of them you know. Françoise Raphaël has recently arrived, just so alive as before: she is looking for a job in Paris. Gilbert also is here, an influential man in the diplomatic world; I met him recently, no more with his fair-haired Finlandaise, alas, but with a black-velvet-eyed Egyptian wife, of really striking appearance. Good luck for him. The Bardac's are expected in a few weeks: but you may see them in America before me. No news from Eleonore. Did I tell you that the first thing I did here in May was to join Faure (now at the Legation of Budapest). I found him still playing with the idea of marrying her, and with a possible scheme to get for her a swiss citizenship (easy to get in her special case). But nothing could be decided, he thought rather wisely, before they could meet again and see how they felt after so many years. He told me that he was writing her a long letter (I did not tell him of course that Eleonore was losing patience and was rather friendly with an American boy). And then my fault was perhaps not to write myself to Eleonore. Now I lost her tracks, and present address. I hope she does not think that I ever forgot her. If by chance you happen to meet Mrs. Wilhelm in Washington, please, tell her the situation.*

*And now good bye, dearest. I must run out for two appointments, this afternoon.*

*Might this letter catch the first plane so that you be sure earlier that I remain so much*

*your*

*P.T.*

---

If Teilhard received Lucile's November letter (the carbon is incomplete and has no closing), there is no evidence of a reply.

---

*1217 34th Street N.W. Washington D.C.*
*November 30, 1946*

Dearest, -

*Your precious letter of Nov. 7 was waiting for me when I returned from New York about two weeks ago. I had been there for nearly 5 days and had a grand time. I saw a number of old friends and Art exhibits etc etc and came home feeling quite stimulated and your letter just put the crown of happiness on the holiday .. I just went up for a change as I wanted to get away for awhile .. Among others I saw Malvina Hoffman, who was SO pleased to have some news of you .. the Jo Davidsons, who had just returned from Paris and were full of enthusiasm about the beauty of it!! also found that neither of those two sculptors had any commissions for work!! so it seems to be with most artists these days .. also Ernestine Evans who had news of Simone!! but you have not mentioned her, which makes me so wonder if you all had not yet met!! I do so hope you have before now, for I know how much she was looking forward to seeing you!!*

*Also I took to Ernestine the translation of "Planetisation" (?) -it seemed to me it read very smoothly and clearly - I do hope I got your proper meanings!!! am anxious to* hear what she thinks of it. Was SO interested in your meeting with Julian Huxley!! I have just received a small book by Aldus Huxley . . "*Science Liberty and Peace*" . . . which I shall send on to you . . am anxious to see what he says . . as you know he has been greatly influenced by Eastern philosophy . .

Pierre I am SO sorry and distressed about the lecture to have been delivered in Bruxelles!! D —— I'm glad it will be published - but that is not quite the same thing!! I heard about this in N.Y.!! and about other lectures in Italy etc. etc. that you will not be able to give!! all of which makes me very cross!! What you are doing and what you have to offer is the MOST important thing in the world today!! Don't those moyen age fundamentalists realize ANYTHING of what is happening in the world today!!! while they are arguing about how many angels can sit on the head of a pin, the whole works will be blown to bits by the atom bomb!!! and what happened at the symposium in Toulouse to discuss the *Phénomène Humain*? Oh Pierre dear I do so VERY much hope that they are going to publish it. They just MUST do so - it must get out into the world!! and I thought everything was going so well and smoothly and that you were really having freedom to talk.

Oh and I'm so glad that you are seeing a lot of Dr Needham and that the "spirit of wandering is not yet dead" . . . and even tho South Africa is so VERY far away, I'm so glad that you will be getting away from Paris by that time!! they appreciate you more when they do not have you for too long . . and it will be good for you to be in the field again!! how I wish it were to be Chou Koutien!! will that be opened again in time for us to be interested?

No dear you did not write to me before about your meeting with Faure . . and it was naughty of you not to write to Eleanor!! but I wrote to Tillie just as soon as I read your letter for she knows just where to get in touch with Eleanor . . I hope she has gotten really seriously interested in some American . . but she did not want to give up Faure . . they seemed to have so much to build on . . well maybe it will work out, but when I last heard Faure had not yet written to her . . how unkind men can be!!! Perhaps women too sometimes . . in fact when you realize how difficult it is to understand those nearest and dearest to us, it should not surprise us that the United Nations do not fully trust each other!!!!! No, man is still very young and has so very much to learn . . why is honesty so difficult?? and decency and kindness . . and greediness so universal? I suppose because it is the only thing that seems to give tangible results . . and we have lost FAITH in a higher purpose . . in the only thing that will bring real and lasting happiness . . Oh I have found it SO difficult lately to keep my hold on what I know and what you have taught me . . You have no idea how I have longed for your letters and for a touch of your Faith and love . . .

I went to see Rhoda de Terra in NY . . I suppose because I wanted news of you!! and I got it!!!!! but I won't do that again - she always acts as if I were a complete outsider, a casual friend and that she was directing your destinies!!! when she said how she was going to have you do this and do that, I remarked that maybe she did not know you as well as she seemed to think - oh and she said so much else; remembering your reaction to that letter of hers that you read to me, I was most astonished!!! and wondered if you knew - as she had much more recent news of you than I had - there was nothing I could say - in fact I did not want to say anything. I was deeply hurt by her and I don't really like her and I don't like - well you will be disgusted with "the ladies" -but I don't understand - she also said she expected to go to France, to Paris very soon!!!-

*Well be that as it may - Pierre forgive me for writing this, but I've gone over things she said so often in those horrible night hours when one can't sleep!! so now maybe I've gotten it out of my system and can see how really unimportant it all is!! and if it had not been such a long time since I'd heard from you etc. etc. etc. I would not have been so vulnerable -*

*However your precious letter saying that the letter of yours of '38 still holds true, is REALLY important and oh so good. You see dear I'm still believing*

*Paris, Dec. 18th, 1946*

**Dearest,**

    I just receive your precious letter of Dec. the 13 (after the one of Dec. 5). Yes, I was just thinking of you when you wrote me, — and my Ste-Lucile mass was actually <u>for you</u>, - and quite naturally I was going to write you the same day when people came to see me. and everything was protracted once more. Now, at least, I am still in time to send you any possible wishes for Christmas and New Year, including prominently this one that we should meet somewhere and somehow during the coming year. Although (or rather because) everything is so much unsettled and so confused in my prospects of future, any kind of hope remains open and is permitted. Another New Year wish (the safest and the sweetest) is that during 1947 we shall grow closer and deeper to each other; and about this point I have no doubt, Lucile because since fifteen years it has been always so.

    Here my life is going on the same way. I had several talks to deliver, these last weeks, to various and interesting groups, including the most secluded and "laïc" Ecole Normale Primaire and Ecole Normale Technique (at the first place I was asked officially for two lectures). And, next January, I shall be still more busy: four scientific lectures in Sorbonne, one for the Musée Guimet (on the Neolithic of China), and two or three more on "human" subjects before large audiences and specialized groups (f.i. the leaders of the Young Workmen Association). That takes time. But on the other hand that obliges me to think over more and more deeply my perspectives on World and Life. The reactionary wave I told you in my last letter is still rolling (a new fundamentalist Review has just appeared, with a nice special article against me), but not dangerous. La percée est faite, I think; and, on the whole, my Order backs me. At the beginning of January I will go to Toulouse in order to start the move for the publication of the Phénomène Humain. I am not yet sure to succeed, of course.

    Nothing substantially new concerning the South Africa business. De Terra can not come, unfortunately. And I have not yet money enough to bring with me young Blanc (from Rome). At the worst, I will go alone, for a first prospection. Abbé Breuil will be there in any case: he is leaving for Kenya and South Africa at the end of the month, and will stay there for a year and a half.

    I have seen a lot the Bégouën since October. Max has come for six weeks only (he is leaving on Christmas), rather overworked, but successful in his business. But Simone is in bed, since two months, with an attack of arthritis, carefully attended by good doctors. Nothing really serious, but a matter of protracted care. She too has overworked herself during the war. She looks just the same, always smiling, vivacious and "angélique" as ever. Both of them send to you *their heartiest regards. Ida Treat-Bergeret is constantly with her. She (Ida) looks very happy with her most serious, almost austere, husband (a very important man, now), and she is busy writing a book for America. Leroy goes on teaching zoology and searching for hormones in a research-laboratory. Françoise Raphaël is with her father in Algeria up to the middle of January.*

*It took me three days to write you this page. I hope you will get it in time for Xmas; may you be happy, Lucile, — and God bless you for all that you give me.*

*your*

*P.T.*

15 Rue Monsieur, Paris
Jan. the 29th, 1947

Dearest,
*Excuse me for being so late in answering your precious letter of Jan.9 which made me so happy, — because I feel so happy when you are. In fact, this beginning of the year was for me a rather hectic time. First I had to go for a week near Toulouse in order to discuss with some influential friends the question of my book. Then I moved to Blois (of a meeting of the leaders of Young Christian Workmen. Then I started a series of public lectures, some about "ideas", and the others on scientific subjects. Among these latter ones, the most interesting are those I deliver in Sorbonne, on Chinese geology and prehistory. People seem quite interested by what I say; and the task for me is really easy, since the only thing I do is to speak about things which I had seven solid years in Peking to mature in my mind. Now however I begin to emerge out of this duty; and, with the exception of a score of talks before various groups of advanced students, I have not much to do except to concentrate on several papers I would like to write. The most tedious work I have to face is to readjust the famous book on "Le Phénomène Humain". My friends positively hope that I shall be allowed to print it. But now it is my turn not to be satisfied with the child. You know, my ideas have developped and improved (I hope) rather much since six years. People insist that I must publish nevertheless. But I do not like so much the idea. Practically, I will do my best to repolish the thing before Easter. And then I shall decide. In fact, I would prefer to write something entirely new. But where to find the time for it? . . I expect any day my last article (rather good, I think) — the non-given lecture in Belgium — , and I will send it to you immediately together with two other things published this summer. So, you see, I keep sufficiently active. Daily talks with various people positively oblige me to go deeper in the questions, always more. And after so many years of seclusion in Peking, I like it. In the meantimes, I must keep my scientific platform. And this is the reason for which I am decided to do my best in order to materialize the trip to South Africa. But in that line things are still rather vague. I have written a few days ago to Camp, asking him whether I might in some way join and help his party. Breuil has left a month ago, and he is now in Kenya. Later on he will be in Johannesburg, for a year. — I was really excited when I read you about the possible prospect to join the Stantons in Siam. And if you would cross Paris on your way. That should be such a joy for me, Lucile. In*

*any case it seems to me that it should be good for you to get once more in touch
with the big world.*

*Here, I see rather often Simone, who looks decidedly better, —so much so
that she hopes to be able to go back to Morocco in the spring. The last time I went
to see her, she had received your last letter, and she told me everything about your
work. I feel it very sweet to talk of you with her, as if she were a common sister,
"on both sides". In spite of her health you find her just the same as before. Ida
Treat is extremely busy with a book she is writing for an american publisher. I do
not meet her as often as I would like. Paris is not as good a place for meeting
friends as Peking.*

*And, finally Rhoda de T. made her appearance, searching some intellec-
tual food for her novels. As you know I am sincerely fond of her. Unfortunately, I
have very little time to spare. I do my best, but it is not easy, to see her. Luckily, if
you think her possessive, she is not "demanding"; and, on the other hand, she is
quite able to find her own ways by herself. I think she will get all right with Ida,
both of them being writers. Since she speaks but very little french, it is not particularly easy to bring her in touch with many people who might be interesting for
her. She did not give me very good news of Hellmut; and I am sorry for it, because
I think he has several exceptional gifts and because I like him quite deeply. One
man more who was not able to discover his faith and his God. Malvina H. wrote
me a nice letter: she is busy helping her friend Mestrovic starting a studio somewhere. But you know it, surely.*

*Good bye, dearest. I will do my best not to be silent so much. But, even if
I happen to be, forgive me, and do <u>never</u> doubt of my deepest thought and "affection".*

*God bless you. +++*

*Pierre*

---

Lucile, however, was not reassured. Teilhard was busy and his letters were infrequent. He
was evidently establishing a life in which she was no longer included. So his prospective
trip to South Africa seemed to her an opportunity to renew their work and talks together.

---

*1217 34th Street NW, Washington 7 D.C.
February 15, 1947*

*Pierre, dearest, -*

*Thank you for your precious letter of Jan. 29 which seems like magic after the
long lean year. It is so wonderful to have such quick communication.*

*You surely have been very busy since the New Year . . but what a good busines-
s!!It must have been quite inspiring to talk to the young workmen. — I can just see what
an inspiration you must be!! how I wish I could slip in and hear you sometime!! And the
book . . Oh I can so well imagine how you feel about the "child" now!! and yet you cannot
abandon it . . I do hope you will find a happy solution that will not require too much work.
Yes I'm sure your ideas have advanced a lot . . One reason why I am SO anxious to get*

*your papers . . and can hardly wait to read the non-given Brussels one . . is it particularly
dangerous!! or just that it was a big meeting or what? I don't understand why it can be
published if you could not speak it!! but I wont question and just be very happy that it has
happened!! I shall make a translation . . principally because it makes me feel as if it were
still "our" work!! Oh, Pierre, I read over a lot of old letters of yours the other evening
(night) and you so often referred to OUR work! What gay, alive, loving letters! full of
hope and discovery - but now I feel I have no part in the work - the separation, physical, we
cannot help - but dear, I DO still have a part?? After all you are now reaping the harvest
of the seeds we planted together those long years - and surely there will be more plantings
and more discoveries - that is what makes our friendship so wonderful - because we are
always searching a higher and clearer approach to the Great Center. Pierre, if I go along
that path to the VERY BEST of my ability - that too is part of the work? I suppose I want
so much to have something grand and wonderful to give to you - and all I seem to have is
a very completely loving and searching heart! which has prayed so deeply and SO sincerely to be helped to keep on the spiritual path - for I KNOW (as you have so often said)
that the more I love God, the more I will love you and the closer we will be. Another thing
you wrote so very many times - "What is born between us is for EVER; I know it". That is
very sweet, PT, and I believe it too with all my heart - but somehow it makes me very
happy to read it again in your very own writing.*

*Oh Pierre, you know me too well for me to pretend that I was not disturbed by a
part of your letter - but perhaps this very thing is making me take some real steps ahead
because I have prayed so earnestly to see everything on a high spiritual level. It is not
always easy - but that is the idea and I'm improving it!! I wish I had never gone to see her
in NY. I don't know why she had to say all the things she did to me. I thought she was not
going to Paris until spring - but I guess by the time she told me of her trip, I was too numb
to be listening very carefully. I am so sorry this happened - and I really do not think that I
could help it - well -*

*I am so glad you are going ahead with your S. Africa plans, Pierre. It will be good
for you to get in the field again -talking to all those people is splendid and now it will be
good to have some time to digest it all - n'est-ce-pas? Oh did I tell you that I have been taking French lessons this winter so I won't forget everything I know of it - you see I too hope
some day to have a need to use it!! When do you expect to go to S. Africa and where
exactly? Jessie Camp told me where they were going but not knowing the country the
name did not stick. I think they plan to leave in July - if you went then I don't suppose you
would be back for 4 or 5 months!! It takes so long to make plans these days that I am thinking about when I MIGHT go to Siam!!! but there is something I would much rather do -
and that is to take the trip down on the same boat with you to S.A. I have had it in mind
ever since I saw Jessie - do you think it fantastic!! it would be SO wonderful with time
again!! tell me what you think. I suppose it is expensive but I can get the money - and I'm
sure I can get a "business" connection so I can get the passports etc.*

*D. St Clair (formerly Peking) was here for dinner last night . . she was in an
American Consulate in Pretoria and told me lots!! she says the country is fantastically
lovely . . is Mrs Waln(?) Susanne, still down there?. D. St Clair is now about to go back to
Peking!! Said Helen Burton is still in Honolulu and will not go back until things have
quieted down a bit . . Rose met Mrs. S.T. Wang in New York . . who said to tell me NOT to*

go back now .. not for several years!!! but China is the kind of place that MAY be quite liveable soon .. and may NOT ..

I heard a lecture Thursday .. went with Mrs Bill Mayer .. by Dr Pfeffer who has just returned from several months in China .. and he was MOST discouraging .. what are Leroy's plans .. will he return to Peking? has the Institut Géo-biologie been given up or only closed temporarily? Oh it is exciting to even TALK of going places again ..

It makes me VERY happy to think of you and Simone talking of me and my work! she is such a lovely person .. how I do want to see her again .. but for her sake I do hope she will be able to go home this spring .. am so very glad that she is getting better. Why not stop in Morocco too!!! I expect to go to NY next week for a few days .. and after looking up the Begouens friend there, I will write to Simone about it ..

I have been making some useful contacts here this winter - last week a landscape gardener, does all the big rich gardens here -came to see my work - which she liked VERY much!! so I am sure I'll hear from her again - and there were other women in the studio to see this or that - and Pierre they ALL without exception were completly taken by your head!!! I do think I did a pretty good piece of work (++) but the subject was rather inspiring too!! Do you remember the first head when you accused me of being Penelope? That was when I first heard you talk - I couldn't always follow exactly - but I always knew it was something I very much wanted .. and how I do bless you and thank you dearest for all that you have given to me .. it is an endless discovery with always something MORE to realize.

Now I must go .. am going for a long walk up the Canal with Erika!! that also is like Peking days!

Pierre please do think well of my idea for a boat ride to SA .. why should I not see that country?? and please let me know when you have anywhere near a settled date as that might make such a difference .. if you plan to go with the Camps, it would be quite easy for me to get information from them ... Your last letter sounded very unsettled .. but soon you will have to be making reservations etc .. all good luck to your plans Pierre .. I do so want them to work out for you .. as you would like them to be,

All my love dearest, always your,

*Paris, March 3, '47*

Dearest,

Excuse me for not answering faster your exciting letter of Febr. 15. Your idea of South Africa is wonderful. The whole question is to combine and to materialize. Precisely I write yesterday to Weidenreich in order to urge a solution. Finally, the Rockefeller Found. has decided (with the nicest possible appreciations) not to back financially a research-trip in Africa with the team I proposed. But I still have money enough for myself alone; and I plan to go (unless something unforseen happens. In which case I should be very anxious to join the Camps group. A month ago, I wrote him to that effect: but he did not answer me so far. I do not know what is the matter; but I am sure he is doing the best for me. In any case, as soon I get an answer of Weidenreich, I will proceed towards execution. I should leave approximately in July. But I have only a faint idea of the practibility of travelling by boat (which I would prefer). Airplanes, of course, *seem easily available. Let me know what you think. Breuil is already in Johannesburg, — for a full year.*

*I was so glad to hear, Lucile, that you can work and that you have so many devoted and efficient friends around you. I should be so happy if I could do more for you. At least, you know, I give you always the best of me. It would be such a dream to meet you again.*

*In the meantimes, life in Paris is going on, pretty busy. I have started readjusting the famous book for a new examination. Work is proceeding sufficiently well, — not so easy though. Since six years, although my ideas did not change substantially, I think my "vision" is better organized, and somewhat differently focussed, this latter factor making the "retouches" difficult. In some way, writing a new book would be more pleasant. Anyhow, I go on; and I hope that, by Easter, the whole thing will be ready for censorship, — good or not so good. I would much prefer to concentrate on the new points of view which some time seem positively to pour in my mind in the course and under the pressure of private talks and lectures. Too many of such talks and lectures, in fact. I must try to reduce the number, henceforth, by all means. Would you think that, led by fortuitous circumstances, I begin to be more and more interested by Art: technically, because I met recently a few quite modernistisc artists; and "biologically" (if I dare say) because I have a sort of feeling that, in a next stage of Mankind, Art will become an essential function of collective "hominisation", just as scientific Research did in the course of a few generations. There is a marvelous and unique exhibition of Van Gogh aux Tuileries, just now. If only we could visit it together, you and me!*

*Concerning Simone, I must give you very alarming news. A fortnight ago, she seemed so much better that she had booked for Morocco. And then suddenly the heart has begun to give up. Between the too numerous "crisis", she looks just the same, just so smiling and sweet. But everybody is anxious. And yet everybody is so used to see her emerging out of any sort of illness that hope remains. But, at the best, she will have to rest for months. Max was in the depths of Western Africa. He has arrived yesterday, in a single day (!), by plane. Ida stood by Simone all the time. She was wonderful.*

*Goodbye, dearest. The letter is a little short, but I have to go fast. People are already at my door.*

> *yours and your P.T. +++*

*Many thanks for the books of Reeves, A. Huxley and the article by L. Corbellier! Such things are "introuvables" here! I am more and more in friendship and intellectual understanding with Julian Huxley. My separates (for the last article on Humanity) have not yet arrived!*

> *15 Rue Monsieur, Paris VII*
> *March 24, '47*

*Dearest,*

*Simone told me that you would like to receive sometimes letters written in french. So will I do this time (tell me what you prefer!).*

- Donc j'ai bien reçu votre chère lettre du 12, si pleine de projets. De mon côté, voici où j'en suis. Le Viking Fund m'a effectivement écrit pour me dire que mon argent m'attendait, et pour m'indiquer comment l'utiliser. Dans ces conditions, je suis pratiquement décidé à partir en Juillet. D'autre part, Cook me dit qu'il ne faut pas songer à trouverplace sur un bateau (tout, dit-il, serait retenu pour un an!), ce qui m'obligera à prendre l'avion, - à moins que je ne découvre quelque cargo (moyen de transport dont Cook fait profession de ne pas s'occuper). Dans le cas de l'avion, la ligne la plus commode semble être Paris-Madagascar (Air-France), avec changement au Kenya. Voilà tout ce que je puis dire en ce moment. Weidenreich m'a écrit pour m'encourager à partir, même seul. Par ailleurs Camp m'envoyé un très gentil mot de "welcome". J'ai été très étonné de ce que vous (et Weidenreich) me faites savoir concerning his feelings à mon égard. En 1939, à Berkeley, j'avais bien cru sentir quelque chose; mais je l'avais attribué au fait que j'étais l'hôte de Chaney, avec qui il ne s'entendait pas bien à ce moment. En tous cas je n'ai _aucune_ idée de n'avoir pas fait en Chine tout ce que je pouvais pour lui (c'est moi qui l'avais fait venir par le Survey). Serait-ce que je ne l'ai accompagné on the field, le confiant à Young (à cause de mon ignorance bien connue du chinois)? . . . Il doit y avoir un malentendu, - car je n'ai jamais cessé de le considérer comme un vrai ami. J'imagine que tout cela se dissipera à la première rencontre. - Le non moins cher G. B. Barbour (toujours dean of Sciences à Cincinnati) vient de m'écrire une lettre charmante. Il ne serait pas impossible qu'il vienne. Ce serait un rêve.

En attendant, ma vie ici continue suivant les mêmes lignes. J'ai l'impression que ma position s'affermit et s'af-

Well, I received your dear letter of the 12th, so full of plans. As for me, here is what I am doing. The "Viking Fund" has indeed written to tell me that the money is ready and how to use it. Under these conditions, I have practically decided to leave in July. On the other hand, Cook tells me that I mustn't hope to find a berth on a ship (they tell me that there is nothing available for the next twelve months!); so, I will have to fly - unless I can find a cargo ship (a means of transport with which Cook has no professional link). If I fly, the best way would be Paris-Madagascar (Air-France), changing in Kenya. That's all I can say for the moment. Weidenreich wrote me and encouraged me to leave, even alone. Moreover, Camp sent me a very nice "welcome" note. I was extremely surprised by what you (and Weidenreich) told me concerning his feelings toward me. In 1939 at Berkeley, I thought I felt something, but I believed it was because I was Chaney's host with whom he was not getting along at the time. In any case I felt sure I did all I could for him in China (I had the Survey make him come). Might it be because I didn't go with him on the field, entrusting him to Young (because of my well known ignorance of the Chinese language)? . . . It must be a misunderstanding, — for I have never stopped considering him a true friend. I believe all this will disappear when we next meet. — The no less dear G.B. Barbour (still dean of Sciences in Cincinnati) has just written me a charming letter. It is not impossible that he will come. That would be a dream.

In the meantime my life continues on the same lines. It seems that my position is getting stronger and asserts

*firme. De plus en plus de followers, mais naturellement aussi certaines oppositions se manifestent, - ce qui ne me déplaît pas. Le point vif du problème est la question de "la foi en l'Homme", sur lequel je me trouve en conflit à la fois avec les pessimistes incroyants ("existentialistes") et les pessimistes religieux (chrétiens vieux-style et partisans des idées hindoues). En fait, la position se clarifie, dans mon esprit et dans les discussions. Avec toujours plus d'évidence il me semble voir que l'Humanité est irré-sistiblement envahie par la nécessité et le besoin de croire qu'elle n'est pas achevée, mais que quelque grand avenir l'attend sur Terre en avant. Si bien qu'aucune religion ne la satisfera plus si cette religion n'incorpore pas et ne sauve pas cette espérance de progrès. Et je trouve une grande force dans cette conviction. - Ces derniers temps, j''ai encore donné bien des conférences sur ce sujet (et j'en ai refusé bien plus encore). Par ailleurs j'ai fini de corriger mon livre de Peking (Le Phénomène Humain). Dès qu'il sera re-dacty-lographié, je l'enverrai à Rome, accom-pagné d'avis français favorables. Et alors on verra. Concerning the result I feel curiously philosophical. In fact, everything I say in the book is already out.*

*Simone est décidément mieux. Mais elle reste faible. On ne voit pas encore bien comment elle va maintenant arranger sa vie et celle de Max. Le Maroc est hors de question pour le moment. Max va y retourner (au Maroc) au début d'Avril.*

itself. I have more and more followers but, of course, there is also some opposition — this doesn't really displease me. The central point of the problem is the question of "faith in Man", about which I find myself in conflict as well as with the non-believing pessimists (the existentialists) as with the religious pessimists (the old style Christians and the supporters of Hindu ideas.) In fact, my position is getting clearer in my mind and in discussions. It seems to me more and more evident that Humanity is irresistibly overcome by the necessity and the need to believe that it is not yet perfected, but that some great future awaits it on Earth. Which means that no religion will satisfy Humanity if this religion does not incorporate and save this hope for progress. And I find great strength in this conviction. — Lately, I have given many lectures on this subject (and I have refused even more). I have also finished correcting the book I wrote in Peking (*The Phenomenon of Man*). As soon as it is retyped, I will send it to Rome, together with some favorable french opinions. And then we will see.

Simone is decidedly better. But she is still weak. It is not easy to imagine how she will organize her life and Max's. Morocco is out of the question for the time being. Max will go back (to Morocco) early in April.

*Good bye, dearest. I have the feeling that we are so close to each other, these days.*

　　　*yours ever*

　　　*P.T.*

*I am sending you, by ordinary mail, the last "egg". So many thanks for the shaving paste!*

*Dearest,*

*Excuse me for being so late, this time. Lot of small things occured at Easter time, and just now I am in the midst of a biologico-palaeontological symposium which keeps me busy morning and evening. Simpson is here, from the American Museum, - so that I have a little the impression to be back in New York. Here I answer both your letters of March 30 and Easter. They were so sweet, both of them! Hope that you have a good time in Chicago.*

*Concerning our plans, a first thing is that your fascinating idea of Paris can not work under the present conditions.*

*Hier encore j'ai parlé avec Simone, très touchée de votre suggestion. Le malheur est qu'elle s'est décidée à prendre une chambre dans l'appartement d'un de ses cousins, qui est en même temps son docteur; et c'est tout juste si elle pourra tenir là-dedans avec Max. Impossible de vous loger. Et cependant la combinaison eût été parfaite. Si un autre plan se développait, je vous le ferais savoir immédiatement. En ce qui me concerne, il est de plus en plus probable que je vais réellement partir en juillet pour le Transvaal, où l'on m'attend. Mais je n'ai pas encore réservé mon passage; et il se peut que je rencontre là de sérieuses difficultés, - même par avion. Je vais dès cette semaine commencer à m'occuper de cela plus activement.*

Yesterday I spoke again with Simone who is very moved by your suggestion. The problem is that she has decided to rent one room in one of her cousins' apartment who is also her doctor; and she and Max will barely fit in it. They cannot possibly take you in. And yet this solution would have been perfect. If another possibility should develop, I would let you know immediately. As far as I am concerned, it is more and more probable that I will leave in July for Transvaal where I am expected. But I haven't made any reservations yet, and possibly there will be some serious difficulties — even by plane. I will begin to do something about it more actively this week.

*Autrement, la situation reste à peu près la même. Avant dix jours j'espère que le manuscrit de mon livre sera à Lyon (il n'est pas encore complètement re-dactylographié). Ces jours-ci aussi je m'attends à une réponse de Rome concernant la possibilité de publier "le Milieu divin", pour lequel il continue à y avoir une intense demande. Je n'ai rien écrit depuis quelques semaines. Mais j'ai accumulé bien des notes et des idées. Ce qui me paraît le plus important, en ce moment, c'est de faire comprendre l'importance prise dans le monde par "la foi en l'Homme", et l'impossibilité d'arriver à un équilibre tant que les chrétiens ne feront pas à cette foi nouvelle une place dans leur*

Otherwise, the situation remains about the same. I hope the manuscript of my book will be in Lyon within the next ten days (it is not yet completely re-typed). In the very near future also, I expect a reply from Rome concerning the possibility of publishing *The Divine Milieu*, which continues to be very much in demand. I haven't written anything these past few weeks, but I have accumulated many notes and ideas. What seems most important to me at the moment is to make people understand how important "faith in Man" has become throughout the world, and the impossibility of reaching a balance as long as Christians will not make room for this new faith in

religion: "The problem of the two faiths", comme je dis. Sans foi en l'Homme, la foi en Dieu est tiède et stérile; et, sans foi en Dieu, la foi en l'Homme est inconsistance et dépersonnalisante. En fait, le problème est "psychologique", encore plus que philosophique ou théologique. Combien rares sont les chrétiens que leur foi ne rend pas mous, tièdes, incompréhensifs en face des événements de la Terre . . . Je pense avoir l'occasion de donner une ou deux "lectures" là-dessus, ce printemps.

Si vous voyez Eléonore, dites-lui ma grande affection. Répétez-lui qu'il y a un an, à mon arrivée ici, une de mes premières visites avait été pour Faure; et c'est parce que lui, Faure, m'avait dit être en train d'écrire longuement à elle, Eleonore, que je me suis abstenu d'envoyer des nouvelles à Péking (ce que j'aurais dû faire, je le vois maintenant). Après quoi je n'ai plus su où atteindre Eléonore. A ce moment là l'idée de Faure était que rien ne pouvait être décidé avant que lui et El. se revoient; et qu'il y aurait sans doute moyen de faire prendre à El. la nationalité suisse (à laquelle elle aurait droit, - même cas que Hoppeli). Such a mess! Leroy va très bien et travaille toujours les hormones. - Madame Raphaël est décidément entrée à l'UNESCO, en qualité de "Welfare officer"! Je crois qu'elle réussit très bien. - Jacques Bardac est aussi ici, avec Marie-Claire, toujours très brillante. On se voit moins souvent qu'à Péking! -

A bientôt, dearest. And God bless you! . . . +++

P.T.

their religion: "The problem of the two faiths," as I call it. Without faith in Man, faith in God is lukewarm and sterile; and, without faith in God, faith in Man is inconsistent and depersonalizing. In fact, the problem is "psychological" even more than philosophical or theological. How rare are the Christians whose faith doesn't make them faint-hearted, tepid and uncomprehending in the face of what is happening in the world. I think I will have the opportunity to give one or two "lectures" on this subject in the spring.

If you see Eleonore, give her my love. Tell her again that, a year ago on my arrival here, one of my first visits had been for Faure; and it is because he, Faure, had told me he was writing a long letter to her, Eleonore, that I held off sending the news to her in Peking (which I should have done, I can see now). Later on I didn't know where to reach Eleonore. At that time, Faure's idea was that nothing could be decided before he and Eleonore met again, and that it undoubtedly would be possible for Eleonore to obtain the Swiss citizenship (to which she is entitled — same case as Hoppeli). Such a mess! Leroy is very well and works always on hormones research. Mme Raphaël did get into UNESCO as a "Welfare officer". I believe she is doing very well. Jacques Bardac is here also with Marie-Claire, as brilliant as ever. We see each other less than in Peking.

---

Lucile abandoned her plans to join Teilhard and George Barbour on the trip to South Africa because she could not book passage that was timely and affordable.

Meanwhile, Teilhard prepared to depart for the Transvaal, but on June 1 he suffered a severe myocardial infarction and was rushed to the hospital where for two weeks he lingered between life and death. Later the sixty-six year old scientist referred to it as "a heart attack which could have sent me to Jesus". He spent several months in convalescence. Lucile did not know of this serious illness when she wrote in May and June.

*1217 34th Street NW Washington*
*May 14, 1947*

*Dearest, -*

*Your precious letter of April reached me out in Iowa where I went to see my Aunt, the one that Mother stayed with . . she is 88 years old and SUCH a dear . . so alive and so sweet . . my, I hope I can be like her when I get old!! But I had a birthday just a few days ago and I AM getting old!!! I was on the train on your birthday the 1st of May and sent you many loving messages . . and had a definite idea for a new piece of sculpture . . which I have started a sketch for.*

*I do so enjoy your letters in French . . it somehow makes you seem closer and I think you go into more detail when you write in French . . I know more how you are think-ing . . I do wish I knew more how you think the "Noosphere" is going to operate? but your faith in Man is the thing that gives hope. All of which is not saying much . . but I do so thank you for sharing your thoughts with me . . and Pierre I am SO SO happy that your position there is so solid and getting stronger all the time. I know that you have an immense number of followers now, more and more all the time. Have you heard yet the fate of the famous book? Those things always take longer than you expect.*

*I am so glad that Simone has such a happy solution for living in Paris . . that seems to me by far the best possible . . I am disappointed not to be able to come there, but SOME day it will work out . . I do hope she is improving all the time . . will Max be able to be with her very much?*

*And I suppose the plans for South Africa are beginning to take definite form . . am enclosing a clipping from a recent Washington paper . . also one from the New Yorker about de Terra . . he seems to have gotten a great deal of publicity about his Mexican finds . . I do wonder what Weidenreich thought about them . . My I do wish they would be important enough for you to come and see them!! but surely you will be coming to the US before too long??*

*A few days later!*

*I have been slow about this because my own plans are so uncertain at the moment and it now looks very much as if I may be going to Mexico very soon. While I was in Chicago there was much talk about it, but I did not take it too seriously. However it now looks as if the plans will materialize . . the man who was my Father's partner in the business is going down, with his wife and a Mexican business man. They have built (and the Mexican wants Mr. Holms to go down, eventually perhaps to live there and run) a factory down there to manufacture the same moving picture projector that they were doing here.*

*1217 34th Street N.W.*
*Washington DC    June 8, '47*

*Dearest, -*

*How are your plans working out?? Mine do not seem to be doing so well . . the trip to Mexico has been postponed until fall(?); Im not much disappointed, it was one of those things that would be nice, I'd like to see Mexico and it probably will happen some-time. This does not seem to be the moment for easy travel!! So I have been wondering how your own South African plans are going . . I hope O.K. and feel sure that they are . . after*

all a single man and some special work . . have you any idea yet how long you will be down there?

The day I got word that the Mexico trip was off (for the time being) I started a portrait head of a young woman, the first COMMISSION I have had for some time . . so I am very busy with that and that is good . . it seems to be going well, but you know how it is at the start of a piece . . THIS time it is going to be the masterpiece!!!! I have been working again lately on my "Spirit of the Earth" . . as there is something good there but I have not yet gotten what I want . . but I guess I already told you this . .

Life is rather quiet these days, just before the summer exodus . . I shall go up to Mary Parton's for awhile and then to Nantucket and then I don't know what . . there are several possibilities . .

*June 11, 1947*

I started this several days ago; but it seems difficult to go on - for a few short weeks when I thought maybe I was going to see you and I talked to your friends at the Museum, you seemed so close and it was all wonderful. Oh Pierre, I've written several pages and they all seem too stupid to send. I'm afraid I will bore you . . so I'm just going to send this on, hoping you will get a bit of a note to me before we all separate again with miles and miles and miles . . . .

I'm working every day on the portrait I told you about . . and I think it goes well . . I hope to finish it so that I can leave Washington about the 26 or 27th of June. That is in about two weeks . . It would be very nice if you would write and tell me something about what you plan to do . . I mean how long you expect to be in South Africa etc etc . . Oh, darling, I'm really so glad that you are going . . I do think it will be so good for you and you always get such a lot of new ideas and inspiration after you have been out for awhile.

...........................................................................................................................................

It is so splendid that you keep on with your splendid words of Faith and creative force - what a joy it would be if I could again feel some small part in that work! Perhaps - some day - who knows-

But enough for today . . this is just to tell you that I will be in this country — probably — for some time . . and if you cannot write for me to get it before I leave. but PLEASE do — then c/o Mrs Lemuel Parton, Palisades New York . . will always reach me — or things will be forwarded from here . . but I'd get it sooner if sent to Palisades . .

Enclosed is another clipping about Africa!! seems to be much interest in all that . . Did you receive my last letter which was full of clippings??

*15 Rue Monsieur, Paris VII*
*July 5th 47*

**Dearest,**

I am just, or almost just, out of bed. So, do excuse my bad handwriting! - I must thank you so much for your two precious letters, the last being of June 26. Yes, it is rather unusual to me to be sick. But here I am. On the whole, it seems that something went wrong with my circulation, somewhere in the pectus, so that the doctors oblige me, for a few months, to a rather remissed type of life. A classical case, they say, — but for which they have a classical routine-cure too.

*Jusqu'au 1 Décembre, il faut que j'évite tout effort physique, etc. Je ne sais pas encore exactement où je passerai tout ce temps-là; mais ce sera sûrement aux environs de Paris; et vous pouvez toujours m'écrire au 15 Rue Monsieur.*

I must avoid all physical efforts, etc until December 1st. I don't know yet where I will spend all that time, but it will probably be in the vicinity of Paris, and you can always write to me 15 rue Monsieur.

*— Just now, I am in a good clinic, with a nice garden, quite close "les Etudes". —*

*To be frank, je n'ai pas encore retrouvé exactement mon équilibre intérieur.*

*Malgré la guérison, je doute de pouvoir reprendre mon existence on the field; et en tous cas l'affaire d'Afrique du sud est manquée. Je crois sentir que la solution <u>constructive</u>, pour moi, est, sera de me tourner davantage du côté de la pensée et de l'action sur les idées. Mais il faut pour cela tout un ajustement aux événements que je ne puis encore prévoir. ——*

In spite of my recovery, I doubt that I will ever be able to work on the field; in any case I missed the opportunity to go to South Africa. I feel that the <u>constructive</u> solution, for me, is, will be to turn more toward thinking and working on ideas. But I cannot forsee how I will adjust to the recent events.

*En tous cas, more than ever, I need you in order to be myself, and to find <u>more really</u> God.*

*Je vous écrirai plus longuement, bientôt.*

*Yours*

*P.T.*

*Clinique des Soeurs*
*St Germain-en-Laye, 28 Juillet '47*

*Dearest,*

*I am answering here your precious letter of July 13. As you see, I have left my former hospital; and I am now simply resting in a confortable clinique, exactly along the border of the Forêt de St. Germain.*

*Les Soeurs sont aux petits soins avec moi; et j'ai retrouvé avec étonnement et plaisir, faisant provisoirement fonction de chapelain dans la maison le P. Merveille lui-même, qui a passé un an avec nous en 1941 Rue Labrousse! Ce n'est pas tout à fait un "ami"; mais c'est un familier et un camarade avec qui parler sur des choses d'intérêt commun. Il a subi une grave opération au foie et à l'estomac; et bien qu'extérieurement il n'ait pas changé du tout, je me demande s'il pourra retourner en Chine. — Ici, je ne m'en-*

The sisters are taking great care of me; I was very surprised and happy to see again Father Merveille himself who spent one year with us in 1941 rue Labrousse and who is temporarily the Chaplain here. He is not quite a "friend", but he is a familiar face and a companion with whom I can discuss things of common interest. He underwent a very serious liver and stomac operation and, although he has not changed at all outwardly, I wonder if he will be able to go back to China. I am not bored here. I read and I think

nuie pas. Je lis et je pense suffisamment (on dirait que je n'ai jamais eu d'autant d'idées et plus claires que depuis mon accident de santé.); et puis, malgré la distance, des amis viennent me voir presque chaque jour de Paris. George Le Fèvre (celui qui a écrit La Croisière Jaune) habite St Germain même; et je le vois souvent. Evidemment, il reste la déception des plans rompus et l'incertitude de ce que je vais faire exactement plus tard. J'ai quelque crainte que le vrai travail on the field ne soit plus très possible pour moi ( ce n'est pas sûr cependant: il semble que je me remette très bien); mais alors il est possible qu'un autre champ (celui de l'Homme Moderne) s'ouvre plus grand en compensation: tout dépend de la réaction des éléments. En attendant, je suis au demi-repos jusqu'au 1 Décembre; et je ne sais pas encore où je passerai ce temps. Les longs parcours ne me sont pas conseillés, et les escaliers positivement déconseillés pour 4 mois encore. J'imagine que je trouverai quelque endroit aux environs de Paris. Mais, jusqu'à Octobre ou Novembre, je ne pense pas pouvoir rentrer à Paris même, — ce qui ne faciliterait pas les rencontres si par chance vous veniez en Europe en automne! . . En somme, je vis encore beaucoup au jour le jour. Et puis, pour tout achever, un grand malheur vient d'arriver à mon frère de Paris (le seul qui me reste, et par conséquent celui sur qui s'est concentrée presque tout mon affection familiale: son fils (le seul, avec une fille), un brillant garçon de 26 ans, vient de se noyer, dans un étang herbu (caught in the weeds) au début des vacances. Pour mon frère, c'est une blessure inguérissable, mais qui, je l'espère, ne l'abattra pas. Mais le voilà forcé de chercher très haut une raison de vivre, - un intérêt à la vie. En somme nous vivons dans un Univers encore largement immergé dans les chances et le hasard, où tout peut arriver, même le

enough (it is as if I never had so many and clearer ideas than since my illness . . .); and also, in spite of the distance, friends come to see me almost every day from Paris. Georges Le Fèvre (the one who wrote "La Croisière Jaune") lives in St. Germain itself and I see him often. Of course, it remains the disappointment of broken plans and the uncertainty about what I will do in the future. I rather fear that the real work on the field will no longer be possible for me (it is not certain however: it seems that I am recovering very well); but it is possible that another field of action (that of Modern Man) opens up a greater compensation: everything depends on the reaction of the elements. In the meantime, I am half working/half resting until December 1st, and I still don't know where I will spend that time. Long walks are not recommended for me and I have been strictly forbidden to climb stairs for another four months. I think I will find some place in the vicinity of Paris. But until October or November, I don't think I can go back to Paris - which would not make our getting together easy if you happened to come to Europe in the fall! . . . All in all, I still very much live from day to day - and then, as the last straw, a great misfortune has just fallen on my brother who lives in Paris, the only one I have got left and, consequently, the one on whom all my family love has concentrated: his son (his only son, he also has a daughter), a brilliant young man of 26, drowned recently in a grassy pond (caught in the weeds) at the beginning of the vacation. For my brother it is an incurable wound but which, I hope, will not defeat him. Now he has to look higher up for a reason to live, for an interest in life. On the whole we live in an universe still very much immersed in accidents and fate, where everything can happen, even the most absurd: but, in this game of chance, we can, it is our

*plus absurde: mais à ce jeu des chances nous pouvons, il nous appartient de donner un sens par notre foi en quelque avenir divin où prend figure, sens et chaleur. En dehors de cette perspective, je ne pense pas que l'existence soit biologiquement possible ( et c'est la seule chose vraie dans l'"existentialisme" . . .). - Simone est venue me voir avant que je ne vienne ici; toujours aussi angélique. Elle espère aller au Maroc en automne(?), et en Bretagne, en août.*

*Tenez-moi au courant de ce que vous faites; et merci tant pour tout ce que votre affection me donne de douceur et de force.*

task, give a meaning with the help of our faith in some divine future where meaning and warmth take shape. Outside this perspective, I don't believe our existence is biologically possible (and this is the only true thing in "existentialism" . . .). Simone came yesterday to see me before I came here; angelic as usual. She hopes to go to Morocco in the fall(?), and to Brittany in August.

Let me know what you are doing, and thank you so much for all the gentleness and strength your affection gives me.

*your*

*P.T.*

*4 Place Louis XIV*
*St Germain-en-Laye, August 20th 47*

**Dearest,**
　　*Yesterday I have received your chère lettre du 10 août. I enjoyed the news you gave me of so many dear friends: the John Carter Vincents, the Grews, and Nathaly (so strange, and yet, à la réflexion, so natural that she should have evolved into another Simone!).*

*Je suis si heureux que vous ayez eu ces belles vacances. De mon côté, rien de nouveau, comme c'était prévu. Je continue à aller normalement bien. Et, n'était l'obscur regret, encore récurrent, du voyage manqué en Afrique du Sud, je n'aurais vraiment pas à me plaindre de mon été. St. Germain, avec ses bois, est vraiment un bel endroit; et je suis réellement gâté par les amis de toutes sortes qui, malgré la période des vacances, trouvent moyen de venir me voir ici. Demain, je vais aller passer l'après-midi à Versailles, où sont présentement réunis nombre de mes collègues appartenant à presque tous les pays du monde. Excellente occasion de prendre la température des esprits, et aussi de faire passer quelques idées. Je dois parler. En fait je recommence à voir presque autant de gens que lorsque*

I am so happy that you had this wonderful vacation. As for me, there is nothing new as could be expected. I continue to be normally well and, were it not for the obscure regret, still recurring, of the aborted trip to South Africa, I would really not have anything to complain about concerning my summer. St. Germain, with its woods, is really a beautiful place, and I have been truly spoiled by all kinds of friends who, although these are the holiday months, manage to come and see me here. Tomorrow I will spend the afternoon at Versailles, where presently many of my colleagues coming from practically every country of the world are gathered. This will be an excellent opportunity to take the temperature of their minds and also to pass along some ideas. I have to speak up. In fact I

*j'étais àParis. Mais n'ayez pas peur: je fais attention à ne pas me fatiguer. En avant, mes projets demeurent juste aussi vagues. J'espère rentrer aux Etudes en Novembre (quitte à y mener une vie plutôt recluse jusqu'à Décembre, époque où les médecins me promettent la liberté. Mais d'ici-là je n'ai aucune idée de ce que je vais faire. Peut-être resterai-je tout bêtement ici? ... Je continue à lire beaucoup, — mais peu de livres vraiment intéressants: surtout les meilleurs romans parus ces derniers temps; et aussi ce que je puis me procurer de littérature existantialiste (La Nausée, de Sartre; La Peste, de Camus, etc. les titres sont gais, n'est-ce pas?). Dans l'ensemble, ce mouvement existentialiste me "hérisse", et me semble de plus en plus un mouvement de snobs, sans racines dans les forces qui mènent aujourd'hui le monde. Néanmoins, il est mené par des gens fort intelligents et il fournit, par opposition, un excellent background aux idées qui sont les miennes. Je me devais de faire plus ample connaissance avec lui; et je dois dire que ce surcroît de connaissance m'a grandement rassuré sur ses points faibles et finalement, je crois, sa stérilité et son impuissance.*

*Pas de nouvelles de Simone, ce semble prouver que tout va bien à Bréhat (l'île de Bretagne, où elle est avec Ida Treat). Barbour m'écrit de Johannesburg (nous devions faire le voyage ensemble!), en me transmettant une bonne lettre d'Eddie Bien, qui a quitté la Chine depuis un an et travaille dans quelque université en Californie. Bien n'a pas l'air le moins du monde surpris par le désordre actuel de la Chine; mais il ne me donne pas ses pronostics d'avenir. Il faut avouer que la Terre humaine n'est pas dans un état bien rassurant en ce moment, ni confortable (du moins en Europe). Mais il me paraît tellement évident, de plus en plus, que, pour des raisons qui dominent ou entraînent la volonté humaine,*

am beginning to see again almost as many people as when I was in Paris. But don't worry; I am careful not to get over tired. My plans remain just as vague for the near future. I hope to return to Les Etudes in November, even if I have to lead the life of a recluse until December, the month when the doctors promise to release me. But, until then, I have no idea what I am going to do. Perhaps I'll very simply stay here? I still read a great deal, but not many really interesting books, mostly the best novels recently published; and also what I can get on existentialist literature (Sartre's *La Nausée*, Camus' *La Peste*, etc . . ., the titles are cheerful, aren't they?) As a whole, this existentialist movement makes me bristle and more and more seems to me to be a snobbish movement without any roots in the forces which today lead the world. Nevertheless, it is led by very intelligent people and it gives, in contrast, an excellent background to my own ideas. I had to find out more about it and I must say that this additional knowledge has reassured me about its weak points and finally, I believe, about its sterility and its impotence.

I haven't heard from Simone which seems to prove that all is well in Bréhat (the island off the coast of Brittany where she is with Ida Treat). Barbour wrote to me from Johannesburg (we were supposed to go there together!), and he passed on to me a good letter from Eddie Bien who left China a year ago and is working in some university in California. Bien does not seem in the least surprised by the present disturbances in China, but he does not make any prognosis as to its future. I must confess that this human world, is neither in a very reassuring state right now, nor very comfortable (at least in Europe). But it seems to me more and more evident, for reasons which control or lead the human will, that this

*le processus ne peut se terminer (de nécessité biologique et planétaire) que sur une unification d'ensemble!*

*Good bye pour cette fois, dearest. Cette lettre a été interrompue par l'arrivée d'amis qui m'ont emmené dans leur auto à travers la forêt, jusqu'au bout de la magnifique terrasse de St Germain, que vous connaissez sans doute. Louis XIV et ceux qui l'entouraient étaient évidemment de grands messieurs.*

*yours ever +++*

*P.T.*

process can only end (because of biological and planetary necessity) in a general unification.

Good by for this time, dearest. This letter was interrupted by the arrival of some friends who took me in their car through the forest to the very end of the magnificent terrace at St. Germain which you no doubt know. Louis XIV and those who surrounded him were evidently grands messieurs.

**St Germain, 24 Sept. 47**

*Dearest,*

*Je viens de recevoir votre longue chère lettre du 19, si pleine de nouvelles et de chose sur vous. Cela m'ennuie de sentir que vous êtes moins entourée à Washington, après tant de départs. Mais j'espère qu'il y aura bientôt des retours pour compenser. Eléonore m'avait écrit avant de quitter la Chine (j'espère qu'elle aura reçu ma réponse, à San Francisco); et j'ai vu Robert Faure lui-même ici, il y a quelque temps. Il espérait en effet trouver le moyen d'aller passer quelques jours aux Etats-Unis pour revoir enfin sa "fiancée". Je l'ai trouvé très gentil. Présentez naturellement toutes mes grandes amitiés à Erica et à Maria Wilhelm. Incidemment, Faure m'a dit que Margaret Tafel avait quitté son mari (Toby), et que cela ne l'étonnait pas. Moi j'ai été péniblement surpris. De Péking je n'ai depuis longtemps aucune nouvelle directe, — sauf une bonne lettre de Nirgidma, qui a l'air tout à fait paisible et heureuse là-bas. Mais évidemment la vie est là-bas complétement changée socialement parlant. De l'Institut de Géo-Biologie je crains qu'il ne faille dire qu'il est mort, - après avoir honorablement joué le rôle pour lequel il avait été créé pendant la guerre. Personne n'est là, ni ne sera trouvé de*

I have just received your dear long letter of the 19th, so full of news and things about you. It bothers me a little to feel that you are less surrounded by friends in Washington after so many departures. But I hope that there soon will be some returns to compensate. Eleonore had written to me before leaving China (I hope she will have received my reply in San Francisco); and I saw Robert Faure himself here some time ago. Indeed, he hoped to go and spend a few days in the United States to finally see again his "fiancée." I found him very nice. Of course, give my best love to Erica and Maria Wilhelm. Incidentally, Faure told me that Margaret Tafel had left her husband (Toby) which did not surprise him. I was painfully surprised. I have not had any direct news from Peking for a long time — except for a nice letter from Nirgidma who seems quite peaceful and happy there. Evidently, life over there is completely changed, socially speaking. I fear I must say that the Institute of Geo-Biology is dead — after honorably playing the role for which it had been created during the war. Nobody is working there, and it will take a long time to find someone who could replace Leroy and me. No news

longtemps, pour remplacer Leroy et moi. Pas de nouvelles du Survey: c'est un peu de ma faute, car je n'écris pas. Mais que pourrais-je écrire, quand mes plans sont tellement incertains? . .

Ici, rien de substantiellement nouveau. Je vais de mieux en mieux, et je pense rentrer Rue Monsieur au commencement d'Octobre, quitte à y mener, comme veulent les docteurs, une vie ralentie jusqu'au 1 Décembre. En somme, le séjour ici aura été bienfaisant et assez plaisant, grâce à un temps magnifique, à de nombreuses visites, à de bons livres, et à un certain travail depensée que je crois assez bon. Je ne me suis pas souvent senti l'esprit aussi vif et lucide: j'imagine que je récolte le fruit des innombrables conversations et discussions de l'an dernier. Tout de même, je continue à sentir que d'avoir manqué le trip en Afrique du Sud a profondément désorganisé mon plan de travail scientifique; et je me sens de plus en plus porté à déserter (relativement) l'Homme fossile pour le Phénomène humain moderne, - ce qui est exactement dans la logique de ma vie. Le malheur est que je me retrouve une fois de plus en difficulté avec Rome, au point que (par une certaine amitié, apparemment, càd. pour me protéger de certains ennuis majeurs avec l'autorité ecclésiastique suprême - quels ennuis? je l'ignore: sans doute la mise "à l'Index") on me donne la consigne de réduire au minimum mes publications non strictement scientifiques. Cela tombe assez mal. Mais j'ai de plus en plus d'amis fidèles et bien placés; et surtout il est désormais trop tard pour arrêter les idées auxquelles je tiens bien plus qu'à la vie: la percée est faite. Je suis donc, au fond de moi-même, suffisamment philosophe et tranquille; - persuadé que je suis qu'une fois de plus le mal apparent tournera au plus grand bien. Je compte sur les événements pour me guider pas à pas; et je continue à écrire beaucoup. Evidemment, dans ces

from the Survey: it is partially my fault because I don't write. But what could I write when my plans are so uncertain?

There is nothing substantially new here. I feel better and better and I hope to go back to rue Monsieur at the beginning of October, even if I have to lead, as the doctors wish, a slower life until December 1st. All in all, the stay here will have been beneficial and pleasant enough, thanks to the magnificent weather, numerous visits, good books and a certain amount of reflexion which was good for me. I haven't often felt so lucid and alive: I suppose I am gathering the fruit of the numerous conversations and discussions I have had this past year. All the same, I still feel that, missing the South African trip has profoundly disorganized my plans of scientific research; and I feel more and more like deserting (relatively speaking) fossil Man for the modern human Phenomenon - which follows exactly the logic of my life. Unfortunately, I am once more in difficulty with Rome, to the point where (out of a certain sense of goodwill apparently, that is to say, to protect me from major problems with the supreme ecclesiastical authority - which problems? I really don't know: perhaps getting me "on the Index") I have been told to limit to a minimum my publications which are not strictly scientific. This is what I needed just now!. But I have more and more faithful and "well-placed" friends; and, in any case, it is already too late to stop the ideas for which I care more than my life: the breakthrough has taken place. So, deep down, I am sufficiently philosophical and peaceful - persuaded as I am that once again the apparent harm will become the greatest good. I count on the events to guide me step by step; and I continue to write a great deal. Evidently, under these conditions, there is very little chance that the manuscript of

*conditions, il n'y a guère de chances pour que le manuscrit de mon livre (Le Phénomène Humain) approuvé en France, échappe à la censure romaine. En somme, peu importe: l'essentiel est que les idées passent, — et elles passent.*

*A propos de livres sur l'Homme, vous savez certainement par Nathaly que Lecomte du Nouy est très gravement malade, à New York. De source directe, je sais qu'il a complétement trouvé (ou retrouvé) Dieu dans son esprit et dans son coeur, ce qui lui donne une admirable sérénité. Je lui ai écrit, il y a peu de jours.*

*Il n'est pas étonnant que vous restiez rêveuse devant l'Existentialisme. C'est un mouvement extrêmement polymorphe qui n'a d'intéressant, à mon sens, que sa tendance générale à sortir la philosophie du monde des abstractions pour nous replacer en face des problèmes de réalité. Ceci reconnu à son éloge, il reste que, d'une manière générale aussi, les existentialistes montrent une tendance malheureuse à vouloir résoudre le problème de la Vie en considérant des individus isolés (dans le Temps et l'Espace) ce qui les incline à déclarer le Monde absurde, avec comme conséquences: ou bien un stoïcisme tragique et stupide (Sartre, Camus, Heidegger); ou bien un Christianisme pessimiste (Kirkegaard, Jaspers, Marcel); ou bien la "littérature noire" et une sorte de "néo-dadaisme" artistique. - A mon avis, sous ces formes, le mouvement n'a pas d'avenir, et il restera une philosophie de snobs et de raffinés. Je crois que nous avons plus besoin de Dieu (et d'un Dieu "aimant") que jamais: mais il me semble que notre foi en lui ne saurait plus naître que d'un excès de notre foi en l'avenir et la valeur du monde (et non d'un défaut de cette foi, comme diraient volontiers les existentialistes chrétiens).*

*Je continue à voir souvent Pierre Leroy, avec qui je m'entends toujours*

my book (*The Phenomenon of Man*) approved in France will escape the Roman censure. But this does not matter much: the essential thing is that the ideas make their way — and they do make their way.

Talking about books on Man, you have probably heard from Nathaly that Lecomte du Noüy is very seriously ill in New York. I know from a direct source that he has completely found (or found again) God in his mind and in his heart, which gives him an admirable serenity. I wrote him a few days ago.

It is not suprising that you are wondering about Existentialism. It is an extremely polymorphous movement which is only interesting, in my opinion, by its general tendency to take philosophy out of the world of abstractions and to place us in front of problems of reality. This being recognized in its favor, it remains that, in a general way also, the existentialists show an unfortunate tendency in wanting to solve Life's problems by considering isolated individuals (in Time and Space) which brings them to declare that the World is absurd with, as a consequence: either a tragic and stupid stoicism (Sartre, Camus, Heidegger), or a pessimistic Christianity (Kierkegaard, Jaspers, Marcel), or a "black literature" and a kind of artistic "neo-dadaism." In my opinion the movement has no future in these forms; and it will remain a philosophy of snobs and the sophisticated. The only philosophy which can and which must penetrate the human mass is a vigorous spirit, exalting human faith and strongly rooted in Matter. I believe we need God (a "loving" God) more that ever: but it seems to me that our faith in Him can only be born from a surplus of our faith in the future and the value of the world (and not from a failing of this faith as the Christian existentialists would readily say).

I often see Pierre Leroy, with whom I still get along very well, or even, if this

*aussi bien, ou même, si c'était possible de mieux en mieux. Il continue à travailler les hormones et a eu de grands succès dans son enseignement. Françoise Raphael est absolument inchangée, et vient régulièrement me voir ici chaque semaine. Elle est toujours "wellfare officer" à l'UNESCO, - très appréciée, je crois. Vous savez que vos anciens voisins, les Dorget, sont également à Paris; eux aussi, je les vois souvent. Je crois qu'ils vont aller tous les deux à Mexico cet automne (pour le congrès de l'UNESCO). Je n'ai pas revu Julian Huxley depuis que je suis immobilisé. Mais nous restons en contact et en grande sympathie.*

*Breuil m'a écrit récemment d'Afrique du Sud, où il s'occupe surtout de peinture rupestres. Quel dommage de manquer une rencontre là-bas avec Henry Field!*

*Vu Simone samedi dernier. Elle a rebondi une fois de plus, et compte retourner au Maroc fin Octobre!! Elle était accompagnée par Ida Treat qui part pour l'Amérique dans peu de jours mais par cargo; ce qui ne la mettra guère à New York avant le 15 Octobre. Elle restera trois mois là-bas et compte vous voir. Comme elle est donc heureuse! . .*

were possible, better and better. He is still working with hormones and has been very successful in his teaching. Françoise Raphaël is absolutely unchanged and comes to see me regularly every week. She is still a "welfare officer" with UNESCO — and is very much appreciated, I think. You know that your former neighbors, the Dorgets, are also in Paris; I also see them often. I think they will both go to Mexico this fall (for the UNESCO convention). I haven't seen Julian Huxley since I was immobilized. But we remain in touch, and we feel a great sympathy for each other.

Breuil wrote me recently from South Africa where he is still working on rupestrian paintings [the cave rock murals]. What a pity to miss a meeting over there with Henry Field!

I saw Simone last Saturday. She has recovered once again and hopes to go back to Morocco at the end of October. Ida Treat, who is leaving for America in a few days by cargo ship, was with her; she probably will not reach New York before October 15. She will stay there three months and hopes to see you. How lucky she is!

*Good bye, dearest. You are such a treasure for me, and I l. you so much!+++*

*God bless you!*

*P.T.*

*Paris, 16 Octobre, 1947*

Dearest,

*I thank you so much for your precious letter of Oct. 5, full of interesting news.*

*Et en particulier je suis si heureux (pour vous et pour elle) que Eléonore soit maintenant avec vous. Dites-lui bien toute ma grande affection. J'ai revu Faure, il y a environ dix jours. Il était donc assez désappointé de n'avoir pu aller faire un tour en Amérique, et ne*

I thank you so much for your precious letter of Oct. 5, full of interesting news. And I am particularly happy (for you and for her) that Eleonore is now with you. Give her all my great affection. I saw Faure again about ten days ago. He was rather disappointed not to

*savait comment rejoindre l'Abyssinie, par suite de la suppression d'une ligne d'avions; mais je pense qu'il a dû finalement partir depuis. Son absence va durer trois ou quatre mois. -*

*Personnellement, je suis donc de nouveau Rue Monsieur, depuis quinze jours; et malgré un certain regret des magnifiques arbres de St Germain, je me trouve très bien ici. Beaucoup de gens et d'amis viennent me voir; et il m'arrive assez souvent d'aller déjeûner ou prendre le thè au dehors, dans le car de quelque ami fortuné. A ce régime, les quelques semaines qui me séparent encore du 1 Décembre (date de ma "libération") passeront vite. Je continue à lire, - mais moins cependant qu'à St Germain, parce que les conversations, ici, sont plus nombreuses. Finalement, je crois que mon hiver va s'arranger et s'occuper facilement. Ce ne sont pas les occasions de parler (de préférence devant de petits groupes sélectionnés) qui me manqueront. Et puis, à défaut d'articles immédiatement publiables, je suis décidé à écrire (sous le titre "Comment je vois") un résumé complet de toute ma perspective (physique, théologique, métaphysique et mystique). Naturellement une telle chose ne sera pas publiée: mais elle pourra être diffusée. Et puis je sens le besoin de fixer, dans un tableau d'ensemble, toute ma pensée. Je continue à avoir cette impression que pour moi la perception de la vraie perspective et le sens des vraies valeurs se sont brusquement super-révélées sont subitement augmenté d'intensité) depuis le mois de juin. C'est cela que je voudrais exprimer; et je crois que ce sera facile, parce que c'est si clair, et si simple . . .*

*Je ne sais encore quel sera le sort de l'article que j'ai écrit en Septembre (sur le "rebondissement" humain de l'Evolution). En attendant j'ai écrit, sur demande, quelques lignes (bien senties) sur Lecomte du Nouy, dont les vues,*

have been able to go to America, and he didn't know how to go to Abyssinia, after the suppression of an Air Line; but I think he must have left finally. He will be away three or four months.

As to myself I have been back to rue Monsieur for two weeks and, although I rather miss the magnificent trees of Saint Germain, I feel very comfortable here. Many people and friends come to see me, and I go out quite often for lunch or tea in the car of some wealthy friend. At this rate, the few weeks which separate me from December 1st (the date of my "liberation") will pass quickly. I continue to read — less however than when I was in Saint Germain because conversations here are more frequent. Finally, I think my winter will take shape and I will easily find occupation. I will not lack opportunities to speak (preferably before small select groups). And then, for lack of articles which could be published immediately, I have decided to write (under the title "How I See") a complete summary of my whole perspective (physical, theological, metaphysical and mystic). Naturally, such a thing will not be published: but it could be circulated. And then I feel the need to set down in a complete picture the whole of my thought. I continue to have the impression that, for me, the perception of the true perspective and the meaning of true values have been suddenly super-revealed (have suddenly grown in intensity) since the month of June. This is what I would like to express; and I believe that it will be easy, because it is so clear and so simple.

I don't know what will be the fate of the article I wrote in September (on the human "rebound" of evolution). Meanwhile, I wrote (I was asked to write) a few (strong) lines on Lecomte du Nouÿ whose views, as you know, are exactly

vous le savez, parallélisent exactement les miennes (excepté qu'il ne va
pas assez "jusqu'au bout", me semble-
t-il). Mme Lecomte du Nouy (la cousine de Nathaly, comme vous le savez)
vient de m'envoyer une lettre bien
touchante. Ma lettre est la dernière qui
soit arrivée à son mari . . .

*Merci* pour le luxueux envoi de cigarettes, que j'ai trouvé dans ma chambre
en rentrant ici. It is too much, dearest.
J'aurais bien voulu voir les Vincent's
eux-mêmes! mais quand ils ont passé
j'étais encore à St Germain. Je suppose
qu'ils trouveront bien le moyen de
venir quelquefois à Paris (ainsi que les
Lago, qui sont nommés à Bruxelles,
m'ont dit le Baron Guillaume et
Scheven).

Dimanche dernier, je suis allé au thé
chez les Dorget (qui vont aller à Mexico pour la réunion de l'Unesco). Il y
avait là P. Leroy, en excellente forme.
Hier, j'ai déjeûné à l'Unesco, avec les
Huxley (en partance, eux aussi, pour
Mexico); j'y ai revu Françoise Raphael,
toujours aussi vive et aussi jeune; elle
ne va *pas* à Mexico. Max Bégouën est
arrivé, mais si anémié qu'il ne repartira
pas pour le Maroc avant Décembre;
Simone est décidée à l'accompagner; je
dois les revoir après-demain. -

*Merci* pour la liste de livres. Je vous
dirai ce dont j'ai besoin.

Good bye, *dearest* +++

P.T.

parallel to mine (except that it seems to
me he does not go far enough). Mme
Lecomte du Nouÿ (Nathaly's cousin as
you know) has just sent me a very
touching letter. My letter was the last
her husband received.

Thank you for the luxurious ship-
ment of cigarettes which I found in my
room on my return. It is too much,
dearest. I would very much have liked
to see the Vincents themselves! But I
was still in St Germain when they came
through. I imagine they will find a way
to come to Paris sometimes. (As well as
the Lagos, who have been sent to Brussels, as I was told by Baron Guillaume
and by Scheven).

I had tea last Sunday at the Dorgets
(who will go to Mexico City for the
UNESCO meeting). P. Leroy was there
in excellent form. Yesterday, I had
lunch at UNESCO with the Huxleys
(also ready to leave for Mexico); I saw
Françoise Raphaël there, still very vivacious and young; she is not going to
Mexico. Max Bégouën has arrived, but
so anemic that he will not go back to
Morocco before December; Simone has
decided to go with him; I will see them
again the day after to-morrow.

Thank you for the list of books. I'll
tell you what I need.

Rue Monsieur
Paris, 21 Nov. 1947

Dearest,

Merci tant pour vos deux lettres du
3 et 15 Novembre (cette dernière
arrivée en même temps que la gentille
lettre d'Eléonore, qui m'a fait un très
grand plaisir, et à laquelle je répond-
rai).

And it is so sweet of you to send me a Xmas package. In fact it did not yet
reach me (the delay is quite normal); but you may be sure that it will be welcome.

Thank you so very much for your
two letters of the 3rd and 15th of
November (the latter arrived at the
same time as Eleonore's very nice letter
which gave me great pleasure and
which I will answer).

*Quoi que vous ait dit Mrs. David-son, il est très difficile de se procurer beaucoup de choses en France en dehors du marché noir (où tout se trouve, en effet, mais à des prix excessifs). Il ne faudrait tout de même pas que vous croyiez that we are starving, et que "vous vous enleviez pour moi le pain de la bouche". La vie, même à Paris, demeure possible, ou même relative-ment confortable (so far!): mais elle demeure difficile, et souvent même très difficile pour les petites et moyennes bourses. Donc, encore une fois, merci, et merci tant: pour la chose, et plus encore pour l'idée.*

*En ce qui me concerne, rien de très particulier. J'ai l'impression d'aller tout à fait bien. Dans quelques jours je vais aller revoir mon médecin pour lui demander quelques avis concernant ma reprise de la vie normale, au début de décembre. Je sais d'avance ce qu'il me dira: "Le moins d'efforts possible". Mais ce n'est pas facile de savoir ce que ceci veut dire. En attendant, j'ai repris quelques sorties en ville; et je m'en trouve bien. Par ailleurs, bien des gens ont recommencé à venir me voir, exact-ement comme avant; et je me suis remis à écrire, aussi comme avant, — de sorte que le temps passe vite de façon intéressante. Mais je ne vois pas encore bien clair en avant, — soit pcq. je ne sais pas encore bien les limites de mes forces, soit parce que j'ignore le rayon des libertés que l'autorité me laissera prendre. De ce dernier côté il est déjà clair que mon action (sinon mes publi-cations) n'a rien à craindre des restric-tions qu'on m'a imposées. Les idées qui me sont chères progressent et se répan-dent juste comme auparavant. Et puis mes amis (bien placés) me soutiennent vigoureusement. Ces derniers jours, dans son discours d'ouverture des cours, le Recteur de l'Université catho-lique de Toulouse has delivered a regu-lar "éloge" of me ... Almost too much!*

Whatever Mrs. Davidson told you, it is very difficult to buy many things in France outside the black market (where anything can be bought at excessive prices). However, you must not think that we are starving and you must not "take the bread out of your mouth" for me. Life, even in Paris, remains possi-ble, or even relatively comfortable (so far!): but it remains difficult, and often very difficult for people with small or average incomes. So, once again, thank you, thank you very much for the pack-age and even more for the thought.

As far as I am concerned, there is nothing very special to report. I have the impression I am really fine. I will see my doctor in a few days to ask advice concerning the resumption of normal life early in December. I already know what he will tell me: "The least efforts possible." But it isn't easy to know what this means. Meanwhile, I have resumed short trips around town -and I have felt well. Besides that, many people are coming to see me just as before, and I have started writing again, also as before — so that time passes quickly and interestingly. But I still don't see ahead clearly - either because so far I do not really know the limits of my strength, or because I do not know the range of freedom which the authorities will allow me to take. From their side, it is already clear that my activity (except for my publica-tions) have nothing to fear from the restrictions which have been imposed on me. The ideas that are dear to me progress and spread just as before. Also, my (well placed) friends are sup-porting me vigorously. Recently, in his opening speech, the Rector of the Cath-olic University in Toulouse has given me a real testimonial — almost too much!

*Pour en revenir à mes projets d'avenir, ce que je voudrais savoir, et ce qu'il me faudra bien essayer tôt ou tard, c'est dans quelle mesure je puis reprendre de longs voyages. Ida Treat (did you see her, by the way?) m'a écrit que Weidenreich était prêt à m'envoyer une lettre d'invitation à venir passer qq. temps à l'American Museum. Bien que je ne vois pas de raison scientifique bien sérieuse pour ce séjour, il y a certainement là quelque chose à considérer, soigneusement. A la rigueur, et si tout allait bien, je pourrais même considérer, en outre, un retour en Europe par l'Afrique du Sud, pour laquelle il est sûrement beaucoup plus facile de trouver un bateau en Amérique qu'en Europe. Ce qui me fait songer à cela est la rencontre, ici, de Henry Field et de Philipps. Le premier m'a apporté de vos nouvelles; et le second m'a chaudement invité à joindre son expédition. Je lui ai dit qu'il n'y avait rien à faire, malheureusement pour le moment, - mais que peut-être pendant l'été prochain . . . Mais que seront les conditions politiques et économiques à ce moment? - Donc, pour finir, et en deux mots: voyage en Amérique possible, vers le printemps; mais rien de sûr.*

*Passons maintenant aux habitants de Paris. Dans ma famille, un évènement heureux: ma nièce (la soeur de mon neveu disparu en juillet) vient de se fiancer, avec un fort gentil garçon. Le mariage se fera juste après Pâques. - Simone, décidément, repart pour le Maroc (à moins que le service des paquebots ne soit interrompu par quelque grève, elle devrait partir dans trois jours, Max la suivant de près, en avion). Ils vont me manquer, tous les deux; mais, pour Simone, c'est un tel progrès sur l'an dernier, qu'on ne peut que se réjouir. Et puis, sur les entrefaites, Rhoda est arrivée. Je crois bien qu'elle ne pouvait se tenir de venir voir*

To get back to my plans for the future, what I would like to know and what I will have to try sooner or later, is to what extent I can make long trips. Ida Treat (did you see her, by the way?) wrote me that Weidenreich was ready to send me an invitation to come and spend some time at the American Museum. Although I don't see any serious scientific reason for this stay, it is certainly something to consider carefully. Eventually, and if all went well, I could even consider a return trip to Europe via South Africa for which it is surely much easier to find a ship in America than in Europe. What makes me think of that is meeting here with Henry Field and Philipps. The first brought me news of you; and the second warmly invited me to take part in his expedition. I told him that, unfortunately, nothing could be done at the moment — but perhaps next summer. But what will the political and economic conditions be at that time? So, finally, in two words: a trip to America, possibly in the spring; but nothing definite.

Now, about people in Paris: in my family, a happy event: my niece (the sister of my nephew who died in July) just became engaged to an extremely nice young man. The wedding will take place just after Easter. Simone is definitely going back to Morocco (unless the steamer service is interrupted by some strike, she should leave in three days; Max will follow her shortly by plane). I will miss both of them. As for Simone, I see such progress in her, compared to last year, that one can but rejoice. And then, meanwhile, Rhoda arrived. I quite believe she couldn't wait to see if I was really alive. Her second stay was made

*si j'étais bien encore vivant. Ce deux-ième séjour lui a été facilité par la présence de son frère et de sa belle-soeur à Paris. Elle repart au com-mencement de Décembre: toujours aussi active et réaliste, et aussi décidée à poursuivre une carrière littéraire. Elle est certainement douée pour la psy-chologie. - Et de la voir a certainement ranimé mon désir de revoir l'Amérique, et plus particulièrement Washington.*

easier by the presence of her brother and sister-in-law in Paris. She will leave early in December: she is as active and realistic as ever, and also has decided to carry on a literary career. She certainly has a gift for psychology. And seeing her again has certainly reawakened my desire to go to Amer-ica, and more particularly to Washing-ton.

*Yes, Lucile, you have been so sweet et so patient, all these years. If only I could do something really good for you and to you! Anyhow, who ever talked to you during the night was certainly from God and heaven, because nothing can be added to the words you have heard, except to realize and to feel their full meaning ever more.*

*Je songeais justement ces temps-ci que toute l'essence de mon "évangile" peut en somme se ramener à ces simples mots: non seulement "Dieu est amour", comme répétait St Jean; mais "le Monde est amour", dans la mesure où il ne s'achève et ne prend de sens que nous subissons et rejoignons Dieu (à travers et sous la forme de tous efforts et de tous événements) par amour. L'amour est la forme supérieure, stable et définitive de toute énergie, - comme nous le disions déjà en traduisant "l'Energie Humaine". Do you remem-ber? (J'ai été si ému en revoyant le petit snapshot de Péking que vous m'avez envoyé. Mais il ne faut rien regretter: ces années ont été riches et fécondes, à Ta Tien Shui hutung; elles ont porté leur fruit; il faut toujours regarder en avant. Je suis content que vous ayez trouvé, pour votre sculpture, un sujet inspirant, — celui-là même, peut-être, que vous n'avez jamais cherché sous tous vos tâtonnements des dernières années.*

Indeed, I was recently thinking that the essence of my "gospel" can be sum-marized by these simple words: not only "God is love," as Saint John used to say, but "the World is love" and it is only fulfilled and takes on meaning to the extent that we submit to God and rejoin him (through and in the shape of all efforts and all events) through love. Love is the superior, stable, and defini-tive form of all energy — as we were already saying when we translated "Human Energy." Do you remember? (I was so moved when I saw the small snapshot of Peking which you sent me.) But we have no regrets: those years in Ta Tien Shui Hutung were rich and fertile and they bore fruits; one must always look ahead. I am happy that you have found an inspiring sub-ject for your sculpture — the very same, perhaps which you never looked for in all your strivings of the last few years.

*Je pense vous écrire bientôt, - en tous cas dès que je recevrai votre package. En attendant, mille douces choses à Eléonore, — et à vous toujours aussi profondément.*

I will write to you soon again, - in any case as soon as I receive your pack-age. Meanwhile a thousand best wishes to Eleonore — yours always deeply devoted.

*P.T.*

1217 34th Street NW, Washington D.C.
Washington, December 13, '47 St. Lucia's Day.

THEIR
1941–48
LETTERS

219

*Dearest, -*

*Again my Saint's day. The first time I remember of writing to you on this day was in '38 when you were on your way, or already in Burma. What a long time ago and yet how close it all is. I wonder if you thought of me especially at Mass this morning. I felt that you did - and it seemed to me I was closer to God and to peace and happiness because of it - and to the real love. It is wonderful, dear, if you can really feel in your heart that "le Monde est amour". Yes, I remember l'Energie humaine (I must reread it) and the role of love. Is it being achieved? Probably we are all too impatient. How grateful I am to you for giving me an understanding of TIME. Of looking at things from the long view, in fact that is the only way that things seem to me to make sense. You say "do not regret those years at Ta Tien Shui Ching"! Regret!! Oh my dear, they are so much the richest years of my life and it is very hard not to long for them - with the war and all it has been especially hard to find a path. Perhaps, for me, they were too perfect; and it seems to me I have not always been wise in putting into practice the things we talked of and believed in. It has been a funny struggle in some ways. Often I feared I would eventually bore you if I became "pious" (which I suppose I have not much danger of becoming), and yet I have had to find my way to God. It is so very important to me - and I still believe so strongly in the sign that you showed me . . and I could not fall too far behind . . well it will be interesting tosee . . where we each have gone . . as a very humble pupil . . I hope you will not be too disappointed in me . . To have a proper perspective of "personal love" . . is still very hard . . The things I have always been taught . . and the way . . . well it will be SO wonderful to be able to TALK with you again . .*

*Pierre, I am so excited at the possibility of your coming here soon. I have hardly dared think about it definitely. You must know what it means to me - the focal point of my existence since we said goodbye in the little house in '41. And it is so strange how I have felt I could not force my coming to France! I am sure my friends think I have been very stupid and remiss - perhaps even you do too, but there is something INSIDE that kept saying to me that the time had not yet come! I hope with all my heart that I have been right. At least, dear, you so surely must know that it was not indifference that kept me away. But now the time is almost here - really and truly almost here! Now I long for it - and yet I am just a tiny bit afraid - but I don't want to convey that idea - so I will not dwell on it now. It is all so very exciting and wonderful. Oh Pierre, you know my heart.*

*It was so good to see and talk to Ida Treat whom I like so much. She also gave me another picture of Rhoda which is good. Rhoda's book was - well I was interested to see that Eleanor objected to it even more than I did - so it was not just ME. However it is splendid that she has been able to DO things. Oh, Pierre, Ida told me that you are not allowed to smoke!! gosh I always seem to be TOO LATE . . and goodness knows when the packages will arrive . . everything seems to take so much time . . please do not wait for that before writing again. I look every day for a letter to say definitely that you are coming . .*

*This is a stupid letter I fear . . I am realizing that we will be together again before very long and I am much too emotional to be very clear . . This is just to wish you a happy Christmas . . and every good wish for the New Year . .*

*My heart is full to overflowing with love of you and all the things you stand for.*

*Thank you infinitely for the things you have given to me and for being you . . God bless you and all my love to you . .*

*Paris, 21 Decembre, 1947*

*Lucile, dearest,*

*Merci tant pour votre chère lettre datée de la Ste Lucile. C'est moi qui aurais dû vous écrire, ce jour-là ou pour ce jour-là. En tous cas, ma pensée était avec vous, - et comme d'habitude ma messe a été dite pour vous, — pour que (suivant votre expression si juste) vous trouviez votre Dieu.*

Thank you so very much for your dear letter written on the day of Saint Lucile. It is I who should have written to you on that day or for that day. In any case, my thoughts were with you and, as usual, my mass was said for you so that (as you so rightly say) you can find your God.

*No, I do not see you (and I would not like you) "pious", Lucile. But it is one thing to be "pious", and another one to see the world at the light and under the warmth of a personal and leading influence. And that you will get, I hope, some day. But do not forget that the discovery of God is something (like Art) which is never achieved, although trying to achieve it is probably the greatest joy man can feel; at least, that is what I am experiencing each year more. So you have to be steady, and patient, and chiefly "confiante". I suppose that the highest form of worship is active "confiance" in Life, — confiance which brings peace.*

*Que vous dire sur Paris et ma présente existence? — Tout va aussi bien que possible physiquement, et, moralement aussi, je me sens bien en forme. La semaine dernière j'ai donné deux lectures (en cercles semi-privés, mais à des auditoires très intéressants) qui m'ont permis de constater que mon "message" était plus clair que jamais, dans ma tête et dans mon coeur. J'ai même rédigé quelques nouvelles pages (one more "egg") ces jours-ci. Finalement, je suis persuadé que les difficultés venant de Rome n'auront aucun inconvénient sérieux pour la maturation et la diffusion de ma pensée, ou même je demande si elles ne seront pas un "incentive" de plus pour la faire accepter. Le Recteur de l'Université catholique de Toulouse, mon ami Mgr. Bruno de Solages vient de faire et publier un long discours où il expose et défend (très habilement) ce qu'il y a de plus incontestable dans ma position. Je ne sais pas encore l'effet que cette intervention aura en haut lieu.*

What can I say about Paris and my life at the moment? Everything is as good as possible, physically and morally as well; I feel very fit. I gave two lectures last week (semi-private circles, but to very interesting audiences), which made me realize that my "message" was clearer than ever in my head and in my heart. I even rewrote a few new pages (one more "egg") recently. Finally, I feel certain that the difficulties coming from Rome will present no serious drawbacks for the maturation and diffusion of my thought; I even wonder if they will not be one more "incentive" to have my thought accepted. The Rector of the Catholic University in Toulouse, my friend Monsignor Bruno de Solages, has just given (and published) a long speech in which he presents and defends (very cleverly) what is most incontestable in my position. I still don't know what the result of this intervention will be in high places.

*Sauf que je continue à me ménager*

Except that I continue to take long

de longues nuits et à éviter le metro (à cause des escaliers) je reprends une existence presque normale, et je vois de nombreux amis. Hier par ex. j'ai rencontré Laurette Dorget, juste rentrée, avec son mari, de Mexico (Congrès de l'Unesco). Mme. Raphael vient de partir pour quinze jours en Algérie. Autrement elle est toujours ici, à l'UNESCO, où elle réussit admirablement (adresse: Hotel Reynold's, Rue Bertie Albrecht, Paris VIII). Je la vois assez souvent, et aussi Leroy, ce dernier très en forme. Avant-hier, vu Ginette Bussière, contente pour le moment avec un petit job. Sa soeur (Mme deSercey) est aussi ici: sa fille se débrouille bien, mais n'arrive pas à oublier la Chine. Le Dr. est toujours à Péking, bien seul. Il paraît qu'il n'y a aucune sécurité hors de la ville. Beianho (maison du Dr. aux Collines) a été en partie pillé. On ne peut plus y résider. Il paraît que les Bréal réussissent très bien. Les Max Bégouën ont finalement fait très bon voyage (à cause des grèves, Simone est partie avec Max en avion). Je n'ai pas encore de lettre d'eux.

Dites à Eleonor ma grande affection et mes voeux de Noël et Nouvel an. Je ne comprends pas que Robert F. lui ait écrit une lettre insatisfaisante. La veille de son départ il est venu me voir, et m'a dit que dès son retour de Somalie (dans l'hiver) il se ferait envoyer à Washington (pour quelques jours) pour revoir enfin Eléonor; et je suis sûr qu'il était sincère.

Rien d'essentiellement nouveau pour mes projets de voyage (j'attend encore qqs autorisations nécessaires). Mais j'ai bon espoir!

nights of rest and avoid the metro (because of the stairs) I am leading a practically normal life and I see very many friends. Yesterday, for example, I met Laurette Dorget who had just returned with her husband from Mexico (the UNESCO convention). Mme Raphaël recently left for Algeria where she will stay a fortnight. Otherwise she is always here at UNESCO where she is extremely successful. (Address: hôtel Reynold's, rue Bertie Albrecht, Paris VIII). I see her fairly often and also Leroy, who is in great shape. The day before yesterday I saw Ginette Bussière quite satisfied for the moment with a little job. Her sister (Mme de Sercey) is also here; her daughter is doing well but cannot forget China. The Doctor is still in Peking, very much alone. It seems there is no safety outside the city. Beianho (the doctor's house on the hills) was partly plundered. It cannot be lived in anymore. It seems that the Bréals are doing very well. The Max Bégouëns finally had a very nice trip (because of the strikes, Simone left with Max by plane). I have not heard from them yet.

Give Eleonore my great affection and my best greetings for Christmas and the New Year. I do not know what to make of the unsatisfactory letter that Robert F. has written to her. The day before he left he came to see me and told me that, as soon as he returns from Somalia (in the winter), he would arrange to be sent to Washington (for a few days) so as to finally see Eleonore again; I am sure that he was sincere.

Nothing essentially new concerning my travel plans (I am still waiting for some necessary authorizations). But I am very hopeful!

Good bye, dearest. I stop here so that this letter should reach you not too late after Xmas!

with love

P.T.

The parcel did not yet arrive. But eventually it will. — I don't anymore smoke, but american cigarettes are a treat for my visitors!!

*Lucile, dearest,*

*Two days ago (that is on the eve of the New Year) your two wonderful parcels have finally arrived, in perfect conditions; and in addition to their rich material content they were so full of your "presence", heart and hands. I could almost feel you . . . Thank you so much for so much you give me. The dressing gown is simply wonderful. But whom did you deprieve (yourself probably?), to be still in possession of this chinese, or even pekinese, product? And everything else is so practical and useful. Really, I feel spoilt.*

*Puisque nous ne sommes encore que le 2 Janvier, je profite de l'occasion pour vous redire (et à Eléonore) mes plus affectueux souhaits de bonne année. Que 1948 vous apporte toutes sortes de douces choses, dearest, et surtout beaucoup de paix, de goût et de chaleur intérieure. Pour moi, ce dernier don me paraît, de plus en plus, ce qui nous est le plus nécessaire. J'y ai souvent songé, depuis quelque temps: ce qui rend, dans son essence, le Christianisme vrai et irremplaçable, c'est que seul il se montre capable (d'une façon logique et cohérente avec l'histoire et la structure de l'Univers) de réchauffer et de rendre à la fois aimant et aimable le Monde par le dedans. On nous menace encore souvent d'une fin de l'Humanité par refroidissement de la planète: moi je pense que ce qui nous tuerait bien plus sûrement, et bien avant, ce serait de "geler" intérieurement par impossibilité de trouver une âme et un coeur aux immensités qui nous entraînent et nous entourent.*

*Mon existence ici continue la même. Je vais très bien physiquement, et reprends une vie presque normale (sauf que je prolonge encore mes nuits et évite le métro). Je n'ai cependant pas repris d'occupation bien régulière (sauf d'écrire un peu tous les jours et de parler beaucoup) par suite du projet, toujours à l'horizon, du voyage en Amérique. Sur ce point, je n'ai pas encore les dernières autorisations: mais ce n'est qu'une affaire de "red tape", et je ne prévois aucune difficulté. Je pense*

Since this is still only January 2nd, I am taking the opportunity to again offer you (and Eleonore) my warmest New Year's Greetings. May 1948 bring you all kinds of nice things, dearest, and especially much peace, zest and inner warmth. For me, this latter gift seems, more and more, what we need the most. I have often thought about it recently: what makes Christianity, in its essence, true and irreplaceable is that it alone is capable (in a way which is logical and coherent with the history and the structure of the Universe) of rewarming the world and making it at the same time loving and lovable from the inside. We are again threatened with the end of Humanity through the cooling down of the planet: I think that what would kill us much more surely and much more quickly would be to "freeze" internally because of the impossibility of finding a soul and a heart in the vastness which carries us along and surrounds us.

My existence here is still the same. I am very well physically, and my life is almost normal again (except that I still sleep longer nights and I avoid the metro). However, I haven't really resumed my regular activities (except that I write a little every day and make a lot of speeches) because of the still-on-the-horizon projected trip to America. For this point I do not have final authorizations but it is only a matter of "red tape" and I do not foresee any difficulties. I probably will leave around

*partir vers le début de mars. Mais rien n'est encore déterminé. Naturellement, je vous tiendrai au courant.*

*Reçu une bonne lettre de Max Bégouën. Simone a bien supporté le voyage en avion; mais les deux semblent avoir été assez fatigués; mieux depuis. Cependant Max renonce à son projet de voyage en Afrique Occidentale Française, où il a de grandes ambitions de nouvelles plantations. Pour Simone, cette décision est ce qui pouvait arriver de mieux. Comme cela, elle ne restera pas seule. — Ici, le P. Leroy va toujours bien, et il me charge de vous envoyer (à vous et à Eléonore) ses meilleurs voeux. Mme Raphael, toujours à l'UNESCO, est en ce moment en Algérie, pour une quizaine. Son adresse à Paris: Hôtel Reynold's, Rue Bertie Albrecht, Paris VIII.*

*Good bye, dearest. Encore mille souhaits de paix et de succès. Et à bientôt d'autres nouvelles.+++*

*En grande affection,*

*P.T.*

the beginning of March, but nothing is yet quite decided. Naturally, I will keep you informed.

I have received a good letter from Max Bégouën. Simone had no problem with the plane trip, but it seems that both were pretty tired; they are better now. However, Max has given up the idea of going to French West Africa where he has great ambitions for new plantations. For Simone this decision is the best thing that could happen. That way, she would not be alone. Here P. Leroy is still well, and he has asked me to send you (you and Eleonore) his best wishes. Mme Raphaël, still working at UNESCO, is in Algeria at the moment where she will stay for a fortnight. Her address in Paris: Hôtel Reynold's, Rue Bertie Albrecht, Paris VIII.

---

Teilhard was still convalescing at the Jesuit house on the Rue Monsieur in Paris when Lucile wrote from Washington. The carbons of this letter are incomplete, with the third paragraph ending in mid-sentence with the word "might".

*1217 34th St Washington DC*
*January 4 1948*

*Dearest, -*
*Thank you so very much for your precious letter of Dec. 21. It did not arrive until the 30th and I was beginning to fear that you were ill again. And I am so very glad to hear that all goes well both physically AND morally . . Pierre, you are, as always, such a wonderful example for the rest of us, not to be discouraged by "set backs" and on the contrary to find in them an extra stimulus . . It is so splendid and will surely bear fruit. And that you find your ideas are more clear than ever . . and that you have another "egg" in the process of making. I hope I shall have the privilege of seeing it before too long. (Of course I realize that it all takes time, copies to be made, etc).*
*And especially I thank you for the things you say to me. You have surely hit the heart of the matter as concerns me when you say I must have confidence . . You have no doubt read through my letters recently that I have been going through a difficult struggle . . and a sort of lack of confidence has been the seat of the trouble. I suppose it has been*

*brought about at least partly by my "impatience". I could not see that I was making any progress and it seemed to me that I was losing some of the things that I cared for most in the world. Even my work has been going very badly. And I realize that I have been mixed up in my relation to you . . Our friendship has always been primarily a <u>spiritual</u> one, a constant seeking together for a closer touch and greater realization of God. That is the thing you have always given to me so abundantly and I hope sometimes I have helped you too, to see more clearly. In the midst of feeling very much alone (and a bit sorry for myself) I thought of how, in His moment of greatest trial, Christ was deserted by his dearest friends. Surely there must be a great lesson for all of us here. His steadfastness has meaning for all of us. For although our trials are not great or dramatic, they sometimes call for our own small steadfastness and LOVE. And I love what you say, I suppose the highest form of worship is "confiance" in Life, - confiance which brings peace" . . I shall try to engrave that on my heart, for I know that is the way I will find peace. I do so much appreciate your constant patience and help with me . . They say that sometimes when you seem to be making the least progress is really when you are taking a step ahead . . so I hope very much that is what is happening to me . . at any rate I feel more peaceful than I have for some time.*

*I am sorry that you have not yet gotten your authorization for the trip to America . . and do hope it will come soon. Especially was I hoping that you might*

*America . . and trust that it will come through soon . . I was so hoping you could escape this winter in France . . which seems to have some hardships. But the present weather in New York, does not sound too good either . . We have not had the heavy snow down here, at least not yet . . but Washington is much more mild than NY. How strange . . and rather marvelous, to have New York without motor cars or buses and people skiing down 5th Ave.*

*I had such a sweet letter from Simone yesterday . . what a really precious friend she is. I'm sure you must miss her very much . . I hope she will continue to be well down there.*

*So sorry the packages have not arrived . . they surely are VERY slow, the first was sent very early November and the other about a week later.*

*And now we have started a New Year . . I feel so sure that THIS year we shall meet . . now I need it so <u>much</u> that I know it will happen. Now I can meet you with <u>confidence</u> in my heart. Perhaps this is the lesson I had to learn first . . and it seems that we only really learn through suffering.*

*Eleanore is well and still working on the same job . . and trying to get used to life over here She has heard nothing more from Faure . . all that is rather a strange business and she has not written but probably he will come over this spring and then they will know what they want. She has had a rather quiet time mostly, but is out this evening with a young man. I think she will try to go to NY soon, to have a "look-see" . . but life is rather difficult and very expensive there now . . well so it is everywhere. I too shall probably go up again before long. I can always stay with an old friend . . and I like to go for a change.*

*Dearest Precious Teilhard, I do hope this New Year will bring you great Peace and happiness and that we will be together again. It would be such a joy for me to see you again!! Yes I am sure that it will happen.*

Dearest,

Thank you so much for your nice letter of Jan. 27. So many things we will have to talk over together! since it decidedly seems that I will soon be in America. Everything seems more or less settled, just now; except that I do not yet have my ticket; but a reservation was made on s.s. America; leaving Cherbourg on Febr. 20 supposedly. My plans are exceedingly vague. Except that I know that I will settle in New York, in order to do some work, and much talking, with the people at the Museum of Natural Hist. Evidently, I would go to Washington and Boston. Nothing definite concerning the duration of my staying there: two months, at least. Le reste des projets s'éclaircira sur place.

Ici, rien de nouveau. J'ai encore écrit un nouveau paper dernièrement, et donné plusieurs lectures semi-privées. Dans l'ensemble, et grâce à l'appui de mes amis, la situation semble se détendre sensiblement (le discours de Mgr. de Solages, distribué à nombreux exemplaires, fait excellente impression: I will bring you a copy, for the fun). Malgré tout, ce ne sera pas mauvais que je disparaisse pour quelque temps.

Socialement parlant, la vie demeure agréable. Je vois souvent Leroy, qui est resté mon meilleur ami, ici comme à Péking. Nous sommes allés l'autre jour prendre un cocktail avec Jacques et Marie-Claire chez Mrs. Coatman. On se serait cru de nouveau àPéking. Les Cosme sont de nouveau ici: Alice [Cosme] pas encore mariée, son père toujours assez triste et nerveux (encore que sa situation politique soit maintenant pratiquement arrangée). Françoise Raphael est toujours à l'Unesco, pareille à elle-même. Elle habite maintenant l'Hôtel Windsor (14, Rue Beaujon, Paris VIII), — le même hôtel que Mme Velloso(!). Celle-ci, veuve depuis un an (son mari est mort à New York, il était à l'Onu) va retourner au Brésil. — Les Lago (maintenant en poste à Bruxelles) viennent de temps en temps à Paris; je ne les ai pasencore vus. - Il y a une semaine, j'ai déjeûné chez les Dorget, avec les Scheven. Toujours Péking!

Here, nothing new. I have written another paper recently and given several semi-private lectures. On the whole and thanks to the support of my friends, the situation seems to calm down perceptibly (Mgr. de Solages' speech, of which many copies have been handed out, has made an excellent impression: I will bring you a copy, for the fun). However it is not a bad thing that I disappear for a little while.

Socially speaking, life remains pleasant. I often see Leroy who remains my best friend here as in Peking. The other day we went to a cocktail party with Jacques and Marie-Claire at Mrs. Coatman's. It felt as if we were back in Peking. The Cosmes here again. Alice still not married, her father still pretty sad and nervous (although his political situation is now practically settled). Françoise Raphaël is still at UNESCO, just like herself. She now lives at the Hôtel Windsor (14, rue Beaujon, Paris VIII) - the same hotel as Mme Velloso (!). The latter, a widow since last year (her husband died in New York, he was with the U.N.) is going back to Brazil. The Lagos (now in office in Brussels) come to Paris from time to time; I have not seen them yet. I had lunch a week ago at the Dorgets with the Schevens. Always Peking!

*Good bye, dearest. I stop here so that my letter will leave this evening. A bientôt, apparently.*

*Yours, as ever,++*

*P.T.*

---

When Teilhard arrived in New York in late February, he found both Lucile and Rhoda de Terra waiting at the dock. That initial reunion was somewhat awkward. Rhoda had helped arrange for his trip and the work at the museum in New York; and Lucile had received Teilhard's itinerary from him in February.

---

*New York, 26 March 48*

*Dearest,*

*Merci tant pour votre gentil petit mot, de Washington. Ce sera bon de regarder fleurir les magnolias, comme jadis les cerisiers du Central Park. Vous verrez que nous nous "retrouv erons", — comme il le faut, — à la mesure des temps nouveaux. —*

*Finalement, je n'arriverai à Washington que mercredi. Dr. Canon (the dermatologist) wants to see me again on Tuesday. La figure va tout-à-fait bien maintenant. Mais j'ai d'autres petits ennuis. -*

*En grande affection et à bientôt. -Fidèles amitiés à Eléonore.*

*P.T.*

*Ida Treat vient peut-être (?) demain.*

Thank you so very much for your nice note from Washington. It will be good to see the magnolias in bloom, like the cherry-trees of Central Park some time ago. You will see that we will "rediscover" one another again - as it must be - according to the new times.

Finally, I will not arrive in Washington till Wednesday. Dr. Canon (the dermatologist) wants to see me again on Tuesday. My face is quite well now. But I have other small problems.

---

Teilhard spent a week in Washington, staying in the Jesuit community at Georgetown University. While there he visited with Lucile and Eleanor Tafel who were living in a house in Georgetown. He also spoke at the American Museum of Natural History and reestablished contact at the Catholic University of America, as well as with many old friends. Then he returned to his work at the museum in New York.

---

*New York, April the 11, 1948*

*Dearest,*

*Ces qqs. lignes pour vous dire combien j'ai aimé, apprécié, enjoyed, la dernière semaine, à Washington. — Un petit Péking! Merci. — You have been perfect, — and always the same. — Ici, j'ai retrouvé une vie assez active: graduellement, les contacts se multiplient,*

These few lines to tell you how much I loved, appreciated, enjoyed last week in Washington. A small Peking!...
. Thank you: You have been perfect, - and always the same. Here I am leading again a pretty active life: gradually contacts multiply in number and I fore-

et j'entrevois mieux la possibilité d'une série de lectures, next year. — Vendredi, j'ai donné ma causerie au Viking Fund. Audience a bit too small. Mais j'étais en forme, et j'ai pu dire exactement ce que je pensais, — en une langue compréhensible. — Je recommence mercredi, sur un autre sujet, àl'American Museum. — Hellmut de Terra est ici; nous nous sommes retrouvés avec joie. — Jouve (des Etudes, Paris) arrive ici vers le 15. — Et ce soir je vois des collègues de Fordham. — Vous voyez que cela va.

see the possibility of a series of lectures next year. Friday I gave my talk at the Viking Fund. Audience a bit too small. But I was fit and I could say exactly what I thought - in easily understood language. I will speak again on Wednesday on another subject at the American Museum. Helmut de Terra is here; we met again with pleasure. Jouve (from Les Etudes, Paris) arrives around the 15th. And I will see some colleagues from Fordham to-night. You see things are moving.

    A bientôt, — et <u>mille choses</u> à Eléonore!

    Your

    P.T.

*New York, Friday, May 14, '48*

Dearest,

    I am back from Boston, — somewhat tired. Evidently, I want rest. Could you come to meet me here, next monday, on about 5 P.M. (five o'clock)? We should have an early dinner somewhere in the vicinity.

    On Tuesday, if I feel OK., I must meet (at the headquarters of "Commonweal") a certain Miss Fremantle, who seems to be a close friend of Mrs. John Wiley. Perhaps you know her.

    Yours, as ever,

    P.T.

---

The following letter from Lucile is marked "Wednesday," but is otherwise undated. We would suggest a date of May 19, 1948 — largely because of the reference to a Washington visit. It would seem that this "May" letter was not sent, nor the slightly shorter version also found among her papers.

---

*Wednesday, New York*

Dear P.T.

    I am very sorry that I "went off the deep end" last evening. I was a poor sport and rotten loser. But I thank you for telling me the truth. I suppose I have really known it for a long time, but in Washington I thought maybe I was wrong and one does not easily accept something that breaks the heart. You say you have not changed toward me.: but of course that is not the truth, though you may believe.: I assure it is not true.

    Years ago when you wrote, not once but several times. "What is born between us is forever . . I know it." I feared you did not know (I think no one can <u>know</u>) but I so much wanted to believe and because of all the circumstances, and also even our ages, made it seem very possible, and so I built my life upon it. You also wrote "If you do not find me it is not any petty foreign intrusion, but the presence of God . . etc. etc . . " and so I believed as you so often said that we would grow closer and closer to each other as we progressed in our discovery and love of God. And so it went on for so many years, and you knew exactly how I felt. (I told you too often for there to be any doubt in your mind) and that last two years did bring this very result of a closer bond and deeper search for all that is Best. I write all this because I cannot bear to have you think I am a foolish woman who has built her life on figments of her own imagination. You speak of Peking as though it were a sort of fantasy or something . . which is not fair . . at least to me they were the most real years of my life. You compare me with Ida. I can only say that if Ida had had the same kind of feeling, it would have been IMPOSSIBLE for her to marry. I know this will change nothing, but I had to try to put my case less emotionally and stupidly than I did last night. You feel sorry for Ida now. I beg you to have charity for me. Life seems to have absolutely no consistency and I need your help desperately . . I am sure you can show me a way to go on.

You say you cannot help what has happened . . Does that mean that there is no such thing as free will, are we just victims of fate to be thrown here and there as chance decides? Then what is the use of striving? Oh no I do not believe it . . Perhaps that is why the Existentialists came into being (at least as I understand what they stand for).

As you can see I am utterly confused, no that is not quite true, but I do need some help very much . . I will be home at 4 on Friday ad I hope you will come as we planned.

Lucile

---

On May 23, 1948 in a letter to Pierre Leroy, Teilhard mentioned ". . . at this moment I am undergoing one of those periods of nervous depression such as you witnessed two or three times in Peking. Everything seems mountainous to me. Patience!" . . .

---

*New York, May 30, 1948*

Dearest,

Thank you for the precious visit with you today. I need you so much and feel that I have found you again, and it makes me deeply happy. You give me faith and hope and love and the courage to go on with a real confidence in the future.

I wish there was something I could do for you; but now I feel sure that things will work out. Those years of working together will go on. Not in the same way, of course but possibly even more fruitfully. So let us go on.

Oh Pierre, I do feel happy and confident. Your strength will come back and your wonderful work and spirit will go on. I am terribly sorry for "the mix-up" here. So many things seem to be necessary to make up Life, perhaps this will serve some useful purpose —hope so. I feel sure that it will for me. I'll build on more solid ground — the ground you always intended - I suppose. But those were such good years. I surely do not regret them, only now we will go on to something else — and better.

And always know that I am your devoted and loving Lucile.

I wanted to put my arms about you and comfort you. I can't bear to see you suffering. Wouldn't it relieve the tension if you would weep on my shoulder and tell me, well only what you want to tell. I am sure dear, that I can give you motherly love and understanding with no remarks of blame of you or of me. I wish you could do it or anything that would help you. You gave me so much yesterday and it is a glorious feeling to know that you are the same you whom I can count on for love and strength and help in all things but *especially in the search of God. Thank you dearest and God bless you and give you peace.*

Lucile

*New York, June the 4th, '48*

*Dearest,*

*These few lines (I am not very much in the mood to write any letter.) to tell you how precious for me was your last letter. — No retreat! Let us go constructively ahead. You can, you must help me. My dearest hope is that now, on a clearer and stronger basis, we can build still higher. — In her <u>last</u> letter, my cousine wrote me this line, which, I am convinced, is the expression of what is growing between you and me: "Devant Dieu j'ai compris que je t'aimais <u>mieux</u> (that is in a better way), et ainsi que je t'aimais <u>plus</u>, ce que je n'aurais pas cru possible". - C'est ce qui se vérifiera pour nous, aussi. ——*

*Today, the feast of the "Heart" of Christ, — c'est-à-dire la fête de l'Amour-Energie! — a good omen!*

*Your*

*P.T.*

*Hope you are feeling better physically!!!*

---

Teilhard had planned on leaving New York City in July, but instead he set out for Paris the day after he wrote to Lucile. Pierre Leroy said that he arrived grief stricken.

---

*340 East 57th Street   New York 22 N.Y.*
*June 15, 1948*

*Dearest, -*

*Now you have been home for several days . . and although New York seems very empty without you, I am so glad that you are there . . and not only hope, but pray every day that you may be feeling well and yourself again.*

*It was so sweet of you to write me that precious note . . I should not have asked you . . again remember the "tippling" monk . . the need was great. How beautifully your cousin expresses herself and how good of you to say that that is what is happening to us too. Most good things have to go through a painful birth . . so I hope and believe that this new relationship . . well really not so new, just more clear . . will be stronger and healthier than ever. I know that this is the basis on which there need be no limit. But sometimes, even tho one knows what is best, it is hard to not get things mixed up. One wants so much in this life!!*

*It took me a few days to feel quite alright again. And then I went to the country for a long week-end. And now feel very well again. And even went over today to make the first steps for getting a passport. And have practically decided to go on the French Liner de Grasse about the 17th of August, so I would be in Paris for a few days on my way to Switzerland to the Vincents . . that would be the latter part of August and I suppose you will be far away in the country at that time. If you are only at St Germaine!! that is not very far away . . Well all that is some time off but still I have to begin to start things here.*

*I think this trip will be good for me. I know I have been dull lately. feel as if I had been living in a sort of strange fog for sometime. I may even study painting with someone this fall. But I think now that I will go to Rome for several months .. and stop in Paris on my way home, probably late December or the first of the year .. of course all plans are subject to change?? but it is fun making them, and this time it will probably go through.*

*I do so hope you will feel well enough to write me a note .. I am so very anxious to hear about the trip .. did your very serious Dutchman cabin mate, prove to be nice and what of the "rich man" who was there .. Im sure they took good care of you .. it is such a pleasure to take care of you Pierre .. you are such a dear precious person who radiates love.*

*How deeply and earnestly I want to be worthy of your friendship.I know that with Time and patience (especially with myself) the joy and confidence in Life are growing .. and that with faith and active love, I shall find and feel a closer tie with God. Which will give me a greater understanding of Love .. Yes, "Je t'aimais MIEUX."*

*Do take good care of yourself and dont start doing too much again. and please, if possible, let me have just a few lines to know how you are and if the trip was good ..*

*Always your devoted*

> *15 Rue Monsieur, Paris VII*
> *18 Juin, 1948*

**Dearest,**

*Your precious letter of June 15 has just arrived.*

*Merci. Elle me dit tout ce que j'espérais, — tout ce dont j'ai besoin. Maintenant, vraiment, plus vraiment que jamais, le futur est à nous, à la lumière grandissante de Dieu. Let us go ahead, — and "no retreat"!*

It tells me all that I hoped for — all that I need. Now really and more than ever, the future is ours under the ever growing light of God. Let us go ahead - and "no retreat".

*Mon voyage s'est effectué assez calmement, mais pas trop gaiement, dans la cabine embaumée par votre souvenir et les fleurs d'Eléonore. Plusieurs relations agréables à bord, mais pas de vrais amis: la solitude dans la foule. Je suis arrivé à Paris plutôt déprimé. Heureusement Leroy m'attendait sur le quai de St Lazare, et il a commencé à me réconforter. Je ne me sens pas encore solide. Mais j'ai un très bon médecin qui vient souvent causer avec moi. Je crois que je commence à me remonter. Je comprends encore assez mal ce qui m'est arrivé. Une affaire purement organique, me dit mon ami, déclanché par un peu d'émotion trop forte.*

My trip was quite calm but not too cheerful in the cabin fragrant with your memory and Eleonore's flowers. A few pleasant acquaintances on board, but no real friends: solitude in the crowd. I arrived in Paris rather depressed. Fortunately, Leroy was waiting for me on the platform at Saint-Lazare and he started to comfort me. I am still not very strong, but I have a very good doctor friend who often comes to talk with me. I think I am beginning to feel better. I still do not really understand what happened. A purely organic problem, says my friend, triggered by strong emotions.

*Naturellement je me trouve pris ici dans un petit tourbillon de courrier en retard, et de gens à revoir, — attendus*

Naturally, I am now caught up in a small whirlwind of letters to answer and people — expected or unexpected *et inattendus: hier c'était J.S. Lee (l'ancien du Geol. Survey, avec Wong et Ting) qui me tombait du ciel. Conversation très affectueuse, mais dont finalement je n'ai rien tiré (ni trop osé demander) sur l'état des choses en Chine, du côté Nanking. Revu mon frère: le jeune ménage semble très heureux et heureusement installé en Auvergne. Demain je dois aller voir Malvina Hoffman dans son studio. Elle est encore à Paris pour une quinzaine de jours, je crois: nous parlerons de vous.*

*J'ai trouvé ici (et je vous envoie par ordinary mail) l'article de moi publié en avril. Il me semble bon; et il ne paraît avoir suscité aucune réaction fâcheuse. C'est bon signe. Il faudrait que je me remette à écrire quelque courte chose (j'ai une idée, venue à N.Y.): ce serait pour moi la meilleure des cures. — Pas de nouvelles des Bégouën. Certains pensent qu'ils doivent revenir pour qq. temps cet été.*

*Good bye dearest. Je doute d'être à Paris, fin-août (rien n'est décidé); mais, à la fin de l'année, ce serait parfait! Pas de nouvelles encore de Rome, pour les conférences d'Amérique.*

*God bless you; —— et je compte tant sur vous.*

*P.T.*

*Grands et affectueux souvenirs à Eléonore. Je n'ai pas encore accroché Faure . . .*

— to see: yesterday it was J.S. Lee (who used to work for the Geological Survey; with Wong and Ting) who arrived out of the blue. Very friendly conversation, but from which finally I learned nothing — nor dared to ask — about the situation in China, of Nanking. I saw my brother again: the young couple seems very happy and happily settled in Auvergne. I must visit Malvina Hoffman in her studio tomorrow. She will stay in Paris for another fortnight, I think. We'll talk about you.

I found here (and I am sending it to you by ordinary mail) my article which was published in April. I believe it is good and it doesn't seem to have provoked any angry reaction. This is a good sign. I should start to write again, something short (I have an idea which came to me in New York): it certainly would be the best therapy for me. No news from the Bégouëns. Some people think they will come back for some time this summer.

Good bye, dearest. I probably will not be in Paris at the end of August (although nothing is decided); but, at the end of the year, it would be perfect! No news yet from Rome, about the lectures in America.

*15 Rue Monsieur, Paris VII*
*6 Juillet 1948*

*Dearest,*
    *So many thanks for your dear long letter of July 2. In some way I am glad to think that you are now resting and working in the country. I hope however that you enjoy a better weather than we here: lot of rain, and almost no heat.*
    *Personally, I have gradually resumed my almost normal life.*

*Essai de travail personnel pendant la matinée (interrompu généralement par beaucoup de visites ou de coups de téléphone) et visites en ville le soir. Physiquement, je ne me sens pas encore*

I try to do some personal work in the morning (generally interrupted by many visitors or phone calls) and visits in town in the evening. Physically, I still do not feel all that well (I have not *très brillant (je ne suis pas encore dégagé de ma dépression nerveuse), et je prends encore des pilules de toutes sortes. Mais je tâche d'y penser le moins possible. Et puis un excellent ami docteur est là pour me surveiller. Je pense toujours aller passer quelque temps chez mon frère en Auvergne en août et septembre; mais rien n'est encore définitivement fixé.*

*Depuis ma dernière lettre, la chose la plus marquante en ce qui me concerne est que le Collège de France me propose une chaire de Préhistoire. J'ai écrit à Rome pour savoir si cette fois on m'autorise. Mais je n'ai pas encore de réponse (ce qui est normal). En fait je ne suis qu'à moitié désireux d'accepter cette situation (ce serait pour deux ou trois ans seulement), qui m'oblige, je trouve à un nombre un peu trop grand de conférences. Attendons la suite des événements. Dans la même lettre, à Rome, j'ai aussi abordé la question des conférences en Amérique; mais sur ce dernier point je n'attends pas une réponse rapide, pcq. je suppose que Rome consultera New-York, et cela prend du temps. — J'ai fini le court Essai dont je vous parlais (sur les Directions et Conditions de l'Avenir Humain): mais je ne sais pas encore si ni où je pourrai le publier. D'ici Octobre, je voudrais rédiger, en une série de courtes propositions bien enchaînées, l'essentiel de ma Weltanschauung (Phénoménologie, Métaphysique, Mystique) sous le titre "Comment je vois". Je crois que j'y arriverai facilement, et que cela m'intéressera.*

*Reçu avant-hier des nouvelles d'Ida. Ses affaires ne paraissent pas s'arranger du tout. Cela me navre pour elle. — Et cela me navre aussi d'apprendre par vous la réponse de Faure à Eléonore. A celui-ci (Faure) j'ai écrit dès mon arrivée; et je n'ai pas reçu encore de réponse, preuve qu'il n'est pas à Paris. Il faudrait que je le vois.*

completely recovered from my nervous depression) and I still take all kinds of pills. But I try to think about it as little as possible. Also, an excellent friend of mine, a doctor, is there to keep an eye on me. I am still thinking of spending some time at my brother's in Auvergne in August and September, but nothing has been definitely decided.

Since my last letter the most important thing, as far as I am concerned, is that the Collège de France has offered me a chair in Prehistory. I have written to Rome to ask if they would give me the authorization this time. But I have not had a reply yet (which is normal). In fact, I am only half desirous to accept this position (which would be for two or three years only) and which would require me to give, in my opinion, too many lectures. Let's wait and see. In the same letter to Rome I also introduced the question of the lectures in America; but to this last point I am not expecting a quick answer, because I imagine that Rome will get in touch with New York, and that takes time. I have finished the short essay I told you about (on the Directions and Conditions of the Future of Man). But I don't know yet if, or where, I will be able to publish it. Before October I would like to compose, in a series of short, well-linked propositions, the essential of my Weltanschauung (Phenomenology, Metaphysics, Mystic) under the title "How I See". I think I will be able to do it easily and that it will interest me.

I received the day before yesterday news from Ida. It seems that her affairs are not working out at all. This grieves me for her. And it upsets me also to hear (from you) Faure's answer to Eleonore. I wrote to the former (Faure) on my arrival, but I still have not received a reply, proof that he is not in Paris. I should see him. But when? At the first

*Mais quand? A l'occasion, dites à Eléonore ma grande et fidèle affection. Je ferai toujours pour elle tout ce que je pourrai, bien sûr.*

*Ici, je vois assez régulièrement Leroy et Mme Raphael (celle-ci toujours à l'Hôtel Windsor, 14, Rue Beaujon, Paris IX, tout près de l'Etoile (Phone: CARnot 73.00), ou à son office à l'UNESCO; 19 Avenue Kléber, XVI, Phone: KLEber 52.00). Le Laboratoire de Leroy est: 4, Avenue Gordon Bennett, Paris XVI, Phone:MOLitor 57.66. -Malvina H. est encore ici pour un mois. Je dois aller la voir dans deux jours: elle s'acharne à mon buste, et m'affirme que la version "souriante" à fait de grands progrès.*

*Merci de m'envoyer les papers sur Einstein et les federalists. Cela me servira beaucoup. Dimanche dernier j'ai recommencé à donner une causerie à un groupe de sympathisants. C'était près de l'Etoile, dans un remarquable studio, où un artiste, Devêche, fait d'étonnantes tapisseries modernes, qui m'ont beaucoup impressionné. J'ai parlé de la nécessité pour nous de re-développer un nouveau "sens de l'espèce" et d'expliciter notre "Mystique de l'Ouest". Samedi dernier, dans une réunion du World Congress for the Union of Faiths, j'ai rencontré qqs instants Aldous Huxley, de passage en Europe. J'espère le revoir plus sérieusement à la fin du mois.*

opportunity give Eleonore my great and faithful affection. I will always do the best I can for her, of course.

I see Leroy and Mme Raphaël fairly regularly (the latter is at the Hotel Windsor, 14 rue Beaujon, Paris IX, close to Etoile. Tel: CARnot 73-00 or at her office at UNESCO, 19 Avenue Kleber, XVI, telephone: KLEber 52-00). Leroy's laboratory is 4 Avenue Gordon Bennett, Paris XVI, telephone: MOLitor 57-66. Malvina H. is still here for one more month. I plan to go and see her in two days: she is working very hard at my bust and tells me that the "smiling" version has progressed very well.

Thank you for sending me the papers on Einstein and the federalists. They will be very useful to me. Last Sunday, I started again giving a talk to a group of sympathizers. It was near the Etoile, in a stunning studio where an artist, Devêche, makes some extraordinary modern tapestries which impressed me very much. I spoke of the necessity for us to develop a new "sense of the species" and to explain our "Western Mysticism." Last Saturday, in a meeting of the World Congress for the Union of Faiths, for a short while I met Aldous Huxley who is passing through Europe. I hope to see him again more seriously at the end of the month.

*Good bye, dearest. On the whole, as you see, things are going sufficiently well. But you must keep on helping me. I need force and élan. I pray (and you, too, do pray) God that under his attraction we "converge" always closer dans sa chaude lumière.*

*your*

*P.T.*

*My best regards to Mary Parton*

*Pas de nouvelles des Bégouëns. Je vous ferai savoir si ils viennent, et leur adresse.*

234

*Dearest,*

*Just received your long and sweet letter from Poughkeepsie. And I want to answer you immediately, before I leave, this afternoon for a weekend in the vicinity of Paris. After which I will stay here for a while (up to August 15), then join my brother in Auvergne for a month.*

*Now, something new has happened in my prospects of the next year. Meaning that, instead of answering me yes or no concerning the american lectures and the Collège de France, my Général asks me (most kindly) to come to Rome sometime in October or November, for a few weeks, so that we could talk: and the meaning of the letter is that he, the Général, is confident that my book might be printed, and everything allowed, both for America and France. To be true, I do <u>not</u> like to go to see the people in Rome; but I can not refuse; — and besides this opportunity of talking with the big wigs down there is perhaps the chance of my life. Consequently I am decided to go (probably on about the 15 of October: what a marvelous coincidence if you were there at the same time! Evidently, I should not be specially free in such surroundings. But still!). The only trouble is that, according to the Général's plan, I would know only at the beginning of November whether I can lecture: and I must answer (both the Viking Fund and the Collège de France) before October. So, three weeks ago, I wrote to Rome on this particular point. And I am still waiting for an answer. But I keep rather confident that everything will be OK. I will let you know.*

*Ici, rien de bien nouveau. Je viens de terminer le brouillon de "Comment je vois": 38 propositions, et une quarantaine de pages. Reste à recopier cela; je tâcherai de le faire chez mon frère. Nous sortons d'un congrès de Zoologie, où j'ai vu Colbert: cela m'a remis à N.Y.! Pas de nouvelles de Simone: on m'a dit qu'elle était déjà en France, chez son beau-père, dans l'Ariège. Je l'avertirai de votre passage à Paris.*

*Bien reçu l'article sur Einstein et le livre de Ralph Linton. Merci tant de <u>collaborer</u> ainsi. C'est très doux pour moi de recevoir cela de vous . . . Puisse cette lettre vous rejoindre à temps à Washington!*

*Ecrivez-moi toujours ici. On me fera suivre.*

*En grande affection,*
*yours*
*P.T.*

Here nothing really new. I have just finished writing the draft of "How I See": 38 propositions and about 40 pages. I still have to copy it; I will try to do this at my brother's. We just came out of a Zoology convention where I saw Colbert; that took me back to New York! No news from Simone. I was told that she is in France at her father-in-law's house in the Ariège. I'll tell her about your coming to Paris.

I have received the article on Einstein and Ralph Linton's book. Thank you very much for <u>collaborating</u> with me so well. It is so sweet to receive that from you. May this letter reach you on time in Washington!

Continue writing to me here. Your letters will be forwarded.

All my affection.

Yours

P.T.

*Ci-joint un mot pour Eléonore*

Enclosed a note for Eléonore.

[?] 8/17/48     à bord  le De Grasse

Dearest -

Now we are nearly in New York - and again one has to start again - finding a place to live and starting all over again: I have done it so often - perhaps that is my Fate - but with all its difficulties I like it better than forever living in the same place -

There is a very small 1st class group and I have met no one who interests me much - so I have been reading and walking - and thinking quite a lot about my work. and I am beginning to see more clearly what I want to paint - It is all quite simple - I'm really very modest - as I realize more and more how difficult it is to create - and all these thoughts make me appreciate what you are doing  - I suppose <u>real creative thought</u>, is the most difficult thing there is - I do think that the original Light or inspiration is God given - but what one does with the inspiration - is pretty much up to oneself - and you have created out of the air - out of yourself - a way of seeing, of thinking of regarding the world - that is full of hope and faith and an always grander future - one that leads to Some One and gives meaning and purpose to everyone - I hope Lecture 5 is progressing to your satisfaction and that the whole series will express your ideas clearly and as you wish them to be expressed, and then, also important, that they will be published and spread far and wide — Pierre dearest - if that does not come immediately it <u>must</u>, it will come eventually. Sometimes that must be rather hard to take, when I know how much you want to do <u>now</u>. But perhaps your role is to give birth to the ideas, and it will later be someone else who will spread them. So often this has happened as you so well know. So my prayer is now that you will have the strength and an always clearer vision of the Truth. I do so hope my dear that you are feeling well again and that you are having a good time, it was so <u>good</u> to hear your gay laughter the last time we were together. Oh Pierre we did have a good time didn't we. I know you enjoyed it to — and the realization that our friendship is so alive and we have so much to give to each other — it makes me very happy and I feel strong for doing good things this winter. St. Francis, or whoever it was who came to me that time and said "to give love, always give love and everything will be alright", was so right and I am very grateful for that vision or whatever it was — it was so clear and strong that it comes back to me at times when I might forget. Life seems so confusing at times.

Like others, this handwritten August letter may not have been mailed. It does not seem to fit with either L's June 15 letter or P.T.s September 3 letter. It may have been written the following year.

Les Moulins, Sept. 3,    1948

Dearest,

Such a thrill to receive your letter from Paris! — And such a happy feeling that you like it! - Yes, let us hope that this new contact with so many old things will rejuvenate you, and show you <u>your</u> line of life, and, <u>ipso facto, your</u> God. — And, concerning this last point, don't be mistaken. It is not for you only, — it is for everybody, I suppose, that the greatest effort and difficulty is <u>not</u> to conceive an attractive face of God, — but to make it real, and alive, and present at the deepest of ourselves and of everything. And, ultimately, He alone can make Himself present to us: we cannot snatch the Light, — but the Light comes to us. At least this is one of the big differences between Christian and Indian mystics that we can not <u>force</u> God to ourselves. But we can ask him, pray him: and the *more I am getting more experienced (or at least older) the more I am convinced that the simplest and the highest of the prayers is to rely actively on the countless events (small and big) of Life — of our own life — with the confidence that these very events, if received and used with "faith and love", are the shortest and the closest way to become One with the Center of everything.*

*But we shall have plenty of time to discuss that. My own plans remain the same. On about Sept.15 I will be back in Paris, and make me ready for the Rome's trip, which has to be advanced rather than postponed, since I am required to answer "yes or no" to the College de France at the very beginning of November: meaning that I should leave Paris on, or rather before, October 10. —*

*Here, I enjoy a complete quietness (I am even making, in a very moderate way, my "retreat"). Yet, I still feel too much this unpleasant physical anxiety, which is, since years, one of my weak points. - The country is beautiful, — and we are here in the deep of the country, at 7 miles of the closest railway station. A wonderful sight too: first the woody rolling hills; and then the plaine de la Limagne; and then the volcanoes; - some forty of them, forming the skyline. — I read a little, I take long walks under the old oaks, and I think a lot. —*

*In the meantime, I hope that you got in touch with Leroy and Mrs. Raphael: they were expecting you.*

*A bientôt, in any case.*

*God bless you, dearest!*

*P.T.*

*Yes, I think I should <u>love</u> the book of G. Green. -*

---

Lucile visited her old friends, Betty and John Carter Vincent in Bern during September and early October. (He was there serving as the American ambassador to Switzerland, a kind of "safe house" post he had been appointed to during an especially troublesome period of "communist" hunting in the U.S. Department of State.) In October Lucile journeyed to Rome where she saw Teilhard briefly. Then she went on to Ethiopia since, as an artist, she was interested in experiencing its much heralded color, light, and beauty .

---

*Roma, October the 7th, 1948*

*Dear L.,*

*These few lines to tell you that I have arrived easily and safely here, last Sunday, at midnight! — I am located a few hundred meters from la place St. Pierre, — at the very fringe of the Vatican! - Got a very charming welcome. But it's too early for having any definite prospects concerning my affairs. — Your letter from Berne reached me in Paris just before my departure. Thank you for everything! — When you are here, let me know. The simplest thing, to start, should be that you call here some day when going to visit St. Peter (better in the morning, — f.i. after 10 a.m. and before noon) and ask for me: they are little reception rooms downstairs (like in Rue Monsieur), — and, in addition, good elevators (like at "America"). ——*

*Have a good time in Berne!*

*Yours as ever*

*Teilhard*

*Roma, Thursday, ? octobre '48*

*My dear L.,*

    *This afternoon I must be back here, at 4 p.m., to meet an influential col-league. — And tomorrow I <u>may</u> have to stay here, more or less the whole day, waiting for possible developments.*

    *The best is perhaps that you should pass here tomorrow morning, between 10.30 and 12. And then I might perhaps go to the Flora at 4 p.m., if I am free.*

    *Would you kindly make sure at the desk of your hotel that the Paris train (via Simplon) is still leaving at 7 <u>a.m.</u>? You could tell me, tomorrow morning.*

    *Your*

    *P.T.*

*If you don't come tomorrow morning, I will wait for you here (as much as I can) in the afternoon, after 3 p.m.*

*15 Rue Monsieur*
*Paris, Nov. 10, 1948*

*Dearest,*

    *Just received your sweet letter of Nov. 6. Thank you so much for expressing so well what we can do for each other. Yes, now, let us look only ahead, — with just this precious memory, as a base and a comfort, of the "Peking's years". To be able to adapt oneself to new circumstances, without dwelling in the past; and also, as we told, to understand that any kind of existence, if imposed upon us by circumstances, may become a unique masterpiece of life and art: those, I think, are two most important rules, — mostly if one is fortunate enough to be able to see the divine influence, the "golden glow", behind every event and element of this world.*

*Voyage de retour facile, sans incident. On m'attendait à la gare, à Paris. Naturellement, je me suis immédiatement trouvé pris dans un whirl de gens à voir et de choses à faire; et je n'en suis pas encore sorti. Mais mes dispositions restent les mêmes que quand je vous ai quittée à Rome. Tout au fond, je me sens plus libre de ne pas avoir à me pré-occuper du Collège de France: je reste davantage "moi-même", me semble-t-il, de cette façon. Et, jusqu'à un certain point, je crois que plusieurs de mes amis pensent de même. De la sorte, je garde mieux, à la fois, ma "physion-*

The return trip was easy and without any incidents. Somebody was waiting for me at the station in Paris. Naturally, I found myself immediately caught in a "whirl" of people to see and things to do; and I have not caught up yet. But my arrangements are the same as when I left you in Rome. Deep down I feel more free not to have to worry about the Collège de France: I remain "myself" more, it seems to me, this way. And, up to a point, I believe several of my friends feel the same. This way I preserve better, at the same time, my "physiognomy," my independence

*omie", mon indépendance, et ma ligne d'action. Et je ne doute guère qu'avant peu de nouvelles formes de travail se présentent à moi.*

*Les Bégouën sont encore ici, pour quelques jours. Ils ont maintenant une belle voiture, et ils repartent (comme ils sont venus) par route et par l'Espagne, ce qui leur donne une grande liberté de mouvement. Simone a encore trop souvent de petites crises de coeur; et Max est toujours très maigre. Cependant ils vont relativement bien; et moralement, ils sont exactement les mêmes; toujours aussi merveilleusement doux et "lumineux". Ils vous envoient tous les deux leurs grandes et fidèles amitiés. —— Je n'ai pas encore revu ma cousine: cela ne va pas bien de ce côté; — frère de plus en plus malade, et belle-soeur, et soeur aussi! De ce fait elle est si prise que nous n'avons pas pu encore nous rencontrer.*

*Hier j'ai traversé le Luxembourg: presque toutes les feuilles sont tombées, maintenant. Et cela m'a fait penser au Pincio. Profitez en bien pendant que vous y êtes. Je suis persuadé que quand vous quitterez Rome vous serez toute surprise de constater combien vous vous y êtes insidieusement habituée, — et combien aussi, peut-être, ce repos dans un beau cadre vous aura spirituellement fortifiée et éclairée.*

and my line of action. I have no doubt that, before long, new forms of work present themselves.

The Bégouëns are still here for a few days. They now have a beautiful car and they are travelling back (the way they came) by road through Spain, and so they are very free to move. Simone still has, too often, small heart attacks; and Max is still very thin. Nevertheless, they are fairly well, and their morale is exactly the same; still as wonderfully sweet and "luminous." Both send you their strong and faithful friendship. — — I still have not seen my cousin [Marguerite Teillard-Chambon]: things are not going well for her — her brother is ever more ill, also her sister and her sister-in-law! Because of this she is so occupied that we haven't yet gotten together.

I walked through the Luxembourg Gardens yesterday: almost all the leaves have fallen now. And that reminded me of the Pincio. Make the most of it while you are there. I am certain that when you leave Rome you will be very surprised to realize how subtly it has grown on you — and how much also, perhaps, this rest in beautiful surroundings will have fortified and enlightened you spiritually.

*I stop here, because I have a crowded morning, and a crowded afternoon. By the same mail (but as printed matter) I send you the few pages I told you (Introduction à la Vie Chrétienne). Some paragraphs will seem to you obscure: don't insist upon them, — we shall discuss them together.*

*God bless you, dearest. We certainly had a few very good days, and, out of them, plenty will remain, I am sure.*

Yours,

P.T.

*Rhoda is due here in 3 or 4 days.*
*Got a telephone call from Faure.*
*He is leaving today by plane to Washington!*
*( to meet Eleonore).*

15 Rue Monsieur
Paris, 26 Nov. 48

THEIR
1941–48
LETTERS

239

**Dearest,**

*Your sweet letter of Nov. 19 came as a great and happy surprise, — not so complete, of course, since you had already a faint idea of the big trip when I left you. Yet, it seems such a fairy tale that you should be by now among the eucalyptus and under the tropical light of Addis Abbeba! As you know, I never went so far as that in Ethiopia (I did not go further than the Aouach river, and I spent most of my time in Harrar). But I saw enough of the country, and precisely at the same time of the year, to realize approximately the surroundings and the conditions of the present life. I am sure that this new experience will actively contribute in giving you the kind of rejuvenation you are searching for. They are places, for us, perhaps, to find better God.*

*I am glad you received the few pages I sent you to Rome (together with a letter; — I suppose you got it too). I did not write you a second time, because I expected to know which were your plans. As far as I am concerned, nothing much to say. A few days after my coming back here, I received a letter from Rome which did not (and could not) say anything new: very kind, but not very hopeful concerning the book, which is still under the final(!) examination, — nor even for the lectures in America. I expect some final answer for Xmas.*

*Two days ago, I saw Faure, on his way back from Washington. A little melancholic, I think. But the question is settled now, by "no", between him and Eleonore. He remains really very fond of her; but, in addition to the reinforcement of the rules forbiding the diplomats to marry foreign girls, he realized that his anti-german feelings had grown so strong during the war that the situation should be unconfortable for Eleonore if they should have to live together. And this is probably true. Eleonor would like to join UNESCO in order to go to Europe, without losing her american citizenship. But I think that she has better first to consolidate her position where she happens to be now. In any case, I will ask Mme Raphael to watch the possibilities. You know that Julian Huxley retires from the general directorship [of UNESCO]: I regret to see him leaving Paris. I liked him decidedly.*

*Elsie Lyons is here. I was so surprised to meet her by chance a few days ago! I did not know that her husband was in the ONU, and sent to Varsovie. [Warsaw] — Rhoda is here up to the 15 of Dec., unless the strikes oblige her to stay longer. She left N.Y. three days only before the beginning of the strike, — by the last boat, in fact! — The Bégouëns are still here for a few days, —not very strong but still going on, as usually. They leave (as they came) by car, through Spain: that makes the journey more pleasant, and they have not to bother for dates and reservations. — My cousin has a very hard time. On the top of her brother's sickness, a large part of the farm in Auvergne (on which the family was living) was accidentally burnt! She keeps remarkably calm. I admire her faith in God.*

*Good bye, dearest. Have a glorious time! and God bless you!*

*yours*

*P.T.*

*1955 photograph / Courtesy of Librairie Hachette, Paris.*

# The Letters of the Last Years:
# from 1949 to 1955

*Dearest,*

*I was so pleased to receive your two letters (the first from Addis, the second one from Asmara). Such a dream that you could visit ces lieux de rêve! As you say, I am sure that such an experience will have helped you to throw away a lot of dust and to discover a new and deeper yourself. You will tell me all that before long; and I will like to hear everything from you concerning a country which has made on me, years ago, a deep impression.*

*Ici, (unbelievably!), rien de nouveau dans mes plans d'avenir, depuis que je vous ai quittée à Rome. C'est-à-dire, aucune décision encore prise à Rome concernant mon livre et les conférences d'Amérique. Rien qu'une lettre de mon général (il y a une semaine) pour me demander, quite kindly, des explications sur certaines paroles qu'on me prêtait dans une conférence (la conférence de Versailles, en Septembre), sans me dire un seul mot du reste, càd. des réponses que j'attends depuis deux mois, et plus! J'ai écrit au Number two (un ami) pour avoir des explications; et, à tout prix, quelques directions. These people, in Rome, are really impossible: as if they were living in another planet.*

*In the meantimes, I keep on going along more or less the same path. In spite of the flu which disturbs many appointments or parties, je continue à voir beaucoup de gens fort variés, - depuis des professeurs de philosophie de la Sorbonne jusqu'à des acteurs ou sociétaires de la Comédie Française; et je continue aussi à donner un certain nombre de private or semi-private talks. De cette façon, la vie passe vite, et assez pleine: mais je trouve un peu gênant de n'avoir pas de job fondamental, précis. En fait, mes idées continuent à avancer; à se préciser, et même à prendre une forme de plus en plus "pénétrante" (je ne veux pas dire "aggressive": mais cependant, quand je parle ou j'écris, j'ai l'impression d'être beaucoup plus affirmatif qu'autrefois). Tout pour moi se ramène maintenant à un si petit nombre de choses*

Here, (unbelievably!), there is nothing new concerning my plans for the future since I left you in Rome. That is to say no decision has been made in Rome about my book and the lectures in America. Nothing but a letter from my general (a week ago) asking me, quite kindly, some explanations concerning some words I am supposed to have said during a lecture (the Versailles lecture in September), but not a single word about the other matters, that is to say about the answers which I have been waiting for for two months and longer! I wrote to Number two (a friend) to have some explanations and, by all means, a few directives. These people, in Rome, are really impossible: as if they were living in another planet.

In the meantimes, I keep on going along more or less the same path. In spite of the flu which disturbs many appointments or parties, I continue to see many very different people, - from professors of philosophy at the Sorbonne to actors or members of the Comédie Française; I also continue giving private or semi-private talks. This way, life passes quickly and quite fully: but I find it a little bothersome not to have a basic and specific job. In fact, my ideas continue to progress, to become clearer, and even to take a more and more "penetrating" shape, (I do not mean "aggressive": however, when I speak or write, I feel I am much more assertive than in the past). For me everything now comes down to such a small number of very simple things: for example, to decide if Humanity is still on the move upon itself ("e pur se

*très simples: par exemple décider si l'Humanité est encore en mouvement sur elle-même ("e pur se muove". . .), - et si ce mouvement est convergent et irréversible, - et si, dans ce cas, Christianisme et Humanisme ne doivent pas se fondre dans une foi rajeunie en un Dieu mieux compris. C'est vraiment, me semble-t-il, un grand bonheur, un bonheur fondamental dans la vie, d'arriver à voir clair et passionnément en avant (malgré une foule d'obscurités, bien sûr), - d'avoir quelque chose à penser et à dire; - and for this kind of fullness or happiness you know how much, Lucile, I am indebted to you.*

*En somme, je suis apparemment destiné à passer ici à Paris tout l'hiver. Plus les jours passent, plus les chances diminuent que je puisse aller en Amérique ce printemps. En tous cas, si la moindre chose inattendue arrivait, je vous le ferais savoir à Rome. I am sure you will enjoy to be again in the Pincio.*

muove"), and if this movement is convergent and irreversible — and if, in this case, Christianity and Humanism must not melt into a rejunevated faith in a better understood God. It is truly, it seems to me, a great joy, a fundamental happiness in life, to succeed in seeing clearly and passionately ahead (in spite of a great many osbcurities, of course) — to have something to think and to say; — and for this kind of fullness or happiness you know how much, Lucile, I am indebted to you.

In short, I am apparently fated to spend all winter here in Paris. The more the days go by, the more the chances of my going to America in the spring diminishes. In any case if the slightest unexpected thing happened, I would let you know in Rome. I am sure you will enjoy to be again in the Pincio.

*Good bye, dearest. I have to prepare a lecture to be given this evening. May this letter reach Rome before you, so that you get it at your arrival.*

*A very, very good new year to you!*

*P.T.*

*Max and Simone are leaving Casablanca the 15, by plane, to Guinea!*

*15 Rue Monsieur*
*Paris, 4 Février, 1949*

*Dearest,*

*Excuse me not to have answered quicker your dear letter of Jan.26. I was so glad to hear about your beautiful trip and to know that you were safely back to old Rome! And I was to answer you immediately. And then a lot of small things came across, -including a semi-private lecture (which I decided to write down, as an article), and an answer to an "enquête" by UNESCO, etc. Et les jours ont passé.*

*Since my last letter, sent to Rome, nothing much new, except a letter from my General (arrived this morning), — a far from being satisfactory letter. Practically "No", to everything, except for an extremely slight chance left to the book. Everything was "gâté" (at some extent) by an infortunate and extremely unwise (and incorrect) report made in Osservatore Romano (December) on the Versailles meeting of last September where I was asked to talk. The whole thing is perfectly stupid. But in Rome they are much less concerned with facts than with the* "impressions" resulting of the facts. And the Osservatore's chronicle is more important for them than anything I may have really told. Well that's that. Nothing to do as far as the lectures in America are concerned. No printing of the Milieu Divin. And I am suggested to refrain, of course, from talking or writing except about pure Science (?). — Don't worry. I am perfectly calm, because I _know_ that "victory" is already mine. Simply I will have to keep on working almost "underground" (as before), — with this good result perhaps that I shall be obliged to concentrate and to focuss still more the points on which I feel that I am right. Obviously, the whole matter, "the heart of the matter", is that (just as in the old times of Galileo) I (and many others with me) we perceive that not only Earth, but Mankind, is in full motion, — whereas the other ones (and more specially the people at the head of the Church) do not see the movement. No possible agreement on such point: one of the two groups has to disappear. And in the meantimes I feel just as deeply as before, that the very motion of Mankind which I perceive is towards the Christ who is in the Church; — so that I can not (en vertu de ma position spirituelle même) fight the Church or leave it! A very curious situation.

Autrement, tout va bien. Je prépare, pour Mars, cinq courses (labelled as _scientific_) en Sorbonne. And I keep seeing and addressing a good number of people, so pathetically anxious to find spiritual light and freedom. Cela console de bien des choses. No prospect of any journey abroad. So you will always find me here when you decide to come north. En attendant profitez bien de Rome: je ne suis pas étonné que vous ayez fini par vous sentir séduite.

J'arrête ici pour que cette lettre parte ce soir. A bientôt d'autres nouvelles. I feel stronger, having you.

Otherwise, all is well. I am preparing, for March, five lectures (labeled as _scientific_) at the Sorbonne. And I am seeing and addressing a good number of people, so pathetically anxious to find spiritual light and freedom. That consoles me in many ways. No prospect of any journey abroad. So you will always find me here when you decide to come north. Meanwhile make the most of Rome: I am not surprised that you finally have been won over.

I stop here so that this letter can leave tonight. I will write soon. I feel stronger, having you.

God bless you!

yours as ever

P.T.

The Bardac's have left a week ago for Peking!

15 Rue Monsieur
Paris, 28 Février 49

Dearest,

Excuse and pardon me for not having answered earlier your two precious letters of Febr. 13 and 15. In fact I have been rather busy the last fortnight, preparing a series of five lectures on Man (structure and evolutionary trends of the human group), — the first one was delivered yesterday with a sufficient success, in spite of the fact that I am precisely experiencing a little attack of flu. The next one will be next Friday, — and so on, from Friday to Friday. And that keeps one rather busy to be ready for the next time. I do not know what is going to come out *of this effort. Perhaps nothing else but the advanced outline of a possible book. In any case I felt that I had <u>to do something</u> to prove myself and to people around that I am still alive.*

*Vous êtes infiniment gentille de prendre aussi à coeur mes affaires "romaines."* Croiriez-vous, à ce propos, que j'ai appris, de bonne source, qu'une des raisons de la vivacité de l'Osservatore Romano en la circonstance tient au fait que le parti "conservateur" avait été inquiet de l'espèce de faveur, rencontrée (ou même d'influence prise) par moi à Rome en Octobre? On a voulu neutraliser l'effet, tout simplement, à la première occasion venue. - Ceci prouverait que la situation, au fond, n'est pas si mauvaise. Toute la question est d'être en possession du "feu". Celui qui aura le feu, c'est celui qui enflammera la Terre.*

*Or, sur ce point d'"avoir le feu", je me sens toujours plus tranquille, — et par conséquent fondamentalement heureux.*

You are infinitely kind to take so much to heart my "Roman" affairs.* Would you believe, concerning this matter, that I learnt from a reliable source that one of the reasons for the sharpness of the Osservatore Romano in these circumstances comes from the fact that the "conservative" party had been worried by the kind of interest I encountered (or even by the kind of influence I had) in Rome in October? They wanted quite simply to neutralize the effect at the first opportunity. This would prove that the situation is not really so bad. The whole point is to be in possession of the "fire." The one who has the fire is the one who will inflame the Earth.

Still, on this point of "having the fire," I feel always more peaceful — and as a consequence fundamentally happy.

*When you are here, I will explain you once more how I see things, — in a still better focussed way since I went to Rome.*

*Besides, — and except for the lectures — life is going on pretty much the same. A kind of routine, with a few extras. I did not see Leroy this week; but I hope to meet him tomorrow. Last Sunday, we met for a cocktail at the house of the pretty mother of Laurette Dorget. Mostly extremely dignified people (ex-ambassadeurs, chefs de Service aux Ministères, directeur de la Revue de Deux Mondes.etc.); but also a few more vivacious elements, including my friend Griaule who claims to have uncovered some unfathomable wisdom (well buried, I must say!) in a tribe, along the Niger. — Dorget et Dorgette ont dû quitter Moscou le 22, on leave. Ils sont en ce moment en Suisse, — et viendront à Paris vers le milieu de Mars.*

*Good bye, dearest. Excuse me for being a bit short: but I want this letter to be sent today (saturday evening) so that you should not think that something is going wrong, avec tout ce silence. I am so happy to hear that you feel more settled internally, - and still more in a creative mood. No better index for the spiritual life!*

*Many regards to the Vincents.*

*And God bless you!*

*P.T.*

*I will explain you better, in a conversation, in which way only I can usefully, or logically, <u>fight</u>, in the present conditions.*

Teilhard wrote the above as a footnote in his letter to Lucile who was still in Switzerland.

After her visit with the John Carter Vincents in Switzerland, Lucile traveled back to Paris with Betty Vincent. They visited Teilhard who gave them an introduction to a Christian Dior showing.

*ÉTVDES*

*Paris, 15, rue Monsieur (7ᵉ)*
*Ségur 74-77*

*Père Teilhard de Chardin*
  *prie M'sieu Christian Dior*
  *de bien accueillir deux de mes amies américaines.*
  *Mrs. John Carter Vincent (femme de ministre d'amerique a' Berne)*
  *et Mrs. Lucile Swan (sculpteur).*
*Merci? . . .*
  *Teilhard, S.J.*
  *11 Mai '49*

*15 Rue Monsieur*
*Paris, 5 Juillet 49*

Dearest,

*Ces quelques lignes, non pas d'adieu, mais de "au revoir", pour vous redire combien, à moi aussi, cette dernière année à été bienfaisante, dans la mesure où, soit ici, soit à Rome (qui eût dit que nous nous retrouverions là!), nous avons pu constater que les heures de Péking étaient toujours bien vivantes, - et que nous pouvons toujours compter l'un sur l'autre pour "couronner" notre vie.*

*Comme je vous l'ai dit, aussi, l'avenir, en avant de moi, est en ce moment particulièrement vague, - ou même obscur. Ce que je continue à voir clairement, du moins, c'est que, de plus en plus, je dois me vouer à l'approfondissement et à la propagation de l'espèce de foi dont la structure s'est précisée pour moi en Chine, - en quelque manière sous vos yeux.*

*Je compte toujours sur vous pour m'aider de toutes façons (par votre affection, vos encouragements, et dans une certaine mesure votre collaboration) à pousser jusqu'au bout cet effort qui me demande, je le sens, de me chercher moi-même de moins en moins, et le Divin Amour de plus en plus. - Et en retour, vous savez quels voeux je fais*

These few lines, not of farewell, but of "au revoir" to tell you once more how much this year has been beneficial also to me, insofar as we, here as well as in Rome (who could have said we would find each other again there), we realized that the Peking hours were still very much alive, and that we can always count on one another to "crown" our lives.

As I told you also the future ahead of me is at the moment particularly vague — or even obscure. What I continue to see clearly, at least, is that I must devote myself more and more to the deepening and the propagation of the kind of faith whose structure became very clear to me in China — under your eyes, so to speak.

I still count on you to help me in many ways (by your affection, your encouragements and, in a certain measure, your collaboration) to pursue to the end this effort which I feel requires that I search myself less and less and Divine Love more and more. And, in return, you know all the wishes I make for your blossoming and your peace -

*pour votre épanouissement et votre* in the Greatest and the most Beautiful
*paix, -dans le plus Grand et le plus* of all.
*Beau que tout.*

    *Bon voyage, dearest, and God bless you for everything!*

    *As ever and for ever*

    *Pierre*

---

Lucile went in early July to England to visit Sidney Cooper, a Peking friend.

---

*Paris, 11 Juillet 49*

*Dearest,*

    *Well received, yesterday your sweet letter of July 7. Two things are particularly true in your lines: the first one, that between us love is <u>better</u>; and the second one that they are some things which you can give me, alone ...*

*Appuyés sur ces deux constatations solides, je pense, as you say, que tout ce qu'il nous reste à faire c'est d'avancer de plus en plus résolument et avec toujours plus de confiance vers le grand Centre lumineux vers lequel notre vie consiste à converger. — Merci encore pour tout ce que vous m'avez donné au cours de ces mois Paris-Rome-Paris!*

*Je vous avais encore téléphoné mercredi matin, vers 10h. à l'hôtel: mais c'est le moment où vous étiez au Luxembourg.*

*Rien de bien nouveau depuis ces derniers jours. Je continue à me sentir plus fort; et je mène sensiblement la même vie. Ma conférence No. 4 est presque finie (typed). D'ici peu, je vais commencer le No. 5. — Vu hier Movius; je dois déjeûner avec lui demain. Il est ici avec sa femme et ses deux enfants!*

*En somme tout va normalement. Je suis de plus en plus décidé à aller passer chez mon frère quelques semaines, à partir du 10 ou 15 août.*

    *Have a good time in England!*

    *yours as ever*

    *P.T.*

Relying on these two sound statements I think, as you say, all that remains for us to do is to go forward more and more steadfastly and with always more confidence, toward the great luminous Center toward which our life consists in converging. — Thank you again for all you gave me during these months Paris-Rome-Paris!

I had phoned you again at the hotel Wednesday morning around 10 o'clock: but you were at the Luxembourg at that time.

Nothing very new these past few days. I continue to feel stronger, and I lead more or less the same life. My lecture No. 4 is almost finished (typed). Very soon I will start on No. 5. I saw Movius yesterday; I am supposed to have lunch with him tomorrow. He is here with his wife and two children.

All in all everything is quite normal. I am more and more decided to go and spend a few weeks at my brother's, leaving on the 10th or 15th of August.

*July 18 - 49*

*Dearest -*

    *Your precious letter of July 11 makes me very happy - I am so glad that you are getting stronger every day and that the writing is progressing -*

*You are a very fortunate person to have been given this understanding of the Evolution of the World and of course the writing is one of your ways of sharing it with others. To so many you have given a renewal of Faith — a real and vital love of the Creator and his Creation and shown them that there is a purpose to it all and that they can help in the achievement of this purpose. With this realization I am sure you can never again have that "empty" feeling, and I like so much what you say in your first letter "de me chercher moi-même de moins en moins, et le Divin Amour de plus en plus" for in that way you will surely get more Light and reach more surely the Truth you have seen much and I am sure you will see more, and more clearly — isn't that a sort of miracle? Sometimes, just now, it is difficult to see how these thoughts are going to reach the many who are longing for them — but I am sure that eventually the way will come. And I have been so fortunate to have been with you so much and have shared these thoughts and seen them grow — you must know how very much they have meant to me in the forming of my beliefs and Faith, and I loved our recent times together — the talks and the walks, in France and in Rome — and the sharing of beautiful things especially the trees, and the sharing of small things too, such as your tea — all this is what makes our friendship so sweet. I miss it all <u>very</u> much but not in a sad way for I have it always with me and that makes me happy and sure of the future.*

*I find London very drab and dirty in comparison with Paris -almost a bit depressing - But I am having a very good time here -we have had 4 or 5 lovely days in the country and I've been about a good bit in town - There are three other ladies in the house and one especially has been a great pleasure to me - we like the same kind of thing and have gone about together and Sydney has been very nice - and it is so pleasant to have a lovely home to come back to - So I am very glad to have come here. But also I shall be glad to be on my way — now that I have left you in Paris — I want to get settled and working again. I do not know just what the winter will bring, but I feel sure that it will be good and creative.*

At the end of July 1949, Lucile sailed from London to New York where she stayed until she left for India in November. Letters flowed between them — his from Paris until mid 1951, hers from New York and India, then from Siam, Rome, England, and New York again, during those same two years.

*Paris, 2 août 49*

**Dearest,**
    *Well received your two sweet and long letters of London (just before your departure) and from the boat (July 27). And I hope that now you are in the quietness of Connecticut, — calmly busy with your experiences of last year and new plans for new work. You are right: creation is the ultimate incentive of any activity, — for the creature as well as for the Creator of the world; but, at the same time, creation is for union and through union. There is plenty to reflect and to think in this mysterious connection between the highest forms of spiritual activity: the one (to create) being mostly a question of intelligence, and the other one (to unite) being finally a matter of love . . .*

*Depuis ma dernière lettre (envoyée à Londres) rien de bien nouveau dans mon existence ici, - sauf que j'ai terminé ce matin la rédaction et même commencé le typing de ma lecture No. 5*

Since my last letter (sent to London) nothing really new in my life here, except that I completed this morning the drafting and I even started the typing of my lecture No. 5 (it is a little *(elle est un peu plus longue que les autres, comme il convient pour la dernière, et je la crois bonne). Il ne me restera plus, quand j'aurai fini le travail fastidieux du recopiage, qu'à revoir et polir un peu les leçons (ou chapitres) 1 et 2. J'aurai tout le temps de le faire en Auvergne, chez mon frère, où je pense toujours aller entre le 15 août et le 15 septembre. Comme projet ultérieur de travail, je n'ai encore que celui de rédiger un rapport d'une dizaine de pages (to be sent to Rome) où j'essaierai une fois de plus d'attirer l'attention de l'autorité sur ce qui, à mon avis, se passe dans le monde en ce moment: apparition d'une espérance nouvelle en l'Homme, en dehors de laquelle la foi chrétienne perd sa puissance de contagion, de consolation et de défense contre les humanismes nouveaux (Marxisme, pour commencer). Tout ce que je pense dire se résume dans ces trois phrases que je compte placer en "exergue" rapport:*

*"Les uns (les "vieux" chrétiens) disent: attendons le retour du Christ". Les autres (les marxistes) répondent: Achevons le Monde. Les troisièmes (les néo-catholiques) pensent: Pour que le Christ puisse revenir, achevons la Terre".*

*A propos de marxistes, la condamnation du communisme ne semble pas faire en France autant d'effet qu'en Italie par exemple. Je comprends l'opportunité politique du geste; mais je regrette que Rome, comme d'habitude, n'ait pas fait plus claire la distinction entre une certaine forme stalinienne de communisme, effectivement matérialiste et athée, et les aspirations communistes, lesquel les sont parfaitement et hautement christianisables.*

*Ici, il continue à faire très chaud et à ne pas pleuvoir. Je n'en souffre pas; mais l'eau manque sérieusement dans les campagnes. Presque tout le monde a quitté ou va quitter Paris, y compris Rhoda (pour l'île de Bréhat, chez Ida).*

longer than the others, as it should be for the last one, and I believe it is good. When I have finished the tedious work of copying it, I'll only have to check and polish a little the lessons (or chapters) 1 and 2. I'll have lots of time to do this in Auvergne at my brother's where I am still thinking of going between August 15 and September 15. As to my plans for future work, I only have that of writing a report of about ten pages (to be sent to Rome) in which I'll try once again to draw the attention of authority on what in my opinion is going on in the world at the moment: the emergence of a new Hope in Man outside of which the Christian faith loses its power of contagion, of consolation and of defense against the new humanisms (Marxism to start with). All that I want to say can be summed up in these three sentences which I intend to place "in the exergue" of the report:

"Some (the "old" Christians) say: let us wait for the return of Christ. Others (the Marxists) reply: let us complete the World. A third group (the neo-Catholics) think: so that Christ may come back, let us complete the Earth."

On the subject of Marxists, the condemnation of Communism doesn't seem to have as much effect in France as in Italy, for instance. I understand the political advisability of the gesture; but I regret that Rome, as usual, didn't make clearer the distinction between a certain Stalinist form of communism, effectively materialistic and atheistic, and the communist aspirations, which can be perfectly and highly christianized.

Here it is still very hot and there is no rain. It doesn't bother me but there is a serious lack of water in the countryside. Almost everybody has left or is about to leave Paris, including Rhoda (who is going to Ida's on the island of

*La semaine dernière, on m'a mené, près de Montparnasse, visiter le musée Bourdelle, récemment ouvert (sur l'emplacement même de l'atelier de Bourdelle). Surtout des répliques, mais un bien bel art. Dommage que Bourdelle ait eu tellement à travailler sur commandes, au lieu de pouvoir suivre son inspiration (comme dans le Centaure ou Beethoven). Et dommage aussi que je n'aie pas su l'ouverture du musée quand vous étiez ici: on aurait visité ensemble. Les honneurs du musée m'ont été faits par la deuxième femme de Bourdelle, une Grecque encore relativement jeune.*

Bréhat). Last week, I was taken to visit the recently opened Bourdelle Museum near Montparnasse (on the very site of Bourdelle's studio). Most are replicas, but very beautiful art. What a pity that Bourdelle had to work so much on commission rather than being able to follow his own inspiration (as in the Centaurus and Beethoven). And it is a pity also that I did not know the museum was opened when you were here! We could have gone there together. Bourdelle's second wife, herself a Greek woman still fairly young, did me the honors of the museum.

*Good bye, dearest, — and God bless you, — and bring us together as soon as possible, somewhere, anywhere!*

*As ever,*

*yours*

*P.T.*

*You can address your letters here. They will be forwarded if I am away.*

*Auvergne, 5 sept. 49*

*Dearest,*
*Just received today your letter of Sept. 1, and yesterday your precedent letter (Aug. 19) with the clippings (I enjoyed reading them). In fact I am so sorry to have been silent so long — for no good reasons: not sure of your address, lazy in the country, busy finishing some work, etc.*
*En tous cas, I loved very much what you wrote me. And I am so thrilled by the idea that you might go to India next winter. Yes, I am sure: Artistically and spiritually you would learn a lot down there, — if only to appreciate more definitely, and at the same time, the need of the West on the East, but also the superiority of the West on the East . . . If you can manage it, take this new trip, by all means.*

*Ce m'est une joie que vous ayez cette nouvelle chance.*

*En ce qui me concerne, rien de bien nouveau. Je suis ici, chez mon frère, en pleine campagne, depuis le 11 août; et je pense rentrer à Paris vers le 15, - à temps, par conséquent pour ne pas manquer Eléonore! Je serai si heureux de la revoir, et je voudrais tant que son avenir s'éclaircisse, à la suite de ce voyage en Europe. - Malgré la redoutable sécheresse, moins grande*

It delights me that you have this new opportunity.

As far as I am concerned, nothing really new. I am here at my brother's where it is completely rural, since the 11th of August; and I think I will go back to Paris around the 15th so as not to miss Eléonore! I will be so happy to see her again, and I hope so much her future becomes clearer after this trip to Europe. In spite of the terrible drought, not quite as bad for the past ten days, *depuis dix jours, le séjour ici m'aura beaucoup reposé. Maison extrêmement calme, égayée par mon nouveau petit neveu (six months old!), un gros poupon qui passe son temps à rire et à gigoter dans son berceau. Et puis l'Auvergne natale m'a repris plus profondément que je n'aurais cru. I positively enjoy looking at the volcanoes skyline, from my window, — chiefly at sunset, when everything is red and gold.*

*Dans ce grand calme, j'ai pu finalement travailler beaucoup, - un peu comme à St. Germain, de douce mémoire (you remember the terrace?). Maintenant mes Cinq Conférences sont complètement finies. Elles feraient un assez bon petit livre. Une fois de plus, je tâcherai de lui faire franchir les censures; et cette fois je ne vois pas trop (quoique je dise les mêmes choses) sur quoi la censure pourrait trouver à mordre: les apparences sont si innocemment scientifiques!*

*Entre temps, je me suis décidé à faire tirer à deux cents exemplaires (au stencil) le "Phénomène Humain"; définitivement arrêté à Rome. Comme cela, le livre pourra passer à quelques amis, et attendre des jours plus favorables. Naturellement you will receive a copy. The work is supposed to be done before October 15. Pas encore de nouvelles concernant l'impression de l'article que j'ai écrit à St. Germain ce printemps. Mais cela ne saurait tarder, et je garde bon espoir.*

*Good bye, dearest. Je dois profiter, pour envoyer cette lettre, d'une occasion, quelqu'un allant à la grande ville de Clermont. -Je vous récrirai de Paris. Pour être sincère, je ne vois pas bien ce que va être pour moi cette nouvelle année. Rien de bien net, ni de bien excitant en vue. Mais j'imagine que le chemin se fera et s'illuminera au jour le jour, — à la grâce de Dieu. Au fond, le seul intérêt de l'existence est de vivre de plus en plus intensément <u>par le</u>*

my stay here will have been most restful. The house is extremely quiet, brightened by my new little nephew (six months old!) a chubby baby who spends his time laughing and wriggling about in his crib. And then, my native Auvergne has got hold of me again, more profoundly than I would have thought. I positively enjoy looking at the volcanoes skyline, from my window, chiefly at sunset when everything is red and gold.

In this complete peacefulness, I was finally able to work a lot, a little like at Saint-Germain of sweet memory (you remember the terrace?). Now my five lectures are completely finished. They could make a fairly good small book. Once again, I'll try to get it past the censors and this time I really don't see (although I say the same thing) what the censor could find to sink his teeth into: the appearance is so innocently scientific!

Meanwhile, I have decided to have 200 (stenciled) copies made of the <u>The Phenomenon of Man</u>, that was definitively held up by Rome. That way, I will be able to give this book to a few friends and wait for more favorable days. Naturally you will receive a copy. The work is supposed to be done before October 15. I still have no news concerning the printing of the article I wrote in Saint-Germain this Spring. But it will not take much longer, and I am hopeful.

Good bye, dearest. I must take advantage of an opportunity to send this letter: someone going to the large town of Clermont. I will write you again from Paris. To be sincere, I really cannot see clearly what this new year will bring to me. Nothing very clear nor very exciting in sight. But I imagine that the way will be lighted day by day — with the grace of God. Basically, the only thing that matters in our existence is to live more and more intensely <u>from</u>

*dedans. Et cela c'est possible toujours et partout.*

the inside. And this is possible always and everywhere.

*10 Octobre 49*

*Dearest,*

*Merci pour votre chère lettre du 26 Sept., à laquelle j'aurais dû répondre déjà, depuis longtemps.* I am extremely glad that your Indian trip's plan seems to hold strong: I am so sure that it will achieve the pacifying work of last year, and enrich you a lot, spiritually and artistically.

*Tenez-moi au courant de ce que vous faites et de ce que vous pensez: cela m'aidera à vivre plus activement moi-même. En ce qui me concerne, je ne sais si, suivant votre expression, "I am setting for the greatest adventure of my life" ... Ce qui est sûr, c'est que je l'ai l'impression que les quelques lignes majeures de ma vision du Monde (quoi qu'elles vaillent . . .) prennent une simplicité et une intensité encore grandissantes. Présentement, elles tendent à se concentrer sur deux foyers principaux, — qui ne sont au fond que le même foyer, focussed at two different depths. Le premier (plus objectif et scientifique) est l'existence, en avant de nous, de ce que j'appelle maintenant un "Ultra-humain", représentant la prolongation biologique de l'évolution humaine. Et le second (plus "mystique") est la présence enveloppante et pénétrante, partout autour de nous, de ce que j'aime à appeler "L'Energie Christique", forme supérieure et ultime de toutes les énergies d'où émerge l'arrangement de l'Univer autour de nous. — En fait, je pense pousser simultanément l'étude de ces deux "réalités", au cours de cette année. L'Ultra-humain serait le sujet des "séminaires" que je compte de plus en plus donner cet hiver àl'Institut de Paléontologie Humaine; et l'"Energie Christique" serait le sujet of my next paper: quelque chose comme la reprise; à vingt ans de distance, du "Milieu Divin". — En ce moment, je suis soutenu dans cet effort par un certain nombre d'indices encourageants. Il y a une semaine, j'ai donné une con-*

Keep me current on what you are doing and what you are thinking: that will help me to live more actively myself. As far as I am concerned, I don't know if, according to your expression, "I am setting out on the greatest adventure of my life". What is certain is that I have the impression that the few important lines of my vision of the World (whatever they are worth.) are taking on an ever growing simplicity and intensity. Presently they have a tendency to converge on two main foci, — which in fact are the same focus, focussed at two different depths. The first (more objective and scientific) is the existence ahead of us of what I now call an "ultra-human" representing the biological prolongation of human evolution. And the second one (more "mystical") is the enveloping and penetrating presence, everywhere around us, of what I like to call "the Christic Energy," the superior and ultimate form of all the energies from which the arrangement of the Universe around us emerges. In fact, I think I will pursue simultaneously the study of these two "realities" in the course of this year. The Ultra-human would be the subject of "seminars" which I more and more intend to teach this winter at the Institute of Human Paleontology; and "the Christic Energy" would be the subject of my next paper: something like resumption twenty years later, of The Divine Milieu. At the moment I am sustained in this effort by a certain number of encouraging signs. A week ago I gave a lecture (on the Ultra-

*férence (sur l'Ultra-humain et ses deux conséquences: un néo-humanisme et un nouveau-christianisme) aux 500 grands élèves de notre école préparatoire aux Grandes Ecoles de Ste Geneviève (Leroy is teaching there), et j'ai été très écouté. Par ailleurs, mon article sur "le nouveau cas de Galilée", écrit à St Germain ce printemps) va sortir sous peu dans une revue scientifique (I will send it to you, of course, avec quelques pages stencilées envoyées dernièrement à Rome . . .).*

humain and its two consequences: a neo-humanism and a neo-Christianity) to 500 students in our preparatory school of Ste. Geneviève for the Grandes Ecoles (Leroy is teaching there) and the students showed great interest. Otherwise, my article on "the new case of Galileo" (written in Saint-Germain this spring) will soon be published in a scientific review (I will send it to you, of course, with a few stenciled pages recently sent to Rome . . .).

*Et puis there is the shadow of a chance that my Five lectures on Man will be accepted and printed here without any recours à Rome. I will let you know. Just now, my text is in the course of being re-typed.*

*Et Eléonore est ici! toute sémillante. I was so pleased to see her, and we talked of you. I am going to have lunch with her today at the small restaurant au coin de la rue Barbet de Jouy. She has a very slight hope to join UNESCO (in a newly open Section for Germany), — and (!) she has been active in helping the fiançailles(?) of Faure with a Dutch girl. She will explain you; I did not understand exactly the case, so far. She bought (first gesture in reaching Paris) a perfectly cute little hat; and she seems entirely in her own element. De son côté, Rhoda is perfectly nice and understanding. By now she has found (for 4 months) a very nice appartment near St Augustin. And Noel seems quite satisfied at the american school. — Leroy is decidedly going to America (with a fellowship) for a year: first to Chicago University. He will leave at Xmas. And I shall miss him. My friend Jouve is away for a month; to rest.*

*Good bye, dearest. Hope everything is OK. with you. God bless you!*

*yours, as ever.*

*P.T.*

*Paris, November 14. '49*

*Dearest,*

*My type-writer being under repair, I have to come back to handwriting. — So exciting to think that this letter is going to reach you in Egypt (in fact, I did not see Alexandria since I left it in 1908, on my way to Theology in England!) Think of me when you pass through the Suez Canal, — an old friend, — shall I see it ever again? I think it is a great luck for you to go back to the East. Upon the East I do not rely much, as you know, as far as the world's vision is concerned. But I still believe (because I have experienced it) in its power of rejuvenation and excitation on our western minds. I am sure you are going to a big experience which will make you more alive, and consequently closer of what is divine in the world.*

*Here, things are going on quietly. I feel quite alive and awake spiritually (as usually in autumn), — and my "ideas" are growing once more, — although always along the same essential lines. D'Ouince has read the new book (the five* lectures), and is quite enthusiastic, — except for the two(!) last pages, which make him a little scared of Rome (complétement à tort, I think). This week he will discuss the case with a great theologian friend (Henri de Lubac) who is coming here; and, if his scruples are persisting, he will send, himself, the manuscript to Rome with a strong letter. — In fact, I do not see how the book could be decently sent to press without letting Rome know it: and then, obviously, Rome will ask for the text. —— So it is perhaps better to jump in the cold water immediately — anyway. My article on the "New Problem of Galileo" is out, and I have a lot of separates, already spreading everywhere. People seem to find it particularly good (but I suspect that in Rome they will not like it so much, — although they can say nothing against it). — My present effort is more and more concentrating on a better analyse of the "ultra-humain" (existence, nature and growth): right at this point, I am convinced, hides the source of every modern conflict and hope; because such an "ultra-humain" cannot be accepted (under the pressure of facts) without accepting, ipso facto, a definite view of the true relationship between Spirit and Matter, — and also a definite "faith" in the future of Man. — — At the end of this week I shall have to develop this idea before a selected group of big business-men at the Royaumont Abbaye, near Paris (for two days).

Otherwise, nothing much new (except that I am publishing an "apparently" harmless article in the next number of Les Etudes, on "La Vision du Passé: ce qu'elle nous apporte, et ce qu'elle nous ôte" — together with a less harmless recension of the Osborn's book ("Our plundered Planet"), — and a still less harmless (but anonymous) page on a Symposium (on Evolution) recently held in Paris (UNESCO).

So, as you know probably, Eleonore is in Italy (or already in Stuttgart?..): not much hope for her at the UNESCO, - but some faint hope, still; - unless she can get something at the Litter. Digest. — Françoise Raphael left for Algeria a fortnight ago: she will be back after ten days. Max and Simone were here for a month, very busy. They finally settled in a free room in my cousine's appartment, rue de Fleurus. Simone is remarkably better (except for the legs, — she can not walk but so slowly!), — and Max has somewhat improved his health in Europe. But he is so thin! Still he keeps enthusiastic and alive (always some new projects), — in spite of serious financial troubles (la rose did not sell well this year, — but le jasmin!). They are leaving this week, unfortunately, — by car, through Portugal. They send you their love. — Rhoda and Noël seem perfectly pleased by their parisian life, - so much more so that Noël seems to be a great success at the American School. — Last Saturday I was invited (at the place of my friend Jouve, — still in the South) to a cocktail given in the Ritz, by Clare [Boothe] Luce (I had met Luce himself in Peking in 1945), on her way back from Rome and the Vatican(!). I had the hope to meet there some interesting U.S. citizens: but nobody, except what I suppose to have been a rather ordinary staff of Life and Time. — Bosshart is in Zürich. He left Peking in May, in disgust (in spite of several "red" friends, he has practically lost all his investments in Peking and Shanghai: could not even go to save anything in his temple in the Hills (where?). - Still, he is leaving in December to Hongkong: the call of the East. I think I still feel it, in spite of everything.

*Good bye and good luck, dearest! —— Have a good time and may India introduce you deeper to a full consciousness of yourself and of God at the center of the great Universe!*

*as ever*

*P.T.*

*15 Rue Monsieur*
*Paris, December 14th, 1949*

Dearest,

*So many thanks for your dear letter of Nov. 28, sent from Genoa! This one is to send you my best and deepest wishes and "affection" for Xmas: a Xmas without snow and tree for you, —but a Xmas still, that is the annual remembrance that we are a part, all of us, of a same growing and loving whole. The great question, of course being to decide what kind of gesture we have to perform, each of us, in order to join this divine Whole: dissolution and identification; or on the contrary, self-achievement and union through love. As you know, I feel more and more convinced that the second way (la "Route de l'Ouest") is the good one; and this is not the way traditionally taught in India. Yet India is a warm and tense atmosphere for any mystics; and I am sure that you are eventually going to feel closer to God (to your God) after this new experience of the East. A few days ago I heard, au Musée Guimet, a good lecture (with excellent pictures) of Ella Maillart, precisely on India. You know that she spent two years down there (near Madras) during the war, in the ashram of a famous guru; and she found there "peace", she told me, — if not "love". By the way, in 1935, I spent two days at the Cecil Hotel of Delhi, in my way to the Narbada, with Hellmut de Terra. The lady keeping the Hotel was a very great friend of Bosshart. Maybe she is still there. I liked the place.*

*Here, nothing much new. The five Lectures, or rather their fate, is still hanging in the air. The chances are that my friend d'Ouince is going to send them himself to Rome with a letter urging for publication. In the meantimes, I may deliver them at the Unesco: this last point will be decided next week when I have a private talk at a dinner with Mr. Torez-Bodet, the present Director of Unesco. My article on "La nouvelle Question de Galiléo" was rather successful: the separates are spreading very fast (I am keeping one for you, of course). Just now, I am thinking of some new Essays: but nothing is actually started. Things have first to mature a bit more in my head. Did I tell you that, at the beginning of November, I went à l'Abbaye de Royaumont, near Paris (a beautiful medieval place, arranged most confortably), in order to talk (during two days) with a group of important businessmen? An excellent opportunity to develop, before an influential audience, my views concerning l'ultra-humain and "l'ultra-christianisme". I think they understood.*

*The Bégouën are still here. The very eve of their departure (a week ago) Simone got a kind of bronchitis, and she is still in bed.*

*In fact, ce retard ne nuit pas absolument aux affaires de Max, qui rencontre en ce moment des gens utiles. Mais*

In fact, this delay absolutely does no harm to Max's business, he is meeting useful people these days. But it is a nui-

*c'est un ennui tout de même. Depuis un mois, ils sont installés tous les deux dans une chambre, dans l'appartement même de ma cousine. Une vraie vie de famille. Très commode pour aller les voir!*

sance all the same. For the past month, they have both been living in one bedroom in my cousin's apartment. True family life. Very easy for me to go and see them.

*Last week, Dr. Wong-Wen-Hao appeared in my room: just the same: the shadow of a little Chinese in a long coat and a big brown felt hat. His wife is in Hong Kong, his daughters in Formosa, his son in Shanghai, — and he on the highways of the world, with a little money for <u>one</u> year. - And the little Mrs. Moser too (did you know her? the daughter of a german lady, married with a Chinese, the maire of Peking during the war). Her mother is sick (cancer) in Peking (attended by Loucks, sheltered by Mary Ferguson), her father in jail in Shanghai, and her husband is divorcing her. Poor little thing! — Mme de Margerie is marrying her daughter (Diane) to an italian prince (Pignatelli).*

*- M. Cosme est réintégré dans tous ses droits d'avant guerre; ce qui le rend tout heureux. Je vais rencontrer chez eux, la semaine prochaine, les Guillaume, toujours ambassadeurs à Paris. Leroy va décidément partir pour l'Amérique (Chicago, first) au début de Janvier. Il me manquera. — Les Bardac sont à San Francisco.*

*Voilà à peu près toutes les nouvelles.*

Mr. Cosme has had all his pre-war rights restored: which makes him very happy. Next week, I will go to their home to meet the Guillaumes; he is still ambassador in Paris. Leroy is definitely going to leave for America (Chicago, first) at the beginning of January. I will miss him. The Bardacs are in San Francisco.

That is about all the news.

*Good bye, dearest. Have a good time, in the glorious East. And may a still more glorious light rise for you inside!*

*En grande affection*

*P.T.*

*Paris, Jan. 22th, 1950*

Dearest,

*I was so happy to receive your long letter of Jan. 3. You must have had such a wonderful time on your cargo [freighter]! And now I am sure that you are slowly collecting and composing your special brand of honey out of the multiple flowers of India. Such a mixture of sweet and bitter, healthy and poisonous vegetation. You will feel your way, and your taste in the jungle. No safer compass or better test, I suppose, to find your way and select your "butin" [goal] but to appreciate things by their actual or potential content in Love. So much of "pantheism", and so little of love, in India (I think): just because they did not catch, there, the "personnalistic" nature of the Universal: the great western Discovery. — Anyhow, I am so keen to know what is happening to you, outside, and mostly inside.*

*Here, life for me is going on, more or less the same. Physically, I was a bit too much "nervous", last month, — for some mysterious reasons, connected with health, weather or God knows what. Better, now. Gave two semi-private lectures, since january, — on Man and what can be expected ahead for Man (sur* l'Humain et l'Ultra-humain). *Clearly, and at the same time, my ideas are becoming more and more simple (reduced to their purest essence) and I can express them with an almost perfect ease. But the danger is to become "monotonous".*

*— Quoi qu'il en soit, je continue à avoir l'impression d'avancer encore in the process of focussing and maturing what I am obscurely feeling and hunting since fifty years: and, in spite of a relatively eventless life, that keeps me interested and alive. Je prépare doucement un nouvel Essay (not for publication) où j'essaierai de suivre et décrire le processus <u>psychologique</u> suivant lequel, - depuis mon enfance -, un sens confus de l'Univers et de l'Universel a graduellement pris en moi la forme du "Milieu Divin" formé par une sorte de "centre Christique universel". Pour le moment, je rassemble mes souvenirs et je tâche de les organiser dans leur suite naturelle. La rédaction demanderait une période de calme: chez mon frère, l'été prochain?*

However that may be, I continue to have the impression of still going forward in the process of focusing and maturing what I am obscurely feeling and hunting since fifty years: and, in spite of a relatively eventless life, that keeps me interested and alive. I am slowly working on a new Essay (not for publication) in which I will try to follow and describe the <u>psychological</u> process according to which - since my childhood - a vague sense of the Universe and of the Universal has gradually taken in my mind the shape of the "Divine Milieu" formed by a kind of "universal Christic center." For the moment I gather my memories and try to organize them in their natural sequence. The writing would require a period of quiet: at my brother's, next summer? . . .

*Le manuscrit des cinq conférences est en route pour Rome. Je demande la permission d'imprimer; et le P. d'Ouince backs me warmly. C'est "fifty fifty", comme chances de succès. In the meantimes, j'ai fait une préface pour un livre (un joli livre) composé sur ma soeur cadette (Marguerite) par ses amies "Les Malades".*

The manuscript of the five lectures is on its way to Rome. I am asking for permission to have it printed; and Father d'Ouince backs me warmly. It is "fifty fifty", as far as the chances of success are concerned . . . In the meantimes I wrote a preface for a book (a lovely book) written about my younger sister (Marguerite) by her friends "The Sick".

*C'est une biographie; mais practically entirely made using letters of my sister: <u>her</u> book, published under her name. If and as soon as the book is printed, I will send it to you, — naturally.*

*Besides, nothing much. Max and Simone had an excellent trip to Casablanca; and now they are on the eve of flying (<u>both</u> of them), by special plane, to Guinea. Eleonore wrote me from Munich. She is deeply interested, but <u>not</u> attracted, by Germany, and plans to be back in Paris (for a last research for a job) on about February 15. I sent her your address in India. — Received a Xmas letter of Rose "Life for me, although ever interesting, is rather difficult as I have no teaching post this year. Tutoring helps, but not enough", she says. — Leroy was delayed by a strike on l'Ile de France. Is leaving tomorrow by an american cargo (a "dry" one!).*

*Good bye, dearest! In my last letter (written at the end of December) I forgot to tell you that on Ste Lucile's day my thought and my mass had been for you. — Thank you so much for the book "Cry my beloved country": it came rather late, but OK. Did not yet read it: but I keep it on my shelf, as a box of candy.*

With love, as ever,

P.T.

15 Rue Monsieur
Paris, February the 16th, 1950

Dearest,

Just received your so interesting letter from fabulous Jaipur. Must have been a thrill, but also a funny impression, for you to get a personal glimpse, just before it dies, on an already condemned type of life, — a kind of luxurious flower grown by a past season of the world! Something still more fantastic will come out of our industrialised and totalizing society, I am convinced. But sous quelle forme? et de quel parfum? I wonder what is going to be, at the end, your final reaction to India, — to its mixture of decaying splendor and swarming population. Looking from outside, I feel more and more convinced that, for a long time, the East may bring its tremendous mass, but will not act as a "moteur" (engine) in the development of the world. So strange that you should go, you too, to beautiful Kashmir!

Here, nothing much since the new year. January was cold, so that I stood wisely at home as much as possible. But now the weather is quite mild: a kind of spring, already. No reaction so far from Rome concerning the manuscript of the "five lectures" on Man, which, I know, was received safely there a fortnight ago. I remain relatively hopeful, and I do not expect a final answer before two months. On the other hand, I have submitted to a publisher, here, in Paris, a book (with une préface written by me) on my sister (la malade) who died in 1935. In fact, the book is mostly made of quotations of my sister, cleverly compiled by her friends de "l'Union Catholique des Malades". I think it might be a success. But I am not yet sure of the publisher's appreciation.

Autrement, je continue à aligner les notes et les idées, — et àvoir un assez grand nombre de gens intéressants, who generally leave my room with a bunch of selected separates or "clandestins". I wonder sometimes how long this type of activity will continue without starting new troubles: because, on the whole, my position is somewhat hardening and my influence spreading. If the book could be printed, things would certainly relax. In the meantime, and in spite of my rather "jobless" situation, life is rather exciting, because I feel still moving inside.

And I have read "Cry, the beloved country". First I had the impression that it was too much sentimental and "goody-goody", — too much a "preacher's work". But gradually I was caught by the whole situation: a clever, and apparently extremely true expression of the whole african human problem. So that I must say that I enjoyed the lecture and got a great deal out of it.

Now, a few news from Paris. Rhoda works steadily on her novel, and begins to search for a new appartment (because she may have to leave the one she has now, in April); Noel is shining as a star at the American School. — The Bégouëns are probably in french Guinée, by now (by air). — No news from Eléonore, so far. En revanche I am having lunch, today, with the Burchart, — back from England, and en route (motoring) to la Côte d'Azur and Italy. I shall give them the last news of your journey. — Laurette Dorget phoned me yesterday; they *are transferred from Moskow to Copenhagen. Françoise Raphael left (lost) her job à l'Unesco (at least provisionnally), and is just wondering whether it is not the best for her to be forced to search for less "bureaucratiques" activities. — Leroy must be in Chicago by now, but I have not yet his address. He will certainly see Mlle Saizeau. He brought a copy of my stenciled book to Dr. Fejos (Viking Fund) who talked very nicely of me, and is ready to help me to come to America for any kind of "unformal" activities.*

*Et voilà à peu près toutes les nouvelles. J'ai trop attendu avant de répondre à votre lettre du 28 janvier; so that I hope that you will get this one very fast.*

*Have a good and fruitful time! and God bless you, dearest.*

*as ever*

*P.T.*

*Paris, 6 Avril 50*

*Dearest,*

*I am awfully late with you, although I have well received your so nice letter from the Hills, and the long one written on your return in Delhi. The last news of you I got two days ago from Eleonore, who came to have lunch with me at the little restaurant you know, near les Etudes. I hope that Kashmir will have super-imposed a deep feeling of majesty and of peace to your so mixed spiritual impressions of India. Last Tuesday I met at dinner the physicist and communist Joliot-Curie, just (or almost just) back from Calcutta-Delhi-Bombay. He is obviously somewhat biased in his appreciations on political subjects. Still, what he says reminds strangely and ominously of kouomintang China. Well, we are living in a quickly and dangerously moving world. We have better to face it, — and chiefly to develop a strong faith (based on a clear vision of things) in the Future of Man.*

*Which brings me to the subject of my "book" (the five lectures). The critics of Rome finally reached me ten days ago (delayed three weeks by the mistake of a secretary). Not too bad. Le censeur was evidently not a understanding man: not on my side. Nevertheless, none of his remarks would require more than a slight éclaircissement of my text. So did I. My proposed retouches will be in Rome for Easter. And then may be I will get the permit of printing; - unless they decide to have "une super-révision" (which would mean an endless processus): but I hope for the best.*

*In the meantime, the last weeks have been for me relatively busy. Five lessons (purely technical) à la Sorbonne, on the Prehistory of the Far-East; and three private talks or lectures, — the most developped of them being a lecture à la Cité Universitaire (students) on what I called "Les Phases (de développement) d'une Planète vivante". I will "rédiger" more carefully this last talk as soon as possible, — although I do not see where to publish it, so far.— Did I tell you that I had written a Foreword for a book written on (or rather by) my sister, la malade, who died in 1935? Finally the book has been heartily accepted by a very good publisher, here, in Paris (it will not be printed however before a few months); and I am very glad. La "transfiguration" de la souffrance is one of the* major problems of human Life; and the living example of my little sister may be extremely illuminating for many suffering people.

On the whole, life is going on rather smoothly for me, — although I have the feeling that something is slowly changing "under my feet", — since my scientific and religious Weltanschauung is unavoidably getting sharper and sharper. Some little crisis may develop any minute; — unless the publication of my book (if permitted) gives a sort of "officielle reconnaissance." In fact, I do not worry. The main thing is that some views which I regard as vital should live and thrive: and they do. And that makes me fundamentally happy.

Besides, not much to say. Eleonore seems quite calmer and happier. A good thing that she is now reconciled with Germany. Leroy writes me frequently from Chicago. He is interested with his work, — although he has to live in a rather narrow-minded house of my order (a new "Chabanel" house (Shih-hu-hutung), he told me!). He has come in touch with Mlle Saizeau, — and also with Claire Hirschberg, who has just lost her father, somewhere in Texas. Here, Mme Raphael is still jobless (she has some definite hopes for the fall). Diane de Margerie is going to marry her italian prince soon after Easter. Rhoda works steadily to her book, and is not yet out of her appartment. Noël shines as the star of the America School. Malvina [Hoffman] was rather sick (flu), and does not seem to plan a trip to Europe this year (her sister is still alive). She does not say anything about the"monument" d'Epinal. Was the project dropped? I hope not.

Et voilà pour cette fois. May you have a good Easter time, dearest, — plenty of light inside of you! I am glad to think that you are going to Siam: the true Far-East, and an impression of China. — I am not leaving Paris before August (the end or the middle of August), — for a month approximately. Such a joy to see you here once more!

yours, as ever.

P.T.

Paris, 9 mai 1950

Dearest,
Thank you so much for the long and sweet letter of April 29 (from Siam), arrived only two days ago. In spite of the perspiration you positively seem quite alive; and I feel so confident that, on your coming back to the States, you shall feel physically and spiritually rejuvenated!

Here, as far as I am concerned, nothing much new. I am <u>still waiting</u> (after four weeks) the answer of Rome to my proposed corrections. Is that a bad or a good omen? impossible to say. In the meantimes I am unexpectedly starting (since a few days) a candidature to the french Académie des Sciences. I did not intend nor exactly like to take this step, — but I was thrown accidentally in the affair; and now I am going on. I am sure to get many favourable ballots; but I start rather as an outsider (at the last minute), a circumstance which diminishes my chances. The vote is expected in a fortnight. The main advantage for me to be elected would be an increase of roman consideration. But such a bore to visit people with the idea of getting "leur voix"!

*Otherwise, days are passing one by one, rather interesting and pleasing. Always some new acquaintance, and some new intellectual excitement, in this parisian environment. In spite of the fact that my ideas seem to have reached by now the stage where they grow simpler, fewer and bigger, rather than multiplying. Presently, two points are practically absorbing the whole of my internal attention: the first being the evidence that, religiously speaking, the major event in our world is a certain change in "the face of God" (God becoming a loving Center of universal Evolution, rather than the big "landowner" of yesterday); — and the second being the vital urgence to watch and feed in Man "Le goût de vivre" (that is the Evolution pressure), which is decidedly the most fundamental of the cosmic energies. — Since a month I have written two short, but rather good, Essays: the one on what I call "Les phases d'une Planète Vivante" (that is, an interpretation of Life and Man in the World), - the other under the little "Le phénomène chrétien" (to show and detect what is probably essentiel and "for ever" in the christian Weltanschauung: that is the idea and gradual rise of a Loving center of the Universe). Both of them I had first "talked", in lectures. The only trouble is that I do not see how to print them.*

Now for some outside events: two days ago, I baptized the second baby of my niece who lives in Paris; and my other niece from Auvergne (Gabriel's daughter) also just had a little boy (her third child in three years!). Mothers and children are all doing very well. Otherwise Diane de Margerie (did you meet her in China?) just married an Italian prince (Pignatelli): a very nice wedding. The Burcharts probably left France last Friday. I had lunch with them only a week ago. Both very happy; Otto like a young man - still mixing very skilfully business and the pleasures of travel (I seem to understand that he now specializes in the curios of the Cyclades — since China is closed). Eléonore is leaving tomorrow, going back to Stuttgart: she is in very good health, quite vivacious, but still in suspense with her undecided lovers. It seems that she wants to stay in Europe as long as possible without compromising acquisition of her the American citizenship. For the 1st of May, she very nicely brought me a bottle of eggnog in memory of Peking (and I had just received a few days before your sprig of forget-me-not from Kashmir! which touched me deeply). Leroy is not hav-

bien touché). — Leroy ne s'amuse pas beaucoup à Chicago, où il a des difficultés matérielles à mettre en train ses expériences. Mais il ne perd pas courage. Sa meilleure consolation est Mlle Saizeau, — assez préoccupée par la perspective de perdre son job, — ce qui la forcerait de rentrer en France. - A propos de job, Françoise Raphael espère trouver bientôt une place dans l'enseignement (aux Colonies); mais rien n'est encore fait. En attendant, elle fait bonne figure. Mais naturellement, au fond, elle est un peu inquiète. Espérons.

Good bye, dearest. Mon plus fidèle souvenir à Delia, — et à Bosshart! Comme cela semble étrange, toutes ces réunions àtravers le monde . . .

God bless and direct you!

as ever

P.T.

ing much fun in Chicago where he has met with financial difficulties in starting his experiments. But he is not losing courage. His best consolation is Mlle Saizeau — quite preoccupied by the perspective of losing her job — which would oblige her to go back to France. Talking of jobs, Françoise Raphaël hopes to find a position soon as a teacher (in the Colonies): but nothing has been decided yet. Meanwhile, she keeps up a good appearance. But, naturally, deep down she is a little worried. Let's hope.

Good bye, dearest. Faithful regards to Delia — and to Bosshart! How strange all these reunions seem throughout the world.

Rhoda est encore dans son appartement; mais elle va sans doute avoir à changer: une amie française la reçoit dans son appartement pour l'été. Ida est attendue, fin Juin.

Rhoda is still in her apartment; but she probably will have to change: a French friend will receive her in her apartment for the summer. Ida is expected at the end of June.

*Paris, 15 July, 1950*

Dearest,
    I just receive your letter of July 6. So you must already be in Rome just now! Almost close.
    As far as my plans are concerned, I am leaving Paris at the beginning of August (about the 10th? I am not sure: depends on my brother), going to Auvergne, as usually. And I will stay there up to the middle of September, approximately. — Let me know what you do and where you are.
    Finally, once more, my book (No. 2) did not get the roman "visa". Reason: nothing to be criticized, but the content is not sufficiently "scientific" (that is, it is too much "philosophic": a point on which I do not agree, of course). Since I was more or less expecting the verdict, I was not disappointed. And, by the end of september, I will probably have a small stenciled edition to distribute to my friends. — In the meantimes the ideas are spreading fast; so that I feel quite satisfied, on the whole.And, in addition, I have some plans of work for the next year. I will tell you.
    Leroy is now well established in his Chicago Lab, — and satisfied. But I do not think that he has found any real friends down there; and he misses it. —

*Here, Françoise Raphael is still jobless: the hopes she had for a teaching position did not materialize. Her situation becomes to be a bit serious: I am so sorry for her! — Did I tell you that Rhoda has lost her brother Charles, — both a "chagrin" for her, and a source of material troubles. She is hunting for a momentary job, she too.*

*Good bye, dearest. I am so glad to feel that you are in good spirits, and so near, too!*

*yours,*

*P.T.*

*Ida Treat is in Britanny (Bréhat) since the end of June.*

---

Lucile visited in Rome about two weeks and then went to Paris. There, at the end of July Lucile saw Teilhard several times, before he went off to Auvergne to visit with his family.

---

*15 Rue Monsieur*
*Paris, 30 Juillet, 1950*

*Dearest,*

*Such a joy to see you again!*

*You are sure to catch me by phone on Friday morning. Early afternoon of Friday I can not easely dispose, but we could join at 6 P.M. (for instance) and have dinner together.*

*If by chance you should once more take a room à l'Aiglon, you would find Nirgidma there!*

*My best regards to the Vincent's. I am so sorry for Betty.*
*A bientôt!*

*yours*

*P.T.*

*Paris, 10 Août, 1950*

*Dearest,*

Ces quelques lignes, en conclusion d'une rencontre douce et féconde au fond (malgré qu'un peu douloureuse et agitée), pour vous dire ceci.

Depuis près de 20 ans, vous m'avez toujours aidé ( et j'ai essayé de vous aider) à monter vers un Dieu toujours plus lumineux et plus chaud.

Je compte, je <u>crois</u>, que cette belle et forte collaboration peut et doit continuer.

Et, en ce qui me concerne, soyez sûre que je continuerai (par besoin personnel interne) à vous tenir au courant de

These few lines as a conclusion to a sweet and basically fruitful meeting (although somewhat painful and troubled), to tell you this.

For almost twenty years, you have always helped me (and I have tried to help you) to go up toward an always more luminous and warm God.

I count on, I <u>believe</u>, that this beautiful and strong collaboration can and must go on.

And, as far as I am concerned, be sure that I will continue (because of a personal inner need) to keep you

ce que je vois, de ce que je pense, de ce que je fais, et de ce qui m'arrive.

Ma grande conviction, je vous le répète, est que rien ne résiste, dans l'Univers, à toujours plus de confiance et à toujours plus de foi.

Je viens de dire ma messe pour vous, — pour que vous trouviez <u>la paix</u>, - dans l'Unique Nécessaire et l'Unique Suffisant. "Dieu seul est pleinement bon", dit le Christ dans l'Evangile.

God bless you, dearest.

P.T.

informed about what I see, what I think, what I do and what happens to me.

My great conviction, I tell you again, is that nothing in the Universe can resist an ever greater trust and ever greater faith.

I have just said my mass for you — so that you may find <u>peace</u> in the One and only Necessary and the One and only Sufficient. "God alone is fully good," says Christ in the Gospel.

Les Moulins, 25 août, 1950

Dearest,

I have just received this morning your nice letter of Aug. 22. The precedent one (written from Paris) came also OK, but I did not know where to answer you. I was delighted that you could meet the Huxleys: I envy you. But perhaps for an exaggerated touch of "orientalism" in his philosophy of positivism or Weltanschauung, I like Julian; and it must be a treat to meet him "at home".

And I must thank you very much for the clippings — the one by Dr. Wright on "Outmoded language" impressed me decidedly:

il contient d'excellentes formules). Ici aussi, en France, toute l'intelligenzia chrétienne est très excitée (et décidément troublée) par les dernières manifestations romaines (Encyclique et dogme de l'Assomption). I get letters or anxious reactions from everywhere. Je crois voir à peu près ce que les théologiens romains ont en vue (empêcher le dogme chrétien de s'évaporer en s'ajustant aux vues modernes du Monde). Mais ils ont pris un bien dangereux langage pour s'exprimer: almost a challenge to the whole and to the most essential core of modern science. Le plus drôle est que, en définissant l'Assomption (qui n'a aucun fondement littéral dans l'Ecriture) ils affirment implicitement que le Dogme peut encore évoluer sur lui-même. Ils agissent en "évolutionnistes" en même temps qu'ils refusent d'accepter l'Evolution!

On savait que ces démonstrations "fundamentalistes" se produiraient à Rome cette année. je n'en suis donc pas

(it contains some excellent expressions). Also here in France all the Christian intelligentsia are very excited (and decidedly troubled) by the latest Roman manifestations (the Encyclical and the dogma of the Assumption). I get letters or anxious reactions from everywhere. I think I almost understand what the Roman theologians have in mind (to prevent the Christian dogma from evaporating while adjusting to the modern views of the World). But they used a very dangerous language to express themselves: almost a challenge to the whole and to the most essential core of modern science. Oddly enough, in defining the Assumption (which has no literal foundation in the Scriptures) they implicitly assert that Dogma may still evolve upon itself. They behave as "evolutionists" at the same time as they refuse to accept Evolution!

We knew that these "fundamentalist" demonstrations would take place in Rome this year. So they did not surprise

surpris, ni déconcerté. Mais si l'importance de continuer mes efforts se trouve accrue par le fait même, le travail n'en est pas rendu plus facile: sauf dans la mesure où les gens, par besoin de trouver une atmosphère respirable, se rapprocheront plus encore qu'avant du point de vue que je représente. Je ne prévois pas du reste encore, en qui me concerne, de "show down". On doit considérer comme mesure de précaution suffisante, à Rome, d'avoir empêché mon deuxième livre (en juin) de paraître. Tout de même; je me trouve un peu on the razor's edge . . .

Ici, vie très calme , dans un très beau cadre. J'ai mis en train un nouvel essai (Le coeur de la Matière: une analyse de mon évolution intérieure, depuis mon enfance) Mais je n'espère pas l'achever ici. La vie ici, malgré l'isolement géographique en pleine campagne, est coupée par toutes sortes de visites et de "parties"; ce qui a l'avantage de me faire mieux connaître l'Auvergne et de renouer avec ma parenté. Il faisait trop sec jusqu'ici; mais la pluie est arrivée hier.

Je pense toujours rentrer vers le milieu de septembre.

Hope to see you!

Good bye, dearest. My best regards to Sydney Cooper.

Yours,

P.T.

me, nor did they disconcert me. But if the importance of continuing with my efforts has increased by this very fact, my work has not been made easier: except in the measure in which people, because of their need to find an atmosphere in which they can breathe, will approach the point of view which I represent even closer than before. Beyond that I do not foresee, a "show down" that will concern me. In Rome they must think they have taken sufficient precautions by preventing my second book from being published (in June). All the same, I find myself a little on the razor's edge.

Here, in very beautiful surroundings, life is peaceful. I started a new essay (The Heart of Matter: an analysis of my inner evolution since my childhood). But I cannot hope to finish it here. Life here, in spite of the geographical isolation in the middle of the countryside, is broken up by all kinds of visits and "parties"; this has the advantage of making me know Auvergne better and of my getting reacquainted with my relatives. It was too dry until now, but the rain came yesterday.

I still think of returning around the middle of September . . .)

Barbour <u>may</u> arrive <u>here</u> this afternoon for a short visit. So strange!

Les Moulins, 9 sept., 1950

Dearest,

Just a few lines (answering, a bit late!) your letter of Aug.29) to tell you that I am decidedly leaving l'Auvergne this coming week. I am planning to come back on the 15th to Paris; so that you can reach me there à partir du 16.

I hope you will get this letter before you leave England!

Nothing new, here: except that my brother, his wife and "le jeune ménage" are back from a five-days motoring trip in the South, so that the house is alive again. Just now, the weather and the light are simply marvelous: almost a pity to leave! But I had a good rest. I could advance my paper. Better now to take a new *plunge in real life. I have no news from my colleagues; and I am curious (if not anxious) to appreciate what is going on in the religious and human world*

THEIR 1949–55 LETTERS

265

     *A bientôt, j'espère!*

    *Yours,*

    *P.T.*

*15 Rue Monsieur*
*Paris, 29 Sept., 1950*

*Dearest,*
    *After circling the world, you are now aiming back toward a beautiful nest in New-York.*
    *May your return be happy and successful. And may life start again for you as a new spring, — because for you (as for me) nothing, less and less, is of any final interest or value outside of the discovery and approach of the "Unique Nécessaire": the Oneness, I mean, into which Earth and Heaven are converging all through the World's joy and pain.*
    *I wish you a happy year, full of ideas, work and contacts; and I hope <u>it will be so</u>. Let me know what you do, what you think, what you see. I will do the same. You can help me tremendously, heart and brain, by this mutual exchange. Life, for both of us, is still going on. Let us always look ahead!*
    *Bon voyage, — et "à bientôt" in your new studio, perhaps!*

    *yours*

    *P.T.*

*I will send you my Essays*
*when they hatch, — of course.*

*Paris, Dec. the 15th, 1950*

*Dearest,*
    *Your dear letter of Dec.12 has arrived this morning, at the very moment I was going to write you, — both for Xmas and for the Ste Lucie feast. — Yes, on the morning of the 13, I said Mass for you, — and for everything in you and around you. And I am sure that God is blessing you; and that He will help both of us in the difficult, but beautiful task (the greatest of the Arts) of reaching and (in some way) achieving Him out of Matter. By the same mail (but by ordinary mail) I send you a copy (just ready) of my last essay, "Le Coeur de la Matière": a sort of history of my spiritual adventure, "the Quest of Spirit through Matter". I wonder whether you will like it, — but I think <u>you will</u>. Anyhow, these pages are an effort to express an internal evolution deeply impressed <u>by you</u>. And I think also that they are a fairly good expression of my present state of mind. — Really, at this point (an approaching terminal point) of my life, I may say that nothing counts any more for me except a passionate interest for a better vision and discovery-of-God-through-evolving-Matter: this effort bringing me to a warm and rich feeling of some mysterious essence of human Research — and love.*

*In fact, and in spite of many unpleasant affairs between French catholic thought and Rome (the Encyclical letter), I feel curiously eager, calm and decided to progress still further along my line. No breaking whatever, I think: but a smiling and stubborn tenacity. It is utterly impossible for me not to see (and to say) what I see. And I am so sure that God cannot be smaller than our biggest and wildest conceptions! Of course, I cannot print. But printing is not essential. I am glad you liked my last booklet (Julian Huxley told me very appreciative things about it). I plan to have its substance published in a scientific memoir next year, - after I have talked it (next january), in the course of five lectures, at the Sorbonne (Geology). — In spite of the present stiffening of Rome, it seems that the people, there, are less suspicious of my doings. Largely, perhaps, because I spoke loudly of taking a scientific trip to South Africa: back to material facts and to field, at last (they think). Concerning this african projects, everything seems to develop favorably, — except that I have still no answer from Dr. Fejos (Viking Fund). Scientifically speaking, I realize more and more that this is for me "the very thing to do". My idea would be, if the plan materializes, to go to America from South Africa, directly, — next autumn (leaving Paris for Africa in July next).*

*I am so glad to think that you are now settled in your new studio, — working once more on ivory and clay. May Inspiration visit you, — and commissions come, too! — I did not see Joe Davidson since your departure. But, last Monday, I had dinner at Mme. de Podestal (with André Billy and Marthe de Fels). A very pleasant party, — where, of course, we talked of you. Another one who talked of you (last sunday) is Julian Huxley, now in Paris for a week. I was extremely glad to see him again. He is developing big plans concerning a kind of Institute "for advanced Research in the line of Human Ideology"; and, of course, I feel deeply interested in the project.*

*Now, a few more news about various people. Leroy is probably staying in the University of Chicago (Dept. of Anatomy) six months more (that is up to the summer). — No direct news from Françoise Raphael (no address!): but, in his last letter, Leroy told me that she was extremely successful somewhere in Egypt (Cairo?). — Guy Dorget is going, as "consul général", to Florence; according to the mother of Laurette (I met her a few days ago) everything is all right now between him and Laurette. And I am so glad!*

*The Bégouëns are still here for a few days, — Max having been delayed for an important question of money. Just the same charming friends. Max has bought a little car for Simone — with the result that her life is going to be entirely improved in Casablanca.*

*I met Jeanine Dubosc in the street recently: just the same, too; except that one of their little boys (who was walking with her) is a big boy, by now.*

*No news from Eleonore!*

*Good bye, dearest! God bless you, — and me.*

*A merry Xmas to you, and a happy new year!*

*P.T.*

*Dearest,*

    *Your precious letter came a few days ago and nothing you could have sent me could have given me more pleasure. And thank you for the St. Lucias day mass. Im sure it will help me. And I shall be so especially interested in your new essay, "Le Coeur de la Matiere." I hope it comes soon.*

    *Oh Pierre, I have recently been reading <u>Le Milieu Divin</u>, and I understand why it has been loved by so many people, and it is of special delight to me because it somehow so vividly recalls to mind the YOU as you were when I first knew you, the eager searcher, the mystic who was so full of the love of the world and to whom God was so so close, so much a part of you that everyone who came in contact with you was aware of His Presence. I like to hold to this picture for it broadens my own feeling and vision.*

    *That same spirit went through your letters and how proud and happy I was when you said how much I helped to clarify your ideas, to talk them over with me and so it was OUR work - and you say so kindly in this last letter "the internal evolution so deeply impressed <u>by you</u>". Perhaps it was something like this that you meant when you wrote over and over again "what is born between us is <u>for ever</u>".*

    *Oh my dear and let me remember one other thing, do you remember our last Xmas in Peking, when we trimmed the little Xmas tree together? It was so gay and so FREE and Christ's spirit was so definitely there too. I believe Bob Drummond came in later and we laughed and had a little drink together. Oh dearest, I drink to you now with all my heart. My wish for the New Year is that you will find God more closely and deeply every day, which will help you to love the World even more than you have done.*

    *One thing you say in your last letter that I do not understand "the discovery of God through <u>evolving</u> matter. as I understand matter it does not evolve.Isnt it always H20 etc? to infinite combinations . . The mind, the spirit evolve; but does Matter? <u>Through</u> matter yes, but <u>evolving</u> Matter, what is that? surely you dont mean such things as the atom bomb. its true that it releases a new kind of energy in the world, which may have enormous consequences, is that the sort of thing you mean? I hope you will some day have time to answer this.*

    *Im deeply interested in this plan of Julian Huxley's to develope an Institute for research of Human Ideology" oh I do hope it will materialize and soon. there have been several such dreams but always something has happened. Maybe now there will be enough people who will realize the importance and necessity of such an Institute. It has always been my dream that you would spend your later years working in such a place with men whose minds and spirits would be an inspiration to you. wouldnt it be wonderful if it should happen?*

    *And I am SO happy that you are going to S. Africa. It will be so good for you to "get your hands in the Earth" again. I do think this is still very important for your spirit. Too long in Paris has never been so good. Will Barbour go with you? I hope you have heard from Frjos [sic] by now. I have not seen Ralph Linton but have heard from him, he seldom gets to New York, but I could make a POINT of seeing him if there was anything to be gained by it. Will it mean some time in the field? Oh Pierre it would make you feel so fres again . . I am more than delighted that it is going to happen.*

    *I had a long talk with Bob Drummond the other day . . . it was fun to talk of*

*Peking again . . I do love it and the city itself is always so <u>beautiful</u>. I can see you now as I once saw you in your rickshaw in your tall fur hat . . . looking rather severe and "catholic" but a beautiful expression on your face . . . as Bob and I talked so many such pictures came to my mind . . . really there was MUCH much that was very beautiful in those days. God bless you dearest, may the New Year bring you (and me too) great Peace.*

*Paris, Jan. 22, 1951*

*Dearest,*

   *Day before yesterday came your long letter of Jan.17, — full of news, one of the best being that you like your studio, and that you are working to interesting things. I was so surprised that you should have met Bob Drummond. I am afraid China is decidedly a closed paradise for him, now. What is he going to do? A week ago, I met Janine Dubosc, and her husband. She is actually running the curios shop of her father, here, in Paris; and apparently she likes it immensely: and she told me that the trade is still good, because there are so many people who sell their chinese things because they need money, and still so many other people who want to buy them!*

   *In my own life, nothing much new. Still a few clouds in Rome's direction, on account of some unwise newspapers articles (about my so called "clandestins"); but nothing serious. Presently I am busy with a series of lectures à la Sorbonne, concerning the phylogeny of Man. Five of them, on the whole, — always in the line du Phénomène humain, but from a slightly different angle, and with some new ideas. Je les rédige à mesure and when they are finished, I will get them printed in a strictly scientific review, so that Rome can say nothing. And I shall have a sufficient number of separates. — Besides, I see a rather large number of various people, of any kind; and discussing with them helps me a lot in advancing my own views. I am so much convinced, more and more, that nothing can be obtained any more in the line of making Man happier and better except by visualizing a "new dimension" of God: the God of a moving and growing World — the true Spirit of Matter. — I am glad you liked my last essay. And I am glad that I have written it out, too. That is certainly something which I had to express une bonne fois. Now I feel plus disponible for something else.*

   *The Bégouëns have left Paris a week ago, only, because Max was detained for some important financial reasons. And they were scarcely in Toulouse when Simone fell sick once more: some trouble in the ears, making her dizzy. I hope she is well again and able to reach Casablanca. But I have no news. Poor Simone! Always ailing somewhere, and yet so sweet.*

   *No recent news from Leroy, who is protracting his staying in Chicago (up to next autumn, I think). I don't think he is particularly happy (too much alone!), but his work is quite successful. I got only one letter from Françoise, who seems to enjoy very much Ismaïliah, her girls (she is teaching french), and le Club du Canal. She is much better there than at the UNESCO, anyhow.*

   *Finally, I got an answer from the Viking Fund. Nothing granted so far (the board does not meet before March); but the prospects are good. Really, going to the Australopithecidae sites would be the best thing to do for me just now: a new and important scientific work; and the best way to keep Rome quiet on my subject. Since I can not hide in Peking any more.*

*Good bye, dearest; and God bless you plenty!*

*Yours P.T.*

*Paris, 19 Février 1951*

Dearest,

Just received this morning your letter of Febr.14. It found me approximately in the same external and internal conditions as those I was in January. So far I have escaped flu (not so bad, but quite extensive, in Paris). And my work is slowly progressing along the same lines. The five lectures à la Sorbonne I enjoyed giving, much more than I could suspect, — probably because, for the first time, I succeeded in displaying systematically, before an audience, the whole of my scientific Weltanschaung as far as Man is concerned. In the last lecture, I emphasized the point that, from my <u>scientific</u> point of view, Man can not reach his evolutionary maturation unless, ahead of him, he can recognise (or at least hope) that the World is <u>not</u> closed, but <u>does</u> open on some higher type of existence (otherwise, he will get discouraged, bored, and stop pushing Life further on by research and creative effort). Rather "piquant" to deliver this kind of teaching in the very Amphithéâtre de Géologie de la Sorbonne. Anyhow, my friend Prof. Piveteau has already in hands my manuscript (fully ready) and the whole thing will be printed this summer, as a scientific memoir, in the "Annales de Paléontologie". So that Rome will not be able to reproach me to wander outside the field of Science.

On the other hand, the book on (or rather by) my sister ("L'énergie spirituelle de la Souffrance", with a preface by me) is supposed to be out on February 28 next. I will have a copy sent to you as soon as possible.

The lectures being finished, I am now slowly busy with the preparation of a small essay, precisely on the fundamental topic I told you the last time. To make people aware of the fundamental psychical change brought in our life by the newly born perception of a converging (or concentrating) Universe, in which, "à force d'organisation", the Weltstoff, is gradually becoming conscious(that is "intérieur" to itself). Really a new World, in which the whole set of human (and christian) problems and values are strangely transformed and "transfigured". My plan is to talk privately the subject before writing it, — for a selected type of readers, as usually.

Recently, a rather small catholic newspaper has still devoted a large number of columns to my ideas (rather nicely, but so stupidly!): two full articles already, and one more to come. But nothing dangerous or even unpleasant: nothing except a new evidence of the utter incapacity of the average catholic mind to grasp the new scientific vision of the Universe (so far).

Otherwise, nothing new. I am slowly preparing my south-african trip; but without still believing that it will actually materialize. And yet, to go down there would give me a kind of new scientific start. I <u>must</u> try to do it, by all means, par fidélité à la vie. God will decide and help.

Give my best regards to Bob Drummond and Rose. No recent news from the Bégouëns.

Met yesterday, in the street, Janine Dubosc. She looked all right, as usually. I did not hear anything about her family situation.

*I wrote to Malvina. Hope that the shock was not to much for her. In a way, she must feel more free for her own life, now.*

*Good bye, dearest,*

*yours*

P.T.

*Leroy is decidedly staying in Chicago University, Lab. of Anatomy, up to August or September.*

*Paris, March the 29th, 1951*

*Dearest,*

*So many thanks for your good Easter letter, — and for the "printed" mail (which has arrived yesterday). I hope that, in turn, you have well received the booklet of (on) my sister, which I sent you some three weeks ago. — I knew, from the newspapers (Time, specially), the de-motion of John Carter [Vincent]; and I understand your feelings. But don't forget how often to be demoted is the price and the indication of a next promotion. Before long, events may throw a new light on what should be the true and sound politic attitude in China. And, in the meantimes, Tangiers is certainly a most remarkable point of vantage. Please, tell Betty my warmest sympathy, if you happen to see her.*

*Here, as far as I am concerned, things are going on rather smoothly. In spite of some new unpleasing publicity (on my ideas) in the conservative catholic press, Rome seems to have lost interest (or hope) à mon endroit; and I keep on writing new Essays, — which however I do not spread except in the most discreet way. Two short papers are actually being stenciled. I will send them to you, when "out of press". On the other hand, my lectures à la Sorbonne will be published this coming summer in a highly technical Revue: so that nobody can accuse me to wander on non-scientific fields. — On the whole, I feel more and more interested (uniquely interested) on the double problem:*

*a) to discover an appropriate psychic energy for the human effort of pushing on evolution towards some "ultra-Human".*

*b) and consequently to "unveil" the face of the God we need for radiating such an Energy (of human self-and ultra-evolution).*

*Last week, I still had a long talk with Julian Huxley (on his way to the Jo Davidson's manoir, for the holidays) concerning the possibility of starting an "Institute (Research Institute) for Human Self-Evolution". Julian is going lecturing in the States next April (lectures at Washington and in Indiana); and he will meet Dr. Fejos (Viking Fund, — a good friend of mine) in New-York. In my mind, the South-African trip (si intéressant soit-il geologically speaking) is nothing else but a step (and a screen) in the direction of this new field of activities.*

*I have read carefully the pages of Swami Nikhilananda. I see quite well why you feel attracted. But at the same time I feel reluctant and unconfortable each time I happen to read these hindu teachings, because I have the impression that they are using our "occidental" words without understanding them properly (two weeks ago, somebody sent me the last publications of late Sri Aurobindo:*

*and I felt the same). — More precisely, it seems to me that, on three major points, the "oriental wisdom" is unsatisfactory:*

*a) on the idea of Matter (regarded as a kind of "jail", and not as a "matrix" of Soul and Spirit;*

*b) on the idea of Oneness (regarded, in spite of verbal statements, as the result of an "identification" resulting itself in a fusion (instead of a re-inforcement, through love) of the elementary "ego".*

*c) on the idea of evolution (implicitely reduced to an individual process of "perfection", — no consideration being given to the probability of a steady and universal birth of consciousness, through a better arrangement of "Matter", in the World as a whole).*

*When Swami Nikhil. speaks of God (what kind of God? "conscious and supra-personal? or unconscious and impersonal"?) "unfolding <u>himself in the World process</u>", I suspect that this expression "World process" has not much more meaning for him than for a Roman theologian.*

*But I know that on this ground I may be prejudiced, and wrong.*

*In a way or another, the only thing which counts, for me, is the development in human Consciousness of a superior form of Love, able to act as a "universal" motor for human activity. What I object to the Eastern mystics is a tendency to undermine true Love by a deep-set confusion between a pantheism of identification (excluding love, by structure "God <u>All</u>") and a pantheism of unification (based upon Love: "God <u>All in All</u>"). If I am unfair to them, I am ready to apologize.*

*Besides, nothing much. Nothing from Françoise (apparently O.K. in Ismaïliah). Nardi (do you remember him) has succeeded in leaving Peking, and is now à Lyon, jobless. He wrote me that Monestier (and Bussière?) could not get their visa (when the visa is granted, one has to leave within 24 hours!). Pei is the head of the Geological Survey(!). — Met Janine Dubosc in the street —unchanged. Leroy will be back from Chicago next summer.*

*And my plans are the same. Leaving Paris at the beginning of July, — if nothing happens before. To watch on me in South Africa, I am counting on Barbour and Rhoda. — Then, if God permits, New-York, — to see Fejos and the Viking Fund.*

*Good bye, dearest. You don't tell me how you can work. Hope that everything is all right in this field.*

*God bless you!*

*Yours*

*P.T.*

*321 East 58th Street*
*New York 22, April 3, 1951*

Dearest,
*The beautiful little book arrived just in time for my Easter, and I do thank you so much for sending it to me. It is very beautiful and I feel almost as if I had a new friend. I have not read it all yet, but enough to get the whole quality of your dear sister. What an inspiration she is.*

*I did not write to you immediately because I guess it is a sort of flu that I've had and just did not feel up to letters last week — and still do not feel very well. It seems so hard to get over it once it really gets hold of you.*

*And yesterday I received your very good letter of March 29. It was good of you to read that thing of Nikhilananda's and to write so fully about it, naturally I'm SO interested in what you say. I don't think your are quite fair to him. He belongs to the same group (?) that Aldous Huxley is interested in — and as I understand him, his beliefs are more like yours than anything that I have found. I want so much to answer your objections, but would like to think more about it first. I realize that some of the things seem to me not important in as far as LIVING is concerned — they seem (your objections) to do with the remote inner workings that are so often interpreted to suit one's temperament. However, as you know I am NOT a theologian, nor very interested in them. The main thing I get is that we have to achieve the world through our efforts of work, research, arts, etc. And the closer we are to God, the better will be the results of our efforts. And they help to show you how to feel God and to be closer to Him. I mean in the way of meditation and reading and thinking and self-discipline — things that I have not found in Christian teaching. Or do you know any books that give one that kind of help? And as for LOVE! I wish I could understand what you mean by it. It seems to me that both Christian nations and individuals TAKE what they want and to hell with the other fellow. But probably I'm feeling pretty low today so this is not the time to answer these things. For I'm really SO very keen about what you say of discovering an "appropriate psychic energy", etc. We MUST find that energy if Life is to go on — or rather Evolution — and to unveil the face of the God needed for radiating that energy, and, Pierre, the USUAL Christian God is NOT big enough for that. We must find a greater face for HIM, and while I admit so much of what you say about the Oriental wisdom in general, it seems to me this group of Vedantists comes closer to something BIG. Oh how I do wish that we could talk . . but I wonder when that will be???*

*Also am simply delighted that you saw and talked of the Research Institute with Julian Huxley . . do you feel that maybe the Viking Fund would be interested in it? Wouldnt it be SPLENDID if it could be realized? You MUST take part in it if it does materialize . . "You must"?? you know dear what I mean, I HOPE you will.*

*So Mrs. de Terra is going to South Africa with you. I suppose I have known all along that she would, so I should not be so upset. I was SO in hopes you were going to have a few months of freedom to be yourself again, but probably this is what YOU want so I should be happy about it. I am so sorry my encounter with her last summer was so unsuccessful. It seems to me that now she has EVERYTHING that used to be mine, the daily visits, the sharing of all the intimate things and friends — well, all that makes life sweet and worthwhile, now that she has it all she could be a little more generous so that I could feel happier about your being with her so constantly. Perhaps this is also a part of the lesson that I have to learn. And you can see I have not yet conquered my EGO or I would not still feel so unhappy about it all. Am glad that Barbour is going, or is he?*

*Malvina Hoffman came in to see me the other day. I thot she looked very tired . . . and she talked all the time about her husband . . which is rather strange as I really do not know her so well . . It seems that he has married his psycho-analyst . . I dont know how recently . . but he is still very dear to her and I could see that her heart was not happy. I guess all Life is like that . . so I dont know why we should expect anything else.*

*As for my work? Yes, I work every day, and sometimes I think it is good - the ivory is very brittle so it goes slowly - but I have just finished a group. The sort of thing that I've had in mind a long time - Brotherhood of Man - only this time I've made female figures representing the Yellow, white and black races: females, clasping hands and back of them a figure - not Christ exactly nor Buddha - but representing the SPIRITUAL side which is absolutely necessary if any "Brotherhood" is going to exist. Most everyone likes it, and some like it very much. The design is good; any way it is the most successful thing of the sort I've done. What am I doing with it???? It is only 20 inches high .. well perhaps SOME day .. Ive done several small things, may be Ill have enough for a small show next fall .. Lilo Komor comes to work with me twice a week,..and I like that. Ive been doing sculpture entirely .. it is so good to have everything to work with .. and I don't know for how long I can have this studio .. in fact I have NO idea what I am going to do, either this summer or next fall .. some how I feel so sure that I will be helped to SEE what to do when the time comes, that I am not worrying .. The people who have the house here are going to California July 1st .. so if the place should be taken by someone who wants the studio too, I'll have to go .. I'm just here from month to month, but I've enjoyed the winter, and I'm sure things will work out.*

*I shall probably write again about the Hindu stuff, and I know we really agree so much .. Forgive this letter, perhaps if I felt better I would not send it .. I don't know, but I guess there isn't anything very much been said . . .*

*God bless you and keep you well and happy.*

*Paris, May the 6th, '51*

*Dearest,*

*So many thanks for your two letters of April 26 and May first, which arrived just in time for my 70(!) years. Yes, I remember so well ten years ago: the cocktail, and the excursion (with Eleonore, I think?) behind Pi yung ssu. Well, it's getting rather old, now. For me (and for you) I pray God that it should give us the supreme gift "celui de finir en beauté" — as a testimony for the vision to which I have devoted my life: the vision of an Universe converging, by its whole power of arrangement, into a loving oneness. — I am so terribly glad that you should now become more sensitive to the "love of God". And, by all means, take light and warmth where you find it. Against the Swami I have nothing; except that (à tort ou à raison) I think that the God-Ocean (of identification) does not "radiate" such a true and efficient Love as a God-Centre (of unification): although I recognize that a supreme Centre has precisely the mystical proprieties of an Ocean (but in a "corrected" way). The essential thing is that you should feel growing, in you and around you, a sort of loving essence of everything, in which you could progress through every effort, every pain, and every joy. This is the road to happiness.*

*Here, in Paris, life is essentially the same. Once more I almost came in serious trouble with Rome on account of some unwise friend candidly showing to the General one of my last essays. But everything seems to be settled, by now. Still, I think it's Providence which sends me to South-Africa (as, before, to China). Better for me to disappear for a short time. Along this line, my plans keep provisionnally the same: leaving in July, reaching N.Y. in November, to report at* the Viking Fund. After what, a blank. Circumstances must decide. In any case, I am glad that you can keep your studio. With so many friends back in America, you will have a pleasant summer. But what about Eleonore? Not a word from her. Leroy is coming back to Paris in August (by l'Ile-de-France). I think he had a successful time (although not particularly cheerful) in Chicago. In a letter (received two days ago) he tells me that Françoise was planning a trip to Chypre, for Easter. I hope everything is all right in her prospects for next year.

From China, news are rather grim. In Tientsin, les Hautes-Etudes are now taken by the new governement, — and, in Shanghai, l'Aurore also is "occupée". A complete end to the missionary work in China. So far, the native priests seem to behave quite well as a whole. Did I tell you that Nardi is back, — jobless and moneyless, in France? Monestier could not get his visa out, so far. Nor Bussière. — Pei seems to be most influential (acting director) in the Geological Survey.

I stop here: Lejay is coming to take me in his car to the Institute.

Be happy, and God bless you!

yours

P.T.

Paris, June the 8th, 1951

Dearest,

I have just received this morning your good long letter of June 5, — and two days before the "Nature of the Universe". No book could bring me more interest and pleasure, just now. Of course, I am not able to have a really personal idea on such astro-physical subjects. But the general perspective supplies me with a good pattern (and the proper scale) for expressing my still growing and improving views on what I call "La convergence de l'Univers": this expression being used to express the peculiar drift towards increasing aggregation and arrangement which pushes selectively the Weltstoff (and forces it, somehow) into living forms. Nothing better than the discovery of this particular and peculiar movement of the Universe in the direction of constantly higher types of arrangement (and consequently of consciousness) is able, I think, to create around us the special atmosphere we presently need in politics as well as in religion.

And, speaking of religion, I am terribly glad that you should feel growing in you the sense of the universal and ever-growing presence of God. Along this direction, go on as freely as possible, — following your own instinct, — collecting your "honey" where you find it. Just keep in mind that "the sense of Unity" is a powerful energy (or, if you prefer, a very strong drink.) to be used with "discernement"; — but that you risk nothing as long as you use this big force as an incentive to be more personal, more active, more "loving".

I am glad that you can keep your studio, — and work. I did not discuss your project of "Brotherhood", because it is not easy to criticize usefully a sketch: but I hope you have materialized some "ébauche" [rough sketch], — and I will love to see it this coming fall. I suppose your "Girl with fawns" is a development of the similar Woman with a fawn you made in Peking, some fifteen years ago. Funny how long it takes for an idea to take its due form. I experience it every day.

Here, I am preparing slowly my departure: leaving England (Southampton) on July the 12th. I was surprised to discover that, because I have been living in China, my american visa has to be delivered by Washington! which means a rather long procedure. People, at the american Embassy, are helpful and charming. But the red tape is there.

Finally, things have settled down peacefully in Rome; largely, I suppose, because they are glad to see me deep again in the study of old bones, down there. Many thanks for the news about Eleonore. Well, everything is all right, since she has got a new car! — Malvina wrote me that she had been quite sick (sciatica,- etc.), but felt well again. Does not say anything about a coming to France. — Barbour will meet me in July in London, and then follow me by plane to Johannesburg. — A few days ago, I met in the street d'Andurain (unchanged) who told me that Roland de Margerie had just had a very high promotion in the Foreign Office. More lucky was he than the Vincents, — who, I hope, will have their lucky time before long, they too.

God bless you, dearest!

yours

P.T.

Johannesburg, Sept. 1, '51

Dearest,

Since weeks I did not write you; — and yet your nice letter of June 20 reached me in Paris just a few days before my departure. But these few days were precisely particularly hectic. And, since this time, I have been more or less continously on the way, — a very bad condition for letters.

In fact (and largely thanks to the helpful and calming presence of Rhoda) the journey is developing all right. Scientifically speaking, I am extremely interested by everything I see here in the line of both continental and human genesis. And, as a result of this new contact with field and fieldwork, I feel a kind of mental rejuvenation (or excitation): the favourable atmosphere for a further (?) development of the ideas (or Weltanschaung) I try so hard to focuss and to express, since fifty years.

Paris had been grey and rainy, from October to July, almost continously. — It was a relief and a joy, therefore, to find here, for a whole month, a perfectly blue sky, and a continously bright sun, with a crisp and dry air. In fact, exactly the Peking's weather in early spring, before the dust wind; and exactly the Peking's colours, too: plenty of pink blooming fruit-trees on a grey landscape.

Since five weeks, I have taken several trips, — either northward (in the direction of the Limpopo), or southward (in the Kimberly area). And I feel really "caught" and lured by this enormous and enormously worn out country, where the roads and the tracks can strike, right ahead, through endless "étendues" of a thorny jungle, — so perfectly similar to the Abyssinian bush. — A curious mixture of contrasts and similarities with dear old Asia.

Since my departure of Paris, I am practically cut from the "thinking" world. Very few letters from America or Europe (this is the holidays time); and

*here, besides technical discussions with geologist colleagues, very few opportuni-
ties for interesting contacts. A big difference with Peking, indeed! — Probably due
to their isolated location at the end of a continent, the people here seem to be
curiously absorbed in their petty dissensions (white against natives, — Africaans
against British, — bigotted Dutch Church against any form of spiritual liberty).*

     *To be stuck here for a long time would be unpleasant. For a few weeks, I
don't mind. On the contrary, I enjoy rather the feeling to be quietly here for a
while, — at a reasonable number of hundred of miles from Rome. A rare and fine
opportunity to collect and consolidate oneself internally, — far from any foreign
pressure.*

     *I wish and hope that you had a resting summer, — and a constructive
one, too. — Substantially, my plans remain the same: to be in New-York before
Xmas. But, due to the uncertain schedule of the boats from here to America, it is
still impossible to fix a definite date for the journey. En tous cas, "à bientôt"!*

     *Bien affectueusement,*

*yours*

*P.T.*

*New York, Nov. 29th, 1951*

*Dearest,*

     *At last, I have arrived, two days ago. As you can see from the envelop, I
am located this time 980 Park Avenue (84th Street) (Butterfield 8.6200) - because
no room for me at Riverside. In fact, the location is quite convenient, since I will
have to work 71st str. at the Viking Foundation. — Apparently, Paris has become
too hot for me these days; and I must try to find a shelter here for the time being.
— I will explain you. — I may be here for months.*

     *Since I am rather much out, in town, give your phone number (and name)
here, at the gate's office, if by chance they answer you that I am not home. —*

     *A très bientôt,
enfin!*

*Yours*

*P.T.*

After working about eight weeks in Africa, Teilhard set out for North America by way of
Buenos Aires, Rio de Janeiro, and Trinidad. As he later explained, this roundabout route
gave him a chance to experience, at least briefly, the geological and anthropological view-
points to be gained from the perspective of those areas. In New York City, for the winter,
Teilhard sometimes had tea with Lucile. These visits became less and less frequent. Apparently she knew he often saw Rhoda de Terra also and told him she felt superseded. He
pointed out that he was an old, sick man who needed care and that the role of nurse did not
suit Lucile. Teilhard's American biographers explain the role of Rhoda de Terra at that time:
"She kept an eye out for his health, arranged his social calendar, deposited him and picked
him up at many of his appointments, took care of his nuisance errands, introduced him to
her literary cousins, the Roger Strauses, and . . . avoided prying into his relations with his
Order. (Lukas, 307)." A selection from Teilhard's letters were published as Letters to Two
Friends. These friends are not identified in the book; the first is Ida Treat (1926-52 letters)
and the second is Rhoda de Terra (1938-50 letters).

*Undated*
[perhaps November 1951]

THEIR
*1949–55*
*LETTERS*

277

*Dearest,*

The last evening you were here, you said that you were concerned with the love of God, and it was said, as I remember, to explain any difficulties that we may have in understanding and agreeing with each other. I have been thinking about it a lot, and at least to me, it makes things clearer. I too am concerned with my love of God; not perhaps to the extent that you are but to an increasing degree. So it is not in the "WHAT" that we have trouble but in the "HOW"!!! There is where all our differences of opinion lie. I believe that by living as I think HE made me, in the midst of all His creatures, with the same problems and the same opportunities to err and also the same opportunities to overcome, by living to the fullest with all the personality that He has given me, that seems to me my duty; and the fullness of my life and its riches are the proof of the depth of my love. (I don't mean that they must be tangible riches, a most humble soul can be a complete expression of love). You have chosen another path, more sheltered and more concentrated. Dearest dont think I am trying to compare us; you have gone so infinitely much further than I . . that if that were all that was necessary to prove the superiority of your WAY, well you would win without an argument . . Also I really am not trying to argue . . Im only writing this out to try to make my thoughts more clear . . and if by chance there is something new, or at least expressed differently, then naturally I want to share it with you. As I want to share everything that is beautiful with you . . That was one thing that was so very hard when you left . . I am so glad dearest that you are going to see that glorious country, and I couldnt help wanting dreadfully to see it with you . . .

It seems to me that your way limits most everything!!! It limits your own possibilities of life - a large and important part of your personality is left untouched or uncultivated . . . Which does seem to matter IN YOU, for you have so much, you are so rich, IN SPITE of this. All our difficulties come through the problem of finding a working ground for these two WAYS. It seems to me that yours limits us - but you do not think that it does, so then perhaps the problem is mine principally — to see always more clearly your way. I know that it is my blindness that makes the difficulty . . not entirely, for you too sometimes do not see clearly. Probably I am too much concerned with temporal things, without realizing how deeply my wants may lead us from the ultimate achievement of a perfect love of God. Through habit I take certain things for granted, just as you take other things. You are trying a new path which you think has greater possibilities, and I still think that the old way of living as completely as we can the ordinary life and rising above it is the greater good. It is all because I do not fully understand your way. You cannot separate your love of God from LIFE, but how much you can give to another Life is still not clear. But the fact that we are really wanting the same end may make it easier for us to understand and amalgamate our two points of view. How much can we share to the greatest good of all is the problem. Which seems to me to mean, how much can we unite, where do you put the limit? You have often said there is no limit to the amount we may love, how is that love to express itself? Isn't love uniting? You have said in "personalistic Universe" "It is most important to give full expansion to the love created by two human beings". It is to understand the deepest meaning of these things that I am giving my thoughts. I know you have not found answers to all my questions but I want you to believe that always I am trying to work with you, not argue against you. You always say "have patience" and you must be right, for surely I see more than I did a year ago, probably next year I shall see even more.

*Glacier Park, Aug. 14, 1952*

*Dear Lucile,*

*I write you without any table under my pad, - so you must excuse my handwriting. Since weeks I have left you without any news, and you may wonder what is happening to me. Nothing wrong, — on the contrary. But the constant agitation of a journey, which, on the whole, has been extremely pleasing, — more interesting, in fact, than I expected. — On my way out, I spent two days with the George Gaylord Simpsons, in their nice little house, in New Mexico; and Dr. Simpson introduced me to the most famous geological formations of the San Juan Basin. — Then, I settled at Berkeley, where I renewed close contact with Chaney, Camp, Stirton, and others. Mrs Camp was near Santa Barbara (where her grand-children had measles), — and I did not see her.— Met von Lessing, twice; — and saw a good deal the Bardacs, absolutely unchanged, — and perfectly happy in a nice appartement. Jacques is now à la Banque d'Indochine, and vaguely hopes to spend a few months in France (Mrs. Coatman is living in the Jacques "garçon-nière" rue Galilée, in Paris, — and has bought for Jacques an appartement in Passy). — Presently, I am spending a few days in Glacier Park, in order to see some critical geological formation (the exact equivalent and replica of the "Sin-ian" beds of Nankou, in the Western Hills). - Then I plan to spend a few more days in Maine (at the holidays place of a sister of Rhoda), — my return to N.Y. being arranged for the first days of September. — By that time, you will already be in Europe (Majorque?). I wish this new experience will give you a fresh creative impulsion. And, knowing you, I think it will. —Personally, I come back from this trip with a still clearer perception of what can be the final contribution of my life: namely to promove in Man a more distinct consciousness of the big "cosmic" movement which forces and attracts Mankind to converge (to "reflect") more and more on himself. — I feel so much more convinced, — even after these few weeks of new experiences — that any advance along the line of this new humanism means a complete "renaissance" of human behaviour and human power of adora-tion. — No news from Rome (I hope the people here will keep quiet, since I am apparently concentrating on Sciences). Aux Etudes, Jouve is more and more sick (now the heart seems to yield.), and is confined in the hospital, rue Oudinot. You know how much I like him. ——*

*Good-bye, good journey! have a grand and fruitful time! and God bless you for everything!*

*En grande affection*

*Pierre*

Sometime in early (?) November, Lucile returned from a painting trip with Flo Davidson (wife of the sculptor Jo Davidson). Subsequently in a brief journal entry she noted that a lunch with Teilhard had been "all wrong."

*New York, Nov. the 30 1952*

*My dear Lucile,*

*Next Wednesday, I am not free, as I expected to be. — Will you not be angry with me if I come only the following Wednesday (December 10th)?*

*In fact, I might force somewhat my schedule of the week, and see you before. — But, after a year of experience, I wonder whether it would not be better and more constructive, for <u>both</u> of us, if I spaced a little my visits. — To see you is good for me. But, at the same time, it still disturbs me.*

*Maybe, with some "spacing" as I say, the strain will disappear and the relationship between you and me will become (as it can and must be) a really conforting and relaxing friendship. — We still have so much to receive from each other and to give!*

*Shall we try? — still going ahead, for God and Peace?*

*Please, do not read in these lines anything but an effort to keep us together in a more stable and constructive way. Pardon me if, unwillingly, I hurt you. ——*

*And in any case believe me*
*always*

*yours,*

*P.T.*

---

Teilhard called on Lucile the day after Christmas; Lucile's note on her calendar was succinct: "Nice".

---

*Jan. 8th, '53*

*Dear Lucile,*

*Finalement, ma fin de semaine est plus occupée que je ne pensais!. (Peut-être même vais-je me décider à un nouvel essai pour me séparer de mon "parasite", — Asmodée, je l'appelle, en souvenir des exorcismes de Loudun, - c.f. A. Huxley).*

Finally, my week end has been busier than I thought! . . . (Perhaps, even, I am going to make up my mind to do another essay to get rid of my "parasite" - I call it Asmodée, in memory of the exorcismes of Loudun, cf. A.Huxley).

*I will telephone you at the beginning of the next week. — Friday the 16th would be a good day for me. — I will bring you the book and a separate.*

*No fresh news from Paris. I hope you have heard, by now, from the Vincent's. And I hope mostly that you are in a creative mood. — Moi-même je tourne autour d'un sujet d'article: but I could not <u>catch</u> it exactly so far. I will explain you.*

*yours,*

*P.T.*

---

The "Asmodée" of Teilhard's January 8th note is the evil spirit known as Ashmadai in Jewish demonology.

*Oh Pierre, I wish we could be at ease with each other! There are so many things I would like to discuss with you. For instance, I was just reading the following, "According to Hindu theory of evolution, nothing is superadded in the course of evolution, but what is only potentially existing becomes unfolded. The whole of the tree potentially exists in the seed. Swami V. rightly defined religion as the manifestation of divinity already in man. To unfold this divinity already existing within is the end of evolution and the goal of life. Does this differ very much from your thought? It seems to me to be the core of what I believe. "The kingdom of heaven is within us".*

*I have no practical suggestions for seeing each other. It seems to me that is YOUR problem. But any real friendship must be built on honesty and MUTUAL consideration.*

*If it is all too difficult for you, at least let us not stop on a note of accusations and confusion. There has been too much creative beauty in the past. And besides we know that above all else we are both trying to realize God in this life, and that our way to this realization is through Jesus Christ, even though I do not always understand His meaning. But to me He means Faith and Hope and Love, and the greatest of these is love. And as you have so often written and said to me, the more we love God, the more we can love each other (and in the best way).*

*May God give you Peace, Pierre.*

*As always,*

*Dear Lucile,*

*I have well received your sweet letter of Sunday.*

*In a few days, I will try to write and suggest you a few constructive views, — with the help of God.*

*In any case, as you say, it should not be (and it will not be) any bitterness, nor any confusion.*

*But only, for both of us, more Peace and a higher vision.*

*Just now, may you be in Peace, too.*

*yours*

*P.T.*

*Lucile dear,*

*Since your letter reached me, I have been thinking (and also praying) over the kind of "impasse" in which we find ourselves: a paradoxical situation, indeed, since it should be so simple for two people who have such deep feelings of friendship for one another to be talking and thinking constructively together.*

*Well, emotions are strange. And the truth is that we still disturb each other whereas, both of us, we need absolutely "peace".*

*Last year, we have tried frequent meetings; and it was not so good. Should we try to meet less often, — let us say once a month? Maybe, if we have a definite, but spaced, time for our meetings we shall have so much to talk about than we can keep, naturally, on an even emotional plane.*

*Now, maybe you will not feel that my solution is your solution. If so, you must tell me. And if, just now, meetings are too disturbing, there are always letters. Write me one of those anyway. And tell me whether we shall meet the next month. And, if we do, let us try to have a grand time chatting about our projects, and about Eastern versus Western conceptions of Evolution, and look-ing at your paintings, which I like more and more.*

*God bless you, Lucile, and may He help our common effort towards the development of an ever loving World!*

*yours always*

*P.T.*

*— The Wiley's have telephoned me. I see them tomorrow.*

*— Received also a phone call (yesterday) from Claire Tadjan (Hirschberg). She is apparently now, with a job, in Brooklyn. I will probably see her before long.*

*January 31, 1953*

*Dear Pierre,*

*Thank you for your nice letter. I also have been thinking and praying about us and trying to understand the situation.*

*I know I have been very much at fault. When I have so sincerely thought that I had conquered my Ego, some little thing happens and it is as if the Devil rushes in and takes possession of me and pulls out all the stops of pride and vanity and jealousy and pos-sessive-love, all of them — as you know only too well. So until I have really mastered myself, there is no use in our trying to meet. I must read and meditate and pray — I don't know how long it will take — a month, two months? Sometimes I get very discouraged at the Slowness of my spiritual progress. But I want it so much, and I know God will help me. IF I do my part. If you have any suggestions for reading or discipline, I should be most grateful for them.*

*And thank you for what you say about my painting. I have just started a new canvas of the arched street in Morocco. It poses a lot of problems, but I am having a grand time with it — am also doing a statuette, small portrait which I had promised some time ago. So I am busy.*

*My darling cousin Mary Wood Gilbert spent a week with me from the 18th to the 25th. I love her dearly — so that was very nice. We had some fine times. This afternoon I go to the Bill Mayers — and then to the Clubbs for dinner. So the days are going too fast.*

*I am sure that you understand my position. It seems to me the only thing to do, and it is I think always wonderful to hear from you. And may I write for a date when I think the time has come?*

*The Viking Fund*
*New York, February 3, 1953*

*Lucile dear,*

*Thank you for your sweet and perfect letter of yesterday.*
*I needed it, and it was full of peace.*
*Because it seems to me that we are now closer to God.*

*Write me when you like (when you feel it is time).*
*I am always there.*

*yours,*

*P.T.*

*Good luck for the new canvas! I am waiting for an inspiration myself.*

---

Three weeks later, on the morning of February 28th, Teilhard telephoned Lucile. Later that day she wrote on her calendar, "He said he was not well so he needed my help." They met in her studio apartment where she showed him her new work — the canvas he had referred to on February 3. She was pleased by his enthusiastic response.

---

*March 2, 1953*

PT, *dearest friend,*

*No word from this morning which I hope means that you are getting along well.*

*I just want to repeat what I said to you the other day, that you must go on as you have been with Rhoda, and there not be any "shadow" between you.*

*At LONG last, I think my prayers are being answered, and I am beginning to feel more free than I have for a very long time, and this will bring a real peace.*

*As for coming to see me this week, you must feel absolutely no pressure about it. Only if you feel well enough and would like a discussion about the East and West — or anything — but there is no hurry about it, so take your time. Only let me know whether to expect you on Friday either by phone or send a note. It would be nice to have a word to know how you are getting along.*

*May God bless you and make you well and happy.*

*I place my hands upon your head and give you my deep and loving blessing — and to Rhoda too.*

*Always*
*your*
*Lucile*

*The Viking Fund*
*March 14th 1953*

*Lucile dear,*

*Just a few lines to tell you that I still do not feel well in my nerves, — but that I do not forget you. In fact, if something may help my cure, it is to know that you are happy and working constructively. Write me everything you are doing, because I should like to keep in touch with you and telephoning seems to be still straining my nerves. I am impatient with myself, and one of the reasons I want so much to be well again is that I feel that when we resume our little meetings everything will be clearer and stronger for us than since a long while.*

*Nothing new as far as I am concerned. I try to advance little by little the scheme of my book. But my ideas are not much clear at this time. Received a letter from my cousin. Nothing about the Bégouëns.*

Très affectueusement,

as ever,

P.T.

New-York, March 24, 1953

Lucile dear,
   Merci, tellement, for your sweet letter of March 18. It brought me warmth and peace: just what I still need so much these present days. Dr. Simard keeps quite optimistical on my condition. In fact I am still the easy prey of the most amazing variety of "anxieties", — an old disease of mine, which (if only I was a more spiritual man!) should force me into an evergrowing "abandon" in the hands of God. Pray for me. I am praying for you.
   Otherwise, I try to keep working and reading in the line of my book(?) on the Future of Man. And, so doing, I become more and more convinced that, "after a million of years" (as Ch. Galton-Darwin puts it in his recent booklet, at Doubleday) the whole human evolutive activity will be so deeply charged with (and transformed by) new energies of a "mystical" type (Sense of the Universe, Sense of Evolution, Sense of the Species, Sense of God) that nothing can be distinctly forseen by us today, — but everything expected. This is the very point overlooked both by C. Darwin and Julian Huxley ("Evolution in Action"). Received lately a very nice letter of J. Huxley, by the way.
   Autre chose, rather annoying. Unexpectedly the doctors have discovered that Rhoda has developped a rather large "fibrome" (not malignant); and she will be operated on April 1st (at the Doctors Hospital, East 86th Str.). In the occurence, she is extraordinary calm, a large half of this calm being derived from a peculiar sense of the presence and the action of "God", which I feel ashamed not to experience at the same extent. I know you will "pray" for her. Normally, she should not stay longer than ten days in the hospital.
   A week ago, I have seen Ida: en excellente forme. She had a letter (a good one) from Simone, who is in Casa (Max was still en Guinée).
   A bientôt d'autres nouvelles, amie. Tell me if you are going to be in town around Eastern. I must see your new paintings.

   En grande affection,

   P.T.

The Viking Fund
New York, April 3, 1953

Dear Lucile,
   Just a few lines on this remarkable paper to thank you for your sweet letter of March 30, — and to tell you that (unless something unexpected does happen) I will come to see you next wednesday, vers 3 o'clock.
   Finally, and for an accidental reason, the operation of Rhoda had to be postponed. She will be operated at the beginning of the next week. I admire more and more her quiet reaction to the "évènements" — in spite, of course, of the disapointment.

*Today I am going to Frick's at Roslyn (Long Island) We did not see each other since a long time; and he is anxious to show me his last palaeontological discoveries.*

*Received a letter from my cousine. No special news, except that she seems to have found an interesting (or even captivating) subject of work (the life of somebody, some hundred years ago, I understand). And that is probably what she needed the most just now: a constructive interest for her mind.*

*A very happy Easter day to you!*

*En grande affection,*

*P.T.*

*N.Y., April 18th, 1953*

*Lucile, dear,*

*Since I saw you the days have passed in such an unpredictable way that I made no plans. — In the meantimes Rh. got a slight complication, — so that she is still in the hospital (much better, however).*

*I will phone you next Tuesday or Wednesday, to decide with you for an afternoon.*

*On the whole, I feel better, and I can work with a clearer mind. Still, there is need and room for more "peace & drive". — You will help me with both.*

*Bien affectueusement*

*as ever*

*P.T.*

*N.Y., May 8, 1953*

*Lucile, dear,*

*Day after tomorrow, you will probably be out town. -*

*These few lines to wish you a happy birthday! And, whatever might be the value of my mass, — to tell you that my mass of the 10th will be for you:*

*— that the Presence of God should keep on growing in you;*

*— that, in the light, the warmth, and the peace of this Presence we should help each other and keep "converging" constructively!*

*To many returns!*

*En grande affection,*

*P.T.*

*Next week, the best day for me to see you
would be Friday (3 p.m.). — Phone me
at the Foundation if the day is inconvenient for you.!*

On June 21st Lucile noted in her Line A Day: "Nice dinner." It was probably their last visit before Teilhard left for South Africa. In August he wrote to her at the Thousand Islands resort area on the upper St. Lawrence where she was vacationing.

*Dear Lucile,*

*Since almost a month, I am back in Africa. It is more than time that I should send you some news about the journey. You, you probably are in the peace of the Thousand Islands. I, I am once more, not exactly in the field, but in close contact with old mother Earth: and you know that, for me, there is no better way for rejuvenation, and even "adoration". So that we are not so far apart as it would seem.*

*So far, everything is going all right in my trip. Between New-York and Capetown, the crossing was long (no stop at all, and nothing in sight, for 18 days, except the small islands of Ascension and St. Helena); but the boat, although small, was perfectly confortable, and we have entered Capetown by a "spring" day. In fact, we had still a few cold winter days a week ago. But here, on the high and dry plateau, the atmosphere is so dry and the sky so blue (exactly like in Peking) that even a little freezing is not unpleasant.*

*Here I have found back, with a real joy, a warm group of fellow geologists and palaeontologists; and I have the comforting feeling that I can really do something in directing the Wenner-Gren financial blood to the right places. Since two years, the problems concerning Early Man have certainly become clearer in S. Africa; and an eager team of young searchers is just there, ready to be used. Somewhat a duplication of the situation I have found in China thirty years ago! A few days ago, I have re-visited (some 300 miles of here) a small "Choukoutien" where exhaustive excavations have been started in april, with the support of the Wenner-Gren Foundation. Most interesting, — although no human bony remains have been found so far. In a week, I plan to go to N. Rhodesia in order to visit another strategic place. All this keeps me busy, — without preventing me (on the contrary) from maturing further on, as much as I can, the "philosophical" and religious side of my ideas. As you know, Early Man, for me, is only the gate leading to "Future" Man, — the existence of such a "Future Man" being, in my opinion, the strongest foundation on which to build the new faith in God which is so urgently needed by the Man of today. — I have outlined, these very days, the sketch of a new paper. One more ——*

*From France, very few news (no wonder, now, with the strike!) Everybody I know is out of Paris, just now. The old Comte Begouën sent me a most touching letter (he is now 90 years old), — but without giving me any news of Max and Simone (I don't even know whether they have come to France this summer). My cousine seems to be quite interested (et même passionnée) by writing a book on Lincoln.*

*Here, as you may suppose, Rhoda is of an immense help for me. In fact she helps me a lot, even in my work for the Foundation, on the most essential social and psychological planes, — a plane where, as you know, probably, I am not particularly gifted. -*

*In the meantime, I hope and pray that you find more and more peace and light. ——*

*God bless you!*

*P.T.*

*New York, Nov. 21, 1953*

*Dear Lucile,*

*God bless you for your kind and sweet letter of yesterday. Your lines brought me strength and peace. —*

*As you know, I am not much interested in myself. — But I am anxious that my whole life should help "everything" to become One, — the <u>true</u> One.*

*Yours as ever*

*et à bientôt*

*P.T.*

---

In late November of 1953, Teilhard learned that "Piltdown Man" was an elaborate hoax. (T. had worked briefly at the Sussex fossil site in 1912–13.) J. A. Wiener, the anthropologist, who uncovered Dawson's apparent forgery dismisses as "rubbish" Stephen Jay Gould's charge in 1980 that Teilhard had collaborated in the famous hoax.

See also Charles Blinderman, The Piltdown Inquest (Prometheus Books, 1986); Frank Spencer, Piltdown: Scientific Forgery (Oxford University Press, 1990); and Philip Tobias, "On Piltdown: The French Connection Revisited," Current Anthropology, Vol. 34, No. 1, February 1993.

---

*New-York, Dec. 13. 1953*

*Dear Lucile,*

*These few lines to tell you that I am just back from the Chapelle, where I said (as every 13 of Dec., "Sainte Lucie") my mass for you. That you should have ever more incentive for your work, — peace in your soul, — "Presence" of God everywhere in you and around you. That we should, up to the end, help each other in the fascinating effort to approach "le Coeur des Choses". —*

*Last week, I have been rather busy (a visit of my friend Alberto Blanc, the prehistorian-geologist of Rome). — I shall phone you on Tuesday, so that we decide for a next réunion, — as soon as possible.*

*En grande affection*

*P.T.*

*My cousine wrote me that the Bégouëns are in Paris, -recuperating. Simone still rather weak.*

*I have been distressed and angry in reading the papers a week ago (J.P. Davies)!!*

---

Teilhard's reference to John Paton Davies was a reaction to the tense, "red" hunting days presided over by Senator Joseph McCarthy. China hands John Carter Vincent, Edmund O. Chubb, and John Service were also smeared by anti-communist zealots.

---

*December 20, 1953*

*Dear Pierre,*

*Do you think that some day we might have a CALM talk about "<u>us</u>." We meet and act as if nothing had ever existed between us . . until just as we are parting some chance remark brings on others and the time being so short and the feeling of pressure so*

great, things are said that are too strong or not explicit and there is never time to understand. so we part with a feeling of frustration and ill ease. you must feel it too.

Is it an impossible situation? You were the strongest influence in my life for
nearly 20 years and a VERY deep one. Since 1948 I have tried to make a whole new picture. I know I have not been very quick nor very clever, but God knows I have tried. And I
have acquired a real inner Peace, which is necessary for me, as well as for you.

I know that we want sincerely to help each other, is that possible? And how? It
was you who put me in the role of mother, but when I have told you things which seemed
to me to be less than your best self, I feel that I have no right to say them, in fact I am so
uncertain of where I stand with you that it makes it doubly hard to act wisely.

I know that you do not like to analyze situations, but don't you think we would
all be happier if you faced this one when you are well and calm? If you do not want to talk
with me, can you write it?

This is only a suggestion. If you do not feel it is good - skip it.

Today after church I stopped in at the Guggenheim museum to see an exhibit of
avant avant gard painters from France, well Europe. Most of them seemed to me so empty,
so thin. I don't suppose we could ever see them together . . but stop in some time and tell
me what you think . . it seems so in line with the Rostand book . . It must reflect what the
young are thinking and feeling . .

The Christmas season makes one feel rather alone and a bit sentimental, I guess
which may exaggerate things. But please believe that this is written with a real desire to
create a constructive relationship between us. If for any reason you think that not possible,
let's face the thing. I do not feel very happy about the way things are now, I am so uncertain about what is wanted or expected of me, so I cannot know how to act and —well, that
is it — can I be ME? I don't want always to have to ACT.

God bless you and give us both wisdom.

Yours,

Lucile

N.Y., January 1, 1954

Dear Lucile

This is to wish you — du fond du coeur — a happy 1954. May God, during
this new year, bring us closer to Him, — and to each other of us.

What I want mostly to tell you today is how much I hope that our
friendship will soon find its true, constructive and progressing form; — and how
much, also, the only ultimate goal and interest of my life remains (more and more
. . .) the "praying discovery" of an ever more divine God. — Along this line, let us
progress, helped by each other, — and converge.

I still feel a bit shaky, these days. So I think it wiser for me (and perhaps
for you?) to wait a little before coming to see you.

But be sure that I am there, just the same; — and tell me if I can do anything for you.

En fidèle affection

P.T.

I was so sorry, and I thought immediately of you, when I heard of the death of
Ralph Linton.

*January 5, 1954*

*Dear PT,*

  *Thank you for your sweet letter — I have wanted to write too. — I was so <u>sure</u> "it" could not happen again — but it did. It was a great blow to me to realize that my grasp of spiritual truths was not stronger. It made me feel very discouraged and depressed for some days, but I suppose it is through mistakes that we learn, and God has helped me to see more clearly and to put my heart more completely into loving Him.*

  *At least I found out that my emotions (though <u>misdirected</u> are not dead!! But I am terribly sorry if you have suffered by this "misdirection".*

  *And thank you for your good wishes for the New Year — I do so wish the same for you and that we both shall find our way to God and can help each other. Surely we can do this calmly and constructively. It is such a strong thing in each of us.*

  *Please believe me your humble and sincere fellow-seeker of God.*

  *L. S.*

*P.S. I have decided to enclose a note I wrote some days ago.* If it does not help, I do not see that it can do any harm — I do so want a really constructive relationship.*

Lucile's "Line A Day" note on January 11th reads "Good final (?) letter to PT". However, it was not a final letter.

*Jan. 14 1954*

*Lucile dear,*

  *I have received yesterday only your sweet letter of Jan.11, — just when I was going to answer the precedent one.*

  *I think you are absolutely right in your diagnosis — except that I would put it in a slightly different way. In the "Chinese phase" of our life, not only you needed me — but we needed each other. - And now, apparently, we need each other (and we can help each other) in a different way, which will show itself with the time: I believe it, and I pray for it.*

  *In the meantimes I am so happy that your heart should be "full". That helps mine to be so.*

  *God bless you (and your work).*

  *yours*

  *P.T.*

*(My book progresses, — slowly ——)*

*New York, March 2, 1954*

*Lucile dear,*

  *So many thanks for your nice letter of yesterday. I was terribly silent, but I pray for you every day too. In fact, my nerves are stupidly somewhat tense these days. But I try to forget it, and to lean on God, — the closer for it.*

---

*No copy of this note was found among Lucile's papers.

*In the meantimes, my booklet advances slowly, but continously. I hope to have finished it on about Easter. But what am I going to do with it? I will discuss the case with my friends and superiors in France, this summer. In fact, in my opinion, the time would be just ripe for a publication, — except for the unfortunate circumstance that the "priest-workmen" affair renders the religious atmosphere pretty tense in Europe, just now. And yet is not the core of the problem right there: "What has to be a priest, henceforth, in order to be a real priest of the New-God for a New-World?" Even if I can publish nothing of my book, I am decided, the coming summer, to write down a completely sincere report on what I feel, hope and believe (in the line of Christianity), and to have this report presented to the highest authorities in my Church (or at least of my Order). I think I was never attached more deeply that I am now to Christ. But never also have I seen Him so clearly and passionately as a "Super-Christ".*

*I am <u>extremely</u> glad to hear that your painting is progressing. Good luck for the next week!*

*At St. Ignatius (Park Ave.) they start new constructions, — so that I am obliged to search for another shelter. A big nuisance. I wonder whether they have a room for me at Riverside. Anyhow, I shall find something, somewhere. I will let you know.*

*God bless you, and your work, and everything for you.*

*yours, as always,*

*P.T.*

*April 16 1954*

*Dear Lucile,*
*These few lines to thank you for your card from Boston, — and to tell you that I do not forget you. — May you have, in the deepest of your heart, a very, very sunny Easter Day! I know you are wishing the same for me. —*

*Why is it I should still feel somewhat too tense? God knows better, I suppose. The main thing is that, in the process, I should feel Him always closer, and warmer, and unique. — And, I think, He does.*

*In the meantimes my booklet on Man is finished; and I am busy re-typing it duefully. I can't really say how good it is. But, at least, compared with the other book published on the same subject since two years, it is "different". This summer, in Paris, I will explore the chances for a publication. – Not much hope.*

*"Fundamentalists" have still the upper hand, it seems, both in France and in Rome. But, underneath, I am convinced that the "new God" is irresistibly growing, — from the very development of the present World.*

*God bless you, Lucile!*

*as ever,*

*P.T.*

*April 24, 1954*

*Dear P.T.*
*Thank you for your sweet letter and Easter greeting.*

*It is splendid that the book is finished and you know how greatly I hope that it will be published — Not only for you but for all the others who would benefit so much by it. I hope I shall be able to read it some day. It is strange that the Fundamentalists should be so strong now — when a vital new vision is so sorely needed. The church here seems a bit less enthusiastic lately about McC [Joseph McCarthy], thank goodness.*

*I am planning to go to Mallorca July 20 for a few months. I hope to do a lot of painting. Floss [Mrs. Jo Davidson] is coming down from Paris to join me. She wants me to stay with her in Paris later, but I doubt that I shall go there at all. However, my plans are not very definite for the return. When do you go to France? and for how long? I do hope I shall see you before you go.*

*I am so sorry, Pierre, that you are still "tense" but if it brings you closer to God, that is much. His ways and man's are not always easy to understand, but it is wonderful when we can realize that they are His Will.*

*Again many thanks to you for all the wonderfully happy times we had together — and even more for helping me to try to realize God and stimulating my desire to find a more spiritual way of life. That is always most precious.*

*As always,*
*Your devoted and loving,*
*Lucile*

*It is almost your birthday again — have a very happy day.*

*The Viking Fund*
*New York, May 7. 1954*

*Dear Lucile,*
*Thank you so much for your nice letter of April 24. — This one to tell you that my mass of May 9 will be for you, — as every year; — for you and some-what, at the same time for me, so that we should at last! find "each other" in the best and the highest possible way.*

*Pardon my silence. I am still groping for myself. — But I am convinced that we are "converging" upward, all right.*

*I am leaving for France at the beginning of June (coming probably back in September — with Leroy — who has to do some work in Chicago). — You can always reach me aux Etudes (15 - rue Monsieur). ——*

*Et, bien entendu, I shall see you before I leave.*
*Bonne fête!*

*Your*

*P.T.*

*P.S. In fact, I am going to France with "mixed" feelings. —*
*My hope however is that this contact with Europe will*
*help me to focuss better where and how to direct the next*
*(and ultimate?) effort of my life.*

*My booklet is finished. I will try to have it published*
*in some technically scientific series, — without having*
*to ask any special permission of my Order.*

Dear Lucile,

I wonder where, when (or even whether) these lines will reach you . . . But I want to write them anyhow in order to thank you so much for your sweet letter from Majorca (august 8!) which has been forwarded to me here only lately. — Yes, I think that we have reached, you and me, this new and constructive type of friendship, — where everything is strength and peace in a closer presence and approach of God. Let us go ahead! I am so happy to feel that you feel, yourself, creative and happy. I shall be much interested, when seeing your new paintings.

As far as I am concerned, I am back to America since August 16. These two months in Paris were useful, but somewhat hectic: too many people to see in too short a time! — And yet, at the beginning of August, I felt that I had better to leave: nobody, practically, was left in town; — the Etudes were closing for a month; — and Rome was not particularly satisfied of my presence in France . . . Better, I thought, not to be too greedy for a first time. — In fact, I was able, during these few weeks, to renew many dear, or useful, connections, — especially with my Order, both in Paris and Lyon. And my friend Prof. Piveteau (Sorbonne) took immediately for his review ("Les Annales de Paléontologie") my manuscript on Man. — The whole thing may be printed and published at the very beginning of 1955. — Evidently, very few people read "Les Annales de Paléont." But, to be published in such a highly technical Revue is a kind of guarantee for me that the theologians will ignore the paper, — or not frown too much at it. — And I have ordered a rather large number of separates. — We shall see . . .

I saw Max and Simone (who spent august and september at Bréhat). Simone's foot was better; but she looks more and more frail. And yet she keeps smiling, - just as before. - My cousin Marguerite was just finishing her book on Lincoln (Lincoln as seen by a French, for the frenchmen . . .); I found her remarkably well —both physically and morally.

Here, I am still out of St. Ignatius (the buildings will not be completed before May). So we have decided (Fr. de Breuvery and me) to settle in a double room appartement at Hotel Fourteen (East 60th St). Everything going all right, so far.-

I hope this letter will reach you.
Be happy, and God bless you!

Yours

P.T.

New-York, Nov. 7, '54

Dear Lucile,

So many thanks for your "lettre d'arrivée"! — I am deeply glad that your summer was such a success, — and that you should come back refreshed for more art, and more "meditation". — Since I wrote you, I had some interesting experiences (at the end of October) in the course of the symposium of Columbia University ("Bicentenary"). — I will tell you that, — and many other things too, — as soon as possible. I am expecting Leroy (from Chicago) at the beginning of the *week; and Wenner-Gren himself is expected at the Foundation, these days (re: some news plans, for a new symposium (!?).*

  *I shall phone you. — Or you can phone me (as usual, before noon, at the Foundation). —*

  *Yours, as ever*

  *P.T.*

                 *November 30, 1954*

*Dear PT,*

  *I might have given you a wrong impression on Friday and, I want to assure you, that what I wish for you above everything else is that you should find Peace and quiet and freedom. My love for you will always be something special; but believe me it is neither demanding nor possessive.*

  *It would not be true to say that I love Rhoda, but I am glad she has found her God and I sincerely wish her well.*

  *I know that I can always count on you as you know that you can always count on me. And I am always here if you should ever need me or want me.*

  *I pray God to bless you and give you peace and quiet and happiness as He has in such large measure given to me.*

  *Yours, etc.,*

  *Lucile*

---

Sometime after the end of November and probably before Christmas, Teilhard suddenly became ill while out walking and fell to the sidewalk. He was rushed to his doctor's office nearby (on the upper East Side of New York). From there, Dr. Jean Simard telephoned Lucile Swan, since the stricken Teilhard had asked for her. Simard asked Lucile to reassure Teilhard and to tell him that she loved him. She came at once and she did. Teilhard's fellow Jesuits had also been called. They came and drove him to the Jesuit residence.

---

              *New-York, Dec. 1. 54*

*Dear Lucile,*

  *Thank you, so much, for your letter of yesterday. — No, you had __not__ given me any wrong impression, when we met, last week. On the contrary, you were very sweet, — and I found you such a strong friend to me. Yes, I count on you, too, — just as you count on me. And, for smaller or bigger things, I am always here for you, and <u>I know</u> that you are there for me. — Let us converge, you and me, courageously and happily, toward the new face of God which attracts both of us. — For this fascinating task of discovery I need you, — and I shall always do the utmost for helping you. ——*

  *Good luck for your work! — and God bless you for all you did and are for me!*

  *Yours*

  *P.T.*

*Dear Lucile,*

*These few lines to tell you that tomorrow (St. Lucia) my "mass" will be for you: that God should give you plenty of his peace (that is of his Presence), — and that we should be "force et douceur" for each other, — you and me — more and more, — and for ever —*

*I hope your work is developping well. — Nothing much new, as far as I concerned, except that the W. G. Foundation is decidedly planning some enlargements, — and that I am likely to be incorporated in the new scheme ——*

*I shall explain you.*

*A bientôt!*

*Yours*

*P.T.*

---

After Christmas he apparently joined her several times for tea. There are no letters nor record of visits during the next three months. But in her calendar on March 25, Lucile commented "wonderful visit". The following letter was probably written shortly afterwards and may be the one that Teilhard dates March 28. This undated copy was found among her papers.

---

[no date / perhaps March 28, 1955]

*Dearest,*

*What a wonderful talk we had on Friday. I have been thinking of it so much — especially about your "atomic theory". It is such a thrilling idea — and so very possibly true and the key to a real Unity which would lead to the spiritual awakening of which we dream. If you write anything on this subject please send me a copy — and I hope we shall* talk *about it again some day, when you feel like it.*

*Dearest it makes me very sad if I am partly the cause of your malaise. Don't let me be. You know I have found Peace and it is the thing I long for you more than anything else — the real Peace of God's presence. If there is anything I can do to help you, please talk. You know I am always here to do anything I can.*

*G.B.Y. Always*
*Lucile*

*P.S. If it would be easier not to see me, tell me.*

---

Lucile's undated letter may be the one that Teilhard referred to in his March 30 reply.

---

*New-York, March 30, 1955*

*Lucile dear,*

*Merci, tant, for your letter (March 28)*

*Yes, stupidly enough, I am still nervous, — more nervous than I would, — than I should be.*

*And, at the same time, I need definitely your presence, your influence, in my life.*

*I hope (I am sure) that things will gradually settle, "emotionally" speaking. — In the meantimes, and as a minimum (or as a provisional "optimum") we might try to see each other at the rate of two-three times a winter. — In any case, we know, both of us, that we "are always here" for each other. — Phone me any time you like. — I will let you know anything important or interesting which may happen to me. And I shall certainly see you before I leave New York for the summer. — My plans are still vague, on account of this awful question of "permanent visa" which I have not got so far!*

*God bless you for all you gave and give me!*

*Yours, very affectueusement,*

*Pierre*

That was Teilhard's final letter to Lucile; he died eleven days later on the evening of Easter Sunday, April 10, 1955. Lucile was among the handful of mourners who attended his funeral Mass at St. Ignatius Church in New York. He is buried in the Jesuit cemetery near Poughkeepsie, New York.

Lucile had made a brief Journal entry on another Easter Sunday in 1943. There was no other entry until 1956 when she wrote in her journal for the last time.

[Journal] *Aug. 20, 1956*

*And Pierre died on Easter day 1955 — Beloved Pierre — how much had changed.*

Ten years later Lucile Swan died, on May 2, 1965. She is buried in Sioux City, Iowa.

**THE EDITORS**

# EPILOGUE: "Teilhard and the Feminine"

In 1950 Teilhard wrote his spiritual autobiography, *The Heart of Matter*, which ends with an account of "The Feminine": "I have experienced no form of self-development without some feminine eye turned on me, some feminine influence at work." He spoke of a "homage which sprang from the depths of my being and was paid to those women whose warmth and charm have been absorbed, drop by drop, into the life blood of my most cherished ideas" (HM,59).

The passage went on to tell of two ways that humanity has formalized sexual energy: 1. In marriage it is ordered to having children and, 2. In the separation of the sexes it has given rise to religious life. But he proposed a "Third Way": a man and a woman would develop a spiritual bond between them that would not involve them physically.* They would both remain chaste in a sort of Platonic friendship. This would allow "the unfathomable spiritual powers that still lie dormant under the mutual attraction of the sexes" to develop, but the man and woman would conquer these "by sublimation." He sent a copy of *The Heart of Matter* to Lucile saying, "These pages are an effort to express an internal evolution deeply impressed by you."

Teilhard tells of being so fascinated by the universal that he was not aware of the Feminine until his thirtieth year. Then he met the Feminine in the person of Marguerite Teillard-Chambon (a first cousin once removed) shortly before he went into military service (December 1914). He wrote Marguerite abundant letters from the Front (published as *The Making of a Mind*) and filled his wartime Journal with references to virginity and the feminine—all the references are philosophical. Journal notations for February 1916 tell of sexual union neutralizing human energies: "there is always a certain dissipation of powers;" "satisfaction always appears *to neutralize* the human individual" (J,40,31).

In March 1918 he finally produced a poetic essay, "The Eternal Feminine." The essay was dedicated to Beatrice, the woman who by her glance alone had inspired Dante to make his journey from the Inferno, through Purgatorio to Paradiso. It again tells of the spiritual appeal of the Feminine. Teilhard's essay explains, "when a man loves a woman he thinks at first that his love is given to an individual like himself whom he envelops in his power and freely associates with himself." But, soon "he is astonished by the violence of the forces unleashed in him," and "trembles to realize" that he cannot be united with the feminine without "becoming enslaved to a universal work of creation." Thus the Feminine was seen as the force that calls man out of himself and into Life.

---

*It should be noted that the "Third Way" is not the same as the "Second Way" (religious life). Twelve years after Teilhard's death, Pedro Arrupe, the then Jesuit Father General, was asked whether young Jesuits seeking personal growth might follow the "Third Way"—a term understood in many ways. In a letter of December 12, 1967, Arrupe, appealing to the texts of Vatican II and the statutes of the Society, said the "Third Way" (understood as the cultivation of an exclusive and intimate relationship with a woman similar to marriage but without conjugal privileges) cannot be justified or approved for Jesuits.

The Christian Gospel recommended virginity, but this did not mean the Feminine was to lose her power. Virginity was not to exile love from a man's heart: "on the contrary it is his duty to remain essentially a man." The Feminine becomes idealized as "Mary the Virgin." She now inspires the spirit to rise beyond the world and unite with God.

After the War Teilhard returned to his work in science and, though he often saw Marguerite, he did not again feel the full power of the feminine until he met Lucile in 1929. Marguerite had shared Teilhard's Catholic faith (where virginity is highly valued), but Lucile did not and challenged him often. The essays he wrote during the 1930s often considered the meaning of chastity in an evolving cosmos; many of these passages are summarized in the present text. In 1931 he wrote "The Spirit of the Earth" which tells of the physical nature of love changing with the appearance of the human. The essay gives some understanding of what he was telling Lucile: love is

> no longer only a unique and periodic attraction for purposes of material fertility; but an unbounded and continuous possibility of contact between minds rather than bodies; the play of countless subtle antennae seeking one another in the light and darkness of the soul; the pull towards mutual sensibility and completion, in which preoccupation with preserving the species gradually dissolves in the greater intoxication of two people creating a world.

The essay went on to tell of the great wastage of energy involved in irresponsible sex.

In 1934 he wrote "The Evolution of Chastity" that again tried to understand chastity in terms of the evolution of life. He told of a woman's power to activate a man, but he added that by the very intensity of sexual expression

> a sort of 'short-circuit' is produced in the dazzling gift of the body—a flash which burns up and deadens a portion of the soul. Something is born, but it is for the most part used up on the spot.

Through the physical expression the lovers have found a deadening of soul and not a rise in spirit. So Teilhard recommended: "No immediate contact, but convergence at a higher level." This resembled the resolution he had written in his Journal in 1916. He ended the essay:

> When men have harnessed the winds, the waves, the tides and gravity, they will harness for God the energies of love, and then for the second time in the history of the world, man will have discovered Fire.

Lucile was not entirely convinced and considered breaking off the friendship. But that same year she wrote in her journal: "I cannot have you. Not really. So I must learn your way of having each other." This "way" became the basis of their friendship. After his death she considered her sublimation of eros and wrote, "it certainly makes the bonds even stronger than in an ordinary relationship."

Lucile originally seems to have believed Teilhard would relent and the relationship could take a more familiar form. But in October 1939 she more or less accepted the type of relationship Teilhard had proposed. By then she was very taken by his religious message and was assisting him develop his ideas; she translated many of his essays into English. They were both in Peiping from September 1949 till August 1941, which Teilhard called "two precious years of constant presence." Lucile reflected on this time, "Never had Teilhard's visits been so regular nor our talks so satisfactory." When Teilhard brought *The Phenomenon of Man* to Lucile, she typed a final copy making two carbons. These years seem to have been the high point of their relationship.

After the War (World War II) Lucile did not see Teilhard until 1948; then he was weak and still recovering from a severe myocardial infarction. It seems he could not respond to her challenges and expectations. Eventually he began seeing more of Rhoda than Lucile; this and his declining health resulted in the strains in their friendship recounted in the later letters.

There were other significant women in the life of Teilhard. One was Ida Treat, an American and pro-Communist political activist with whom Teilhard had studied in the laboratory of Marcellin Boule. She was in New York in Teilhard's final years. Another was Léontine Zanta, a feminist and Catholic much influenced by Henri Bergson. She was the first woman to receive a doctorate in philosophy from a French university. During the 1920s and 1930s Teilhard frequently attended the literary salons at her apartment just outside of Paris. He wrote to her with the same warmth found in many letters to others: "I owe you so much, dear friend, and it is such sweetness, both for my mind and my heart, to find you there again on each return from Europe." There was also Jeanne Mortier who had studied scholastic philosophy for ten years at the Institut Catholique without finding satisfaction. She was overwhelmed when she read a typed copy of *Le Milieu Divin* and then met Teilhard in January 1939. He told her he appreciated her support in his "vague lights and aspirations in the meaning of a higher comprehension of chastity." In 1942 she dedicated herself to spreading his message—at first by mimeographing and distributing his texts. But on July 2, 1951 he appointed her his literary executrice and she arranged publication of his works after his death. There was also Claude Rivière, a broadcaster who in 1942 interviewed Teilhard on the air in Shanghai; and they kept in contact. He would thank her for her "precious inspiration" and explain, "We will communicate in the BECOMING. It is there we will converge." Again his message was spiritual: "I want to be able to help you discover for yourself and by your own path the One Thing Necessary and his universal Presence."

In Paris in July 1954 Teilhard read again the final passages from *The Heart of Matter*. He began weeping "at the memory of all the reproachful 'Beatrices' he knew and he had hurt unwittingly" (Lukas,337). One of these was Lucile. But by this time Lucile had become reconciled to their changed relationship and had been continuing her own spiritual search. After his death she treasured what he had said and written to her and the time they had spent together. She wrote, "The privilege of knowing and having the friendship of this great man continues to be the most important and most beautiful part of my life."

*Georgetown University*
*August 1993*

T.K.

*Lucile Swan with Mary Wood Gilbert's daughter; photograph taken in the early 1950s.*

# CHRONOLOGY

| Pierre Teilhard de Chardin | | Lucile Swan |
|---|---|---|
| *May 1*: Teilhard born in the Auvergne, France | 1881 | |
| | 1890 | *May 10*: Lucile born in Sioux City, Iowa, U.S.A. |
| *March 20*: Teilhard entered the Society of Jesus | 1899<br>\|<br>1902 | *School years*: attended Episcopal boarding school |
| | 1903 | *During year*: moved to Chicago |
| | 1908 | *During year*: Chicago, began study at Art Institute |
| *August*: ordained priest in England | 1911 | |
| | 1912 | *December*: married Jerome Blum, artist |
| | 1916<br>\|<br>1923 | *During 7 years*: worked and traveled in Corsica, Japan, China, Tahiti, and France |
| *May*: began scientific exploration work in China's Ordos desert | | |
| | 1924 | *During year*: divorced; worked on Frank Lloyd Wright commission in Wisconsin |
| | 1926 | *Autumn*: closed Chicago studio and moved to New York City |
| *April*: accepted post at National Geological Society of China in Peking | 1929 | *March*: New York / exhibit at Anderson Galleries<br>*September–December*: Peking |
| *January–August*: Tienstsin, Shensi & Shansi, Peking, Mongolia & Gobi Desert<br>*September–December*: France | 1930 | *January–December*: Peking |
| *January–February*: in the U.S.A.<br>*March–April*: Peking<br>*May*: joined Citroën's "La Croisière Jaune" expedition | 1931 | *January–December*: Peking |

*February*: ended "La Croisière Jaune" work in Peking
*July*: Shansi
*August–December*: Paris & London

*January*: France
*February–April*: Peking
*June–September*: U.S.A.
*November*: Peking

*January–February*: Kwangshi & South China
*February*: Peking
*May–July*: Yangtze Valley
*August–December*: Peking

*January–February*: Kwangshi & South China
*March–April*: Peking
*May–August*: France
*September–December*: Kashmir & India
*December*: Peking

*January*: Java
*February–June*: Peking
*July*: Shantung
*August–December*: Peking

*January*: Peking
*February–March*: U.S.A.
*April–August*: France
*September–November*: Peking
*December*: Burma

*January–March*: Burma & Java
*May–September*: Peking
*September–November*: U.S.A.
*November–December*: France

*January–June*: France
*July–August*: U.S.A.
*August 30–December*: Peking

*January–December*: Peking

1932  *January–December*: Peking / worked on Chinese figures (wrestlers, acrobats, children) & first bust of Teilhard

1933  *January–July*: Peking / exhibit at Lloyd Studio
*August*: Dairen, North China
*September–December*: Peking

1934  *January–February*: Peking
*March*: Shanghai
*April–July*: Peking
*August*: Mongolia
*September–December*: Peking

1935  *January–February*: Peking

*March–August*: U.S.A. / exhibit in Chicago
*September–October*: Europe
*November–December*: Peking / exhibit in Shanghai

1936  *January–August*: Peking / exhibit at Hanforth Gallery

*September–December*: Hankow

1937  *January–June*: Peking; worked on "Nelly" under Weidenreich
*July*: Peitaho, North China
*August–December*: Peking

1938  *January–July*: Peking
*August–December*: U.S.A. / exhibits in New York, Washington, D.C., & Sioux City

1939  *January–July*: U.S.A.

*August–December*: Peking

1940  *January–June*: Peking
*July*: Peitaho, North China
*August–December*: Peking

*January–November*: Peking
*December*: (confined in Peking by Japanese occupation)

1941 *January–August*: Peking
*August–December*: U.S.A.

*January–December*: Peking

1942 *January–December*: Chicago

*January–December*: Peking

1943 In Chicago for the year

*August*: P.T. and other internationals released from Peking "detention" after Japanese surrender

1944 *January–September*: Chicago
*October–December*: New York

*January–December*: Peking

1945 *January–September*: New York
*October–December*: Washington, D.C. (exhibit at Chattel Gallery in December)

*January–March*: Peking
*May–December*: France

1946 *January–December*: Washington, D.C. (exhibit at Worth Gallery, Palm Beach, Florida)

*June–December*: France (June: major heart attack)

1947 *January–December*: Washington, D.C.

*January–March*: France
*March–June*: New York
*June–August*: France

1948 *January–April*: Washington, D.C.
*May*: New York
*June*: Washington, D.C. / exhibit
*July*: Poughkeepsie, N.Y.
*August*: France
*September–December*: Switzerland, Rome, Ethiopia

*October*: Rome
*November–December*: France

*January–December*: France

1949 *January*: Rome
*February–April*: Switzerland
*May*: France
*July–August*: London
*September*: U.S.A.
*October–December*: India

*January–December*: France; elected to Académie des Sciences

1950 *January–April*: India
*May*: Siam
*July–August*: Rome
*August–September*: England
*October–December*: New York

*January–June*: France
*July–November*: South Africa
*November*: South America
*December*: New York

1951 *January–December*: New York

*January–July*: New York

*August*: Glacier Park
*September–December*: New York

*January–June*: New York
*July–August*: South Africa
*August–September*: Rhodesia
*November–December*: New York

*January–May*: New York
*June–August*: France
*September–December*: New York

*January–April*: New York
*April 10*: Teilhard died in New York

1952   *January–July*: New York (exhibit at Black, Starr, & Gorham and Worth galleries)

1952   *August–October*: Mallorca
*November–December*: New York

1953   *January–July*: New York
*August*: Thousand Islands, N.Y.
*September–December*: New York

1954   *January–June*: New York
*July–October*: Mallorca
*September–December*: New York

1955   *January–December*: New York (worked in studio & taught )

1965   *May 2*: Lucile died in New York

# SELECT BIBLIOGRAPHY

*GENERAL REFERENCES*

Cuénot, Claude, *Teilhard de Chardin, a Biographical Study*, translated by Vincent Colimore. London: Burns & Oates, 1965.

Lukas, Mary and Ellen, *Teilhard*. New York: Doubleday, 1977.

Speaight, Robert, *Teilhard de Chardin*. New York: Harper & Row, 1967.

Teilhard de Chardin, Pierre, *Human Energy*, translated by J. M. Cohen. New York: A Helen & Kurt Wolff Book, Harcourt Brace Jovanovich, 1969.

Teilhard de Chardin, Pierre, *Letters from My Friend Teilhard de Chardin*, translated by Mary Lukas. New York / Ramsey: Paulist, 1980.

Teilhard de Chardin, Pierre, *Toward the Future*, translated by René Hague. New York: Harcourt Brace Jovanovich, 1975.


*REFERENCE FOR THE PROLOGUE*

Davies, John Paton, Jr., *Dragon by the Tail: American, British, Japanese, and Russian Encounters with China and One Another*, p. 173. New York: W. W. Norton & Company, 1972.


*REFERENCES FOR THE EPILOGUE*

HM Teilhard de Chardin, Pierre, *The Heart of Matter*, translated by René Hague. New York: A Helen & Kurt Wolff Book, Harcourt Brace Jovanovich, 1979.

J *Journal*, Tome I, texte integral publié par Nicole et Karl Schmitz-Moormann. Paris: Fayard, 1975.

*Lettres à Jeanne Mortier* [de Teilhard]. Paris: Editions du Seuil, 1984.

*Letters to Léontine Zanta* [from Teilhard] translated by Bernard Wall. New York: Harper & Row, 1969.

*Letters to Two Friends: 1926–1952* [from Teilhard to Ida Treat and Rhoda de Terra]. New York: The New American Library, 1968.

Lukas, Mary and Ellen. *Teilhard*. New York: Doubleday & Co., 1977.

**Note from the Editors**: Wherever a first name or a last name is used alone in the correspondence, we have attempted to identify each of those persons by referring to other documents or to the Chronology in this volume. We regret any errors that may ensue and ask your help with revisions.

Please send corrections to the Georgetown University Press.

**Akabori**. Japanese Anthropologist

**Alice**. *See* Cosme

**Amadeus**. *See* Grabau

**Andersson**, J. Gunnar (1874–1960). Swedish geologist and archaeologist who predicted discovery of Peking Man; active in Chou Kuo Tien excavations, 1927

**André**. *See* Bergeret

**Andrews**, Roy Chapman (1884–1960). American naturalist, explorer, and writer on staff of the Museum of Natural History in New York (1906–41) and its director 1935–41); headed the Mongolian Expedition on which Teilhard served as a geologist and a paleontologist.

**Aragonnès**, Claude. Nom de plume of the writer, Marguerite Teillard-Chambon, a cousin of Teilhard.

**Arrupe**, Pedro (1907–1991). Jesuit father general (1965–91).

**Arthur**. *See* Ringwalt

**Aurobindo**, Ghose (1872–1950) Sri. Indian philosopher.

**Aven**, Marc. Ida Treat-Bergeret's nom de plume.

**Balbo**. *Probably* Italo Balbo (1896–1940). Italian aviator and statesman; attended Chicago World's Fair, 1933.

**Barbier**, Miss. Person who typed manuscript of Teilhard's scientific papers.

**Barbour**, George. American paleontologist who taught at Yenching University, Peking. He worked with Teilhard on various expeditions from 1929 to 1953; after the war, professor of geology at

Columbia University in New York; wrote *In the Field with Teilhard de Chardin*, (Paris, Le Seuil, 1965).

**Bardac**, Jacques. Frenchman and director of the Banque Franco-Chinoise in Peking during the 1930s.

**Bardac**, Marie-Claire. American wife of Jacques Bardac.

**Baudet**, Philippe. French consul in Shanghai during the Japanese occupation, later Ambassador to Moscow.

**Béchamp**, Dr. French consul at Chentu.

**Bégouën**, Comte Henri de. Father of Max Bégouën and professor of prehistory at the University of Toulouse.

**Bégouën**, Max and Simone. French businessman and philosopher. Max met Teilhard on the battlefield in 1915. Simone, his wife, typed and distributed Teilhard's essays in 1937.

**Bergeret**, André. French writer and naval officer; husband of Ida Treat.

**Betty**. *See* Tucker; *see also* Vincent.

**Bien**, M. N. "Eddy". Chinese geologist. He worked with Teilhard at Chou Kuo Tien.

**Billy**. Staff member at American Museum in New York City.

**Billy**, André (1882–1971). French journalist. Member of the Académie Goncourt. He wrote articles about Teilhard's ideas (cf. Leroy *Lettres Familiéres*, p. 71).

**Black**, Davidson (1885–1934). Canadian scientist and director of Cenozoic Laboratory (1934) and head of the anatomy department at Peking Union Medical College; organized and directed research at Chou Kuo Tien. Wife, Adena.

**Blanc,** Baron Alberto Carlo. Italian prehistorian and paleontologist; member of the Société Préhistorique de France.

**Blanc,** Dr. Teilhard's physician in Peking.

**Blum,** Jerome. American artist and Lucile Swan's ex-husband.

**Blum,** Leon (1872–1956). French writer and politician. Prime Minister in 1936 Front Populaire.

**Boas,** Franz (1858–1942). American anthropologist and ethnologist; taught at Columbia University (1896–1936).

**Bonnet,** Mme. Wife of French Minister in Peking.

**Bosshart,** Walter. Swiss reporter in Peking.

**Boule,** Piérre Marcellin (1861–1942). French paleontologist and professor Musée National d'Histoire Naturelle (1902–36), Paris.

**Bourdelle,** Antoine (1861–1929. French sculptor, student of Rodin.

**Bowen,** Trevor. Peking Union Medical College controller.

**Boyden,** Amanda, "Peggy". American officer (*probably* a WAVE); in Peking in the 1930s.

**Branch,** Miss. Malvina Hoffman's friend.

**Bréal,** Michel. Member of the French Legation in Peking; married to the Mongolian princess, Nirgidma de Torhout.

**Breuil,** Henri (1877–1961). French priest and archaeologist, authority on paleolithic art; Professor Collège de France (1929); member of the Académie des Sciences.

**Breuvery,** Emmanuel de (1903–1970). French Jesuit, an economist in the Université Aurore, Shanghai; member of the U.N. Department of Natural Resources in New York (1952–70); shared an apartment in New York with Teilhard (1954–55).

**Burchart,** Otto and "Poney." German art dealer and wife living in Peking.

**Burkitt,** Miles C. English archaeologist.

**Burton,** Helen. American proprietor in Peking of clothing and curio shop; interned during Japanese occupation (1941–1945).

**Bussière,** Dr. Physician of the French Legation in Peking; father of Ginette Bussière and Mme. Sercey.

**Bussière,** Ginette. One of Dr. Bussière's daughters.

**Camille.** Niece of Teilhard by marriage.

**Camp,** Charles. American paleontologist who worked in China and South Africa. Wife, Jessie.

**Canon,** Dr. American dermatologist in New York.

**Carrel,** Alexis (1873–1944). French surgeon and experimental biologist. Nobel Prize (1912); worked at the Rockefeller Institute for Medical Research (1906–39). He introduced new techniques for the culture of embryonic tissues; published *Man, the Unknown* in 1935 (the MS is in the Special Collections of Georgetown University Library).

**Carter,** Francis. Cousin to Lucile Swan.

**Champeaux** Monsieur de. Director of Franco Chinoise Bank in Peking (1934–36) and Hong Kong (1937).

**Chaney,** Ralph W. American geologist and explorer in China.

**Chang.** Professor of geology at Sun Yat-sen University in South China.

**Charles.** Brother of Rhoda de Terra, died 1950.

**Charles,** Pierre (1881–1953). Belgian Jesuit who studied philosophy with Teilhard in Jersey; Professor of theology at Louvain; original writer and thinker; a specialist in modern evangelization of pagan countries.

**Charvet,** René (1883–1978). French Jesuit missionary in China; superior of Jesuits in North China.

**Chase,** Sabin. American foreign service officer serving in Peking in the 1930s.

**Christian,** Billy. Manager in the 1930s and early 1940s of the British-American Tobacco Company in China.

**Clubb,** Edmund. American minister in China during the 1930s; served in Moscow; author of *20th Century China.* Wife, Marian.

**Coatman,** Mrs. American living in Peking; detained by Japanese during the war.

**Colbert,** Edwin Harris. American paleontologist, Museum of Natural History in New York.

**Collings.** Prehistorian and director of Raffles Museum in Singapore. (P.T. mentioned him in a December 1937 letter from Rangoon.)

**Collings.** Worked with Teilhard in Malaysia. (This colleague whom Teilhard mentions in an April 1938 letter as a "friend of Malaya" is *probably* the same person as the Raffles director.)

**Commisso,** Msgr. Member of the Apostolic Delegation in Peking (1930–31); secretary to Msgr. Zanin.

**Cooper,** Sydney. Englishman who lived for a while in Peking. Lucile modeled a portrait bust of him before he returned to England.

Carnegie-financed excavations he directed in 1937.

**Komor**, Lila. Austrian wife of a Hungarian art dealer.

**Kullgren**, Mr. and Mrs. Swedish couple living in Peking.

**Kunkel**, Ruth. American nurse at Peking Union Medical College.

**Lagarde**, Jean de. French consul in New York.

**Lago**. French diplomat. Delivered a letter from Teilhard to Lucile during the war.

**Lamon**, Miss. Aunt of Marguerite Teilhard-Chambon.

**Laurette**. *See* Dorget.

**Lebrun**, Albert (1871–1950). President of the French Republic 1932–1940.

**LeComte du Noüy**, Pierre (1883–1947). French biophysicist and writer.

**Le Corbellier**. Professor at Harvard and author of an article that Lucile sent to Teilhard.

**Ledochówski**, Wlodzimierz (1866–1942). Jesuit father general (1915–42).

**Lee**, C. V. Chinese paleontologue in Peking.

**Lee**, J. S. Chinese paleontologist, director of Nanking Geological Institute in Peking.

**Lefèvre**, Georges. Historian of the Citroën Expedition "La Croisière Jaune" which traversed Central Asia.

**Leighton**. *See* Stuart.

**Lejay**, Pierre (1898–1960). French Jesuit. Geophysicist and director of the Jesuit observatory in Shanghai; member of the Académie des Sciences.

**Leroy**, Pierre (1900–1992). French Jesuit. Biologist, director of the Tientsin Museum of Natural History (1938); director of the Institut de Géobiologie in Peking (1940). Lived with Teilhard in Peking during the Japanese occupation. Wrote *Lettres Familière de Pierre Teilhard de Chardin, Mon Ami, 1948–1955* and *Le Centurion* (1976).

**Lessing**, von. German sociologist and ethnologist.

**Licent**, Émile (1876–1952). French Jesuit. Naturalist and explorer of Yellow River Basin in North China; founder of the Museum-Laboratory in Tientsin.

**Lichnowsky**, Countess Ellinor. Daughter of Prince Karl Max and a German agriculturist.

**Lin**, YuTang (1895–1976). Chinese author and philologist.

**Linton**, Ralph (1893–1953). American anthropologist and author; contributed to development of cultural anthropology.

**Lippmann**, Walter (1889–1974). American journalist and essayist.

**Lloyd**, Madgalen. Dutch owner of curio shop in Peking.

**Loucks**, Harold. Professor of Surgery at the Peking Union Medical College.

**Lubac**, Henri de (b. 1896). Professor of theology at Fourvière in Lyon; member de l' Institut Catholique; author of *The Religion of Teilhard de Chardin*.

**Luce**, Clare Boothe (1903–1987). Member of U.S. Congress, Ambassador to Italy, wife of Henry Luce (founder of *Life* and *Time* magazines).

**Lynn**, Bob. Staff member at American Legation.

**Lyons**, Cecil and Elsie. American diplomat and wife stationed in Peking before the war. Elsie was the daughter of Ambassador and Mrs. Joseph Grew.

**Mac**. *See* MacDonald.

**McCarthy**, Joseph R. (1908–1957). U.S. Senator.

**McCown**. Scientist.

**MacDonald**. Scottish officer stationed on an English gunboat on the Yangtze River during the early years of the war.

**MacHugh**, Maj. James and Mrs. U.S. Marine Corps couple stationed in Peking in the 1930s.

**McKenzie**. British consular service officer in charge of education in the Cook Islands.

**Maillart**, Ella. Dutch author of travelogues.

**Malvina**. *See* Hoffman.

**Marcel**, Gabriel (1889–1973). French philosopher and dramatist.

**Margerie**, Roland de. French Ambassador in Peking. Daughter, Diane

**Margetts**, Mrs. Widow of American Marine officer in Peking; interned by Japanese.

**Marguerite**. *See* Teillard-Chambon.

**Marie-Claire**. *See* Bardac.

**Marin**, Georges. Canadian-born American Jesuit; the Apostolic Vicar in China. Founded in 1937 the Maison Chabanel, a school of Chinese language for missionaries in Peking.

**Martel**, Mrs. de. Jacques Bardac's sister.

**Mary**. *See* Ferguson.

**Matthews**, F. American paleontologist.

**Max**. *See* Bégouën.

**Maxwell**, Dr. Member of the executive committee of the Peking Union Medical College.

**Mayer**, Col. William. American military attaché in Peking during the 1930s.

**Mayo**. *See* Newhall.

like, was used by Teilhard to mean the current Jesuit father general.

**Romola.** Lucile sculpted a bust.

**Rose.** *See* Jameson.

**Rostand.** (*Possibly* Maurice R (1891–1968) writer and son of Edmond Rostand's brother, Gèrard).

**Roy.** *See* Andrews.

**St. Clair,** Dorothy. American friend of Lucile Swan in U.S. foreign service (Peking).

**Saizeau,** Fernande. French artist. Sold Chinese curios in Peking. After the war she taught French in Chicago.

**Scheven.** Staff member at Belgian Legation in Peking.

**Schlemmer,** Christian and Françoise. Members of the Institut Franco-Chinois d'études sinologiques in Peking.

**Scott,** Delia. Married Peter Tyrwhitt.

**Seaholm,** Carl. Swede and American wife who lived in Peking during the 1930s.

**Sercey,** Mme. Married daughter of French Legation's physician, Dr. Bussière.

**Sickman,** Laurence. Connoisseur of Chinese artifacts; developed Chinese collection of paintings and furniture for Nelson Gallery in Kansas City.

**Simard,** Jean. French physician practicing in New York.

**Simone.** *See* Bégouën.

**Simpson,** George Gaylord. American paleontologist and biologist, curator of fossil mammals and birds at the American Museum of Natural History, New York.

**Smith,** Dick. American in China who forwarded mail from Lucile Swan to Teilhard in 1943.

**Smuts,** Jan Christiaan (1870–1950). South African statesman, soldier; active in organizing the U.N.

**Smythe,** Jane. Husband worked at American Legation.

**Snow,** Edgar Parks (1905–1972). American journalist, author of *Red Star Over China*.

**Solages,** Msgr. Bruno de. Rector of the Toulouse Catholic University; wrote a good analysis of Teilhard's main ideas.

**Spencer,** Betty. Later Mrs. John Carter Vincent.

**Stanton,** Edward and Josephine. Friends of Peking years whom Lucile visited later when they were posted to Siam.

**Stein,** Sir Mark Aurel (1862–1943). English archaeologist and orientalist.

**Stein-Callenfels,** Dr. Pieter Vincent Van (1886–1938). Dutch archaeologist and prehistorian.

**Steinen,** Diether von den. German sinologist and translator of Chinese poetry. Wife Erika.

**Stirton,** Ruben Arthur. American paleontologist, curator of paleontology at American Museum, New York.

**Straus,** Roger. New York publisher and cousin of Rhoda de Terra.

**Stuart,** Leighton. President of Yenching University; interned in Peking by the Japanese during war.

**Tadjan** (Taschdjian), Claire Hirschberg. Teilhard's secretary at Lockhart Hall in Peking. Husband was professor of biology at Fujen University.

**Tafel,** Eleonore. German national living in Peking; daughter of famous German explorer.

**Tarnowski** (Tarnowsky), Count John. Polish national who lived in Peking.

**Teilhard** de Chardin, Gabriel. Brother of Pierre Teilhard.

**Teilhard** de Chardin, Joseph. Brother of Pierre.

**Teilhard** de Chardin, Marguerite Marie (Guiguite). Teilhard's younger sister. He wrote the preface for the book, *Les Malades*, which recounted her work among the sick.

**Teillard-Chambon,** Marguerite. Cousin of Teilhard (pen name Claude Aragonnès) whose writing includes a work on Abraham Lincoln. Letters that Teilhard wrote to her from 1914 to 1919 were published as *Genèse d'une Pensèe*.

**Terra,** Helmut de. German national of French origin; geologist and explorer in Tibet, Central Asia, Burma, India, Java; professor at Columbia University in New York; wrote *Memories of Teilhard de Chardin*. Wife, Rhoda. Divorced.

**Terra,** Noël de. Science writer and daughter of Helmut and Rhoda de Terra.

**Terra,** Rhoda de. Novelist and American-born wife of Helmut de Terra.

**Thorez,** Maurice (1900–1964). French Communist leader; vice premier of France (1946–47).

**Tillie.** *See* Hoffman.

**Timp.** Englishman living in China.

**Ting,** V. K. (d. 1935) Geologist. One of the founders of the Chinese Geological Survey in Peking and the Museum of Natural History in Peking (1934). Director of Academia Sinica, Nanking.

**Torez-Bodet,** Jaime. At Mexican Legation in Peking; later director of UNESCO in Paris.

Torhout, Nirgidma de. Princess of Mongolia who lived in Peking; married Michel Bréal.

Trassaert, Maurice. Professor of science and mathematics at Collège des Hautes Etudes Commerciales in Tientsin.

Treat-Bergeret, Ida. Student with Teilhard in Marcellin Boule's laboratory. Married first to French Marxist Vaillant-Coutrier; then to André Bergeret, author.

Truda. Dr. Grabau's secretary.

Tucker, Betty. Friend of the Bégouëns.

Tyrrel, Ross. English journalist; friend of Miss Petre.

Tyrwhitt, Delia Scott. Wife of Peter.

Tyrwhitt, Peter. English army officer, killed at Singapore.

Valensin, Auguste (1879–1953). French Jesuit. Philosopher and literary critic; professor in the Catholic faculties of the University of Lyon and the Mediterranean Institute (Centre Universitaire Méditerranéen), Nice.

Valéry, Paul (1871–1953). French writer, poet, and intellectual.

Vargassov. Russian photographer in Peking.

Vayron. An officer of the Banque Franco-Chinoise.

Velloso. Brazilian minister in Peking, 1930. After World War II, United Nations official.

Vetch, Henry. Publisher and owner of the French Library in Peking. He edited scientific essays by Teilhard and Leroy from their work at the Institut de Géobiologie.

Vincent, Betty. Formerly Betty Spencer; wife of John Carter Vincent.

Vincent, John Carter. American diplomat in China during the 1930s; member of Chiang Kai Shek's advisory group during the war; U.S. Ambassador to Switzerland.

Volange, Mrs. The "Flying Angel" of Dr. Grabau's household.

Walsh, Edmund A. (1855–1956). American Jesuit and founder of the School of Foreign Service at Georgetown University; director of a papal mission for famine relief in Russia.

Wang. Lucile's Number-One Boy in Peking.

Wang, H. S. Chinese paleontologist. Collaborated with Teilhard.

Wang, S. T. Staff member at Peking Union Medical College.

Weaver, Dr. Head of the department of the Rockefeller Foundation in charge of Chou Kou Tien.

Weidenreich, Franz (1873–1948). German anatomist and paleoanthropologist; succeeded Davidson Black in 1935 at PUMC for the study of fossil man in China. He directed Lucile Swan's sculptural reconstruction of the head of "Nelly," using a cast made from one of the Sinanthropus skulls excavated at Chou Kuo Tien in 1929.

Wells, H. G. (1866–1946). English novelist.

Weltfish, Mrs. Anthropologist, Columbia University.

Wenner-Gren, Alex (1881–1961). Swedish industrialist and founder of the Wenner Gren (Viking) Foundation for Anthropological Research.

Wiley, John. American diplomat.

Wilhelm, Hellmut (b. 1905). German sinologue. Published a commentary on I Ching. Wife Maria.

Williams. On staff of "La Croisière Jaune" expedition.

Williams, Roger. Director of Institute of Biochemistry in Austin, Texas.

Willis, Bailey. American geologist.

Wong, Anna May. Chinese actress who starred in The Good Earth and other Hollywood motion pictures.

Wong, Wen-Hao. Chinese paleontologist. Member of the Geological Survey of China.

Wood, Mrs. Kay. Friend of Lucile Swan.

Worton, Gen. W. A. American Marine Corps commander in pre-war Peking.

Wright. American student from Harvard College.

Wright, Arthur F. (1913–1976). Headed committee on Chinese Thought for Association for Asian Studies. Author of Outmoded Languages. Wife, Mary Claybaugh, published China in Revolution: The First Phase, 1900–1913 (Yale, 1968).

Wu Pei 'fu. Chinese scientist and administrator at the P.U.M.C.

Yang Kieh. Chinese geologist.

Young (Yang), Chung-Chien. Chinese paleontologist and colleague of Teilhard's in China.

Zanin, Msgr. Apostolic delegate at Peking.

Zanta, Léontine. First woman to receive the doctorate in philosophy from a French university.

# INDEX OF NAMES

**Note from the Editors:** Wherever a first name or a last name is used alone in the correspondence, we have attempted to identify each of those persons in the Guide to Indexed Names which precedes this Index.
Please send any corrections to the Georgetown University Press.

Toward the Future: The Evolution of Chastity

Comment je crois

Essays of a Biologist: Julian Huxley

L'union différencié (1935)

Fountain: Ch. Morgan pg 50
The Personal Universe — pg 54 & see pg 57–58 ✳
Christ & Evolution
Réflexions sur la Conversion du Monde pg 63